Bc

BX 5937 .C662 G73 1994
Colton, Albert J., 1925-1988.
A grace observed : sermons by the
Reverend Canon Albert J. Colton

A Grace Observed

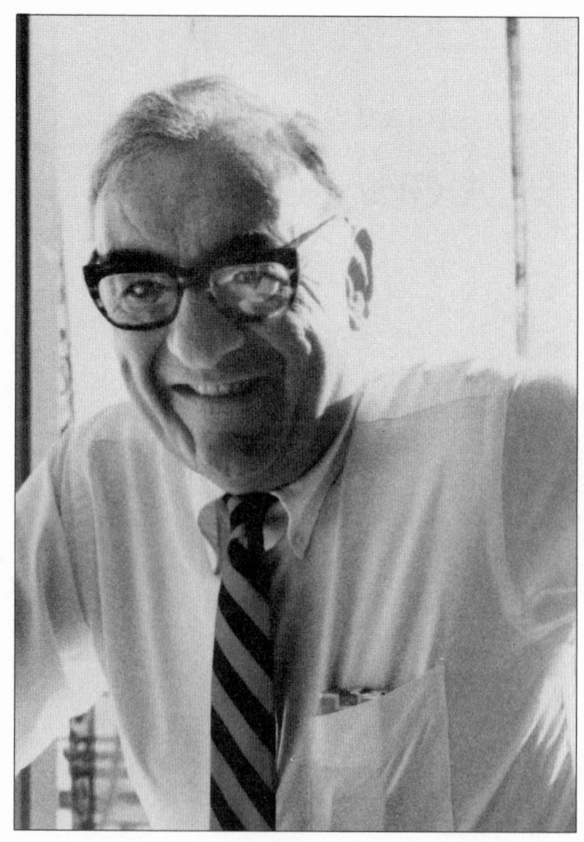

"So good people, my message to you this day is a very simple one. Go out and love one another."

A Grace Observed

Sermons by The Reverend Canon
ALBERT J. COLTON

Edited by
Bradley S. Wirth

With a foreword by The Very Reverend
William F. Maxwell

THE ALL SAINTS TRUST
SALT LAKE CITY
1994

BX
5937
.C662
G73
1994

Jacket and interior design by Connie Disney
Typesetting by Brent Corcoran

© 1994 by The All Saints Trust
All rights reserved.

∞ *A Grace Observed* was printed on acid-free paper
meeting the permanence of paper requirements of the
American Standard for Information Sciences.
This book was composed, printed, and bound
in the United States.

Colton, Albert J., 1925-1988
A grace observed :
sermons by the Reverend Canon Albert J. Colton
\ edited by Bradley S. Wirth ; with a foreword by the
Very Reverend William F. Maxwell, Jr.
p. cm.
Includes bibliographical references.
ISBN 1-56085-075-2 :
1. Sermons, American. 2. Episcopal Church–Sermons.
3. Anglican Communion–United States–Sermons.
I. Wirth, Bradley S., 1955 - .
II. Title.
BX5937.C662G73 1994
252'.03–dc20
94-34438
CIP

Dedication

With deep love for Albert and Elizabeth Colton,
this work is dedicated to
my daughters, Jennifer and Christine,
who now can know Al through these sermons,
to my wife, Jeannine,
who maintained a sense of humor through it all
and supported me with her love,
to my parents, Raymond and Delaine,
who gave me tremendous encouragement,
and to Oliver and Molly,
who were companions along the way.

In Memoriam

Raymond L. Wirth
who entered life everlasting
April 27, 1993

Contents

Foreword xi

by The Very Reverend William F. Maxwell

Preface xv

Acknowledgments xix

Introduction xxv

I. The Body of Christ

Introduction 3

1. The Third Sunday in Advent, 1964 13
2. Whitsunday (Pentecost), 1967 24
3. The Third Sunday after Epiphany, 1986 37
4. The Third Sunday in Lent, 1986 44

II. Belief

Introduction 55

1. Laymen's Sunday, 1956 65
2. The First Sunday after the Epiphany, 1966 76
3. Whitsunday (Pentecost), 1966 88
4. The Eleventh Sunday after Pentecost, 1979 97

III. Sin

Introduction 107

1. The Fifth Sunday after the Epiphany, 1965 119
2. The Eleventh Sunday after Trinity, 1966 128
3. The Twenty-second Sunday after Pentecost, 1984 135
4. The Second Sunday after Pentecost, 1985 143

IV. Grace

Introduction 155
1. The Ninth Sunday after Trinity, 1963 161
2. The Second Sunday in Lent, 1964 172
3. Quinquagesima Sunday, 1966 183
4. The Seventeenth Sunday after Trinity, 1966 . . . 194
5. The Fourth Sunday in Lent, 1988 204

V. Despair and Suffering

Introduction 213
1. Good Friday, 1965 223
2. Good Friday, 1965 228
3. The Second Sunday in Lent, 1968 233
4. The Seventh Sunday of Easter, 1981 245

VI. Death

Introduction 257
1. The Octave of All Saints, 1961 267
2. The Third Sunday in Advent, 1966 275
3. Easter Day, 1967 286
4. Easter Day, 1985 296

VII. The Ministry

Introduction 305
1. The Fourth Sunday after Trinity, 1964 313
2. Septuagesima Sunday, 1968 322
3. The Tenth Sunday after Trinity, 1968 330
4. 1968 (Otherwise Undated) 337

VIII. Witness
Introduction 345
1. Palm Sunday, 1965 353
2. The Seventh Sunday after Pentecost, 1979 361
3. The Feast of the Epiphany, 1981 367
4. The Second Sunday of Easter, 1987 375

IX. Stewardship
Introduction 389
1. The Twelfth Sunday after Trinity, 1962 399
2. The Twentieth Sunday after Trinity, 1967 407
3. The Nineteenth Sunday after Pentecost, 1986 . . 418
4. The Twenty-sixth Sunday after Pentecost, 1986 . 425
5. The Eighth Sunday after Pentecost, 1987 429

X. Church, State, and Law
Introduction 437
1. The Sixth Sunday after Trinity, 1967 451
2. The Second Sunday in Advent, 1967 462
3. Trinity Sunday, 1968 475
4. The Sixth Sunday of Easter, 1983 486

XI. The Faith Speaks to Society
Introduction 495
1. The Twelfth Sunday after Trinity, 1963 505
2. The First Sunday after Easter, 1967 515
3. Palm Sunday, 1968 530
4. The Eighth Sunday after Pentecost, 1986 538

Afterword 545

Foreword

The Very Reverend William F. Maxwell, Dean Emeritus
The Cathedral Church of St. Mark, Salt Lake City, Utah

My teenage children were severe sermon critics as they sat in the acolytes' pew in the Cathedral Church of St. Mark, Salt Lake City. They heard preaching which I am sure was as good as any in the Episcopal Church Sunday after Sunday, year after year. It was my conviction that every priest needs to preach, and every preacher can count on the Holy Spirit's opening the heart and mind of someone in the congregation to the Good News of Jesus Christ, so like the rest of us the acolytes had to take their chances with the preacher of the day. There were exceptions to the level of excellence, of course: preachers with marginal terminal facilities, preachers who thought that gimmicks provided a way to the hearts of their hearers, preachers who beat an invariable and favorite drum. And when the teenagers saw that such a preacher was scheduled, they groaned, feigned assorted illnesses, and tried their best to manage to stay home that morning.

They never complained when Albert Colton was scheduled to preach. Perhaps their acceptance of Al was simply the result of his unique presence, for that was compelling.

Tall, sturdy, with a great booming voice that never depended on the sound system's functioning, Al spoke with an intensity and conviction that demanded to be heard. Perhaps they were simply waiting for the story, sometimes funny, sometimes emotionally compelling, that almost always appeared at some point. Perhaps they were aware that Albert could be counted on to talk about a book he had just read or an event reported in the paper that gave a sense of immediacy to the sermon, an immediacy that meant that the words were important and not just pseudo-pious verbiage. I don't know precisely what drew those teenagers; I do know that they never tried to escape Fr. Colton's preaching.

I know that I shared their high expectations, with a few additional hopes of my own. Albert was in many ways a renaissance man. He was a practicing attorney, a patriot committed to civil rights and civil decency, a humanist who read widely and with enthusiasm, a Christian who knew the saving power of Jesus Christ in his own life, a priest who stood in awe of the willingness of the Holy Spirit to use him as a channel of grace. He was a somewhat romantic conservative, who could argue successfully in the General Convention of the Episcopal Church for the retention of the lovely prayer for a birthday–"Watch over thy child, O Lord, as her days increase . . ."–which was threatened with removal from the 1979 *Book of Common Prayer.* He was an opinionated Democrat who suspected deep in his heart that all Republicans had emerged from the shallow end of the gene pool. He loved the United States with a passion that had become unfashionable but which he proclaimed in season and out of season. He was a sinner, who like each of us had his favorite assortment of foibles and alienations that he found difficult to overcome and that his friends found just as irritating and frustrating as they find yours and mine. But he was a grand and lovely man, who spoke of Gospel and tradition and justice and truth with a grace and power that were always enriching to those who heard him.

As he came to his dying, he showed a level of faith and grace that was a proclamation of the Good News to all of us who were blessed by sharing those months and days with him. He wrote about his approaching death to the people of St. Mark's Cathedral, opening to his friends in Christ his feeling and his convictions and the sureness of his faith in his crucified and risen Lord. As I celebrated the Eucharist at his bedside the day before he died, the priest in Albert broke through the coma and he opened his hands during the Great Thanksgiving, as he had opened them so many times standing before the altar. As we stood with him at the moment of his dying, the man who was Albert came through the distance as he whispered, "I love you!"

Some people, when they die, simply disappear. Others, like Albert Colton, leave a void which refuses to go away. I miss his sermons, and I am grateful to have the opportunity to read them again. I miss his great barks of laughter, his tears of compassion, his uninhibited indignation at yet another sign of injustice. I remember some of his jokes and some of his stories. I pray that he may rest in peace, and somehow I suspect that his version of God's peace is just as active and powerful and funny as it was when he was preaching from the pulpit of the Cathedral he loved so much. Most of all, I miss a dear friend and fellow priest, who was a sign to me and to hundreds of others of God's love.

Preface

The style that I chose for this book is not unique to this project. Selections of sermons and speeches are often arranged by subject. Perhaps the first thing to note is that I selected the subjects used for chapter headings and chose the sermons for those chapters from the total collection of Albert Colton's sermons. In his files, sermons were not collected under headings of "Belief," "Sin," "Death," and the like.

The introductions to each of the chapters containing Al's selected sermons are a combination of bits and pieces of his other sermons and my own transitional statements and interpretations. Readers will note that my words are in italics and quotations from Al appear as indented blocks in regular print. Throughout each introduction I tried to be faithful to what I perceived as his articulation of theology rather than advancing my own beliefs and understanding. Even so, obviously, I could not escape being subjective.

In working through these sermons, I noted occasions where Al identified only the name of an individual he was quoting. In most cases we have been able to identify the source of the quotation. However, there are some citations which we could not verify or identify from a particular text. In those instances, a footnote acknowledges that. Additionally, there may be quotations from other sources not identified as such. Al's handwritten sermons were at times difficult to read and therefore hard to transcribe. It is possible that in transcribing them we unintentionally omitted a citation.

Finally, I wish to say something about the dating of these sermons. Since most sermons given in the Episcopal Church do not have actual titles, the calendar and liturgical dates serve as their reference. For example, Al preached at St. Peter's Church in Clearfield, Utah, on September 8, 1985 (the calendar date), which was the Fifteenth Sunday after Pentecost (the liturgical date). The calendar date grounds the sermon in our history; the liturgical date dictates the biblical readings used on that Sunday.

There may seem to be some inconsistencies in liturgical dates used throughout this volume. For example, some Sundays are Sundays in Advent and some Sundays are Sundays of Advent. Al's earlier sermons given in the summer and fall were given during the season of Trinity. Since the mid-1970s, sermons given at that same time of the calendar year were given during the season of Pentecost. The reason for these differences is that the Church changed prayer books several times during Al's thirty-two years of preaching. Besides the 1929 and 1979 prayer books, we also had at least two experimental prayer books and one proposed *Book of Common Prayer.* These books determined the form used to name the liturgical year and governed the selections of readings available to preachers.

Added to this means of dating is the less tangible stylistic dating in Al's use of grammar. For example, in earlier sermons, he consistently capitalized the letter "h" in the word "He" in referring to God or Jesus. In later sermons, while not dropping the practice, he was less rigorous in not only capitalizing the letter but he also used masculine pronouns less frequently when referring to God. I have left his style as he presented it originally, preserving for the reader one more aspect of the flavor of Church oratory for the era in which it was given.

Acknowledgments

This has been an extraordinary project. Not only did the scope of this labor of love exceed my wildest imagination, but the amount of help, constructive criticism, and advice I received was nothing short of God's grace. Given that this was a central theme in Albert J. Colton's life, it is appropriate that grace governed the beginning, the middle, and the end of this entire effort.

The Right Reverend George E. Bates, Bishop of Utah, gave me the gift of a sabbatical of four months to get the project off the ground. During that sabbatical, fellow clergy on the diocesan staff "covered" for me in a myriad ways, and to them, I am grateful.

This book would have been but a thought and not a reality had I not enjoyed the phenomenal insight, support, and love of Elizabeth Colton, Al's wife and partner in faith. Her working every week with me for over four months, and then regularly during the subsequent years of research, gave me the encouragement and the holy spark which kept the project alive.

In the beginning stages of this work, Ms. Mary Ann Fowler, one of Al's legal secretaries, transcribed almost two decades of his sermons. Al had a most creative penmanship, and Mary Ann was one of the few who could decipher it. Mr. Robert M. Gordon, Ms. Lucie Glenn, my wife, Jeannine, and my parents, Raymond and Delaine Wirth, suffered through the earliest drafts of this book, gently offering criticism, advice, and correction. Ms. Toni Sutliff, an attorney, gave me special insight through her reading of the manuscript. Ms. Mary Elisabeth Rivetti read the drafts and offered corrections as well and provided editorial advice when it came to submitting the manuscript for publication. My colleague in ministry at All Saints Church, Ms. Lyn Briggs, was immensely helpful in reading the manuscript as well.

The Reverend W. Lee Shaw, The Reverend Dr. Alan Tull, The Reverend Mary L. Allen, and Ms. Theresa Anderson helped locate some of the more allusive quotations in Al's sermons. I appreciate as well the Reverend Malcolm Boyd for assisting me in recalling a reference involving him.

A great many people across the country, whose names I never knew, helped me locate many of the sources Albert used. I wish to thank the library staffs of the University of Utah, Westminster College, the Salt Lake City Public Library, the Lamont Library and Widener Library at Harvard College, the Andover-Harvard Theological Library at Harvard Divinity School, the Cambridge (Massachusetts) Public Library, the Episcopal Divinity School-Weston School of Theology Library, the San Diego City Library, the San Francisco City and County Library, the John F. Kennedy Presidential Library, the archives of KGO Radio, San Francisco, the archives of the State of Minnesota, the archives of the University of Pennsylvania, the archives and the Library of the University of Texas at Austin, the archives of the Diocese of California, the archives of the Diocese of Michigan, the archives and library of the Cathedral Church of St. Mark, Salt Lake City, and the archives of St. Francis Episcopal Church, San Francisco. At St. Francis' Church, Ms. Jean Mackenzie and The Reverend Charles L. Ramsden were especially helpful in arranging a visit to their archives.

Much of my interest in working on a book such as this is having the opportunity of appreciating the inspiration gained by studying under people receptive to the marriage of rhetoric and theology. I am grateful to rhetoricians Mr. Ivan R. Hunt, Dr. Thomas R. Nilsen, Dr. Barnet Baskerville, and mentor, Dr. John A. Campbell. Significant theologians in my life, who also were interested in rhetoric and rhetorical criticism, include The Reverend Dr. Owen C. Thomas, The Reverend Dr. John E. Skinner, The Reverend Dr. Daniel B. Stevick, The Reverend Dr. Dieter Georgi, The Reverend Dr. George H. Williams, and my mentor and tutor in seminary, The Reverend Dr. Eugene Van Ness Goetchius.

Any collection of sermons are inherently a part of the

community which inspired them. The members and clergy of Grace Cathedral and St. Francis Church in San Francisco and the Cathedral Church of St. Mark in Salt Lake City were a significant part of the liturgical life of Albert Colton. I am especially grateful for the contribution of The Very Reverend William F. Maxwell, Dean Emeritus of the Cathedral Church of St. Mark, to this project. He served as the one who not only has been the greatest influence on my life as a priest but also nurtured the wonderful relationship the clergy of the Cathedral had with Al.

There remains one person on whom the vast majority of this work of prayer has rested. Ms. Ellen Tracy has been a source of unmeasurable energy, encouragement, humor, advice, technical skill, and insight. Without her constant presence in all aspects of this work, this project would never have been completed.

I wish to thank three of Al's long-time friends and "companions along the way." Anonymously, they underwrote this project allowing the publisher, The All Saints Trust, to realize all proceeds from the sale of this book.

Finally, I wish to thank Ms. Connie Disney for her design work and Mr. Gary J. Bergera for serving as editor. With this being my first attempt at such a project, I tremendously appreciated their humor, grace, expertise, and patience.

With so many talented people, having worked so joyfully hard with me on making this a reality, it seems difficult to imagine that mistakes and omissions still may remain in the text. They are, of course, my own.

Introduction

I have no photograph of her that's any good. I cannot even see her face distinctly in my imagination. Yet the odd face of some stranger seen in a crowd this morning may come before me in vivid perfection the moment I close my eyes tonight. No doubt, the explanation is simple enough. We have seen the faces of those we know best so variously, from so many angles, in so many lights, with so many expressions–waking, sleeping, laughing, crying, eating, talking, thinking–that all the impressions crowd into our memory together and cancel out into a mere blur. But her voice is still vivid. The remembered voice–that can turn me at any moment to a whimpering child.
–C. S. Lewis, A Grief Observed *(New York: Bantam Books, Inc., 1976), pp. 16, 17.*

C. S. Lewis, Albert Colton's favorite author, in *A Grief Observed,* wrote the above about "H" (Helen Joy Davidman), his wife of four years, on the occasion of her death from cancer. Those of us who knew Al feel much the same way about this scholar, lawyer, and priest. I find it nearly impossible to remember an accurate picture of Al. I momentarily see him in his alb, preparing for a 7:00 a.m.

Wednesday morning Holy Eucharist, but that blurs into an image of him wearing his "I've Climbed the Great Wall" sweatshirt he bought in China and his sitting in my backyard sipping a cool drink. When I am sure that is who he was to me, I see him turn into a scholarly man wearing his "going to court" dark suit in preparation for a trial.

And yet, as uncertain as I am about how I envision him, I join hundreds, maybe thousands, who recall his voice saying "Take, eat: This is my Body, which was given for you. Do this for the remembrance of me." During those small, simple, early Wednesday morning services, Al sounded not unlike a careful chef reciting the recipe for making a pie as though it were the first pie he ever baked. But in Al's case, he was reciting the recipe for holiness or, as Dom Gregory Dix said in his monumental work, *The Shape of the Liturgy,* he did this celebrating the Eucharist "just to make the plebs sancta Dei"–the holy common people of God.[1]

The Reverend Canon Albert J. Colton in sixty-three years of life temporal left a significant mark. He was born on June 3, 1925, in Buffalo, New York. He received his Bachelor of Arts degree in History, summa cum laude, from Dartmouth College, where he was elected to Phi Beta Kappa and was class valedictorian. He received his Master

1. Dom Gregory Dix, *The Shape of the Liturgy* (London: Adam and Charles Black, 1945), p. 744.

of Laws degree from Yale Law School and he earned his Bachelor of Civil Laws from Oxford University where he attended Balliol College as a Rhodes Scholar. He married Elizabeth Wright in 1948. Two children, Mary Elizabeth Colton and Thomas Spencer Colton, rounded out their family. Various beloved dogs added punctuation.

At the time of his death, Colton was Director and President of the Salt Lake City law firm, Fabian and Clendenin. At the same time, he was the Canon Chancellor (priest and legal advisor) of the Cathedral Church of St. Mark, Salt Lake City. During the decade of the 1960s, Colton left Fabian and Clendenin to pursue theological education at the Church Divinity School of the Pacific, Berkeley, California, where he received his Bachelor of Divinity with Distinction. Following graduation and ordination, he served as Vice Dean and Canon Chancellor of Grace Cathedral and as Rector of St. Francis' Church, both in San Francisco, and the Diocese of California. In 1968, Colton returned to Salt Lake City to resume his law practice and enjoy his new clerical relationship with the cathedral and diocese he left as a lay person. The marriage of lawyer and priest in Colton was seen in his serving as Canon Chancellor to the Cathedral and in his ministry of several terms as Chancellor of the Diocese of Utah. In those roles he served with distinction as a priest of the Church and advisor in both civil and canon (church) law.

But that is not who Albert Colton was where it counted,

at least in his eyes. He was, O merciful Savior, "a sheep of your own fold, a lamb of your own flock, a sinner of your own redeeming."[2] What made Colton who he was, in fact, was his having been washed in baptism, his being nourished by the Body and Blood of Christ, and in his death, being raised to new life.

About two weeks before he died, I had an opportunity to talk to him about his preaching. With some timidity, I asked him if I could catalogue and publish a collection of his sermons. He was pleased with the suggestion, embraced it with vigor, and then attempted to explain his labyrinthine filing "system" of twenty-five years of sermons and related (and unrelated) documents, the rationale of which followed him to the grave.

When Albert Colton died on the evening of November 7, 1988, many of his friends and his brothers and sisters in Christ knew three things for certain. First, the terrible cancer which had taken his strength and wind was no longer of any power. Second, he, a confirmed and loyal Democrat, was spared the election results of the next day—a moment of mercy in his life, joked many teary-eyed Democrats and Republicans alike. Finally, he rested, with his voice, in the arms of a loving God. While his political

2. "The Burial of the Dead: Rite Two," *The Book of Common Prayer* (New York: The Church Hymnal Corporation, 1979), p. 499.

vote could never again be counted, the same could not be said of his preaching. True, he would not stand in the grand brass-and-oak pulpit of the Cathedral Church of St. Mark on Sunday mornings, but his words, inspired by Christ, could fall the way of pilgrims and inquirers once more through print. He had been careful to construct those sermons in manuscript form.

A sermon is more than print on a page. As my own speech professor at the University of Washington, Dr. John A. Campbell, wrote, in reviewing the Reverend John Leffler's collection of sermons, *Go Into the City: Sermons For A Strenuous Age* (Seattle: Madrona Press, 1986),

> Few preachers, however, even good ones, should collect their sermons in a book.
>
> A living sermon is not a creature of print, but of an occasion. Eye-contact, gesture, intonation and timing all play a role in the mutual evocation of meaning which is a sermon. Nor is a sermon literature. One may be profoundly moved by what, if read, would be a very bad essay, and one may be left cold by hearing a well composed sermon. Some of the best sermons pass unremembered with the moment which called them forth. The worst are forgiven, or at least forgotten, in the course of an ordered service which a merciful Providence has not left to the chance gifts of those who conduct it.[3]

---

3. John A. Campbell, in a longer, unpublished version of the review,

I believe that Albert Colton shared that distinction Campbell identified when he wrote, "John Leffler's sermons belong to that small class of addresses which are moving when heard and repay reflection when read."[4] That, quite simply, is the reason for this book.

I became a colleague of Albert Colton on August 21, 1955, when I was baptized a Christian at the age of seventeen weeks. Colton strongly believed in the Body of Christ, the Body of the Baptized, as the company of saints, fellow pilgrims on the way, fellow workers of the vineyard. Twenty-five years later I met Colton for the first time when I joined the staff as Curate of the Cathedral Church of St. Mark. On Sunday we sat next to one another in the chancel of the Cathedral. Because I was that close to him each Sunday for the next seven years and five months until I left the employ of the Cathedral to become Canon to the Ordinary for the Diocese of Utah, I never saw him preach. Due to the placement of our chairs and the pulpit, I could only see his back. And from that vantage point, I could observe only that he shined the back of his shoes, never

---

the shorter of which appeared in the *Olympia Churchman,* a newspaper of the Diocese of Olympia. Campbell is Associate Professor of Speech at the University of Washington and a communicant at St. Clement's Church, Seattle, Washington.

4. Ibid.

really got his stole and hood of his alb synchronized, and occasionally let his left hand fly in a gesture.

But there was that booming voice, the remembered voice of which C. S. Lewis spoke. Unfortunately, for several years our old public address system, a true relic, kept intelligibility at a premium for those of us sitting in the chancel. By the time words traveled the 160 feet from the pulpit to the Narthex and back to the chancel, much inflection and considerable timing was lost. Sadly, he rarely gave homilies during his mid-week chapel services which he celebrated for two decades. So even for many of us who were "there," we have only his written texts remaining.

But "there and then" are not "here and now." And it is not the attempt of this book to duplicate the setting in which those sermons took place for the first time. That event is over. This publication of those sermons, initially given over the span of a quarter of a century, is a brand new experience of the word becoming discernible. More important than seeing these sermons as offerings of past days is viewing them as the "eloquence" of the church.

The great rhetorician and apologist for the Christian faith and Christian oratory, St. Augustine of Hippo, drawing on Cicero, said, "It is necessary therefore for the ecclesiastical orator, when he urges that something be done, not only to teach that he may instruct and to please that he may hold attention, but also to persuade that he may be victorious."[5] In that light these sermons are not offered as a historical picture of Albert J. Colton. Rather, they are part of a new rhetorical event in which Colton's words, as passionately and as fervently as is possible, try to persuade people to deepen their belief and challenge their thoughts as he rehearses for them the 2,000-year-old story of Christ.

I am not suggesting that Colton's sermons are moments of some romantic immortality whereby he speaks from the "great beyond." He would have been the first to point out the sentimental nonsense of such a premise. What I am saying is that when the "word" is offered prayerfully, and in the name of God, the oratory becomes the sacred possession of the Body of Christ with a vibrant life centered in the glory of God. As such, it remains a living testimony of God's salvation focused on those eager for delight and hungry for grace.

This view of Christian oratory is not a new theme by any means. After all, the Christian church has recognized in its canon of Holy Scripture other sermons, including those in the Acts of the Apostles traditionally attributed to St. Peter and St. Stephen. The Book of Hebrews is thought

---

5. St. Augustine (of Hippo), *On Christian Doctrine,* trans. D. W. Robertson, Jr. (New York: Bobbs-Merrill Co., Inc., 1958), p. 138.

to be largely a "written sermon."[6] The Catholic tradition has treated not only sermons found in the Bible as holy literature but also those of the Church Fathers as well. True, the sermons of Cyril of Alexandria, St. Athanasius, and St. John Chrysostom do not enjoy canonical status, but they are treated as a moment of prayer and are read in such a spirit by the faithful.

All Christian orators' sermons, from what ever age, are subject to Campbell's observation: they are a holy and sacred blend of the times, the text, the orator, the listeners, and the Spirit, never to be repeated in the same manner. And yet, if one accepts that Christian oratory is the property of Christ, provided that it is offered to the greater glory of Christ, Colton's sermons can be as, or more, significant, powerful, and prayerful in their reading as they were in their short life from the pulpit. It all depends on how they are interpreted. This introduction is offered in the spirit that the thoughts contained within may help readers interpret, appreciate, and participate in the sacred dialogue with Al's oratory offered for the sake of Christ.

The reading of Scripture, the reading of the Early Church Fathers, and the reading of contemporary sermons all require special attention. In fact, reading this volume

---

6. F. F. Bruce, "Hebrews," *Peake's Commentary on the Bible,* eds. Matthew Black and H. H. Rowley (Ontario: Thomas Nelson and Sons, 1962), p. 1008.

requires interpretation. David E. Linge speaks of this discipline:

> The dialogical character of interpretation is subverted when the interpreter concentrates on the other person as such rather than on the subject matter–when he looks at the other person, as it were, rather than with him at what the other attempts to communicate. . . . The interpreter must recover and make his own, then, not the personality or the world view of the author, but the fundamental concern that motivates the text–the question that it seeks to answer and that it poses again and again to its interpreters. This process of grasping the question posed by the text does not lead to the openness of a genuine conversation, however, when it is conceived simply as a scientific isolation of the "original" question, but only when the interpreter is provoked by the subject matter to question further in the direction it indicates. . . . We understand the subject matter of the text that addresses us when we locate its question; in our attempt to gain this question we are, in our own questioning, continually transcending the historical horizon of the text and fusing it with our own horizon, and consequently transforming our horizon. To locate the question of the text is not simply to leave it, but to put it again, so that we, the questioners, are ourselves questioned by the subject matter of the text.[7]

7. Hans-Georg Gadamer, *Philosophical Hermeneutics,* trans. and ed.

Obviously, if this representation of Colton's sermons is to be meaningful, readers will have to resist the temptation to simply "understand Colton" and move to a plane where his questioning invokes the same in reader or listener. If that movement happens, the resulting dialogue among the moment of the text, the intervention of the Holy Spirit, and the reader-listener become a holy venture and sacred pilgrimage.

What is Colton, aided by the power of the Trinity, saying? If Linge is right, much of that question can be answered by the individual pilgrim who chooses to take a journey with this book. Some initial understanding can be gained through identifying four intentional audiences of Colton's oratory. Those "congregations" include the churches full of people on the day the sermon was presented, the readers of his sermons or those who heard later on what he had to say (including people reading these sermons at this time), Colton himself reacting to his own words now strengthened by the invocation of God, and finally, God, in that Colton offered his sermons as a prayer to God rather than as a performance about God.

He was speaking to a church full of people from all walks of life. They willingly came to worship the Savior, and

---

David E. Linge (Berkeley: University of California Press, 1977), pp. xx-xxi.

as part of that worship of Christ they had the opportunity to hear a sermon. It makes sense to consider the congregation which was privy to this initial homiletical prayer. It is as varied as the number of people themselves multiplied by twenty-five years of sermons. He knew that he was preaching to anyone and everyone. He knew that his offering could possibly be the first sermon one would experience and at the same time the last sermon another might hear. Even though it is impossible to characterize completely his initial hearers, one can gain an understanding of whom he hoped the congregation was at that time or was becoming through his homiletical spiritual direction.

He wanted them to be inquiring. "We don't park our brains at the narthex of the church when we arrive!" was his familiar statement to congregations he served. Colton was a thinker. And while he was a first-class thinker, an accomplished thinker, he didn't require all to be academic scholars. He was comfortable with people stretching their minds to new horizons and that meant different things to different people.

He wanted them to be truthful about themselves. They had to know and accept that they were sinners, that they were imperfect, that they could be downright rascals–just as he believed he was. He wanted them to acknowledge themselves, "warts and all," just as he saw himself with his "big nose" and with similar imperfections noticeable and hidden on and in every person. So central to his sermons was comprehending sin, one of his understandings of sin bears repeating: "Selfishness, self-centeredness, self-congratulation–this is the basis of what the church calls 'sin.' It is the magnification of ourselves, which if it is carried far enough, makes it impossible for us to relate to anyone else."[8]

But these same folks, if they desired to be honest, also had to acknowledge the fact that they were counted as righteous in the sight of God. They were redeemed. They were holy. They were sisters and brothers in Christ. It follows most powerfully that it was a challenge to be in Colton's congregation. One had to confess sin and faith at the same time. There was no middle ground.

Finally, he wanted his listeners to believe. It was one thing to show up and another to believe the outrageous statement that Christ died for us and rose from the dead defeating the sting of death and the power of sin. The Church was not a club for the "really good and holy people" but a place and a living organism where the challenge of Christ could lead the worldly-comfortable people to holy discomfort and at the same time guide the

8. Sermon preached the Eleventh Sunday after Trinity, August 21, 1966, St. Francis' Church, San Francisco, California. The whole of this sermon is found in the chapter entitled "Sin" in this volume.

restless and contrite sinner to the peace made possible by the cross.

The second audience of Colton's sermons includes a wider assembly than the first. Undoubtedly, people who occupied the pews, such as myself, are interested in reading his sermons and "hearing" them for a second (or third, or fourth . . .) time. This audience's character is similar to the initial audience which sat in the pews and heard the sermon first delivered. But there is another segment of this second group of people which deserves special attention. They were those who "overheard" Colton's sermons.

He lived in great hope, as is seen most poignantly in his discussions about his "unchurched" friends who were never mentioned by name. He wanted them, in one way or another, to hear what he had to say. Since Salt Lake City, Utah, for example, is too small a place to hide from something one has said, one with confidence may believe that they, the unchurched, were an intentional secondary audience. He appreciated the fact that his sermons would get back to those in his social and legal circles. Often he would report that he had been in conversation with them over the issues presented by the readings for that Sunday and that they were at odds with the Catholic Christian tradition, or at least unaware of it.

There is no doubt many knew he may be talking about their belief or lack of belief. Colton was cognizant that a sermon was not given in confidence, and it was that realization that gave him this second intentional audience to his message. A good example of this can be seen in his sermons concerning stewardship and pledging money to the church. Colton believed one should tithe, or at least strive to tithe. He felt a communicant's problem with disagreeable personalities of the clergy or lay leadership in a parish was not an adequate excuse for not pledging. And he believed that stewardship also involved one's attendance in church.

If people didn't pledge and didn't come to church but still considered themselves "members," he had them in his homiletical sights. He tried to assist his fellow clergy and lay leadership to prepare canvassers with the most powerful and persuasive sacred ammunition he could give them and then they were cut loose to go after those who had fallen away. And the canvassers did just that. Much of what Colton said, combined with exhortation from others, made its way into the homes, hearts, and minds of those who darkened the doors of the church with dedicated infrequency. Colton's cadre of canvassers took his articulation of prayer and holy exhortation door to door. The receptive householders, vulnerable enough to listen to those bringing his message, became an extended audience.

Colton did not lack courage in preaching the faith to those who did not believe. His hope that his unchurched friends would "overhear" him was not a dodge from the responsibility of being evangelical in a direct and engaging way. Many of his sermons display a passionate disappointment in his ability to convert people, especially those closest to him. Without question, he grieved for them. However, Colton was one who respected people and God's ability to work through other means and through other evangelists than himself. He did not shove a Bible or *The Book of Common Prayer* down the throats of those he encountered. He assumed God had the ability to engage in persuasion in ways which respected the freedom of even those who chose not to believe.

It also needs to be mentioned that Colton reserved a strong passion for the Anglican way, which holds, among other things, that the Episcopal Church is not the only avenue to appreciate the efficacious grace of God. He believed that not all were attracted or called by God to be Episcopalians. Some of his unchurched friends probably were waiting in the wings, whether they knew it or not, for a good Lutheran, Methodist, Roman Catholic, Presbyterian, or other pilgrim of the faith to come along and bring them home to enjoy spiritual friendship with their creator.

To these unchurched, Colton desired that his words would someday help bring them into an honest relationship with Christ within the community of Christ.

Another part of this wider audience to his sermons included his political friends. Why would he want them to have access to his sermons? Quite simply, God had claim on politics and economics just as legitimately as on all other aspects of human life. He intended them to understand that God could claim liberals and conservatives as well as Republicans, Democrats, and Independents but that it didn't work the other way. No party could claim the exclusive membership of God. This part of his potential secondary audience was a tremendously significant circle of people for whom he cared deeply.

His sermons took two tacks when it came to the wider audience of those interested in politics. For those who claimed him a conservative, as did some conservatives and many liberals, he could reclaim, to the chagrin of that branch of politics, the discourse and symbolization of the Christian Church which had been appropriated unjustly, in his mind, by ultraconservatives. The American flag, the "Pledge of Allegiance," freedom, American troops in foreign lands, his distrust of communism, and his respect for the United States were given over to God's claim of creation. Therefore they were subject to God's nurturing and when necessary to God's chastisement through the prophetic oratory of the Church. Such symbols and articles of belief were not the possessions of the right wing but rather were gifts of God under God's stewardship of love and charity.

For those who claimed that Colton was a liberal, as did some liberals and many conservatives, he had a surprise for them as well. He believed in the liberating power of

Christ rather than in what might be perceived as the "Liberal Agenda."

Having said this, Colton received posthumously an award from the American Civil Liberties Union for his championing of various causes of freedom and safeguarding liberties guaranteed by the Constitution and the Bill of Rights. Would he, in good conscience, have accepted a similar award while alive from what many believe is an ultraliberal organization? Certainly! Again, Colton was a champion of the liberating power of Christ. And Christ had a claim on the American Civil Liberties Union just as powerfully as he had a claim on the Republican Party's efforts to elect George Bush, a man who dreaded the "L" word. What was important to him, and somewhat disarming to liberals and conservatives who vied for his loyalty, was the fact that he could switch sides at the blink of an eye if the other political party's efforts better reflected his understanding of the liberating power and compassion of Christ. This switching bothered Democrats more than Republicans because Colton was a strong Democrat.

He lived, as do most political people, in tension between the possibilities of ideals and the constraints of being human. An added dimension, not necessarily shared by all political people, was that Colton's first canon of living in a world of relationships was that of loving God and loving one's neighbor as one's self. Obviously, before he could concentrate on being the perfect politician, he had other concerns before him, namely living the life made possible by the grace of God through Christ. For those who complained that Colton was not the liberal (or conservative) they had thought or hoped him to be, they were right. He was more interested in the vocation of living a Christian life. His goal, although never perfectly met, was to intersect his life as a Christian with the political drives and aspirations of Republicans, Democrats, conservatives, and liberals, when he perceived himself called to do so by God. He acted out this sense of ministry with Jeffersonian conviction in that he felt the one who loved his or her country best was the one who worked hardest to make it better.

Now we get to the discussion of the most fascinating human listener of Colton's Christian oratory. We get to Colton himself. Who was he addressing when he was addressing himself in his sermons? Much of what we know of his image of himself can be gained by what he chose to say to his congregations.

To begin, Colton, when addressing himself, was speaking to a redeemed sinner. He understood sin and redemption. As opposed to general perception, he did not see "sin" synonymous with "bad acts committed." Rather he knew sin as a state of separation and alienation caused when people believe themselves the center of the universe, around which all things and meaning revolve. Colton understood that humanity was not content with being "a little lower than the angels" but rather desired to be endowed with the knowledge, authority, and power held only by God.

In several sermons he asked why people would bother to get down on their knees to say the confession if they had no sense of sin to confess. All of us are sinners and that included Colton. He saw this desire of people, including himself, to try to be more than they are as the gravest and most over-arching aspect of sin. This, in a nutshell, was the understanding he gained from the story of the "Fall" of humanity in the third chapter of Genesis. He claimed the story of Adam and Eve and the "Fall" as his favorite passage of scripture on which to preach.

One might think it odd that he relished the opportunity to preach on "the Fall." True, it served as a great setup for talking about the redemption of Christ and Christ's buying back by his death on the cross all those who suffered and groaned in travail. However, his sermons suggest more than just a fascination with the text. They speak in a tense of confession. His sermons dealing with sin are impacted tremendously with not just words about sin, confession, grace and forgiveness, but about the brokenness of the sinner, the humility of the one confessing, and the overwhelming joy and gratefulness of a lost sheep now found.

Clearly, Colton struggled with believing what he heard himself say. He often needed to be reminded of and persuaded by his argument as well as by the faithful reasoning offered by Christ, the prophets, the apostles, the

Early Church Fathers, theologians, and *The Book of Common Prayer* that God would be there again and again to forgive, redeem, and love. He was too creative a preacher to dwell on the same message of sin, forgiveness, and grace year after year, were there not good reason to do so.

Why did Colton pursue the themes of grace, salvation, and redemption as defeating sin through the dialogue of the sermon? This "dialogue" existed between God and Colton in the construction of the sermon in terms of revelation and response. It existed between Colton and himself in discerning the available means of persuasion consistent with his ability to present his arguments. And the dialogue existed between Colton and his congregation because of necessity: those who heard his sermons responded in one way or another. Had not people in the pews heard it before? Probably. Did they need to hear it again? Perhaps, but in Colton's case there were special reasons for his dwelling on God's justification of us all by grace.

To best persuade himself of God's desire for reconciliation, Colton participated in a rhetorical practice as old as Christianity itself. He gave a speech and released a thought–a thought which hurled itself to a congregation as well as to himself. As a result, he gave the congregation a chance to believe all over again. He also gave himself the same opportunity by continually reflecting on what he was thinking and saying in his sermons.

It was Colton's practice to write his sermon, rewrite it, deliver it to his wife, Elizabeth, receive constructive criticism from her, rewrite it again, and then deliver it to his congregation. His being open to criticism is akin to allowing one's idea (and self) to exist in community for a time and to return again, polished or perhaps just scratched. Rewriting a sermon is not the same as "fixing" it. Rewriting a sermon implies engagement with a community or a spiritual friend who adds a part of herself or himself (or the "community's self") to the process of discernment. From that practice a clearer articulation of the faith follows.

Once the sermon left Colton's lips he became part of the community of faith that heard it simultaneously. He couldn't escape it. He heard it as a member of his congregation because he believed he was drawn into that status by Christ. Even as the preacher, he was inherently part of the Body that received the words of the sermon delivered in the name of God.

In that sense he believed that the preacher was not a guru. People didn't, or shouldn't, flock to the preacher as a result of his or her preaching. Rather, he hoped they would gather in the name of Christ. And in this gathering they would find Colton as a fellow pilgrim sharing their yearning to follow Jesus.

The evidence of his hearing his own sermons in the company of a congregation is seen in his growth and in many penciled alterations on sermons given several times. Often these sermons were subjected to holy and prayerful editing by Colton and then given again. And once more the Body of Christ would engage in his journey of faith.

The final audience, addressed by Colton, was God. In his sermons Colton used many titles, names, attributes, and qualities to describe and address God. One which shines above all the rest is that of God who knew Albert Jay Colton, warts and all. He knew that God was mindful of him, loved him, would advocate for him, and had committed to walk the roads of anticipation, joy, sorrow, despair, trial, death, and resurrection with him. That brought into being, for Colton, an interesting, delightful, and passionate partner in homiletical prayer.

These four audiences–the congregation, the extended audience (including the reader), Colton himself, and God–were those for whom he cared deeply and with whom he desired to share his journey in Christ.

What was said by Colton in these sermons (thankfully) lies beyond the scope of this introduction. Besides, in any rhetorical event the meanings are many, and those understandings are even more complicated by the fact that he considered his sermons moments of prayer. Therefore the engagement of the people in the meaning of the sermon was impacted by the unique presence of God.

We should not be surprised that the meaning of Christian oratory, the eloquence of the church, is held to be perfected by Christ in such a way that through prayer, each listener, each reader, and each orator becomes organically connected to the Word that became flesh and dwelt among us full of grace. For so it is with the Body of Christ.

Before readers of this compilation are forty-five of the hundreds of sermons Colton gave during the three decades through which he served Christ as a preacher. My task involved selecting these sermons from his "sermon barrel," as it is called by preachers who keep their sermons. Why did I choose these sermons and not others?

When I began this project I thought long and hard about the method I would use. Time and time again my thoughts mysteriously were drawn to an epochal book, Charles Darwin's *Origin of Species.* I say that because I am persuaded that Darwin had a great gift of observation. He paid attention to creation with such intensity that God was able to disclose to him all that was necessary for him to discover, articulate, and expose such a vivid picture of God's handiwork. And as a result of this wonderful communion with his Creator, as well as creation, Darwin changed forever the way we think of ourselves.

I felt a kinship with Darwin in this project because I sensed myself engaged in a similar, albeit more modest, task. The boxes of sermons and, quite frankly, "stuff" seemed to elude any obvious display of order. There also were distractions within Colton's writings. (The most obvious and disturbing of those was Colton's use of "exclusive language.") I, as an editor, wanted to fix that but didn't feel the license to alter his sermons. I'm sure Darwin might have wanted to "fix" parts of creation that also struck him as odd or even annoying.

Then, spiritually, something began to happen to me, even as it became more and more frustrating to capture the essence of Colton's prayer. It was a feeling Darwin seemed to be able to make intelligible in his conclusion to the *Origin of Species:*

> It is interesting to contemplate a tangled bank, clothed with many plants of many kinds, with birds singing on the bushes, with various insects flitting about, and with worms crawling through the damp earth, and to reflect that these elaborately constructed forms, so different from each other, and dependent upon each other in so complex a manner, have all been produced by laws acting around us. . . . There is grandeur in this view of life with its several powers, having been originally breathed by the Creator into a few forms or into one; and that, while this planet has gone circling on according to the fixed law of gravity, from so simple a beginning endless forms most beautiful and most wonderful have been, and are being evolved.[9]

---

9. Charles Darwin, *The Origin of the Species,* 2d ed. (New York: Hurst and Co., 1860), p. 474. I am thankful to Dr. John A. Campbell for

It occurred to me that I was privy to the evolution of a pilgrim on the way. These sermons were evidence of the struggle and growth in which Colton engaged as he prayerfully wrestled with God. The questions of the ages became his questions. And when one deals with such questions, it does not promise to be a tidy endeavor but a wonder-filled excursion wherein one is moved and changed. Again my thoughts turned to Darwin for guidance in discovering Colton's rhetorical prayer. Darwin introduced the process whereby he was able to discern the mysteries of the means of natural selection with these words:

> When on board *H. M. S. Beagle,* as naturalist, I was much struck with certain facts in the distribution of the organic beings inhabiting South America, and in the geological relations of the present to the past inhabitants of that continent. These facts, as will be seen in the latter chapters of this volume, seemed to throw some light on the origin of species—that mystery of mysteries, as it has been called by one of our greatest philosophers.[10]

The key, I believe, to Darwin's brilliance was his allowing himself to be "struck" by something and then having

---

introducing the "Rhetorical Mr. Darwin" (the title of one of his essays) to me through his scholarly writing and lectures.

10. Darwin, *Origin,* p. 1.

the patience to allow that which "struck" him to "throw some light on the . . . mystery of mysteries."

I have tried to imitate Darwin on my smaller voyage through some thirty-two years of Colton's sermons. Many of those sermons, I found, impressed themselves upon me. They survived the imperfect, perhaps callous and overly-subjective, process I used to "weed" out some for the sake of others. As a result, I like to believe I was left with sermons that throw light on the relationship of God with God's creation, as seen and interpreted by my brother in Christ, Albert Colton.

I suggest Darwin's method of discovery to you. Allow yourself to be moved by what you see. And after you are done, and you have allowed God and Colton to touch you, you might feel as I did when I believed I had completed work on this book: God tossed me a ball, which I held for a while and which then evolved into a new ball, of new life, which is now tossed to others. Maybe someday it will be pitched my way again. If so, I look forward to catching it anew.

I
The Body of Christ

Introduction

The Church, as Albert Colton knew and lived it, was rarely seen as a private possession or an experience of just one person. The sacraments depended upon the gathered community. The moving events or revelatory moments that one might encounter needed the discernment of others for interpretation and meaning. As a result, the concept of the "Body of Christ" was of tremendous importance. Colton believed that Christ died for all people, regardless of their profession of faith. The Body of Christ was composed of those people who were brought into the community of the faithful through baptism. That Body exists for the express purpose of ministry and of telling the world of the salvation made available to them by the grace of God:

> One aspect of the Christian Church since its inception has been its visibility. We start with the basic Christian principle that God makes Himself known through outward and visible forms. God Himself was invisible and unknown, until He made Himself known and visible in the flesh and blood of a man.
>
> A Christian becomes a Christian not by thinking good thoughts, but by a very visible dash of cold water poured on his head. (In the good old days, before the church lost too many people by pneumonia, etc., this

was done even more dramatically and visibly by immersion in the flowing waters of some nearby stream.)

The "church," the *ecclesia,* was a collection of people gathered together in one place to pray, to give thanks for the healing of their separation which God had accomplished through Jesus Christ, and to break bread. All these things were very visible.[1]

Colton adopted an expression of the concept of "universalism" in that he was convinced that Christ lived and died for all people. More often than not he expressed the opinion that all, even those who desired at this time not to be enfolded into the Body of Christ, were securely in the caring arms of a loving God. Occasionally, he was in tension with that belief. In some sermons he expressed the belief that one ultimately could say "no" to God and therefore reject God.

While wrestling with that tension, he clearly denied that any church body had the right or credentials to limit the scope of the Body of Christ:

I started to prepare this sermon last Sunday in a cabin on top of a peak overlooking the Wind River Range in northwestern Wyoming, a magnificent setting. The group we were with was unchurched. I read them today's gospel [Luke 13:22-30, RSV] and especially verse 25 which reads: "When once the house-

1. Sermon preached the Second Sunday after the Epiphany, January 15, 1967, St. Francis' Church, San Francisco, California.

holder has risen up and shut the door, you will begin to stand outside and to knock at the door, saying, 'Lord, open to us.' He will answer you, 'I do not know where you come from,'" and they all groaned. The advice given me was to stay away from it. Referring to the "closed door," someone said, "That's the original bad news–'knock–knock, 'who's there?' joke."

At first blush, the passage seems to be saying that salvation is for the select few. Historically, this message has great appeal to some. . . . Certain religious groups proclaim themselves as the only "true" church. But the idea of a select few runs totally contrary to what has been proclaimed as the central core of the Gospel proclamation–a message of good news to all mankind. Thus the comfortable words, "Come unto me, all ye that travail and are heavy laden, and I will refresh you." "God so loved the *world*" (not a select few) "that he gave his only begotten son . . ."[2]

Colton had great fondness for and admiration of those who were confident in their faith. He was energized by those who firmly believed and acted saved because they knew all creation was saved by the grace of God. At the same time, he had little patience or

2. The emphasis is Colton's. "The Comfortable Words" are found in *The Book of Common Prayer* (New York: The Church Hymnal Corporation, 1979), p. 332. Colton quotes from Matthew 11:28 and a portion from John 3:16. Sermon preached the Fourteenth Sunday after Pentecost, August 24, 1986, the Cathedral Church of St. Mark, Salt Lake City, Utah.

time for those who were haughty or proud, taking, as it were, the credit from Christ and appropriating the great sacrifice on the cross as their own idea and accomplishment. "And you will weep and gnash your teeth, when you see Abraham and Isaac and Jacob and all the prophets in the kingdom of God and you yourselves thrust out. And men will come from east and west, and from north and south, and sit at table in the kingdom of God. And behold, some are last who will be first, and some are first who will be last" (Luke 13:28-29, RSV). Those who make up the Body of Christ are a curious lot.

> The conclusion is thus not that of an exclusive, elite club—there are folks there from the east bench, the west side, central city, and even from Logan and Nephi and Tooele. One thing is sure, it is not a guest list that we would have thought of. And that is perhaps the kernel of this little vignette. . . . We dare not exclude others. . . . If you know you are in, you may be in the process of going out, and if you think that you are unworthy of being admitted, you may already be inside. There is in this gospel passage a call to continual newness. In a way, I think, Jesus is bidding us to go out the door and come in again, to discover with fresh eyes the feast and the kingdom.[3]

Colton rejoiced in a church that contained its share of

---

3. Sermon preached the Fourteenth Sunday after Pentecost, August 24, 1986, the Cathedral Church of St. Mark, Salt Lake City, Utah.

scoundrels. To have defined the Body of Christ exclusively as the most acceptable and decent in society would have taken away from the whole power of the gospel. The same held true for the radicals of the world. They were included by virtue of their baptism. The institution needed all people to give justice to the name, "The Body of Christ."

The Church can look back on a fabulous heritage of countless thousands of men and women who have devoted their lives to the message of Jesus Christ. It has had its share of rascals too. It does us no good to gloss over this. Acts which would shock a horse thief have been committed in the name of the love of God. St. Paul, himself, in this very letter [2 Corinthians] admitted that he was not following his Lord's advice. And yet the wonder of it all is not this, but that for two thousand years in all sorts and conditions of cultures and places, this institution has existed–a string of continuity and common cause binding together as nothing else has ever done.

The woods of the church today are full of angry young men demanding radical reformation of the church's structure and attitudes. . . . But angry young men, or angry old men, are nothing new. They go back to the Old Testament prophets (who were, incidentally, in most part laymen, not clergy). The prophetic and reforming note should always be present to keep us from smugness and complacency and to remind us that Christianity is essentially a scandalous and revolutionary assertion which always should shake the foundations.[4]

And yet Colton believed it essential to have us summoned back to community, a community called to worship together, and join in the sharing of a cup and the breaking of bread.

Take an example from our own day. If the Christian faith is true, then God has commanded us to worship Him in community–the family gathered together in one place. This does not mean that we cannot worship Him in our solitude, but only that worship in solitude alone is never enough. Man was made to worship God and love his neighbor, and he can never really do the one without the other, and loving one's neighbor means living in community with him, seeing him, hearing him, touching him. The Holy Communion, for example, is a *communal* act (the very word suggests this), something we do together.

But there is something in us that resists this requirement. It is an awful nuisance to become involved with other people, and make no mistake, if you become involved, people will make demands upon you, and if you expose yourself to other people, they may hurt you. (Of course, unless you become involved, unless you expose yourself, you will have no opportunity to reach

---

4. Sermon preached on Sexagesima Sunday (the Second Sunday before Lent), February 21, 1965, St. Francis' Church, San Francisco, California.

out and touch them in love and they of course can never love you. I cannot love what I do not know.)

But just because this demand is a nuisance we tend to fudge as much as we can. We are told we should worship in community—and I guess we have stretched this about as far as we can go with what I gather is a spreading idea—the drive-in church—as perfect an example of phoney community as any I know.

We are told we must be together, but we make sure that there is no real possibility of any confrontation [in the drive-in church] by appearing safely encased in our steel womb where we can stare out our window at other people in their steel womb, each of us secure, each of us unaffected by others around us. . . . In other words, everything is done exactly on our terms.

Some of these drive-in churches apparently administer Holy Communion from time to time, with the sacramental elements delivered from car to car. People roll down their windows if they wish to receive and partake of the sacrament in the comfort of their own front seat.

The symbolism is a grotesquely perfect one of community which is not community at all—of worship as something which is done to and for you, not as something in which the worshipper brings of himself to give and participate in. It has become an event where people come together to get rather than to give.[5]

5. Sermon preached the Sunday before Advent, November 26, 1967, St. Francis' Church, San Francisco, California. Also preached at

What an obvious tool, one would therefore think, this rite [the Holy Eucharist] would be in promoting unity in the splintered Christian Community. But the tragedy is that this one uniting thing has not been that at all, but rather a means of further disunity.

In fact it leads to certain grotesque things. For example, the Roman Catholics in San Francisco a few months ago [in 1964] during the "Octave of Unity" invited a number of Protestant clergy to attend a service and then to have dinner with them afterward in the basement of Old St. Mary's Church. The service was a Eucharist at which it was made quite clear that we were not expected to communicate. The result—Christians could break bread and drink wine together down in the basement, but not in God's house.

Or of course the same problem comes up amongst Protestants themselves. At many an ecumenical meeting, the delegates can sit and eat together for days on end, but each one runs off to his own little group at the time they are to receive Holy Communion.[6]

Being a united, practicing Christian family is our number one priority.[7]

St. Stephen's Church, West Valley City, December 1964.

6. Sermon preached Maundy Thursday, March 26, 1964, St. Alban's Church, Albany, California.

7. Sermon preached the Third Sunday after Epiphany, January 25, 1981, the Cathedral Church of St. Mark, Salt Lake City, Utah.

Great energy can be expended in trying to maintain the Body of Christ with integrity reflective of the truth that Christ died for all people. However, Colton believed we had no choice but to press on for an inclusive church.

> Of course, running a church is like dancing with a gorilla. You don't stop dancing when *you* are tired–you stop when the gorilla is tired.[8]

This Body of Christ, that is the worshiping, praying, loving community of Christ, was a life and death matter for Colton. It was that serious.

> The Church teaches that a man cannot live by himself–this is death. He needs to live in community with other persons and with his God. The parish church provides for both of these needs, as a community of people sharing each other's concerns and attempting to live together in love and charity (not always easy), and as that place where the Eucharist is celebrated and the sacrament of God's presence is distributed for our nourishment. A person who refrains from regular participation in the Lord's Supper can starve to death spiritually.[9]

---

8. Ibid.

9. Sermon preached Sexagesima Sunday (the Second Sunday before Lent), February 21, 1965, St. Francis' Church, San Francisco, California.

1

Tempting as it may be for each of us to found our own little church of one person, and certain as it is that God still loves us even if we do this, I suggest that this is not the Christian faith once delivered to the saints. This faith is by its very nature a corporate thing. It is a recognition of what life really is. Whether I like it or not, I am related to you. What you do affects me, and what I do influences you. No man is an island.

The Third Sunday in Advent December 13, 1964

St. Francis' Episcopal Church San Francisco, California

From the collect for today: "Grant that the ministers and stewards of thy mysteries may likewise so prepare and make ready thy way . . . that we may be found an acceptable people in thy sight. . . ."[10]

Like any revolution, the Protestant Reformation brought to the Christian world many blessings, and also many things we could do without. Again, as is so often the case in the history of revolution, it was not the initial

10. *The Book of Common Prayer* (New York: The Church Pension Fund, 1928), p. 93.

revolutionaries who caused the difficulty, but those who projected, to an extreme, the premises upon which the original revolutionaries started.

Certainly one of the great problems we have inherited from the Reformation is the conception of the invisible church. Let me translate this into modern terms, in its presently abused form: "I can find God where I am; I don't need any super-organized group of do-gooders (who are incidentally pious hypocrites) to help me find God. I can find Him on the golf course, or out on my boat. I don't need any man or institution to stand between me and God."

Having spent some time on a golf course and on a boat (not as much as I would like), I honestly doubt if I have ever "found" God there. I've been too busy enjoying myself. Mind you, I have no doubt that God is there, and there are those moments of solitude before the magnificent splendor of some portion of God's creation– whether it be a mountain waterfall, or in a sleeping bag staring at the summer sky, or when you see the sun sink as your boat bobs quietly in the water, or when you see the great power of the ocean surf–at these moments you are brought up suddenly with awe and wonder at this phenomenon we call life and existence.

But so often the man who claims he finds God on the golf course is using this as a rationalization for do-

ing what he really feels is important, which is really not finding God at all, but to enjoy himself and perhaps, in the process, make "contacts" with those who may assist him along the way.

After all, we usually do what we think is important for ourselves. A southern priest once told me the story of the white southern congregation which was confronted with the request of some Negroes to join their congregation. They decided that as Christians they could not turn them away from the altar rail, but that they would cancel the social or coffee hour after the service until further notice. As the priest suggested, was it not that, to this congregation, the sacrament that *really* counted, was the coffee hour, and not the Body and Blood of our Lord? This is why they really came, and this was the ultimate value they would not share.

The God on the golf course is one's own God, made in our own image. It is not the God of Abraham, Isaac, and Jacob. It is the God of our own individualism, subjectively determined. If I like a God of vague general principles who doesn't intrude in my own personal life, by some strange coincidence I will find Him on the golf course, and no one will say me "nay." If I like a God who is really nothing more than a few sappy platitudes which dissolve any time I meet the hard, gutty substance of life, or suffering and death, there is no one in my little church of one to say me "nay"—until it is too late, and I find I am spiritually bankrupt.

Tempting as it may be for each of us to found our own little church of one person, and certain as it is that God still loves us even if we do this, I suggest that this is *not* the Christian faith once delivered to the saints. This faith is by its very nature a corporate thing. It is a recognition of what life really is. Whether I like it or not, I am related to you. What you do affects me, and what I do influences you. No man is an island.

God's concern is with all men, each one of infinite value, whom he desires to live, not as islands to themselves, but in a relationship of love toward each other. Men respond ideally to God in the same sense of love and relationship they should show to each other. Indeed, the one is like unto the other. A man who says he loves God and hates his neighbor is a liar, as Scripture tells us.

The early Christian could not conceive of a person claiming he was a Christian and yet refusing to identify with the rest of the Christian community. Christians were by definition those who were indeed involved with one another. They were people who, through baptism, had undergone true death and were reborn into a new family, the family of the church with Jesus Christ at its head. They were people who shared—shared one of the deepest things imaginable—the sharing in the breaking of bread which brought them to the Risen Lord. This was an act they could not do alone. They had to do it together.

The Eucharist has been called the Holy Mystery. Mystery is defined in the dictionary as something which cannot be fully explained, or as beyond human comprehension. There is much mystery in life. Science gives us ever-increasing answers to the "how's" of things. But the great riddle of the "why" and of ultimate purposes remains unanswered. Why and for what purpose do I exist? Why do the innocent suffer? Why (if it is true) did God choose to manifest Himself uniquely and completely in the person of one human body instead of generally in all humanity? Why (if it is true) did God choose to continue His presence through a simple ritual of breaking bread and drinking wine?

We can suggest reasons, and others can use logical arguments to refute them. But no one had been won to Christianity solely by logical debate and no one leaves it for this reason either.

The Christian knows that he meets his Lord and King uniquely in the sacrament of bread and wine, and that he partakes of this sacrament in the company of other Christians. The very word "communion" requires "community," not just of God and a man, but God and men. And through this sacrament we are tied not just to men at this altar rail, but to all men at all altar rails at all times and in all places.

Tied we are, therefore, to all other Christian men, and

to the King of the Universe who has chosen this way to communicate with us in community.

Corporateness is built into the very essence of this faith. A corporateness built upon a two-fold mandate, one given to certain people, initially the Apostles, "He that receives you receives me . . ." [Matt. 10:40, RSV], and the other, the command to "Do this in remembrance (and recalling) of me" [cf. Luke 20:19, RSV]. And in the Catholic tradition to which Anglicanism adheres these two are closely tied together. The Risen Lord continued to live and evidence Himself through His church, the Body of Christ. And this body is no self-validating body. Its validation is the commission it received from Christ Himself. Just as Christianity is an immensely physical religion (in theological jargon we call this sacramental), so it is immensely physical in how it senses it is tied to all other Christians throughout time. We break this bread and share the cup in this church this day not because someone found an old book, dusted it off, and read about this ritual and thought it would be a good idea to start again, but because we are inheritors of a commission passed along by physical means through the centuries. We had been told and taught to do this by other people.

The sacrament (in other words) is dispensed as the result of a commission from the Lord Himself, and Anglicans feel that the agency through which this dispensation is made was also commissioned by our Lord. This we call the Apostolic ministry, which we feel has been handed down through the church to this day, embodied in the office of the episcopate or bishop, a person not a principal.

This does not mean that when our Lord commissioned Peter he whispered in his ear, "This means you will be the first Pope–the Bishop of Rome." The very word "bishop" is a terribly elusive one in Holy Scripture and in other ancient writings. *What it does mean is that a means of human personal continuity of remembrance was also preserved together with the institution of the sacrament itself.*

There was within this corporate visible church an agency of continuity, of recommissioning from those who received the original commission. This agency of continuity and re-commission may have, in the earliest years of the church, been known by different titles and names. Although from very ancient times this role was seen to rest upon the shoulder of that man known as the *episcopos* (over-seer–bishop). It is not so much the title which is significant as the fact that this element of passing on the original commission was seen as important. Ministry and sacrament were intimately tied together.

Up until four hundred years ago all Christians operated under the episcopal structure. Today over 75 percent of the world's Christians still accept it. Many of the bishop's functions have varied over the centuries. Bishops in the past were often powerful secular princes. Recently they have been saddled with crushing administrative duties.

Their jurisdictional authority within the church itself has varied greatly. Thus in the ancient Celtic church in the British Isles, bishops had no jurisdictional power at all, the church being run by abbots of monasteries. But even there the bishop was preserved, as sort of queen-bee to be sure, to perform the essential sacramental acts (ordination, consecration, and confirmation) assuring continuity to this remembering community.

It is for this reason that it is felt that where the Bishop is, there is the church. His chair or *cathedra* is what determines what is the principle church of a diocese. A cathedral church is not determined because it is the largest and grandest structure (although it is often this, some Cathedrals are quite modest), but because it is the place where the Bishop sits.

Thus it is the Episcopate which, as St. Cyprian said, is "the glue of the church" [Epistle lxvi.7].[11] Embodied in this person is the outward and visible sign of the church's unity and continuity. It is through this office that the leadership and the thrust of the church has come. We have at times

---

11. From the sentence, "Where as, in truth, the Church forms one single whole; it is neither rent nor broken apart but is everywhere linked and bonded tightly together by the glue of the bishops sticking firmly to each other" (Epistle lxvi. 7, in *The Letters of St. Cyprian of Carthage Vol. III, Letters 55-56,* trans. and ann. G. W. Clarke [New York: Newman Press, 1986], p. 122).

forgotten this lesson, to our sorrow. Bishops are not those who arrive *last,* to establish their pomp and ceremony when all of the backbreaking drudgery has been done, but they are the ones who arrive *first,* and under whose direction the back-breaking, heart-breaking work of mission is accomplished. Our missionary thinking is still handicapped to some extent by our confusion here. We sometimes think that a new missionary area must work to earn a bishop, when if we review our Christian history we see that at times of Christian greatness it is the other way. The bishop is the first to earn the missionary area for Jesus Christ.

And as the bishop has been the first in a geographic area, so often he is the leader in other frontiers as well.

Bishops are men, drawn from the lower orders of the ministry, and as the men in these orders vary, so not surprisingly, will our bishops. There is no generalization about the ministry. At a clergy conference where the priests of this or any other diocese gather together in mufti or sports shirts, it is impossible to distinguish this group by their faces or mannerisms from any other group of men. They could be a group of insurance salesmen or physicians.

It is not surprising therefore that different bishops will have different views as to what is significant to be done during their time on this earth. Often this turns on what they themselves do best. Some bishops are known for their great pastoral gifts (an essential to some extent in every bishop) but are wretched preachers. Others use superbly the gift of the preached word of God. Some are first rate administrators. Others carry the business affairs of their diocese around in their hats. Each hopefully utilizes to the fullest those unique gifts which are his.

Many bishops have been saints. A few have been outright rascals. No one of them has been worthy, any more than any priest is worthy to celebrate the Holy Communion or any communicant is worthy enough to receive that sacrament.

Fortunately for all of us, "worthiness" is not a criterion for membership in the Christian family. But this does not relieve us of our duty, with God's help, to strive to worthiness or to let God help us do that which is pleasing in his sight.

And it does not relieve a bishop of the most awesome responsibility of all, one which he assumes upon consecration and which he can never again rid himself of, to be a minister and a steward of the mysteries of God. He is handed the awesome responsibility of passing along this treasure, along with counseling and leading his flock.

There has probably never been a bishop with whom everybody agrees all the time. In fact, if ever there were such a bishop, it would be pretty good evidence that he wasn't doing his job. But this one man personifies in himself the unity of all Christians under his jurisdiction.

It is much like the President of the United States. There probably never should be and certainly never will be, a president with whom all Americans at all times and places agree. But there are those moments when we are aware that this man, fallible as all men are, still represents in an almost sacramental sense, the unity and the strength which are ours.

2

The church has a navel, just as we do, a rather inelegant part of the body which indicates that we came from and were tied to someone else. The navel's function ceases within a few minutes after birth, but the mark remains with us till we die–a reminder of our unity with and total dependence upon that which went before.

Whitsunday (Pentecost)	*St. Francis' Church*
May 14, 1967	*San Francisco, California*

ACTS 2:1-12; JOHN 14:15-31A

This Pentecost is many different things to me. It is Mother's Day, the anniversary of my ordination to the priesthood, and the day when one of my God-children is confirmed. However, the Prayer Book in its propers for today doesn't make any reference to any of these.

It talks rather about the culminating event in a series of events which began in Advent around which the Christian faith must stand, the last of a series of God's actions in space in time by which God showed Himself to us in His fullness, when the significance of the Risen Lord became so suddenly and dramatically apparent to a group of followers that they appropriated to themselves this significance and the result was a power and a zeal which transformed the world.

Whitsunday or Pentecost has been called the birthday of the church, and to the extent that we talk of the church as consisting of such fallible creatures as you and me, this is surely true. Or as John Krumm, Rector of the Church of the Ascension in New York City, pointed out in a helpful sermon, "The reason why Whitsunday is so important in the Church calendar is because it is the day when you and I became important in the story of Christianity."[12]

And if you think about it, this is absolutely true. If you take a look at the Nicene Creed, as Dr. Krumm says, "the first part of (it) takes no account of you and me. God created the world; Christ came into the world. What you and I think about that makes no difference at all. Those things are quite independent of us."[13]

In one sense this should be very comforting to you and me. If God is God, then it really doesn't make any difference to the ultimate nature of things whether you or I *think* God exists, or say that God is dead, or remain wholly indifferent to Him. He is still there. Sigmund Freud might

12. John M. Krumm, "The Spirit in Church and World," *The Witness* May 11, 1967, p. 8.

13. Ibid.

contend that God is merely an invention of man, a projection of our own desires and needs, but if He is what the Christian says he is, then it really doesn't matter in the least what Sigmund Freud or anyone else says or thinks. The same objective argument might be made for Christ's entry and departure from this world. But, as Dr. Krumm points out, "the last part of the Creed begins, 'I believe in the Holy Ghost,' and that is when you and I come into the picture. The Holy Ghost is God's presence and power working in your head and mine. He it is who leads us to believe and trust in the God who created us and came to save us; and how we respond to his leading and guiding and illuminating work is all-important, so you and I count for a great deal in this last part of the story of the Creed."[14]

Up to the time of Pentecost, the Christian story is basically one of God's action at Pentecost, and thereafter the emphasis is placed upon man's response to this action.

I am not suggesting that God at that time dusted off His hands and walked away, leaving things completely to us. If God is the God we say He is, He would never abandon His church, or absent Himself from His people. Indeed, we describe the church, in one biblical metaphor, as the "Body of Christ." Tainted and besmirched as such a body might sometimes become, it is still a unique instrument of

---

14. Ibid.

God's presence. God's love would never allow Him to leave His church. And here is one of many doctrinal points on which, say, the Mormon church departs from Catholic Christendom, for the Mormon contends that because of man's evil God left and abandoned His church, only to return with a new dispensation in upstate New York in the first half of the nineteenth century.

Such a concept does violence to many traditional ideas of Godhead, but most particularly with the concept of Unity which underlies that of the Holy Spirit. The Holy Ghost, as "God's presence and power working in your heart and mine,"[15] is also that force which ties you and me together.

St. Luke illustrates this in his story of the first Pentecost read as our epistle this morning. He pictured men and women of many different languages and nations (a pretty good cross-section of the then-known world) all united together and all understanding each other.[16]

This unity of the Spirit extends through time. We here today are tied in union to all Christians who have gone before us. The Spirit has never left His church, our Mormon friends to the contrary. God is absolutely faithful and reliable, no matter how faithless

15. Ibid.

16. Ibid., 9.

and unreliable individual Christians have been, and as we have this assurance of continuity in the past, so we can be assured of it in the future.

In other words, the church has a navel, just as we do, a rather inelegant part of the body which indicates that we came from and were tied to someone else. The navel's function ceases within a few minutes after birth, but the mark remains with us till we die, a reminder of our unity with and total dependence upon that which went before.

To bring Mother's Day in, in quite a backhand way, much of the secular propaganda of this day is not just the florist and candy and greeting card lobbies, but an honest feeling of overwhelming and primordial gratitude for the person who thanklessly took us, nurtured and cared for us, through that period when we could not even understand what gratitude could mean to this chief family dispenser of love. (As an historical footnote, for what it is worth, it might be interesting to note that in 1908 the U.S. Senate voted *against* declaring a National Mother's Day, 33 to 14. It was not until 1914 that it was officially approved by Congress and the President.) The ideal mother (and most of you mothers approximate this much more than your conditioned guilt feelings will allow you to admit) is also quite faithful and reliable and loving to her children no matter how faithless and unreliable they may seem to be in return. Mothers serve as a haven of warmth and security when the world becomes too much, and also a goad and a prod to get out into that world and stand and witness to it. And it is no coincidence that the church is also referred to as Mother Church. The Holy Spirit may be described as "He" (never "It"), but the Church, the protector of the Spirit's unifying love, is referred to as "She." Protestants may rebel at what they feel is an over emphasis upon the devotion to the Virgin Mary by our Roman Catholic brethren. But classic Protestantism has also been made poorer by its cold intellectual masculinity without the recognition of the need for us all to see the fruit of the Spirit, the Church, as a "she" and not as an "it."

The Spirit creates unity not only in time, but in space. The Spirit proclaims the unity of all men, despite their differences. He proclaims the capacity of men to speak together in one common language of love and concern. This indeed is the story related in the book of Acts of the first Pentecost.

Against man's inherent drive to *separate* himself from his neighbor, to build up walls of false smiles and false distinctions, (a drive which we call sin, because the result of all sin is separation and loneliness), there is the persistent and relentless drive of the Spirit to pull us together.

The unity which is achieved is ideally that of love, of forgiving love and acceptance in unity despite those things we each have done which have meant to separate us. Sometimes it is only a unity evidenced by our acknowledgement of our common sin, our separation, but even this unity is a great big step from those who sit either frightened or arrogant in their loneliness.

The church today has many blots on her escutcheon (Cervantes, *Don Quixote*) to be sure. There are many churches where the unity of all men is not allowed to be observed by common worship together by the law of the nation where they are. There are other churches where such lack of unity is expressed not by law but in the much more subtle but equally effective way of hostility and social pressure.[17]

And while there is no question that such deliberately caused separation is a scandal and a blasphemy against the Holy Spirit, it is also fair to say that this is by no means the general course of Christian conduct, nor is such disunity and separation unique to the Christian Church. One need only observe that secular causes have the same problem. Take, for example, the civil rights movement, a great and good cause, which in a few short years has splintered itself into a number of competing, rival factions.[18]

In a day when Christians seem to take some sort of masochistic delight in self-flagellation, when the greatest terms of abuse of the church seem to be com-

17. Ibid., pp. 9-10.

18. Ibid., p. 10.

ing from inside the church itself, it is sometimes helpful to point out some of the more positive aspects of the Christian community. One of these is surely the miracle of the church as the one truly working and operating international community, uniting people of every race and culture throughout the entire world in a common allegiance and a common world view.

In a period when we are involved and concerned about many different forms of political, military, and economic international organizations, we tend to lose sight of a truly international miracle, the Christian Church. Within the past weeks this was brought home forcibly to me because I had the pleasure of meeting Bishop Chiu, the newly consecrated Anglican bishop of Singapore, a native of his diocese and a brilliant former lawyer. I also met, at Diocesan Council, the Roman Catholic Bishop of Kenya, again a native of his country, who expressed great interest in the extent laymen were involved in decision making in the Anglican church and expressed a warmth and love of his Lord which is surely an international trait.

The last conference of the World Council of Churches held in Geneva, where the delegates were predominantly from the laity, was reportedly somewhat of a shock to the delegates from Europe and North America, who found themselves in a minority and very much on the defensive on many issues. This is surely evidence that the gospel of Jesus Christ is beginning to break the strait jacket it has been locked into for the past five hundred years as merely a chaplaincy following the flag of western imperialism. Christianity is no longer identifying itself with western cultures and western values, and those Christians from other cultures are not at all hesitant in saying this. This will probably make us all uncomfortable for some time. Bishop Chiu, for example, made it quite clear that he was concerned about certain churches in his diocese now staffed by American clergy, who see much closer ties to the American church than to him. He pointed out with tact and courtesy, but firmness, that this must end. Either he was the bishop or he was not, and this should have nothing to do with financial support from the outside.

The day has arrived when we can almost say that the gospel has been proclaimed to every race and every nation on the face of the earth. Like a mighty wave moving westward out of the Near East, it engulfed western civilization and then moved on to the farthest corners of the globe. And as with a wave, it picked up characteristic items from each of the lands it passed over. But also, to continue the analogy of a wave, the very height and force of its outer crest left a shallowness and inertia on some of the land previously covered.

It is most probable that in our own country we must realize that the wave has passed over us. The power of the crashing surf is now elsewhere and we are in a period of shallowness and eddy and complacency. But we can take solace from the fact that the water of a wave eventually returns. It is never quite the same, however, because it has picked up and incorporated items from the new beaches it has fallen upon. I am confident that our period of shallowness and complacency in this country is only a temporary thing (although "temporary" in God's eyes may well be measured in generations or centuries). But we must also realize that when depth returns to American Christianity, it will never be the same water we remember nostalgically in the good old days of the so-called Protestant establishment. It will be a depth enriched by the contributions of the peoples of Asia and Africa and South America, and indeed of Europe, which experienced its period of shallowness before us, and now shows many indications of renewal.

The work of the Spirit is by no means confined to the Church. God is at work in His world to unify in many, many areas indeed, including totally secular and non-religious groups. And one of the interesting things is that many of such groups are staffed and sponsored by those who were born and raised as Christians, who now proudly proclaim that while they are grateful for such background, they have now graduated into more important things.[19]

---

19. Krumm, in his article, speaking of that which was written by

There is a fallacy here. At least if the Church is what it says it is, there is no graduating from it. Or to put it another way, to say that one has graduated from the church is like a college graduate saying that now he has graduated he need never open another book or think another thought the rest of his life.[20] Both are equally silly. A college education is not for the purpose of earning a sheep-skin, but rather to be able to have a deeper and fuller experience in living for the rest of your life. So with the church. It is that context of life and value which equips you to live all of your life more fully and deeply. Unfortunately so many of our young people see their confirmation as a graduation in this wrong sense. They see it as a time when they can leave something rather than as a time when they can enter something. To leave is contrary to the Spirit's will, for He wills that we live and act together in unity, and I hope that this day my newly confirmed God-son is reminded of this by his bishop.

The Spirit is indeed at work in the non-church structures of this world, which is perfectly logical when we recall that we describe Him as "the Lord and giver of life"[21] . . .

Bernard Berenson (p. 9).

20. Ibid., p. 11.

21. The phrase "The Lord and giver of life" is contained in the Nicene Creed, *The Book of Common Prayer* (1928), p. 71; cf. Acts 17:24-25.

of *all* life, not just of church life. But I would suggest that there is a uniqueness to life within the church not found elsewhere, which goes more deeply to the center of the human problem than anything else in the world.

There are many organizations where men are joined together by their professed virtue. There are fewer who join together because of a recognition of common weakness and failure, who assert that even heros have flaws and shortcomings that need forgiveness and mercy too. There are fewer still who combine this inclusiveness with the assurance of forgiveness and acceptance, despite these failings, of God Himself. No other organization even makes this claim, and surely no other organization claims to provide the continuing, sustaining nourishment of the sacrament to help us do something about our problem in the future. This organization provides:

A recognition of our common weakness and our needs.
An absolution from our past wrongs.
The feeding of our newly cleansed selves.
The newfound strength to get up and get out into the world.

For all its shortcomings, the Christian church alone has the secret of what creates real fellowship, i.e., the overwhelming and unconditional love and mercy and forgiveness of God in Jesus Christ. "(F)or all of our differences, Christ loves us all, forgives us all, and calls us all into the universal fellowship of his Church."[22]

But we happen to live in the age of the Spirit, that period of history when God's action and love is made known and transmitted through the fallible responses of you and me. No man becomes a Christian on his own. He becomes one because he is told about it by someone else. This is our job.

The unity of man under God's common love is the will of the Spirit. We must ask ourselves this Pentecost what we have done in the past year to effect such unity, confess the failings of our response, and pray that we can open ourselves to a more effective response in the year to come.

---

22. Krumm, p. 10.

3

Our suffering body now stretches beyond Selma, Alabama, to Johannesburg. I don't like it when I get stretched that far. But then I look at that black bishop and I remember his Christian eloquence at the Episcopal Church's General Convention in New Orleans (before he became a Nobel laureate and world figure), and I realize his toothache is mine. We are part of the same body.

The Third Sunday after Epiphany
January 26, 1986

The Cathedral Church of St. Mark
Salt Lake City, Utah

1 CORINTHIANS 12:12-27; LUKE 4:14-21

St. Paul's analogy of a Christian and the Christian Church is that of a human body. What a great common sense analogy to what holds us together.

Our body. What a magnificent piece of machinery it is! Think of the miracle of this. Just for the fun of it, right now, subtly, move your right little finger. Think of that. An audible suggestion comes to us through our ears, it comes to some decision making function in our brain, and we then decide, "I'll be darned if I'm going to let Al Colton make me wiggle my little finger," or we do it. This has been a marvelous audio, mental, and physical process which we go through thousands of times a day. Our body is our only real physical companion. We spend endless hours caring for it. It indeed defines who we are.

Despite the two obvious distinctions in our humanity, we all share certain commonalities. We were born (and can't remember this, the most significant event of our lives). We eat. We breathe. We excrete. Some of us reproduce. And we die. On an emotional plane we each share the experiences of fear, of frustration, of guilt and inadequacy, of love, and of joy.

Each day our newspapers give us lists of those who have just started this journey of sharing in the human phenomenon and those who have just left it.

Now some people in their search for meaning are not content with, or indeed, are dissatisfied and do not approve of the marvel of our physical life. They might concede the marvel of wriggling our little finger on suggestion. They know of the memories of the *smell* of a rose or, in my day, a small gardenia pinned as a corsage on a pretty girl, or a lovely perfume scent; or the smell of incense in a great high church celebration of whatever; or they know of the view of a spectacular sunset (yes, Virginia, they will return to Salt Lake City!); or of the interior bold thrust toward heaven of a Gothic Cathedral.

These folks are not content with this marvel of God's creation. They wanted something more than this crass physical existence because, of course, there are imperfections in this system.

There are those without right little fingers to wiggle and there are those who cannot see sunsets, or whose capacities to do so are very limited. Creation isn't all that good. The smell of gardenias admittedly mixes with other awful smells; the view of a great cathedral can be countered by the structure of a cardboard box, the only cover for a old woman sleeping in freezing weather over the heat exhaust outlet of an executive office building.

So later Jewish thinkers and Greek philosophers discovered the concept of the *soul.* This was something above and beyond that bag of bones we each haul around everyday, above and beyond the crassly physical. It was *this,* they felt, which God our creator truly loved and recognized. So we still pray for "the soul of John departed." We pray for the souls of the faithful departed, and it all sounds so wonderfully pious.

But let me be an idol smasher (an iconoclast) for a few minutes. Isn't that whole idea a bit of pious superfluity? I don't know *you,* and you don't know me, because of our *souls.* We know each other (and I hope love each other) in the garment we wear this minute and the way we use this garment of flesh and bones to act out, in physical and verbal ways, our journey through life.

I have a big nose; Michael Shelton conducts beautiful music; Peg Rowsell handcrafts marvelous vestments;

Bradley Wirth and Rush Duer run our food kitchen; Bill Maxwell preaches a great sermon without notes; Connie Cowan happened to show up and bring order out of chaos at a large funeral the other day; Esther Frank keeps the Episcopal Nominating Committee happy (and the Committee keeps meeting, spending hundreds of hours we hope for the glory of God).

These are not souls, they are people, acting now. I am personally more comfortable with the older Jewish view of personhood, which I also suggest is much more compatible with the Christian proclamation of the Resurrection of the body (*not* the Greek concept of immortality of the soul).

This is best described in present jargon by the term "holism"–coined, irrevocably, by Jan Christian Smuts[23], that great political leader of South Africa (also a philosopher), defeated politically in 1948 by his own people, the Afrikaans, because of his plea for moderation in racial and other issues. "Holism" states that the determining factors in nature are *wholes* (obviously skin pigmentation is by definition the most superficial of distinctions).

We are seen and known, and indeed are ourselves in our wholeness. I cannot close my eyes and imagine the soul of my beloved but you bet your life I can close my eyes and

23. Jan Christian Smuts, *Holism and Evolution* (New York: Macmillan Co., 1926), p. v.

imagine the reality of such a person. The Resurrection of the Body proclaims that we will, in our totality, be recreated.

That of course has its pluses and minuses, but at least it is immensely comprehensible.

It is the *antithesis* of becoming part of some big, pulsating, unusual blob. Our uniqueness will be celebrated forever. The Lord God Almighty, Creator of Heaven and Earth said, "I *love* you, Suzy Jones, and you are ultimately worthy in my sight. Your fingerprints are yours forever. Keep them and use them forever, to my glory and yours."

There are pluses and minuses in that statement. Perhaps I'd rather quit altogether, and be totally forgotten. But I'm sorry, little right finger. You can't quit, even if you wish. Because, like it or not, you are part of a body. *If your body's tooth aches, your little right finger will share that distress and even your "soul" will turn sour.*

This is a physiological truth which St. Paul develops into the concept of the Body of Christ.

I suggest that this physiological truth is also a theological reality. We *are* our brother's keepers. John Donne, convert from Roman Catholicism and Dean of St. Paul's Cathedral in the early seventeenth century, wrote truth when he said:

"No man is an island, entire of itself; every man is a piece of the continent, a part of the main . .. any man's death diminishes me, because I am involved in mankind;

and therefore never send to know for whom the bell tolls; it tolls for thee."[24]

As an Anglican Bishop Desmond Tutu said last Monday, "The great majority of South Africa will some day be free. It is only a question of time. We will then look and see who have been our friends."[25] South Africa is a Christian toothache. White Christian witnesses were present when Martin Luther King called; I think we can be proud of this.

Our suffering body now stretches beyond Selma, Alabama, to Johannesburg. I don't like it when I get stretched that far. But then I look at that black bishop and I remember his Christian eloquence at the Episcopal Church's General Convention in New Orleans (before he became a Nobel laureate and world figure), and I realize his tooth-

24. "No man is an *Iland,* intire of it selfe; every man is a peece of the *Continent,* a part of the maine; . . . any mans death diminishes me, because I am involved in *Mankinde;* And therefore never sent to know for whom the *bell* tolls; It tolls for thee" (*Devotions XVII,* in John Donne, *John Donne – Dean of St. Paul's – Complete Poetry and Selected Prose,* ed. John Hayward [London: Nonesuch Library, 1955], p. 538).

25. Colton was quoting Bishop Desmond Tutu, recipient of the Nonviolent Peace Prize, who actually said the following when he received the award from Coretta Scott King: "When we are free, we want to be able to say the leaders of the free world were on our side . . . When we are free, we will remember who helped us" (Kathy Sawyer, "An Outpouring of Tributes to King–National Celebration Marked By Calls for Apartheid's End," *New York Times,* 21 Jan. 1986, p. A6, Col. 4).

ache is mine. We are part of the same body. And I hear what our Lord selected to read at the synagogue from the prophet Isaiah:

"The spirit of the Lord is upon me, because he has anointed me to preach good news to the poor. He has sent me to proclaim release to the captives . . . to set at liberty those who are oppressed, to proclaim the *acceptable* year of the Lord" [Luke 4:18-19, RSV].

"And he closed the book and gave it back to the attendant, and sat down; and the eyes of all the synagogue were fixed on him. And he began to say to them, 'Today this scripture has been fulfilled in your hearing'" [Luke 4:20-21, RSV].

This is outrageous stuff! Said 2,000 years ago (Isaiah's quotation of course much older), it is a strong mandate to see what we can do about healing toothaches in the body of Christ, before the toothache becomes a serious hemorrhage.

But remember always that this mandate is basically one of love and justice. "I love you, Suzy Jones (and Desmond Tutu), now and forever. You are ultimately worthy in my sight and your fingerprints are yours forever."

But do wriggle your little finger, and then your whole hand, and use this as part of the body, in whatever manner you feel appropriate, for the goodness and healing of the common body and life in Jesus Christ our Lord.

4

The most frequent prayer you will ever hear from a pulpit is the vegetable prayer–"Let us" etc., etc. But in the hearts of each of us, including the preacher, the most frequent non-publicly articulated prayer is the "gimmie" prayer–Lord, give me this, Lord, give me that.

The Third Sunday in Lent
March 2, 1986

The Cathedral Church of St. Mark
Salt Lake City, Utah

"Give us this day, our daily bread."

A phrase repeated by hundreds of millions of people each day as a part of the Lord's prayer.

A petition made each day by millions of others who have never heard of the Lord's prayer.

I have learned a great deal by reading and thinking about this particular preaching assignment, as we continue these Sundays in Lent examining the Lord's prayer.

First, as to prayer in general: The most frequent prayer you will ever hear from a pulpit is the vegetable prayer. "Let us etc., etc." But in the hearts of each of us, including the preacher, the most frequent non-publicly articulated prayer is the "gimmie" prayer. "Lord, give me this, Lord, give me that." We cloak these selfish requests of course with the requisite piety, "If it be thy will"; "If I, an unworthy person, deserve such a request"; but underneath this pious coating, we are still saying, "Lord, gimmie."

Is this phrase of the Lord's prayer just another concession to the "gimmie" prayers? The selfish little kernel loaded to make it easier to justify by pious disclaimers both before and after?

I submit that this is not so, but I also submit that the meaning of this simple petition takes on more meaning the more we ponder it.

First, consider the context in which it appears. As Dean Maxwell and Canon Wirth have so eloquently explained in the two prior sermons, we have a prayer which begins by making certain awesome and loving ascriptions to the nature of God and then it touches upon the kingdom which is coming, and in one sense is here now.

This is not a typical gimmie prayer. And, of course, on its face, it isn't a gimmie prayer at all. It petitions, "give *us*" our daily bread.

By definition, this has to mean more than "me." It is broader than this. It can be as narrow as an immediate family, a tribal group, a nation, or all of mankind. But at least that very supplication draws us from the hell of ego-centrism which is so magnificently described in myth form in Genesis III; that which we call original sin, and which with the term "pride" or "selfishness" the medieval church aptly described as the "queen of sins."

Give *us,* not just me. I've moved a little way by using just that single phrase.

"*Daily* bread." With the word "daily," my research led to something fascinating. The New Testament was, of course, written in Greek. We can find no earlier Aramaic or Hebrew texts of the Lord's prayer. The Greek word *epiousion,* which we translate as "daily," appears nowhere else in Greek literature and is therefore of uncertain meaning because there are no parallels. Some scholars suggest it comes from the Greek word which means "for the following day" and would apply to the daily rations issued to slaves, soldiers, as well as others.

It clearly refers to essential needs, not a surplus. Not a three year's supply, but enough for tomorrow. We are reminded of the manna of the Old Testament. You couldn't keep it and store it. You must consume God's gift when given it and wait upon his grace to replenish you again tomorrow, tomorrow, and tomorrow.

This is obviously, then, a principle of *trust*–"sufficient unto the day is the evil thereof" . . . "be not anxious" . . . "For what does it profit a man to gain the whole world and forfeit his life?" [Mark 8:36, RSV]

"Daily," in this sense, is an echo of the parable from Luke of the rich man whose great surplus led him to tear down his old barns and build bigger and better ones into which he could store his bounty and then say to himself, "Soul, you have ample goods laid up for many years; take your ease, eat, drink and be merry." But God said, 'Fool, This night your soul is required of you; and the things you have prepared, whose will they be?' So is he who lays up treasure for himself and is not rich toward God" [Luke 12:16-21 RSV].

So much for "daily," how about "bread"? That's an obvious one. The dictionary and the encyclopedia answer this for us. It is the oldest of all foods manufactured by man. It is a worldwide staple. At least in the United States and Western Europe since World War I, it is something which we eat which is made by someone outside of our family unit.

Is that *all* that is meant? Bread is called the staff of life. Jesus described Himself as "the bread of life" [John 6:34-58, RSV]. He was recognized as the risen Lord to the two travelers to Emmaus "in the breaking of bread" [Luke 24:35, RSV]. He miraculously fed the multitudes with bread. He told the devil that man cannot live by bread (the staple) alone. Our central act of worship centers around *bread* and wine.

Clearly "bread," in this context, must mean more than mere fodder for the bowels. It covers, in a generic sense, all those things which sustain us, physically, but also in the world of value and of spirit.

But let us not flee from a literal meaning. After all, the

Christian proclaims he lives in a *sacramental* world. God acts and is made known through his physical world, and the judgment upon us is how we handle the physical things which we are allowed to influence.

Ask an American slum kid, third generation from a fatherless homelife (and a child of God), what "bread" means. "Bread? Man, that means money, and money means power."

And we are staring at a different world to which all of the pious, scholarly words I have just spouted are meaningless.

Underlying all of my rhetoric I assumed certain concepts of fairness and compassion which we can recognize and comprehend. However, fairness and compassion (whether they be Christian or not) are part of a *comfortable* culture.

Don't dare talk fairness and compassion to a streetwise slum kid who has never known *any* family, who has never known fairness and compassion in his life.

Think of little gnarled lives, who in their memory have never been held or cuddled, either as babies or as adults. And these little gnarled kids grow up into gnarled adults, hard to touch, because they have never been taught to respond as most of us have.

If we have fairness in the basics, not in a surplus, but in our daily bread, then perhaps the surplus can take care of itself.

4. THE THIRD SUNDAY IN LENT, 1986.

My first image of fairness was in the movie *Mutiny on the Bounty* staring Charles Laughton in about 1935. Terrible Captain Bligh, the bully, the tyrant, was driving his crew to mutiny. They cast him in open boat with a few loyal followers, and miraculously hundreds of miles later, they arrived to safety, but not without almost dying of hunger and of thirst. One day, at the depth of despair, someone batted down a gull with an oar. "Give it to me," the Captain ordered. And he cut the bird in equal portions starting with the beak and ending with the tail. Then he made the first mate turn his back, and as he held up a piece he would say, "Whose portion, Mr. Jenkins," and this part would be given to the person named. And the Captain carefully ate the beak, his only nourishment for many days. *That,* I think, is fairness of bread.

Forget Ethiopia. We, in this country, have become so unfair in our concept of daily bread. Each one of us could easily leave a loaf of bread each day at the door of this Cathedral church and not miss a thing, yet meet this petition of the Lord's prayer for someone else.

But rather than that, we catch ourselves fighting over thousands of dollars, fighting over what is surely surplus.

The concept of "daily" bread has been totally forgotten–they are defining bread in the terms of the deprived street boy, and the *trust* of the term "daily" forgotten. They are back to Genesis III, perhaps without ever knowing it.

My oh my—isn't there much to think about in a mere seven words!

A friend of mine once told me, "I could never get much mileage out of the Lord's Prayer." Having repeated it myself endless thousands of times, often at a mile a minute (God forgive me, but I have found that without a watch on, ten "Our Fathers" is about the appropriate time to perform certain tasks; having as a child heard with admiration a Roman Catholic priest rattle off Ten "Hail Mary's" in almost one breath), I know the dangers and fallacies of rote prayer or of any fixed liturgical form. Why can't we just pray spontaneously and from the spirit?

But a wise and great Jesuit priest, Gustave Wergel, gives what for me is a satisfactory answer:

> the Catholic reacts very badly to the spontaneous prayer spoken at Protestant gatherings. Certainly the idea of spontaneous prayer is unassailable but the way it works out frequently is uncomfortable. Some "spontaneous" prayer is evidently well prepared and rehearsed before the moment of pouring forth. In some cases it is written and read. When it is strictly *extempore,* there are many interspersals of *uhs* and *ahs,* betraying a conscious struggle in the man who is supposed to be uttering an overflow of thought and feeling. Those who are really masters at it, are frequently artificial and theatrical. And in spite of all its supposed spontaneity, it is remarkable how it usually comes out as a mosaic of King James Bible English, with *thees* and *thous* and

> *lookdowns*. Spontaneous it may be, but it is not the spontaneity of our daily existence but a labored attempt to achieve a studied biblical language expression.[26]

We can hear our liturgy every Sunday and send back the responses with fervor. We can enjoy a well-sung litany or a *Sursum Corda,*[27] and it is all too often, water off a duck's back. (That is not meant pejoratively, because I assume that usually a duck *enjoys* water on its back.)

But we do things often by rote, and in a liturgical church that is how it is done. Yet there come those flashy moments in our life when rote becomes suddenly reality. A few words we have so often said suddenly crash into our head and perception, and we say, "This is true; this has meaning."

Give us this day our daily bread. Amen.

---

26. Robert McAfee Brown and Gustave Weigel, S.J., *An American Dialogue: A Protestant Looks at Catholicism and a Catholic Looks at Protestantism* (Garden City, NY: Doubleday and Co., Inc., 1960), p. 136.

27. The *Sursum Corda* is the portion of the Thanksgiving in the Eucharist which begins with the words "The Lord be with you . . . ," e.g., *The Book of Common Prayer* (1979), p. 361.

II
Belief

Introduction

There is not one answer only as to why we believe what we believe. Albert Colton wrestled with this in a variety of ways and lamented, perhaps tongue in cheek, God's not just blasting humanity with the only option for belief and truth. Certainly faith would have been much less complicated and religious argumentation would have been kept at a minimum. However, that was not to be. Therefore we have been left with the option of choice governing belief. Colton thought this was a direct result of God's love for us, allowing us to wrestle with truth.

Every American has heard the term "Doubting Thomas," but as evidence of our present biblical illiteracy, when I asked around my office as to its origin, almost no one knew.

We have just heard the story from the Gospel of John [John 20:19-31]–"Unless I physically see and physically touch, I will not believe," said Thomas. Thomas was then given the opportunity to see and touch and he then uttered the classic Christian profession of faith, "My Lord and my God!" [John 20:28, RSV]

And Jesus responded, "Have you believed because you have seen me? Blessed are those who have not seen and yet believe" [John 20:29, RSV].

And of course that category includes all of us here today.

God could have acted otherwise. If God is omniscient and omnipotent, as we believe He is, He could, for example, arrange a spectacular show of power say every noon throughout the world–say a darkening of the sun and a booming voice understood by everyone demanding obedience.

Such a celestial power show would, I bet, result in a substantial increase in church attendance, and if we could get God to use portions of *The Book of Common Prayer,* it would be a great boon for our Cathedral.

But God has chosen not to do this. He does not say, "love me or I'll knock your block off." Rather He says, "I'll leave you free to either accept or reject me."[1]

Colton found two avenues to begin his contemplation of belief. The first, and less significant, was all of the components we seemingly control when believing or attempting to believe. That includes all the feelings and categories of recognition we foster when we approach the world. The second, and more significant element contained in belief, contributing most to our sense of commitment, is the breakthrough of God into our lives. That comes from beyond our own little world and sometimes it makes sense and sometimes it scuttles our limited understanding of the world by turning the world on its head.

---

1. Sermon preached the Second Sunday of Easter, April 10, 1988, the Cathedral Church of St. Mark, Salt Lake City, Utah.

"O all ye works of the Lord, bless ye the Lord, praise Him and magnify Him forever."[2]

Despite the bugs and the mosquitos, I find my faith reaffirmed by my encounters with the majesty and wonder of the physical life I observe.

Yet, this is not a totally rational reaction. In one sense, I have already made up my mind, and am using this as buttressing for what I have already decided I will believe.

An English fellow named Anselm about a thousand years ago put this thought process into a formula. He said, *"Credo ut intelligam"*—"I believe so that I may understand."[3]

I know this is a terribly unfashionable thing to say in our day and age when scientific rationalism is clearly supposed to lead us to truth.

I know that certain religious bodies emphasizing this formula, even though they don't have the foggiest idea that it came from one of the members of our

---

2. The opening line of Canticle 1, "A Song of Creation" (Benedicite, omnia opera Domini), *The Book of Common Prayer* (New York: The Church Hymnal Corporation, 1979), p. 47.

3. "*Neque enim quaero intelligere ut credam, sed credo ut intelligam. Nam et hoc credo: quia 'nisi credidero, non intelligam.'*" ("For I do not seek to understand so that I may believe; but I believe so that I may understand. For I believe this also, that 'unless I believe, I shall not understand.'") In St. Anselm, *St. Anselm's Proslogion,* trans., intro., and phil. com. M. J. Charlesworth (Notre Dame: University of Notre Dame Press, 1979), pp. 114-15.

church, and pervert it to mean, "Park your brains with your car as you enter this house of worship."

I, of course, don't mean this at all. The issue I am proposing, however, which is impossible to discuss in any depth in even the twenty minutes which is the ultimate heretical limit of any Anglican sermon, is *how* we come to commitment to *anything.*

I can find my lost credit cards by the use of pure reason. If my credit cards are indeed the answer to my ultimate questions, then the use of reason is enough.

But I would venture to say that no one here is a Christian, an Episcopalian (or a Democrat or Republican), on the basis of sheer reason alone. These decisions are made because of a mix of many, many things–family tradition, a sudden loss, frustration, grief, guilt, a love of beauty, a smell of incense, social pressure, a yearning for meaning, and certainly a feeling that this commitment makes sense.

Each of us, not in our lips but in our lives, whether we know it or not, reflects a commitment to that which we hold to have ultimate value. This commitment is really quite transparent and obvious to those who know us well.

St. Paul, 2,000 years ago confronting a group of hard-boiled rationalists, suggested that the first step to an ultimate commitment came from outside–not something we found on our own by use of our own facilities.[4]

---

4. Sermon preached the Second Sunday after Pentecost, May 28,

While believing that God reveals God's self to us, thereby leading us to believe, Colton was not overly impressed with the miraculous moments out of the ordinary. God came to us more powerfully by the cross.

> I really should be preaching this Sunday on the miracles of God–after all, two of our three appointed lessons deal with these. But quite honestly, miracles don't turn me on. I do not worship a person because he turns water into wine at a party even though he'd be cheaper than caterers generally.
>
> As the Dean suggested last Sunday, what Jesus Christ taught and acted through in his life makes one a believer without the need of miracles.
>
> He went to a cross and into hell, and he said he did this for you and me. And he conquered death–also for you and me. Once this truth is appreciated, there is a fire lighted and reflected in the power of words such as those of St. Paul in today's epistle [Gal. 1:11-24].[5]

Neither would Colton be taken in by the temptation of being overwhelmed by numbers. Just because millions of people believed this or that was not enough reason to form beliefs, change beliefs, or abandon belief. Growing religions and sects impressed him very little.

1978, the Cathedral Church of St. Mark, Salt Lake City, Utah.

5. Sermon preached the Third Sunday after Pentecost, June 8, 1986, the Cathedral Church of St. Mark, Salt Lake City, Utah.

We all like to be on a winning team. I want to be pastor and preach over TV at the Crystal Cathedral in Southern California, or be with Billy Graham, with thousands cheering, or have Brother Falwell's following of millions. Yet we sit in this lovely small Cathedral Church with a boiler ready to blow up, and our parish hall kitchen a tribute to the culinary state of the art of the early 1920s.

Aren't *numbers,* either of people or of dollars, the best test there is of commitment?

Should we load up with a little more hell-fire and brimstone? Two of our four official nominees for Bishop of Utah in their presentations a few weeks ago commented on the "graciousness" of Anglicanism. Perhaps we should bag this, roll up our sleeves and start eating peas with our knife.[6]

Colton believed we should not be so tempted. The substance of belief begins and ends with God's claim on the whole of one's being. It does not live and die by the fancies of humanity. Even our belief in belief is not ours but is Christ's.

(T)he Christian claim is a pretty gigantic one. It is a claim on the totality of a person's life.

It is first of all the assertion of a God who is Creator and Sustainer of all life. It says that every breath we draw is a gift of God. All of our life is within the concern and purview of God. Now a psy-

6. Ibid.

choanalyst said to me last week-end, "Isn't that pretty presumptuous of you to make such a claim?" Well of course it is—but certainly if I am going to believe in a God, I want a first class one—as the Venite says, perhaps referring to polytheism still present at the time, our God is "a great King above all gods."[7] Not only is the claim presumptuous in this sense, but of course if true, then it restricts the significance of each individual.

If God is Lord of my life, then of course I can't be Lord of my life, or of your life. I can't be God because God is God. If God is Creator of all things, then I am merely a creature. And as Genesis III reminds us, man doesn't like this kind of restriction on himself. It is hard, hard, hard, for us to acknowledge that we are dependent. "I need you" is a true statement, but it is something difficult to say.[8]

Belief for Colton was something beyond our capabilities to construct. Taking pride in one's belief was foolishness. Rather, belief was finding one's self included in the "arrogance" of the Gospel. Colton believed Jesus' willingness to die, as well as his death and resurrection, changed forever all of the cosmos. Faced

7. *The Book of Common Prayer* (New York: The Church Pension Fund, 1928), p. 9.

8. Sermon preached on the Sunday Next Before Advent, November 20, 1966, St. Francis' Church, San Francisco, California.

with that fact, Colton then, and only then, was able to respond with belief and commitment.

Many of us view our church and our faith as a nice club—one we are pleased and proud to belong to—but of necessity recognizing other clubs which other people are equally pleased to belong to. And because we are nice tolerant folks, or because we know that one way for others to tolerate us is for us to tolerate them, we shy away from making any claims that set us aside as unique or special.

So we make statements such as "I don't care what you believe in, so long as you believe in something," or "we're all going in the same direction," or "each to his own taste; religion is a personal matter and whatever makes you feel better is right for you."

And then BAM!—along comes intense, passionate, brilliant St. Paul and says, "All of this is nonsense!" "The Christian proclamation is just not for those who are made to feel better because of it; it is not just for those who decide to belong to the club; it is a proclamation that applies to all men; not only to all men, but to all of creation and to the entire universe—to the whole creation."

Of course, this sounds downright arrogant, or to some people, preposterous and silly, and I think most of us try to shy away from this incredible claim of universal uniqueness—certainly, most of us are appalled at religious sects that claim that they alone have all the answers. To these groups, Archbishop Geoffrey Fisher had an appropriate answer: "The Anglican Communion does not claim to have all the answers, but it has enough for me."[9]

However, St. Paul raises a slightly different issue than the claim of infallible superiority. St. Paul is proclaiming the unique and cosmic influence of an event in history. He is saying that the life, death and resurrection of one man knit back together the universe, whether that universe knows it or acknowledges it or not.

This, to many, is absurd arrogance. To some, this does not deter acceptance. Tertullian, an early Christian theologian, said, "I believe because it is absurd."[10]

---

9. Citation uncertain.

10. Colton quoted Tertullian as saying, *"Credo quia absurdum."* However, some doubt that Tertullian actually said this. For example, Arthur McGiffert wrote: "We are to believe the rule of faith not because it is true and not because it appeals to us, as expressing the mind of Christ, but because it is commanded. The more unreasonable it appears to us, so Tertullian seem to think, the greater the merit of our faith (f.n. 3, cf. *Adv. Marcionem,* II.2; V.5). In his tract, *On the Flesh of Christ,* he declares, 'The Son of God died: it is absolutely worthy of belief because it is absurd. (f.n. 4 *Prorsus credible est, quia ineptum est.*) And having been buried, he rose again; it is certain because it is impossible.' (f.n. 5 *Certum est, quia impossible est* [*De carne Christi,* 5] The particular words, *Credo quia absurdum,* often attributed to Tertullian are not his.)." In Arthur McGiffert, *A History of Christian Thought* (New York: Charles Scribner's Sons, 1947), Vol. 2:16. Sermon preached in Lent, 1981 (otherwise undated), the Cathedral Church of St. Mark, Salt Lake City, Utah. Also preached in Lent, 1981 (otherwise undated), All Saints Church, Salt Lake City, Utah.

1

I submit that it may well be that it is more difficult today to be a Christian than at any other time in history, and that even we as laymen, avowedly Church members, cannot be too sure of our allegiance. It is a time when we should each carefully ask ourselves, "Is our life based on a Christian choice, or some watered down version of 'do-goodism'?"

Laymen's Sunday — *The Cathedral Church of St. Mark*
October 14, 1956 — *Salt Lake City, Utah*

[Note: In 1956, Albert Colton served the parish as a church school teacher and clerk of the Vestry. This was his first sermon.]

The feeling everyone has that he has at least one hundred sermons up his sleeve better than the one being given disappears rapidly when time comes to deliver one. Yet all sermons essentially concern our God, our Church, ourselves, and the relationship among them. Our clergy, once a year on this Sunday, ask the laymen to wrestle with these problems and try to present them in concrete form, without benefit of the clergy.

Sermons concern wondrous things. Sometimes, indeed, familiarity with the words blind us to the true marvel of the concepts. It never hurts, therefore, to restate these as laymen without professional theological help.

In our endless universe and on this insignificant speck called Earth is an ant-hill, and human beings have frequently worked with great diligence to destroy one another. But throughout this ordeal they have always longed for something more. They have shown an appreciation for a greater force than that realized by their senses, and have worshipped this.

On this speck of earth, within a devout religiously developed people 2,000 years ago, arose a group which made the non-logical and what has been called the scandalous assertion that this divine force, vaguely worshipped by all men, has come to earth in human form to redeem all men from their fallen state.

This group was not to hide its light under a bushel. They were to be proselytizers–salesmen. As Matthew said, they were told: "Go ye therefore and teach all nations, baptizing them in the name of the Father, and of the Son, and of the Holy Ghost" [Matt. 28:19, KJV].

This "cult" has grown in 2,000 years into the largest and most influential organized religious force on the face of the earth. Most of us have been brought up to pay lip-service to its authority.

Yet in this nation which has achieved unequaled material power and splendor, we find fear, neurosis, and loneliness. W. H. Auden, the poet, reminds us that we are:

> Lost in a haunted wood;
> Children afraid of the night
> Who have never been happy or good.[11]

Our novels often reflect a moral bankruptcy. Our non-fiction list is filled with books promising peace of mind, material success through "positive thought"–combining easy nostrums and abracadabra which our eager public gobbles down between doses of *Miltown*. How often we see the ulcerated American, caught in a "rat race" without a goal, or without reason.

Now this observation, if accurate, suggests either that religion is incapable of coping with these problems, or that while it can cope with them, it is really not a significant force in this country. I suggest that it is not a significant force.

W. Norman Pittenger, the noted Episcopalian writer and teacher, makes this observation: "(W)e are now living in a world which is essentially non-Christian, both in its assumptions about the meaning of life and in the actual

---

11. W. H. Auden, "September 1, 1939, *The Collective Poetry of W. H. Auden* (New York: Random House, 1945), pp. 57-61, see p. 58.

conduct of life itself. It is time that all of us were aware of this fact and that silly chatter about America as a 'Christian land' were silenced. America is *not* a Christian land."[12]

I submit that it may well be that it is more difficult today to be a Christian than at any other time in history, and that even we as laymen, avowedly Church members, cannot be too sure of our allegiance. It is a time when we should each carefully ask ourselves, "Is our life based on a Christian choice, or some watered down version of 'do-goodism'?"

We are all aware of the forces which make Dr. Pittenger's comment accurate. We are, first of all, a people who have harnessed the world of science, yet we often refuse to see that with its benefits it takes its toll. Our children, for example, rather than labor through the miracle of the printed page and the individual imagery which it necessarily involves, turn to the TV résumé of the same story, done with much greater technical accuracy, and also done in one-half hour. It is a world made so blasé by the super-colossal that basic truths lack their dramatic impact.

We are a people that seem to have a real fear of being different. As David Reisman said, "We are a nation of the lonely crowd, each member basing his values on nothing

12. W. Norman Pittenger, *Christ in the Haunted Wood–The Christian Foundation for the Good Life* (Greenwich, CT: Seabury Press, 1953), p. 167.

he deems inherent in all things, but only on what the other fellow thinks."[13] This moral relativism is reflected in the Kinsey report. What is classified as "normal" is what most people actually do. If enough people do a thing, by this logic, we are all excused.[14]

This moral relativism is a clear result of our scientific conquests. Healthy skepticism is the basis of the scientific method. The revered rule of yesterday is today reposing in the scientific garbage can, supplanted by new rules which are tested, and which work better. This skepticism in the world of science is then transferred to the world of moral values. All doctrinaire statements are treated with suspicion. Thus, the boldness of the Christian assertion becomes a source of embarrassment. "Surely," the skeptic says, "I can see much good in your religion. Your moral code is a fine one. But you really can't mean it when you say that it is the answer."

Nevertheless, the malaise of our time drives even the skeptic to seek comfort somewhere. Having repudiated his

---

13. It is uncertain where Colton found this quotation. The subject, however, is well covered in David Reisman, *The Lonely Crowd* (New Haven, CT: Yale University Press, 1950). Over a dozen magazine articles also portrayed a similar impression in reviewing Reisman's theme expressed by Colton's citation.

14. Alfred C. Kinsey, Wardell B. Pomeroy, and Clyde E. Martin, *Sexual Behavior in the Human Male* (Philadelphia: W. B. Saunders Co., 1948), pp. 384-86, and esp. p. 678.

religious heritage, he seeks help in some form of ethical code–in some "do it yourself" religion. His eyes grow misty as he gazes into the distance and assures us, "I have my own religion." It is frequently a collection of unthought-out abstractions. It was C. S. Lewis who told of the young lady who finally discovered that in her self-made religious system she had formed a mental image of God which was terrifyingly similar to tapioca pudding.[15]

These home-brewed concoctions are often based upon shallow and unreal optimism that evaporates the first time "positive thinking" doesn't lead to positive results. Often it is wholly pessimistic, leading only to a life robbed of zest and joy.

In the midst of all this stands the Church, saying that God has revealed Himself once in time in human form, and that for a period of thirty or so years Time and Eternity, Divinity and Humanity were one. This is a staggering assertion.

If true, it is the most fantastic and important event in the history of the world. There is no compromise with it. Yet despite the fact that we recite our belief in this every

---

15. "A girl I knew was brought up by 'higher thinking' parents to regard God as a perfect 'substance'; in later life she realised that this had actually led her to think of Him as something like a vast tapioca pudding. (To make matters worse, she disliked tapioca.)" From C. S. Lewis, *Miracles* (New York: Macmillan Publishing Co., Inc., 1947), p. 75.

time we say the Creeds, it would be interesting to know how many laymen believe this or have thought through its implications. Many of us, I am sure, are honestly a little embarrassed by the assertion of the Incarnation, and prefer to discuss the Beatitudes and the Golden Rule.

But is Christianity really incompatible with the thinking of our scientific skeptic? I think not. He must concede that we, as finite minds, can never conceivably comprehend the Infinite. Dogs, however smart, will never learn to read, or lobsters to give sermons. We can never, therefore, presume to prove anything about God. Infinity is beyond our comprehension. Whatever our skeptic wishes to believe or disbelieve about God, it is not because he has proven anything. He, like everyone else, must make the leap of faith when it comes to the Ultimate. Whatever God wishes to make known to us about Himself must come from Him, not us. It must, whether the skeptic likes the word or not, be *revealed.* The Christian says that God has already revealed Himself in human form in our dimension of time-space. There is no way that we can logically prove the truth of this revelation.

In fact, the assertions of Christianity are probably immensely illogical. Indeed, is not this lack of logic "logical"? Should a loving God appear more readily to the Phi Beta Kappa than to the peasant? From the viewpoint of divinity the difference in intellectual ability between the two is nothing. Brains and logic are in fact often hindrances, because they are tools which we, in our pride, pathetically use to lead us to think that we can analyze the Infinite.

But there is one form of proof which should appeal to the skeptic: Christianity works! To those who give up using the Church as a hedge against Eternity—to those who stop keeping one foot on shore and one in the boat, ready to jump either way—to those who cast out completely from the shore with faith, there is a comfort not to be found anywhere else.

We laymen who are avowedly Church members should ask ourselves whether we are aship or ashore, or conveniently trying to stay in both places at once. How relentless a theological "third degree" can we stand? While, for example, we may dismiss the zeal of the missionary from some other faith who visits our home, are we really as well equipped as he in knowledge of Scripture so that we may discuss knowledgeably points of dogma on which we differ? How many good serious religious books ("meaty" ones) have we read recently?

If we feel strong in our faith, have we tested it with a few non-Christians anecdotes? How well can we resist the works of the iconoclast—the Elmer Gantry type of fiction, or some good Socialistic harangue on religion as "the opiate of the people"? Or how well does your faith stand up against the gentle yet sub-Christian humanism of a philosopher like Alfred North Whitehead? If we must stand these tests (and the battle against doubt is a perpetual one) we must then ask, do our *actions* reflect the Christian *conviction* which we claim we have, or do they show doubt?

The average St. Mark's Cathedral layman must have more doubt than he will admit. The largest church fund raising organization in the United States classes church congregations into three groups: the core, the body, and the periphery. The core is about 15 percent of the congregation. It gives from 60 percent to 75 percent of the financial support needed by the Church. The body, about 50 percent in numbers, contributes 20 percent of the money, and the periphery, which is the remaining 35 percent, contributes 5 percent to 10 percent. I am told that this breakdown is born out at St. Mark's. About 15 percent of the congregation give about 75 percent of its support.

Now while it may be argued that the core group, because of their churchly diligence, is rewarded with more of the world's goods to give, we all know that Christianity (despite the testimony of certain modern writers) is not a guarantee to riches. The differences, therefore, must be in one's conviction.

The Episcopal Church has been, in the eyes of many, the church of the "nice people" where the debutantes are married and where (as one member of the vestry of a wealthy California parish told me) the "educated gentlemen" go. By "nice people" is clearly meant people who think that they are nice people, or of course, not nice people at all. This stigma is grossly and patently unfair, but as a relative newcomer to the Church, I find it is an opinion that is widely held. It is perhaps some evidence that our actions reflect Christian doubts instead of Christian conviction.

These are aspects of our life in the Church. What our personal lives show we alone know best. We must all remember that Christianity does not require unattainable perfection. Such would be a religion of despair, not hope, for imperfect creatures like ourselves. It requires a seeking for an acceptance of God's forgiveness, and a constant moral effort to bridge the unbridgeable gap between our actuality and the perfect.

But we may well examine our motives. Many of us made the choice to Christianity in search of emotional peace not to be found elsewhere. If this is our goal, we may be disappointed. If we are not willing to love God unless we get something out of it for ourselves, we are secretly making ourselves the center of things rather than God.

As Arnold Toynbee suggested in his *Study of History,* one of the great miracles of life is the inability to attain a goal by aiming directly at it, yet attaining it unknowingly while striving for something else.[16] A person who works

---

16. Arnold J. Toynbee, *A Study of History,* Vols. 7-10 abrdg., D. C. Somervell (London: Oxford University Press, 1957), pp. 1-3.

only to achieve personal happiness may find nothing. One who strives to identify as closely as he can with his God and with his church may find he has attained the same happiness without knowing it. This has been the experience of devoted laymen over the centuries. Through work in their church, the vehicle of Christ on this earth, they have found a satisfaction unobtainable elsewhere.

It would be well for each of us on this October 14, 1956, as we live on our portion of that speck called Earth, to ask ourselves frankly what choice we have made in our life. Despite our scientific progress, the choice is the same one man has always had to make. Does he choose to worship his God with all his heart, all his soul, and all his mind, or does he put it off until tomorrow? Does he strive to accept the tenets of the Apostle's Creed, praying all the while, "Lord, I believe; help Thou mine unbelief" [Mark 9:24, KJV], or does he consider this (if he considers at all) as a mere meaningless bit of ritual?

It is a choice each must make alone. By failing to choose, we in fact make a choice. Relentlessly we are driven to decide whether we wish to be another of the scurrying ants on the ant-hill, or to partake wholeheartedly of what Our Lord tells us is the Way and the Life.

2

Let those who froth at the mouth over what they feel is the church's excessive involvement in the affairs of the world ask themselves the reason for their great concern. Could it not possibly be that they have little carved-out areas of their life where they do not want God or judgment or anything else to enter?

The First Sunday after the Epiphany — *St. Francis' Church*
January 9, 1966 — *San Francisco, California*

Epiphany is the great feast of the celebration of the manifestation of God's truth to the whole world. It is an essential part of the Christian faith, this making manifest, this showing forth, this preaching and proclaiming. For as St. Paul states in one of his very logical developments:

> How then shall they call on Him in whom they have not believed? And how shall they believe in Him of whom they have not heard? And how shall they hear without a preacher? [Rom. 10:14, KJV]

And yet preaching has become a nasty word. One frequently heard complaint in a domestic situation that has gone sour is that one spouse is always "preaching"—

"Preach, preach, preach all day long," and the comment is not made in terms of endearment.

The word "Preacher" has a bit of the taste of southern corn-pone, a florid faced man with a mane of white hair and a booming voice, or a skinny, pointed-nosed man with an angry whining voice.

It is remarkable that the preached sermon has survived at all. It doesn't do any good to remind you of what you are being spared. Only a hundred years ago, a man who couldn't preach for at least an hour just wasn't worth his pay. Even then it was suggested by some that the purpose of a sermon was not so much to communicate God's truth to the faithful as it was to bore the devil to death.

Anglicanism has indeed had some great preachers, but as a whole it is not noted for the strength of its preaching. This is partially because we can become seduced by the great beauty and majesty of the rest of our liturgy and feel it is not necessary to rely upon the sermon to add anything. This was surely true until the great Reformation now taking place in the Roman Catholic Church. Until Pope John XXIII, of sainted memory, the Catholic Church had, without question, the worst preaching in Christendom. The pulpit was used principally for harangues, mercifully brief, either for money or on the sins of the flesh. Once again the Roman Church's liturgical emphasis had perhaps made the ministry of the preached Word seem unnecessary. This was not true of most of Protestantism, whose less elaborate and dramatic liturgical structure tended to give a greater emphasis to the sermon. But even here the question is being asked, "In a time when almost all congregations are literate, and where most of them have more brains and intellectual equipment than the preacher, if he has anything to say, why not have him write it out, mimeograph it, and let the congregation take it home and read it on their own?"

It is surely true that the day when the preacher was the best educated man in town is well passed. One of the great revolutions, which the church must face, is that the brains are now in the pews. However, once having said that, let me make two observations. One of the things you pay us clergy to do is to study.

Phillips Brooks wrote one hundred years ago, "In many respects an ignorant clergy, however pious it may be, is worse than none at all. The more the empty head glows and burns, the more hollow and thin and dry it grows. 'The knowledge of the priest,' said St. Francis de Sales, 'is the eighth sacrament of the Church.'"[17]

With the competing demands on time of pastoral, administrative and liturgical duties, study is sometimes difficult to work in, but this is our fault. The pile of

---

17. Theodore Parker Ferris, intro., *Phillips Brooks on Preaching* (New York: Seabury Press, 1964), p. 45.

published material, much of it good and exciting and significant, that comes into a church office each week is overwhelming. It is impossible to expect the average layman to keep abreast of this anymore than it would be to expect a priest to keep abreast of current events in your specialties. But it is surely one of the roles of the clergy to keep informed and to select from and submit to his laity portions of this material which have direct relevance and bearing on their present interests and concerns.

While I readily agree that today the brains are in the pews and not in the pulpits (and of course there is a great quantity of brain power that is *neither* in the pulpit or the pew), it is still quite obvious that there is a great deal of difference between innate, inert brain-power and brain power which is mobilized and working at a particular problem. Somehow this brain-power and capacity sitting in the pews has to be mobilized, and inspired to go to work, and while I have been properly humbled by the hortatory powers of my preaching, I am absolutely convinced that the effectiveness of exhortation from the pulpit is hundreds of times more effective than it is through the printed word of the parish mailing or Sunday bulletin.

(I may have mentioned before a story an older priest told me about the Sunday he put into the bulletin, buried among the other announcements, that "the rector will give five dollars to each person who mentions this notice to him after the service," and he left the church Sunday none the poorer. I'm not sure that I believe the story, but then again, maybe so.)

Preaching is as old as the Christian Church. Several of the sermons of St. Paul and St. Peter are preserved for us in the book of Acts. A sermon of St. Stephen, which caused his martyrdom, is set forth in the 7th chapter of Acts. St. Philip, on one occasion, preached to a congregation of one–the Ethiopian eunuch [Acts 8:35].

Nor should we be led to think that preaching was used then because the hearers were illiterate rustics. Most of the listeners could read well enough, and we know that St. Paul sent out a steady stream of correspondence to church congregations. But it is also certain that St. Paul, when he arrived at a church to which he had written, would not merely refer to his letters, he would preach. Part of the process of communication and proclamation of the Good News was the person-to-person confrontation, flesh to flesh, eyeball to eyeball. (I have heard stories of people who have been converted to the Christian faith solely by reading the Bible, but I have never met such a person, and I am sure that they are rare. I have met a number of persons who have read the Bible thoroughly, but not having anyone to discuss it with, or hear it expounded and interpreted, have remained completely unmoved. The great mathematician and philosopher Alfred North Whitehead spent many years in a study of Holy Scripture, but he viewed this as an academic exercise and never became involved in the flesh and blood of the church as such.) Words, by themselves, are dry bones until life is breathed into them.

The function of preaching has never changed. It is to proclaim the Good News of God's action in Jesus Christ which reconciles men to God and to themselves. It is to make Epiphany—to make this manifest to the world. But how this proclamation can be done is another matter, and this varies from time to time and place to place. The two hour sermon which was standard fare in the seventeenth century would only lead to another crucifixion (this time justifiable) in our busier times. The bombastic, arm-waving oratory of William Jennings Bryan, which moved thousands to tears in his day, would only seem humorous to us today. Preaching, which assumes a ready knowledge of the details of the Bible, today only succeeds in presenting to the preacher a sea of glazed and sleepy eyes.

Today I would suggest that one of the basic functions of preaching is that of education in the basic elements of the Christian faith. Most modern Christians are woefully ignorant of the essentials of the Faith, let alone some of its nicer details.

As an example, let me read to you from an article from *Time* magazine of December 31, 1965, on proposed revision of the Prayer Book of the Church of England, which *Time* does acknowledge is "one of the glories of the English language." The article discusses the proposed new Psalter, which the author obviously doesn't like. He writes:

> Somewhat less felicitous is the new Psalter, which can also be used by churches next May. A modernization of the King James translation of the Psalms prepared by a team of Anglican scholars (among them T. S. Aloud), it suffers from the same kind of drab, bureaucratic writing that mars the New English Bible. In the 23rd Psalm, for example, "The Lord is my shepherd, I shall not want," now reads, "The Lord is my shepherd; therefore can I lack nothing."[18]

Now, just for fun, open your prayer books [*The Book of Common Prayer* (1928)] to page 368, where you will find the 23rd Psalm. Note that it says "The Lord is my shepherd; therefore can I lack nothing." This is not so because we wily Americans in some way beat poor old T. S. Aloud and other drab bureaucratic writers to the punch, but because this is how the 23rd Psalm has been in the Prayer Book since the very beginning. *The Book of Common Prayer* [(1928)] uses the translation of the psalms of the Great Bible of Miles Coverdale rather than the translation of the King James version for at least two good reasons. First, the King James version wasn't in existence at the time the Prayer Book was put together and the Coverdale version was, predating the King James by over seventy-five years; second, the Church has historically preferred the Cover-

18. "ANGLICANS - Changing a Way of Worship," (Religion Department) *Time*, December 31, 1965, p. 50.

dale because while it may lack something of the fluid beauty of the King James, it is felt to make it up in simple directness, and moreover the Coverdale lends itself more easily to singing and chanting.

I point this out not because it is a blasphemous error of *Time* magazine, but because it is such a sloppy one, and yet my hunch is that most Episcopalians who read the article did not catch it. The good old religious editor can fog 'em over the point knowing that the letters to the editor from his department will only be from crack-pot clergy who will argue with whatever he writes anyway. But my hunch is that an equivalent mistake of fact, say in the sports section, would never be tolerated, and would lead to sacks of irate mail. Any baseball fan in this congregation knows that our home team had its origin in New York, and that the Baltimore Orioles were formerly the St. Louis Browns, and that the Minnesota Twins were just created. But my hunch is that few can give much of an analysis of the points of origin of the liturgical strands of our Prayer Book which we spend at least an hour a week reciting.

Hopefully, the sermon can be a tool which, to some extent, can fill the need for education. Hopefully it can be a tool to encourage people to look more deeply into the basics of the faith. Such preaching can't do too much, but it can do something, and I would submit that in a day and age of religious illiteracy, the teaching sermon is essential to the preservation of a strong, vigorous church.

Another function of modern preaching, as I have suggested, is exhortation. We have a first-rate example of the need for exhortation coming up, our Parish meeting. The laity fought long and hard for their right to have a voice in the government of their church. Each member is entitled to a voice at the annual meeting on the state of the parish, and a vote for those who will manage its affairs. The vestry has nominated an outstanding group of people and it will be up to those attending the meeting to choose between them. This is going to be a difficult choice and I know that marking my own ballot will be a hard thing to do. All who have agreed to run, whether they win or not, deserve our deepest thanks for their devoted service to the parish.

But if things go as they have in the past, these significant decisions will be made by only about 10 percent of the congregation. Think what political commentators would say if this were the voting figure in secular politics. Happily even an election for a dog-catcher gets a better turn out than this. One parishioner the other day observed that the only time this parish has had a significant attendance has been when we have seen trouble, or are having a fight. If so, then the lower the turn-out the better I ought to feel.

But I don't think this need be so. We are not, to my knowledge, in trouble, and I hope we aren't going to have a fight. We merely have a lot of exhorting to do–starting here in the pulpit, and hopefully spreading to each of you.

And on this issue we must return again briefly to education. It would be of little value if 100 percent of the parish attended the meeting to vote, if they didn't know what they were voting about. This means that in the case of candidates for the vestry that you make some attempt to educate yourself about them. No one of them to my knowledge is handing out campaign buttons, but they are all faithful attenders of our services. If you don't know them (and you each have a list of their names and a brief resume of their backgrounds) ask someone who they are and go up and introduce yourself. Whatever the results of the election, the fringe benefits would be tremendous.

A third function of modern preaching is double-barrelled. It is to provoke and comfort. As the old saw goes, the preacher's role is to comfort the afflicted and to afflict the comfortable. Perhaps in this diocese recently, we have been a little long on provocation and a little short on comfort. But let those who froth at the mouth over what they feel is the church's excessive involvement in the affairs of the world ask themselves the reason for their great concern. Could it not possibly be that they have little carved-out areas of their life where they do not want God or judgment or anything else to enter? We each have such little pockets, and we each get a little uncomfortable when they are approached. But, of course, when we think about it, what sort of God do we worship who can be kept out of anything? The Christian knows a God who is Lord of all life—who is closer to us than our breathing—a God unto whom all hearts are open, all desires known, and from whom no secrets are hid. Preaching in the mid-twentieth century hopefully helps us to face our little secret pockets of selfish interest and to examine ourselves more honestly.

But preaching, however we might slant it to a particular needs of a time, is first and last proclamation. It is not merely educational, or it would be a lecture. It is not merely exhortation, or it would be a harangue. It is not merely provocative, or it would be a speech. The sermon conveys the personality and the reality of the author as the printed word cannot. Although it also clearly shows his weakness and limitations. But behind even these stands the Word of God. A lady told me the other day that she had given up coming to church when there was a sermon because after thirty years she had heard them all. Perhaps so, in one sense but not so in another. If you are like I am, there are times when I have left a church completely unable to give you a diagrammed outline of the content of the sermon, and yet aware that the preacher had in some way connected himself to a tap-root of great power and had conveyed that to me. It may not happen very often. I have sensed it sometime in the most bumbling and inarticulate, and have not felt it from the gifted, silver-tongued. Some in the same congregation will sense it while others hearing the same sermon will not.

Epiphany, the making manifest of the Word of God,

comes to different people at different times and places. What may move and stir you at a particular time may have no effect on another.

But it is the task of every Christian to celebrate Epiphany–to make manifest–to spread the light–to preach and proclaim the Good News.

Our solution is not to abolish the preaching from the pulpit, but to supplement it and to help us realize that each of us is preaching and proclaiming each day by thought, word, and deed, educating, exhorting, provoking and comforting.

In the words of Scripture, "Exhort and preach to each other daily, while that word 'today' still sounds in your ears so that not one of you is lost" [Heb. 3:13, translation unknown].

This sermon was also preached:
During Epiphany
January 1975 (otherwise undated)
St. Stephen's Church
West Valley City, Utah.

3

I had a friend in seminary who was a cattle rancher. He detested sheep. Every time he saw a Tiffany stained glass window of a beatific pretty-boy Jesus surrounded by a herd of beatific, pretty-boy sheep, he'd shake his head. "That gospel won't sell in my country." And he was undoubtedly right.

Whitsunday (Pentecost) | *St. Francis' Church*
May 29, 1966 | *San Francisco, California*

Today is the great feast of the Holy Spirit—the Lord and Giver of Life—one of the three great days in the Christian Calendar. And yet because tomorrow is a secular holiday, church attendance will be down at least 30 percent.

Yet, indeed, the very sparsity of our numbers may help those of us here to understand better what it is which we commemorate this day.

The concept of the Holy Spirit is an elusive one. We can understand a baby born, and one of the reasons why Christmas is to so many *the* great Christian feast is because we can comprehend this. (Although, interestingly, Christmas was a relatively late arrival on the Christian calendar.)

We even have a vague picture of what it means for a person to rise from the dead, and thus Easter becomes somewhat meaningful. But the Holy Ghost eludes our grasp. If we are honest with ourselves and try to picture Him, I am sure we will come up with some variation of a spook in a Halloween costume.

And yet elusiveness is one of the attributes of the Spirit. When you look directly at Him, He is not there. We are aware of His presence only in the peripheral areas of our perception, much like an optical illusion I saw the other day. In this illusion there is a grid work of black blocks interlaced by white streets. And at the intersection of each street, except the one you were looking directly at, there is a gray dot. But if you looked directly at any particular gray dot, it disappears, popping up at the intersection you were just looking at.

There is a hidden nature to God that goes along with His revelation of Himself, and this is nowhere more apparent than in the concept of the Spirit. We cannot count or measure this. His effect and influence have no relationship to numbers or size. It was the Spirit to which the early church attributed the miracle of its very existence. There they were, a handful of rustics in the outskirts of empire. They had all heard first-hand the *teachings* of this man, Jesus of Nazareth, and yet these alone had not galvanized them into action, to get out and do something about them, any more than the mere teaching of Jesus will do this today.

The teachings alone are an idealistic, pleasant, and unrealistic ethic, much like childhood fairy tales. How nice it would be if they were true! Even the resurrection experience itself, which this handful of people had personally been through, was not enough to mobilize them to do anything. It was well enough that the one they had known, and loved, and followed had conquered death. But it was still a vicarious experience to them. What was there in it for them?

But then a momentous thing happened. This handful of people sensed that these teachings, the presence of this man, and the significance of his conquest, were incorporated into themselves. These were no longer abstract or detached or vicarious observations. *They* were the source of a strength, of a dynamic power in the lives of each one. And this handful of people transformed the history of the world. And the later church, in trying to describe this aspect of the reality of God, recalled the words of the Lord in His earthly ministry. He would send the Spirit of truth, and this was the Spirit, the experience of life, of vitality, of purpose.

What was particularized in this man Jesus was now to be shared by many. *Not* however in terms of broad general principles, but in the specific life and particular problems of each different person. Jesus in his earthly ministry did not carefully propose universal truths for the benefit of all men everywhere in all times, but talked directly to particular people with explicit reference to their particular situations. But we are not they, and their problems aren't ours, so how can he speak meaningfully to us? Precisely this is what the doctrine of the Spirit helps answer. If God in Christ speaks to us *as* he did to his contemporaries, he will not say to us *what* he said to them. Instead he will speak to us particularly.

I had a friend in seminary who was a cattle rancher. He detested sheep. Every time he saw a Tiffany stained glass window of a beatific pretty-boy Jesus surrounded by a herd of beatific, pretty-boy sheep, he'd shake his head. "That gospel won't sell in my country." And he was undoubtedly right. The fact that Jesus used the imagery of a sheep man to speak to sheep men 2,000 years ago doesn't require that American cattle ranchers have to become sheep-lovers. My friend is back in his old area, now a devoted and beloved priest. My hunch is that he still very carefully picks his texts on Good Shepherd Sunday and I don't think he's abandoning the faith at all. He preaches the Gospel to his people and to their problem, and this the Spirit has freed us to do.

What is this Spirit? As St. Paul said, in his first letter to the Corinthians, there are diversities of expression of this liberating, life-giving force, and it is expressed in many different ways. Let me use one example, that of the dance.

Many of you saw the film *Zorba the Greek.* It captured very well the rough, almost savage zest for life of one man, who, when his emotional strings became too taut, when he was on the verge of great joy, or great sorrow, found his release by dancing. His dancing allowed the body to participate in what the mind alone was incapable of doing.

We all need to dance at certain times. We need to let our whole body give vent to what we feel. (I say this as unquestionably the world's worst dancer, having been washed out for incompetence by several dancing schools in my childhood.)

Alexander Pope wrote from the intellectual aridity of the eighteenth century:

> Not to go back is somewhat to advance,
> And men must walk, at least, before they dance.[19]

I would disagree. I have seen babies dance spontaneously to music when they could hardly walk. It is only when they get a little older that they lose this spontaneity–when, like Adam and Eve, they become self-conscious–then their dancing becomes "cute," something to gain the approving beams of other people, and consequently unbearable.

After we lose our age of innocence, we pretty well lose our ability for honest, spontaneous action–whether to

---

19. Alexander Pope, "The First Epistle of the First Book of Horace," lines 53, 54, *Selected Poetry and Prose,* ed. with intro. William K. Wimsatte, Jr. (New York: Holt, Rinehart and Winston, 1951), p. 244.

dance or to express ourselves from our depths in other ways as well. Yet we still have a need to do this. But in our maturity we need specific form and structure for such expression, because as we grow old we realize that we have a need not only to express ourselves, but also to communicate this expression to others.

I realize that there are certain contemporary artists who claim that art should not be concerned with communication, but only with expression. But I cannot see how this, when pushed far enough, doesn't reduce expression to a lot of grunts and groans.

Modern trends in dancing seem to be going that way. The volume of the music makes conversation impossible. Of course you don't dance the "Frug" or "Watusi" with anyone anyway. It's a solo performance in tandem–high on self expression, low on communication. In this Age of the Lonely Crowd,[20] it surely must say something about our culture when you see a dance floor packed with young people expressing themselves like crazy, but communicating with no one.

The Church has its own dance–the Dance of the Spirit–by which we join our emotions, our bodily actions and our voices in expressing our love and thanks to God. We call it the Eucharist (which means "thanksgiving") or

20. An expression of Reisman, *The Lonely Crowd.*

the Holy Communion or the Lord's Supper or the Mass, or in the Orthodox Churches, the Divine Liturgy.

The basic structure of this Dance or Rite is the same for all Christians, although variations are infinite. Protestants approach their Dance of the Spirit much like a middle-aged couple at a formal dance–infrequently, and with a minimum of frivolity and expression. The Orthodox bring to theirs the rich opulence of a royal ball in an Oriental court. The Roman Catholics (until their recent great liturgical reformation) celebrated with an esotericism that made outsiders feel like middle-aged adults, ill at ease and completely lost, observing a high school dance. The Anglicans approach the Eucharist with the simple dignity of a well-chaperoned dancing class run by an old-fashioned Victorian lady who still wears white gloves, a Gibson Girl neck choker and clicks castanets.

But with all the variations, two elements should be built into any such Holy Dance–the opportunity to *express* some of our deepest emotions–and the *communication* of these depths to others. The very word "communion" assumes the latter. We not only "communicate" with the power of Almighty God through this sacrament, but we should also communicate this power to others.

There is nothing more depressing than to watch a listless, half-hearted, poorly done dance. This goes for the Dance of the Spirit as well. If there is a sin against the Holy Spirit, perhaps it is that of a priest who mumbles through a Eucharist, enunciating the magnificent language of our Prayer Book Liturgy with the clarity of a tobacco auctioneer. The very title he has at such time belies this sort of thing. He is called the "celebrant," and we say that a priest "celebrates" the Eucharist. These very terms suggest strength, vigor and power, that which is the gift of the Holy Spirit, Lord of Life.

At the other side of the altar rail we sometimes find the same problems–mute congregations, who seem to have forgotten that "Amen" is an essential part of this service–that it means "I agree," "so be it," "me, too."

Bishop Rusack [late Bishop of the Diocese of Los Angeles], in a sermon at Grace Cathedral, San Francisco, pointed out the irony of listless congregations singing some of the great fight songs of Christendom, e.g., "Rise up, ye men of God," "A Mighty Fortress Is Our God," as though they were funeral dirges.

We Episcopalians have been given a particular form of expressing this Sacred Dance. It reflects our particular heritage in the Church of God and it has its limitations, but it is ours to use until it is legally changed by appropriate process.

Thus the *form* of our particular expression is pretty well fixed. But the style and the flair by which we *communicate* this form is left up to us.

To paraphrase the ancient first collect of Whitsunday, the Holy Spirit is He who first illumines our minds with true and righteous courses of action. In this case we meet here today to break bread pursuant to our Lord's earthly commandment, guided here by the Holy Spirit, and we say that it is meet and right to do so. The collect continues, that the Spirit, once having guided us into right courses of action, strengthens our wills so that we can accomplish this with *joy* "and evermore to *rejoice* in His holy comfort."[21]

Joy is the keynote of the Spirit. It is there for our asking, the result of our knowing that the power of love of God may indwell each one of us in our individuality through the Spirit.

The Dance of the Spirit–the Eucharist–is at the same time a purveyor of the gift of the Spirit and also a grateful response for His presence with us.

So let us indeed lift up our hearts and give thanks unto our Lord God for the gift whereby the *power* of the *cross* is made known to *each* of us–through the Holy Spirit, the Comforter, the Strengthener.

21. *The Book of Common Prayer* (1928), p. 180.

4

Then the organ hit a big chord and everyone jumped up. It was the beginning of the most complex hour of jumping, sitting, standing, and kneeling I have ever known. I just watched my friend and did what he did (except for the kneeling, of course). Then down the aisle came a bunch of folks all dressed up in the same kind of garb as the apocalypses I had seen light the candles, although the fellows at the end of the line seemed older.

The Eleventh Sunday after Pentecost August 19, 1979	*The Cathedral Church of St. Mark Salt Lake City, Utah*

[Note: This sermon is allegorical in nature and assumes a fictitious author.]

I've been getting a little religious lately–well, I wouldn't say "religious," but after my best friend (or my wife or child) died and I had a stroke both in the same week, I thought I had better examine my hole cards.

I was amazed to find, after I had examined my hand, that there wasn't much there. Being perfectly honest with myself for the first time in a long time, I realized that my basic ground rules were pretty superficial. As long as the sun shone and the sales came in, and the breaks went my way, I could be Happy Harry. I found my god in the "85" I shot, in a new car, in a good steak, in beautiful mountains, some moving music, in a view of the moon over city lights.

But that didn't quite take care of the gnawing for something more. And of course I knew that some time, ultimately, I'd have to have some member of the family go to some religious guy to bury me, because I didn't quite have the guts to say that I wanted to throw my carcass out with next Monday's garbage. (In fact, I buried my old dog in my own backyard, and because I couldn't think of anything else, I said the Lord's Prayer over him.)

So I thought I'd better at least give some of those churches a try. They claim they have an answer to some of the questions I was always asking myself. Who? Why? Whence?

Let me tell you about one Sunday. I had a friend who was an "Episcopal." Not a bad guy. I noticed that he went to church every Sunday, although he never talked about it to anyone else. He still seemed to enjoy a Bloody Mary at our Sunday brunches although he was usually late. He always said that he was too lazy to hit the 8 o'clock service, and therefore had to attend the 10 o'clock service. Obviously any good Sunday brunch starts at 11 o'clock, and I could never understand my friend's obtuseness on this point. When I asked him whether he couldn't just show up, be seen, and then leave so that he could get to my party on time he mumbled something about the fact that he felt an obligation to make an appearance at the coffee hour and greet some of his Christian friends–a very inconsiderate type.

Yet I secretly admired this, and as I was saying, I finally asked him if I could join him one Sunday.

He was delighted and picked me up about 9:40, an ungodly hour if you didn't have a golf game or a party to go to.

We walked into what I must acknowledge was a handsome small building. I missed air conditioning but the organ prelude which was in process was first rate. My friend barked my shins by pulling down a kneeler, and knelt upon it, and did something with his right hand just like Catholics I have seen in the movies do.

There was no suggestion that I do the same, and of course there was no way I would. I came to this church to see what it had to offer to enlighten me intellectually. I certainly didn't come to *kneel*–the most degrading, humbling posture I can think of.

O.K. Some kids came out dressed like angels and lit some candles. I thought the girls were better looking in that garb, and my friend said that it was only recently that females had been allowed to do this. He called them "apocalypses," I think.

Then the organ hit a big chord and everyone jumped

up. It was the beginning of the most complex hour of jumping, sitting, standing, and kneeling I have ever known. I just watched my friend and did what he did (except for the kneeling, of course). Then down the aisle came a bunch of folks all dressed up in the same kind of garb as the apocalypses I had seen light the candles, although the fellows at the end of the line seemed older.

We sat after a while and some lessons were read. I couldn't hear all of what was said, but I especially liked the psalm where it read:

> Great is our Lord and mighty in power;
> there is no limit to his wisdom.
> He counts the number of the stars
> and calls them all by their names.
> He covers the heavens with clouds
> and prepares rain for the earth;
> The Lord lifts up the lowly,
> but casts the wicked to the ground.
> He provides food for flocks and herds
> and for the young ravens when they cry.
> How good it is to sing praises to our God![22]

---

22. The Psalm for that Eleventh Sunday after Pentecost was Psalm 147. Perhaps to emphasize the rhetorical license Colton was taking in this sermon, he chose to repeat Psalm 147, but in the order of v.5, v.4, v.8, v.6, v.10, and v.1b using the numbering and translation found in

Now that I can buy! If there is a God at all, he is obviously the boss. And as the psalm suggests, he is not only the boss, but a loving boss. I liked that! I was beginning to feel I could almost become religious.

But then the organist started some music and everyone jumped up again and a bunch of those apocalypses started to come down the aisle headed right toward me. My friend whispered that sometimes on special occasions they whirled a smoke pot of terrible gases, but fortunately this did not happen on this Sunday.

But it was what that fellow said when he got in the middle of us all that really got me. He read something from the Gospel of John (it was printed in the leaflet) that turned my stomach:

> unless you eat the flesh of the Son of man and drink his blood, you have no life in you; . . . [John 6:53, RSV]

After he finished reading I noticed there was a fellow in the pulpit and we all sat down.

As this was now becoming one of the more ridiculous experiences I have ever had, I began to take notes, and this is what he said, if you can believe it:

> The drinking of blood was abhorrent to any good believing Jew at the time of Jesus. Rigid dietary restric-

---

The Book of Common Prayer (1979), p. 804.

tions prevented any possibility that this could happen. Thus the suggestion to a Jew that blood should be drunk was absolutely scandalous, let alone human blood. (Christian persecutors used this command as a ground for the death penalty, alleging that Christians practiced cannibalism.)

Yet this is what the Christ, God who became man, commanded us to do. It is a typical example of the upside down world view that he espoused–the weak are strong; the mild are more effective than the boastful; power comes from the insignificant; death, the ultimate defeat, can be a triumph; bodily death is not the end.

"He who eats my flesh and drinks my blood abides in me . . . " [John 6:56, RSV]

(That preacher and all those folks sitting there are crazier than I thought, if they believe that stuff. I'll buy Psalm 147. I already told you I thought that was truly uplifting and comports with my own quest. I *like* the idea of a God who is the creator of all, including the stars of the universe. But in all honesty, I like the stars because they are so far away, and I like to believe in a Creator of the stars because he must be even *further* away–so he won't meddle with *me.*)

The preacher, reading my mind, continued:

Obviously this assertion by a human being can not be considered rational. There are those who say, "I believe in the lovely teachings of Jesus, but I certainly can't stand the statements made by the *Church* about Him. Why don't they just let us alone to just try to follow his good example?"

But Scripture won't let us do that. As C. S. Lewis, one of the great Anglican lay apologists has pointed out, you can't have this man just meek and mild, or just look to his teachings. He made incredible claims about Himself. He was either what he claimed to be, or he is as crazy as the fellow you met on the street who says he is a fried egg.[23]

The Christian gospel does turn lots of things upside down. A second-century Christian, Tertullian, wrote, "I believe because it is absurd."[24]

---

23. C. S. Lewis actually said, "I am trying here to prevent anyone saying the really foolish thing that people often say about Him: 'I'm ready to accept Jesus as a great moral teacher, but I don't accept His claim to be God.' That is the one thing we must not say. A man who was merely a man and said the sort of things Jesus said would not be a great moral teacher. He would either be a lunatic–on a level with the man who says he is a poached egg–or else he would be the Devil of Hell. You must make your choice. Either this man was, and is, the Son of God: or else a madman or something worse. You can shut Him up for a fool, you can spit at Him and kill Him as a demon; or you can fall at His feet and call Him Lord and God. But let us not come with any patronizing nonsense about His being a great human teacher. He has not left that open to us. He did not intend to" (C. S. Lewis, *Mere Christianity* [New York: Macmillan Co., 1960], pp. 40-41).

24. As mentioned earlier, Tertullian did not say this, but rather said, "The Son of God died: It is absolutely worthy of belief because it is absurd" (in McGiffert, p. 16).

The preacher continued:

> I preach to you a God of blood and guts, not of abstraction; I show you a symbol above our altar of a person who was born as we were, who lived as we do, and who died as we will–all to show us that He loves us and walks with us this very second.
>
> In a few minutes we will have the opportunity to be present with Him in an incredible thing–we will drink wine and eat bread and he will be with us. If this is not true, then I guess we would all be better off buying a Winchell's donut and a cup of coffee and enjoying a view of the Wasatch Mountain Range.

That was enough for me. I smiled at my friend and got up and left (fortunately before the offertory).

I *did* go to Winchell's and defiantly bought a donut and a cup of coffee and looked at the Wasatch Range.

But that blood reference wouldn't go away, and I remembered in my boyhood the old shack where we cut ourselves with a knife and spread the little spots of blood on our arms.

We were blood brothers–eternal comrades.

That blood imagery is tough stuff, powerful stuff. I'll bet those folks at that church coffee hour don't know what dynamite they're playing with.

III
Sin

Introduction

The reality of sin was of paramount importance to Albert Colton. Acknowledging sin allowed him to talk more fully about grace. A great sadness of Colton's was the fact that so many people resisted confessing their sins, either in conversation or in church, and thus could not appreciate the gift of God's forgiveness of their sins.

The other evening I gathered with a group of dear friends–this group has been meeting for over twenty-five years–we were one of Mortimer Adler's *Great Books* groups that followed his curriculum and have continued together. This year we decided to find out what the "world" is reading and undertook a series of best sellers. Our assignment that evening was Lawrence Sander's *The Third Deadly Sin.*

One thing led to another. We wanted to know what were the "Seven Deadly Sins." According to my ecclesiastical dictionary, these go back to Gregory the Great (sixth century) and they are 1) pride, 2) covetousness, 3) lust, 4) envy, 5) gluttony, 6) anger, and 7) sloth.[1]

---

1. F.L. Cross and E. A. Livingstone, eds., *The Oxford Dictionary of the Christian Church* 2d ed. (New York: Oxford University Press, 1974), pp. 1264-1265.

From this we went to the Ten Commandments. It took us a little while to find them in our guest's ancient family Bible. After a little searching we found them.

From this our discussion led to a talk about sin generally, and of original sin. Eyes either glazed over or glared angrily. Our beloved pediatrician proclaimed that he could never see his beloved children as "sinners."

Others pointed out that there were certain parables of the Gospel that were just plain "sappy." The parable of the Prodigal Son was the worst (they identified themselves with the *good* son [or daughter] who stayed home and tended their parents and their property). They were outraged at the story of the workers in the vineyard, where the last to work got paid as much as the fellow who showed up at the crack of dawn.

It was obvious that my argument that *all* people are sinners in need of God's healing forgiveness was a total bust–strike three for orthodox Christianity in a group of lovely, brilliant Americans.[2]

We tend to build callouses around the real meaning of words in the same sense as we tend to build callouses around the really nasty and vicious actions of our world. Thus, the other day I referred, jokingly, to

2. Sermon preached the Fourth Sunday after Epiphany, January 30, 1983, the Cathedral Church of St. Mark, Salt Lake City, Utah.

someone (a very dear person, incidentally) as a "miserable sinner." The reply was, "Oh, now, Father, she is *not.*" But of course, she is, and she and everyone else in this congregation have been calling themselves this every time we say the General Confession.[3]

Colton identified the word "sin" as a great stumbling block for people. Unless seen for what it is, he believed people would continue to try their best to fix their lives sufficiently, living in a morally upstanding way, and thus thinking they have no need for the salvific act of Christ on the cross.

Most people equate "sins" with "sin." I suggest there are basic differences. Sins are specific acts committed by the person who places this description on them as wrongful. There is tremendous divergence of opinion as to these, e.g., some religious groups say that drinking wine is inherently wrong, and it is a sin. My church (as well as the majority of Christians) utilize the drinking of wine in their central act of worship. We can each recount various *acts* which are considered "sins" by some, and not by others.

"Sin" on the other hand, is a condition or a state of being. In the Judeo-Christian tradition, it is described in mythical terms in Genesis III. According to that

3. The term "miserable *offenders*" is found in the General Confession in "Morning Prayer" in *The Book of Common Prayer* (New York: The Church Pension Fund, 1928), p. 6. Sermon preached the Fourth Sunday of Easter, May 16, 1965, St. Francis' Church, San Francisco, California.

great story, men and women came into existence as *creatures*–they, as well as all else they can sense and see, were made by something else–they were created by a God who made all creatures *ex nihilo,* i.e., out of nothing. Thus, they were creatures, not creations (although they were meant to participate with God in his amazing action of continuing and sustaining creation)–and as creatures, they were dependent, not independent.

In this sense of naive dependence, they really had all they would ever need–and as a symbol of this dependence and a reminder of their creatureliness, they were given a tangible restraint–all was theirs except *one* thing–the fruit of one tree. But this one restraint gnawed on man. Why should there be any restraints at all? And as the serpent said, "Forget that restraint, go ahead and eat, and then *ye* shall be as gods" [Gen. 3:5]. And poor old man tried this and from that day to this, Adam (which means me) has been doing the same thing. He is pretending to be more than he is.[4]

A rhetorical devise used by Colton was to force people to choose between classifying themselves as "sinners" or without sin. There was no middle ground. In that light, members of his congregations who enjoyed pointing out the sinful behavior of others often found themselves stung by their own actions.

4. Snowbird Conference, Snowbird Resort, Utah, October 1979.

> And Aaron said to them, "Take off the rings of gold which are in the ears of your wives, your sons, and your daughters, and bring them to me." So all the people took off the rings of gold which were in their ears, and brought them to Aaron. And he received the gold at their hand, and fashioned it with a graving tool, and made a molten calf; and they said, "These are your gods, O Israel, who brought you up out of the land of Egypt!" When Aaron saw this, he built an altar before it; and Aaron made a proclamation and said, "Tomorrow shall be a feast to the Lord." And they rose up early on the morrow, and offered burnt offering and brought peace offerings; and the people sat down to eat and drink, and rose up to play [Ex. 32:2-6, RSV].

Wow! Weren't *they* wicked! When the cat's away, the mice can play! When the boss is on vacation, it's one long coffee break. Isn't that just like some people. The minute you take your eyes off them, they go running away pursuing some form of golden calf or another.

Then, to change metaphors, these people become lost sheep. Now, if this happened frequently enough, I imagine most of us would say "good riddance to bad rubbish" and forget about them.

But as we are told in today's Gospel, this is not how God works. He never gives up in his pursuit of the lost sheep, and rejoices more at the rediscovery of one of those than of ninety-nine of the righteous that have never strayed.

God, as seen by the Christian, has been called the

"Hound of Heaven."[5] He is ceaselessly pursuing all, with his love, to come to Him.

And our epistle for today [1 Tim. 1:12-17] shows the reaction of one person, St. Paul, when the true significance of this fact finally sinks in. As he wrote in his first letter to Timothy, Christ Jesus came into the world to save sinners "and I am the foremost of sinners" [1 Tim. 1:15, RSV], "I formerly blasphemed and persecuted and insulted Him" [1 Tim. 1:13a, RSV]. He ends this passage with a statement of majestic praise. "To the king of ages, immortal, invisible, the only God, be honor and glory for ever and ever, Amen" [1 Tim. 1:17, RSV].

This whole message was obviously great and *good* news to Paul. He had a deep need, and it was met. However, this whole process seems a little unfair to the *good* sheep who were always proper and obedient. They didn't have any fuss made over them.

Of course, this type of unfairness crops up time and time again in the parables of our Lord. In the story of the Prodigal Son, a great big fuss is made over the return of the no-good wastrel, and no one pays heed to the good faithful son. In the parable of the workers in the vineyard, those who came late and only worked a short time were paid just as much as

5. Francis Thompson, "The Hound of Heaven," *The Literature of England: An Anthology and a History,* Vol. Two, rev. ed. George B. Woods, Homer A. Watt, and George K. Anderson (New York: Scott, Foresman and Co., 1936), pp. 963-65.

the good and faithful who had worked in the hot sun all day long.

There's something strange about all of this. We call the Gospel "good" news, but I can only see this as *good* news for those who are bad ones. It is only good news to the lost sheep.

But what does it have to say to all of us good little sheep, dutifully and righteously sitting in our pews this morning? Well, let me let you in on a secret. Whether we know it or not, each and every one of us is a lost sheep, not a good sheep, and we are constantly in need of God's pursuit and his loving acceptance.[6]

And I must say I am generally chary of hard-liners. It is so easy to say "throw out those evil smelly goats, and let us nice holy sheep play together."

But I am always uneasy in classifying myself as a nice holy sheep, when I know I too am in so many respects an evil smelly goat.

That very issue was faced by St. Augustine in the Fourth Century over the question of ordination. A group of hard-liners (the Donatists) wanted a group of priests excommunicated because in a time of weakness they had fallen and were no longer "worthy." Augustine thundered that *no* man is worthy. Despite the scriptural adjuration "Be ye perfect,"[7] the

6. Sermon preached the Sixteenth Sunday after Pentecost, September 14, 1980, All Saints Church, Salt Lake City, Utah.

only thing that makes a man "worthy" is the grace of God.

I believe this to be true. That indeed is the essence of the gospel. That does not mean we do not need rules and regulations and standards, because of course we do. And these rules, regulations and standards should be followed. But the rules, regulations and standards are not the gospel.

Important as they are, we each break the rules, regulations and standards at one time or the other. We cannot just wink at this, but on the other hand, I have come to believe that the one only unforgivable sin against the Holy Ghost is to deny and reject the presence of God's loving and forgiving power in our midst every second of every day of our lives.[8]

Colton believed the difficulty of acknowledging our sin is made more so by our inability to receive and give gracefully. Such trouble causes separation, or a state of sin, in that we believe ourselves to be independent from one another. We neither have to give to others nor to receive from others. This separation is contrary to the way Colton understood the holy dependence we must have upon one another in the Body of Christ.

---

7. Colton probably is making reference to Matthew 5:48, KJV, which reads "Be ye therefore perfect, even as your Father which is in heaven is perfect."

8. Sermon preached the Seventeenth Sunday after Pentecost, October 7, 1979, the Cathedral Church of St. Mark, Salt Lake City, Utah.

The bishop of an eastern diocese tells the story of being approached by a destitute man who asked him for something to eat. The bishop obliged and took him to a restaurant where he bought him a big breakfast, and sat with him until he finished the meal. The bishop then took out a package of cigarettes and offered the man one. The man replied with a sneer on his face and egg on his chin, "And I thought you were a Christian!"

It is difficult to receive with grace. As St. Vincent dePaul said, "You must give smiling, hoping that in some way your love will overcome the hate they feel that you have something to give."[9] Our pride makes us resent the fact that he who gives has something to give which we by taking have to admit we do not have. Thus older people often resent the fact of their growing dependence on other members of their family. This very human problem very often leads to cynicism. It was Mark Twain who said, "If you pick up a starving dog and make him prosperous, he will not bite you. This is the principal difference between a dog and a man."[10]

But, you may rightly say, very often what is seen as ingratitude is the natural result of the ungracious attitude of the giver. And this is true, because it is not only hard to receive, it is difficult to give. The militant

---

9. Citation uncertain.

10. Mark Twain, Pudd'nhead Wilson's Calendar, in Mark Twain (Samuel L. Clemens), *Pudd'nhead Wilson and Those Extraordinary Twins* (New York: P. F. Collier and Son Co., 1920), p. 142.

reaction of the working class in the last century to the lady bountiful type of charity was probably justified, and certainly understandable, because the giving was so often tainted with condescension. The Christian mission itself unfortunately has not been immune from this. Some missionaries confused the Gospel with the supplying of foundation garments to Hottentot women and other so-called superior virtues of western civilization, and where this was done indigenous people often rose and rejected the mission altogether.[11]

Colton believed the only remedy for the sinner was forgiveness. Forgiveness had to be gracefully given and gracefully received. That it was given as a free gift from God made it, by definition, gracefully given. Only by seeing forgiveness as an unearned gift could the penitent sinner appreciate the gracefulness of God, the efficacy of confession and the power of the once and for all sacrifice on the cross.

In the end there is really *nothing* an offending party can do to *compel* forgiveness. Forgiveness is not earned by making monthly payments, at the end of which time the person who has been injured must, willy-nilly, whether he wants to or not, hand over a notarized certificate of forgiveness. Forgiveness is not earned. It is freely given by the forgiver, although often at great cost and hurt to the forgiver. If there is a sacrifice to

11. Sermon preached the Third Sunday in Advent, December 16, 1962, Grace Cathedral, San Francisco, California.

be made to heal the relationship, it must be done by the forgiver, not by the one seeking forgiveness.

Hosea was one of the first to grasp the great truth about Almighty God–he was not only Creator, lawgiver and judge, but he could be approached as Father–his love was enduring.

As Hosea writes in our lesson for this evening: "God will heal us; He will bind us up; He will revive us; He will raise us up that we may live before Him."[12] It is *God* who will do this, and not we ourselves. It is in this sense that Hosea can hear God say, "For I desire steadfast love and not sacrifice, the knowledge of God rather than burnt offerings."

This whole approach seems to turn our customary values upside down. Does it mean *we* can do nothing to cure this malaise within our inner-most being–this sense of loneliness, of inadequacy, of guilt and anxiety? Not at all. Anyone reading all of Hosea will find his consuming concern with the failure of God's people to abide by His will, and he senses the doom which is bound to come as a result. Good works, acts of love and concern for others are essential. Without them, formal sacrifice is little more than blasphemy. But the difference lies in the *purpose* seen

---

12. Colton drew from Hosea 6:1-2, RSV, which reads in total: "Come, let us return to the Lord; for he has torn, that he may heal us; he has stricken, and he will bind us up. After two days he will revive us; on the third day he will raise us up, that we may live before him."

in such acts. God is not to be bought and wheedled. He is sovereign king of all.

Well now, this is fine theory, Hosea, perhaps you're right. You seem to plumb deeper than the sterile intellectual, but how do I know?

The author of Hebrews, in that portion read as our second lesson [Heb. 10:1-25], gives an answer, still using the language of sacrifice.

The sacrifice has indeed been made. And it has been made once and for all. " . . . Christ had offered for all time a single sacrifice for sins . . . " [Heb. 10:12, RSV]. The forgiver has forgiven, in the only way that forgiveness is ever possible, by his own sacrifice.

We are healed not by any act of our own, but by Almighty God's one oblation of Himself, once offered, a full, perfect and sufficient sacrifice, oblation and satisfaction for the sins of the whole world.

As true forgiveness always involves pain, so does the Christian accept the cross as the symbol of the pain which God willingly bore for us. The cross is the great cosmic sign not of a fine theory, but of an objective fact of our history, and it is this which gives meaning to our individual lives.[13]

---

13. Sermon preached on Passion Sunday (the Fifth Sunday in Lent), March 31, 1963, at Grace Cathedral, San Francisco, California.

1

I, for one, am not very fond of a bee's sting. It is to me only an instrument which inflicts pain and suffering. But to remove the bee's stinger is to remove the bee. It is integrally connected to the bee's body. And I fear that in the same way all of us are weed-infested. To remove the weeds would not remove just a few bad guys, it would remove all of us.

The Fifth Sunday after the Epiphany *St. Francis' Church*
February 7, 1965 *San Francisco, California*

MATTHEW 13:24-30

The parable of the wheat and the tares (or to give it a more understandable title, "of the wheat and the weeds") has been variously interpreted. Experts do not agree. But all can agree that it is a good, graphic story. The farmer had prepared his land and sown his wheat. And in the dead of night an enemy came and sowed the same field with weed seeds. This was not discovered until both the wheat and the weeds were well-grown. (At this point I'm not sure what this says about the farmer's skill–one would think he might have detected the weeds at an earlier time–but doubtless he was busy with other matters. And the purpose of the story is not to give advice to 4-H Clubs anyway.) When confronted with the problem the farmer ruled out the suggestion that the weeds be pulled out then, "lest while ye gather up the tares, ye root up also the wheat with them" [Matt. 13:29, KJV]. Rather he advised letting both the wheat and the weeds grow until harvest, at which time they would be gathered and separated and the wheat alone be put into the barn.

Many scholars believe that this was a story describing one of the problems of the early Church, and a problem which the Church still has and doubtless will have as long as earthly time is measured. What do we do about the weeds in the Church? There is, for example, the Easter and Christmas blooming dandelion, resplendent in golden finery for a few days of the year and at that time crowding out the faithful grass which is around all year long, but then disappears in a puff-ball blown wherever the winds take it. There's the night-crawling crabgrass, busy sending out its tentacles and blending innocuously with the rest of the grass, which it then slowly strangles, leaving eventually only an ugly brown stain.

Each one of us could have some fun inventing analogies from particular kinds of weeds to certain types of people we know in the life of the Church.

And the common-sense attitude of at least anyone who has fought the battle of the lawn is very simple. What do you do with a weed? Answer: you pull it out and throw it away.

But our Lord, in this parable, does not appear to be suggesting this obvious answer. In fact, He suggests exactly the opposite. Leave the weeds alone until harvest.

The Church has, on occasion in its history, failed to heed this advice. From the very beginning there are those who have insisted that the Church is a place only for the pure and holy—holy people doing holy things in holy places. And those who are not sufficiently holy should be pulled up and cast out, so that the pristine nature of the club is preserved.

Time and time again those who feel that they have "cornered" the "truth" and are alarmed at what they feel are the perversions and distortions of others have sought either (if they are great enough in numbers and power) to throw out the unclean, or if they cannot throw them out, then they themselves will withdraw to avoid further contamination. They will then often take upon themselves some name which emphasizes their purity from the rest of the Christian unwashed—"the really genuine and pure 100 percent apostolic church," "the true Christian believers," etc. Or, in our day, as we become splintered, such people will not find anyone else who is sufficiently pure to join with them in their breakaway, and they will found a new church of one person—themselves.

"I won't go to church and associate with those hypocrites," suggests, of course, that the person saying this is quite confident that within himself, as opposed to "those other persons," there is no trace of hypocrisy, and he rejoices in the possibility of withdrawal to contemplate his own impeccable navel.

But while the Church has, at a few weak moments, seen itself as an exclusive club which people "join" if they wish (and if they meet appropriate standards) this is not, thank God, what the Church in its deeper moments says it is. It is not a club or voluntary association at all. Indeed, in the technical sense, one should not even use the term "joining" the Church.

One does not "join" the Church. One is born into it. The Church is not a contractual society. It is an organic body. The Church is a family into which one is born through the sacrament of baptism, in which one dies and is born again into a new family. This is very similar to a natural family. No one asked you whether you would care to be born into this family, or in this country. But, by reason of this, you are given a surname and a nationality. Now you may hate your parents, you may disown them or they you, you may defect from your country and go work for the Russians. But kick and squirm as you may, reject and repudiate as we all do at one time or another, you are still organically derivative of this family and this country.

Let us say we wished to form a club, and because we are very pious people we would call it the "God Worshipping Club." This could not be the Church, because the Church existed before we pious people ever decided to get together, or indeed, before we decided anything–in the same sense that our parents did.

The Church is not our creation, rather, we, as Christians, are creations of the Church. And the creations of the Church are marvelously varied, just as they are in any family. There is always in every family an Uncle Louie, whom nobody ever mentions, the black sheep horse thief, who, in the only time you ever met him found him to be an utterly charming, very romantic figure. There is cousin Bessie, the Great Disappointment. Everyone mentally tiptoes around her bemoaning the fact that she could have married a Texas oil millionaire and instead ran off with a guitar-playing folk singer. And there is cousin Charles, the Great Success, whom you have had thrown into your teeth as an example to follow and whom you can't stand.

Some care about the family–some don't. Some are weeds, some are the wheat of the earth.

And most are neither. They are a mixed bag of wheat and weed seeds. And this is where we must be careful with our parable. It is terribly tempting to divide the world into good guys and bad guys, until we walk up to a mirror. Which category are we in? Are you wheat, or are you weed?

If you accept the Christian view of man the answer is not easy. You have been made in the image of God–so far all wheat. But you are also one whose first and prime concern is the magnification of yourself. I don't want to be made in the *image* of God, I want to be God. "I want what I want when I want it," and this is all weeds. And we find that our life is an interesting tension between these polarities. At some times we are no different than the three-year-old who has a temper tantrum because he didn't get the biggest piece of cake at a birthday party. At others for a few fleeting moments we can comprehend the sense of perfect freedom and release that comes from acknowledging our total dependence on that Being whom we acknowledge as the Creator and Sustainer of all things. And *most* of the time we are in a state of civil war between these two–*praying* hopefully that through the process of sanctification we may work toward a fuller sense of where our true freedom lies.

Now if this is true, if we pulled out all of the weeds right now and threw them into the fire, we would all be committing suicide. I, for one, am not very fond of a bee's sting. It is to me only an instrument which inflicts pain and suffering. But to remove the bee's stinger is to remove the bee. It is integrally connected to the bee's body. And I fear that in the same way all of us are weed-infested. To remove the weeds would not remove just a few bad guys, it would remove all of us.

And thus perhaps we can see the wisdom of the parable in at least two ways. Because the Church is an organic family of all sorts and conditions of men born again to

Jesus Christ through Holy Baptism, we can no more eliminate the desirable from the undesirable than we can in our own family. And, moreover, it is really almost impossible to say who is really wheat and who is really weed. Men are really a strange hybrid of both.

Nor should we neglect another interesting point. I'm no farmer, but I am interested in the response of the farmer in this parable. I would assume that an abundance of weeds would choke and deprive the wheat of its growth.

And yet the suggestion is here that there are some good and redeemable elements in this field, even if it is also infested with weeds. To destroy the weeds would be to destroy the entire field. Rather than do this we are told to work within the context we find ourselves.

This is considered a parable, or better an allegory, about the Church. And it may be helpful here to recall that the Church has been called the bride of Christ. This suggests that it is not out of line to use an analogy from the marriage bond itself. Despite the ecstatic look upon the face of the bride and groom as they walk joyfully out of the church, we all know that the life of these two people together will not always be one bowl of cherries. There will be weeds with the wheat.

The marriage vows are pretty solemn things. They cover all of the bases. And yet when the weeds arrive there is often that bewildered reply, "Oh, yes, but I didn't expect this." And one seemingly easy way to get rid of these weeds is through divorce, until one realizes that there is no field that does not have weeds. At times the whole challenge of living may be to live fully in a weed-infested jungle. But whether the context be the husband and wife union, or the church itself, to live with weeds is all but inevitable.

The question really is what to do about it. And we are smack back at the core and center of the Gospel. Our Lord did not flee from the field of life because there were weeds in it. He accepted it fully, weeds and all, and sought by working within the rich earthiness of life with all of its problems, to redeem and use it.

Your share of weeds may include a nagging wife or an unfaithful husband. It doubtless includes your own personal guilt and inadequacies.

But let's remember that we are not the harvester of this crop. God is. Our judgments on other persons, or even on ourselves, can never be ultimate judgments. As St. Paul wrote: "But with me it is a very small thing that I should be judged by you or by any human court. I do not even judge myself . . . It is the Lord who judges me. Therefore do not pronounce judgment before the time, before the Lord comes, who will bring to light the things now hidden in the darkness and will disclose the purposes of the heart" [1 Cor. 4:3-5, RSV].

And we know that God can use even weeds to effect his purposes. The cross itself shows us this. Here was an immensely evil thing which God used for the healing of all mankind. Weeds are the price we pay for a free existence. A sterile field would have no weeds, but it wouldn't have any wheat either.

The weeds of life (or to switch the analogy, the crosses of life) are an integral part of life. And yet in the supreme paradoxes of the Gospel, it is through the Cross that full life is found.

This is summarized beautifully in the collect for the Monday before Easter:

> Almighty God, whose most dear Son went not up to joy but first he suffered pain, and entered not into glory before he was crucified; Mercifully grant that we, walking in the way of the cross, may find it none other than the way of life and peace; through the same thy Son Jesus Christ our Lord.[14]

---

14. *The Book of Common Prayer* (1928), p. 138.

2

Oh what sweet relief it is to be able to blame someone else for the ills of the world and to bask in our own virtue. How sadly humorous it is to watch ourselves cling to our little ragged list of virtues and try to disentangle or disassociate ourselves from all else.

The Eleventh Sunday after Trinity *St. Francis' Church*
August 21, 1966 *San Francisco, California*

1 CORINTHIANS 15:1-11; LUKE 18:9-14

It's a good thing that today's gospel doesn't come later in the church year when we start talking about money and stewardship and every member canvasses, because at first blush it seems to fly in the face of much of what we say at that time.

Let's look at the parable again. Here is a man who is the pillar of his congregation. He comes to church to pray. That is surely a good thing in itself. (I am sorrowful at how few people during the week come in to this church to say a prayer. And in driving around making calls the other day I was amazed at the number of Protestant churches whose doors were locked tight. But I took a visiting priest to see a local Roman Catholic church and found ten or twelve people in it praying, including three men.) No, we cannot fault this man for coming in to pray. And how did he start his prayer? "God, I thank thee . . . " [Luke 18:11, KJV]. There is surely nothing wrong with this either. Thanksgiving is at the *base* of *any* kind or real response of the human creature to Almighty God, just as the Eucharist, the thanksgiving, is the basic service of worship of the Christian. So far we cannot fault this man.

He also makes some statements of fact as to what he does. He fasts twice a week and gives a tithe of all that he possesses. Fasting, now too often ignored even though it is set forth in our own Prayer Book, is an ancient and excellent discipline to remind us that we must keep in control and balance the demands of the body and the spirit. And *surely* there is nothing wrong with *tithing* as such. If I suggested this, I'd have the chairman of our canvass down upon me in an instant, and we would have to abandon a basic element of church teaching. But again, there is no suggestion in the parable that our man didn't fast or tithe, nor any suggestion (fortunately) that fasting and tithing are bad things.

But the rest of his prayer *is* interesting. He says, "I am grateful that I am not like the rest of mankind–extortioners, unjust, adulterers, or even like that tax collector over there" [Luke 18:11]. (Tax collecting was not considered a very savory business.) Now again, there is nothing in the parable to suggest that the man really did commit extortion or adultery, or collect taxes, so he wasn't lying when he said he did not do these things.

And yet we are told that this man, the pillar of the community, went away unjustified before God. What had he done wrong?

"Lord, I am grateful that I am not like the rest of mankind" [Luke 18:11]. I am good, they are bad. The problems of the world are caused by other people. Thank God I'm not involved.

Father Malcolm Boyd has a new record called *Are You Running With Me, Jesus?* One of the meditations in it is entitled, "It takes away my guilt, Jesus, to blame the Jews for killing you."[15] Oh, what sweet relief it is to be able to blame someone else for the ills of the world and to bask in our own virtue. How sadly humorous it is to watch ourselves cling to our little ragged list of virtues and try to disentangle or disassociate ourselves from all else.

Selfishness, self-centeredness, self-congratulation–this is the basis of what the church calls "sin." It is the magnification of ourselves, which if it is carried far enough, makes it impossible for us to relate to anyone else. The other extreme from selfish pride is unselfish humility. And, yet

15. The two-record set was a product of Columbia Records and recorded guitarist Mr. Charles Byrd accompanying Fr. Boyd as he read his meditations. From a telephone conversation with Fr. Boyd.

as the old saying goes, in its paradoxical way, "There is no more prideful man than he who thinks he is humble." True humility is one of those qualities that only can be seen in you by other people. The minute you start thinking you're humble, look out. It only means that you've become insufferable.

How then do we become humble? Some Christians have indeed viewed humility as a goal which a person can consciously set out to achieve. "Today I'm going to be humble." The regimen recommended is replete with hair shirts and much grovelling and conscious self-denial. One problem with this approach, however, is that you are caught in the dilemma of consciously seeking a goal which you shouldn't think about. It's much like telling a little boy to go stand in the corner and not think about a white elephant. And, of course, when the moment comes when you say with Jack Horner, "What a good boy am I," you promptly lose all your humility cards you have worked so hard to earn.

Rather, I would suggest that the attribute of humility is something like certain fairy stories I recall as a child, where the thing sought could never be sought directly, because the minute you went directly toward it, it would get further away, or the minute you looked directly at it, it would disappear.

We cannot *seek* humility. It comes only when it is not sought directly. It comes in those moments and to the extent we apprehend and appropriate in the depths of our being what D. M. Baillie calls, in his book *God Was in Christ,* "the paradox of grace." "Its essence," he says, "lies in the conviction which a Christian man possesses, that every good thing in him, every good thing he does, is somehow not wrought by himself but by God. . . . Never is human action more truly and fully personal, never does the agent feel more perfectly free, than in those moments of which he can say as a Christian that whatever good was in them was not his but God's."[16]

For, you see, to the extent we are aware of this, we are free from the limiting shackles of self-justification and self-pride. I take the first step when I acknowledge that I, left to myself, can do *nothing* good. By ourselves there is no health in us. But this is not a faith of despair, but of freedom. It does not mean that I never do anything good, but only that the good I do is God working through me.

As long as we can remember this, there's nothing in the world wrong in rejoicing over things that you have done. A man who has been given the gift of working with his hands can rightly rejoice at a beautifully or carefully done piece of wooden cabinet work. A woman who has been given the skills of cooking may quite rightly be proud

16. D. M. Baillie, *God Was in Christ: An Essay on Incarnation and Atonement* (London: Faber and Faber Limited, 1960), p. 114.

of a magnificently cooked dinner. The teacher is justly entitled to enjoy the obvious spark that his skills light in the eyes of his pupils because these good things are God's action through him, not his alone. This isn't selfish pride. It is rightful thanks for a gift given to us which we can share.

The Russians, I notice, have a custom whereby when a speaker is applauded, the speaker joins in the applause himself. I'm not sure what the reasoning behind the custom is, but I don't believe that even atheists would do this merely as a public form of self-congratulation, and I imagine the custom goes back before the communist regime. Rather I would think the idea is that to some extent the performer's offering, whether it be a speech or a recital, or what have you, stands to some extent apart from the person giving it and if people indicate by their applause that they enjoy it, then the speaker can also rejoice.

Much the same is true of the paradox of grace in a Christian framework. There is nothing in the world wrong with rejoicing in the good things we ourselves have done, if we keep aware that these things occur when we allow God to work through us.

This is why St. Paul can seem to extol his own virtues at certain times, because as he writes in today's Epistle, "But by the grace of God I am what I am: and his grace which was bestowed upon me was not in vain; but I labored more than abundantly than they all: *yet not I. But the grace of God which was with me*" [1 Cor. 15:10, KJV].

This is what is true humility, and it is this which the man that came in to pray did *not* acknowledge. His virtues were admittedly many, and there is just cause to give thanks to God for them. If he had only recalled that they were not his alone, but the result of God acting through him.

And sadly, when this essential ingredient is lacking, then this man is further from God, despite all his good works, than the poor tax-collector, who while he had no good works at all, was willing to open himself up and admit that he needed God's help–"God be merciful to me, a sinner" [Luke 18:13, KJV].

He asked for God's mercy and forgiveness and came close thereby to the greatest power in the universe, because strangely enough, God did not show the true scope of his majesty and power in his mighty act of creation. The really vast power of Him comes from the seemingly atom-sized qualities of this world. As our collect for today, written over a thousand years ago, puts it so well, "O God, who declarest thy almighty power chiefly in showing mercy and pity."[17]

True humility is letting this almighty power work in joyful acknowledgment through us.

---

17. "The Collect for The Eleventh Sunday after Trinity," *The Book of Common Prayer* (1928), p. 204.

3

If it is true, as I believe it is, that all of us are to some extent hypocrites and falsely righteous, why are we such masochists that we faithfully come to church every Sunday to be hit over the head with our admitted inadequacies? Why not go bowling and get away from the lecture?

The Twenty-second Sunday after Pentecost
November 11, 1984

The Cathedral Church of St. Mark
Salt Lake City, Utah

AMOS 5: 18-24; MATTHEW 25:1-13

In this sermon I would like to concentrate on two of today's texts, the Old Testament lesson from Amos, and our Gospel: one about hypocrisy and judgment, the other about preparedness.

The Old Testament lesson is a reading from Amos 5:18-24, to be exact. It illustrates the problem of reading the Scripture in snippets.

This section by itself makes God sound like a petulant old man. What is the reason that Amos perceived this woe and condemnation to be levied upon the people of the

Lord? Why is it that he suggests that the day of the Lord is "darkness, and not light, and gloom with no brightness in it" (Amos 5:20 [RSV])?

Let's go back a few verses in Amos's book, and perhaps we can see what he meant.

> He who made the Pleiades and Orion, and turns deep darkness into the morning, and darkens the day into night, who calls for the waters of the sea, and pours them out upon the surface of the earth, the Lord is his name, who makes destruction flash forth against the strong, so that destruction comes upon the fortress. They hate him who reproves in the gate, and they abhor him who speaks the truth. Therefore because you trample upon the poor and take from him exactions of wheat, you have built houses of hewn stone, but you shall not dwell in them; you have planted pleasant vineyards, but you shall not drink their wine. For I know how many are your transgressions, and how great are your sins–you who afflict the righteous, who take a bribe, and turn aside the needy in the gate. Therefore he who is prudent will keep silent in such a time; for it is an evil time (Amos 5:8-13 [RSV]).

Our culture views God as "Good old God," whose business is to forgive, accept, give us a peppermint candy and forget, and who is easily placated by a superficial "I'm sorry." This is the present day equivalent of burnt offerings which cost a few shekels at the temple but no expenditure of emotional sweat.

In fact, to those who seek to cleanse themselves by superficiality and yet who oppress the poor and abhor those who speak the uncomfortable truth about ourselves, Amos says there is no hiding, no cover-up. For God, who is love, is also a God of justice and righteousness. It is served up in those great lines used with such telling effect during the civil rights movement: "But let justice roll down like waters, and righteousness like an ever-flowing stream" (Amos 5:24 [RSV]).

The civil rights movement makes us, who have been sitting on the sidelines, squirm and eventually abandon the superficial burnt offering. It makes us stop giving only lip service to the words of our Constitution, and as a nation to try to give them real meaning.

I am always amazed at those who inveigh against the institutional church and eschew participation in it on the basis that it consists of a bunch of hypocrites saying one thing and doing another. The response to these people is, "Of course we are hypocrites; join the club. The only difference between us and you is that at least every Sunday morning we go out of our way to gather together and admit this fact, *as all honest people must.*"

Moreover, we church goers are reminded of our condition with great frequency, as, for example, in our lesson from Amos today.

One lesson from last Tuesday's election [November 6, 1984] is that one who is upbeat will win hearts and minds better than one who is downbeat.[18] If so, I'm glad my living is not dependent upon a ministerial salary and that I'm not running for a political office. Upbeat, downbeat, I'm not sure what this means. But the function of the preaching ministry is to afflict the comfortable and to comfort the afflicted. As Amos says, people need to know the truth about themselves, even if they reject it. And we never like to hear it.

Jesus never thundered more loudly than he did against the comfortable if they lived in hypocrisy and self-righteousness.

Most of us here today, by the luck and accident of birth and environment, are very blessed. We could have been given our existence as starving Ethiopians. Let's be honest.

---

18. On November 6, 1984, President Ronald Reagan carried all but one state (Minnesota) and the District of Columbia in his landslide win over Democrat Walter F. Mondale. "One of the lessons of the Reagan years had been that politics of pleasure played better than politics of pain. Every candidate understood the price that Walter Mondale had paid for candor in his losing race four years before. Mondale had told Americans that taxes would have to be raised to pay for the services they wanted and that Reagan would also be forced to increase them even while denying it. That is exactly what happened, but Mondale barely carried his own state of Minnesota, while Reagan won all the rest." In Haynes Johnson, *Sleepwalking Through History–America in the Reagan Years* (New York: W. W. Norton and Co., 1991), p. 391.

Despite our incredibly unique abilities, we've also been very lucky in the lottery of life. The poorest of us is at least physically comfortable by the standards of the rest of the world.

But, taking a page from Mr. Reagan's incredibly successful book, it does little good to lay a guilt trip on anyone. Indeed, if it is true, as I believe it is, that all of us are to some extent hypocrites and falsely righteous, why are we such masochists that we faithfully come to church every Sunday to be hit over the head with our admitted inadequacies? Why not go bowling and get away from the lecture?

The answer, of course, is because this is not all there is. This confrontation is only the first step in the journey to reality. But, like all steps, it is an essential one. Unless we accept the truth about ourselves, then we are unprepared; we are incapable of going any further.

The Christian faith proclaims that God is ceaselessly seeking for each of us, to love and accept you and me. But for this to be good news, we must not only be aware of it, but also of our need for it if we are to become fulfilled persons.

It is like the person who is exposed to a glorious vision, but refuses to open his eyes. Until he opens and looks, the vision is meaningless.

Which, of course, brings us to our gospel story of the wise and foolish maidens (Matt. 25:1-13).

Remember that our Lord's parables have a single, central point. Don't fret as to why the bridegroom was late, or don't wonder if the unprepared maidens could have found a merchant open at midnight to sell them oil for their lamps, or what the light of the lamps might symbolize, or who the bridegroom was.

The point here is quite simple. Five of the ten maidens did not go to the trouble of being prepared for the joyful event which they knew was to happen, at one time or another, and were not present when it occurred. When they *did* arrive the door was shut.

How harsh and unfair, we say. Is this not directly contrary to the basic Christian concept that God's love and grace are free? One needs no good works to be eligible to enter in. God loves us where we are.

This is certainly true, but here we must recognize a delicate distinction. It is indeed heresy to say, for example, that we have to *earn* God's love. The requirement would totally abuse the heart of the Gospel.

Let's use another story to explain this one. In his book *The Great Divorce,* C. S. Lewis portrays hell as a vast grey city. Every day at an appointed time a bus leaves from this Greytown to Paradise. No fare is charged. Anyone may board the bus. The only requirement is that you *want* to board the bus and that you *be there* when it leaves. But once that bus is gone, it is gone. It does no good for your neighbor or friend to save you a place. You must be there for yourself, willing and prepared to go. (There is an obvious exception, of course, for babes in arms, who are in fact totally dependent upon their parents to get them on the bus.) We need no money with which to go; we need only bring our own pathetic bag of elements which constitute ourselves, plus our longing. But nobody can go for us.[19]

And here is the tragedy of the closed door in the parable: it is the judgment built into the very nature of God's righteousness and love.

No one is theoretically beyond the reach of God's redemptive love. But for those who each day coat themselves in one more layer of phoniness and selfishness, their ability to wash away these accretions becomes harder all the time.

If I don't play bridge or golf with any frequency, my skills in those areas when suddenly called upon will leave me flat on my face. The same rule applies to ultimate values.

A person who has never prayed will usually find this great gift not available at the time of extreme need. He who does not know what he is looking for will not be prepared to recognize it when it does arise.

---

19. C. S. Lewis, *The Great Divorce* (New York: Macmillan Co., 1962), pp. 60-82, see esp. p. 69.

Theologians talk about the *process* of sanctification. While I have no doubt that instant and total conversion experiences have occurred (St. Paul being the foremost example), I will guess that for most of us the process of becoming holy is a slow, hard journey: two steps forward, one step back, and sometimes the other way around.

The Anglican tradition is especially geared to speak to those who see sanctification as a process–not one immediate lightning bolt, but a way of life that constantly lays before us the options we have, yanks us up short when we become prideful and complacent, comforts us when we are distressed and sorrowful, and lifts us up if we fall.

By following such a course, it is impossible to be a foolish, unprepared maiden. By following such a course, we can follow our Anglican love for liturgical beauty, decency, and order, and yet keep it in perspective, knowing it too can be abused, and that it can never be a substitute for, but only a complement to, God's command:

> Let justice roll down like waters, and righteousness like an ever flowing stream [Amos 5:24, RSV].

4

Genesis III describes us all. We are in the middle of our horizon. We don't like sharing things in our playpen.

The Second Sunday
after Pentecost
June 9, 1985

The Cathedral Church
of St. Mark
Salt Lake City, Utah

GENESIS 3:1-21

I'm no gambler, mainly because I'm not very good at it. When leaving Nevada I drop two quarters in a slot machine just to prove that my anti-gambling prejudice is not fanaticism, and the machine, knowing this, has always promptly gobbled them.

But this Sunday I won. The appointed propers include Genesis III once every three years, and I have been assigned to preach. The odds against these two events occurring at the same time are staggering.

Genesis III is one of my favorite Biblical texts. It tells us so much about the human condition, and it is a myth so terribly ancient and so much misunderstood. Outside of the proclamation of Jesus Christ as Lord of all in the New Testament, it is surely one of the most provocative texts in all of Scripture.

Genesis III–the Fall of Man–Man's Alienation from God. We all know the story, the wily serpent, tempting and saying "Ignore the rule. Go ahead and eat. The only reason for the rule is that the Boss is jealous. Go ahead and eat and then you too shall be as God!" You too will be unlimited, omniscient, omnipotent, omnipresent. You will have the three "O's." And Eve bit, and Adam bit, and we all bite [Gen. 3:4-7].

Adam, after all, means man. And whether we like it or not, this story is an attempt to describe each one of us.

There are many different theories as to what is our basic nature. There are those who contend that we are basically good. Left to ourselves, and without corrupting outside forces, we are kind, happy, given to good works and devotion. It was the mind set of the Enlightenment and the French Revolution–the Noble Savage, the honest toiler, the Benevolent Monarch; and along came Stalin and his hideous purges, and Hitler who made scrap of millions of human bodies, both products of Western Civilization.

There are those who believe we are created as a *tabula rasa,* a blank slate. We are formed only by the forces and values of our environment. But the best environment in the world has sometimes bred monsters, and the most squalid has produced saints.

There are those who say we are created with basic, primeval drives, hatreds, and loves. There's the joke about the analyst who asks his patient about her feelings about her parents, "I love them both." Whereupon he writes in his notes: "Suppresses hatred of parents."

Others have taken the Adam and Eve story and put an emphasis upon it which is different than that of the traditional Christian one. Thus Elder Bruce R. McConkie, in his book *Mormon Doctrine,* does not see the story as an attempt to explain the tragedy of the human condition, but as the great emancipating event in man's history. Before the Fall, blood did not flow in Adam's veins and he could have no children. Adam fell "(in) conformity with the will of the Lord" so that the opportunity for eternal progression and perfection might be offered to all the Spirit children of the Father.[20] This explains of course why when I gave a paper on the relationship of the Fall and Genesis III to the capitalistic system to a group of predominantly Mormon businessmen, my whole thesis fell on totally deaf ears. We drew totally different conclusions from the same story.[21]

Despite other possible descriptions of our basic state, or variants on the Adam and Eve story itself, let me give you what I believe is the "kosher" mainline Christian concept of the meaning of this myth, a meaning which

20. Bruce R. McConkie, *Mormon Doctrine* (Salt Lake City: Bookcraft, 1979), p. 268.

21. Snowbird Conference, Snowbird Resort, Utah, October 1979.

from my personal point of view is the best interpretation of human nature as I have observed it, and which portrays man's need which the gospel of Jesus Christ then meets and answers.

Genesis III as so construed tells us a great truth, the truth of our limitation. We are *not* God, we are creatures of God, with failings, needs, guilts and limits. This is a reality and when we accept it, it is good.

But it is not that easy to accept this truth, because like Adam and Eve, we would each like to be God without checks and limitations. Listen to what one Archbishop of Canterbury wrote in describing each one of us.

> When we open our eyes as babies we see the world stretching out around us; we are in the middle of it; all proportions and perspectives in what we see are determined by the relation–distance, height, and so forth–of the various visible objects to ourselves. This will remain true of our bodily vision as long as we live. I am the center of the world I see; where the horizon is depends on where I stand. Now just the same thing is true at first of our mental and spiritual vision. Some things hurt us; we hope they will not happen again; we call them bad. Some things please us; we hope they will happen again; we call them good. Our standard of value is the way things affect ourselves. So each of us takes his place in the center of his own world. But I am not the center of

> the world, or the standard of reference as between good and bad; I am not, and God is.[22]

Archbishop Temple has just described that terrible thing which most so-called "enlightened" people refuse to accept, the concept of original sin. The term conjures up pictures of a harsh Puritan teacher beech rod in hand, forcing his students to recite from the *New England Primer*—"In Adam's Fall, We Sinned All." What nonsense! That sweet little blissful baby in my arms is a sinner? That's sick!

But it all depends on how we define "sin." Obviously this sweet little thing doesn't smoke, drink, or carouse, but to ask a very delicate and sensitive question, has it ever really yet learned how to *love?* Oh, I know, baby loves Mommy. But why? Because Mommy loves baby and takes care of baby.

When Baby has become a toddler, put Baby in a playpen with *another* toddler, and put one toy in that pen. Does Baby *share* with love and concern that toy with the other? Only if the other is a 50-pound gorilla toddler who can take it away.

Genesis III describes us *all.* We are in the middle of our horizon. We don't like sharing things in our playpen.

And yet to the extent we insist on being the center of

22. William Temple, *Christianity and Social Order* (Baltimore: Penguin Books, Inc., 1956), p. 52.

the universe, we are not only insufferable, but we are lonely. Loneliness is the specter which haunts unredeemed humanity.

Good parents recognize this. The little darling who is the center of the world must for his own fulfillment be taught that this is not so.

He is taught to share with his brothers and sisters, and then with his friends. He is taught to eat when the family is ready to eat, and not before or after, and to eat what has been prepared. Because the one thing the world cannot stand is a spoiled brat and yet left to our own designs, this is what we all would become. We need the help of others to bring us out of ourselves. We can't do it alone.

And despite the best of all care, nurture and wisdom, all of us, no matter what our age, revert to spoiled "brattism." We want what we want, and we want it *now!*

Our basic problem is best illustrated when we analyze that deepest of human relationships, *love.* We all want to be loved, appreciated and accepted. Indeed, we really would like to love, appreciate and accept others. Yet the first step in this journey, to quote the late Ma Bell, is that we have to "reach out and touch someone."

But there are risks involved in this process. We can get a wrong number, we can be rejected, we can be *hurt.* Love requires the opening of yourself, yet this also makes us vulnerable. The catatonic schizophrenic curls up in a fetal ball. The poor person cannot be hurt that way, but of course it cannot make love either.

The ultimate symbol of vulnerable love is, of course, the cross, the tragic risk that love always runs.

For this reason, many unconsciously flee from the cross and all that it represents. After all, it's much safer to follow our basic Adam and Eve instincts, that is, play it safe, look out for Number One. The woods are full of such folks, and they're not only selfish, they are *dull.*

The Gospel calls us out of this rut. It says, go ahead, take a risk. But, you ask, why should I? One answer is because it leads to a much more fulfilled life. I believe this to be true. However, you must be warned, it also can lead to a cross. Your heart can be broken.

A more unprovable, yet more ultimate answer as to why you should do this is because this is the way that the ultimate power of the universe is. If the crazy, topsy-turvy, upside down proclamation of the Gospel is true, forgiving love is more powerful than invincible might; little is more powerful than big; the insignificant is significant; dying on a cross in a two-bit provincial town was an ultimate victory; illiterate fishermen can change the face of the world; the death of a Dorothy Martin depresses us as much as the death of a head of state.[23]

---

23. Dorothy Martin was a well-known and longtime member of the

Our natural state, if Genesis III accurately portrays us, leaves us in a cocoon. But we were not made for this. As Genesis I tells us, we were made in the image of God (not *as* God, which is the Genesis III dictum of that truth). We were made for more than a ball of ego.

Jesus Christ made some outrageous statements. As C. S. Lewis said, in one sense they are as crazy as someone who says they are a fried egg.[24] "I am uniquely in the father, and the father uniquely in me" [John 14:11]. "I am the way, the truth and the Life" [John 14:6a, KJV]. "Come unto me, all ye that travail and are heavy laden."[25]

Cathedral Church of St. Mark, Salt Lake City, Utah, who died shortly before this sermon was given.

24. As was mentioned earlier, C. S. Lewis actually said, "I am trying here to prevent anyone saying the really foolish thing that people often say about Him: 'I'm ready to accept Jesus as a great moral teacher, but I don't accept His claim to be God.' That is the one thing we must not say. A man who was merely a man and said the sort of things Jesus said would not be a great moral teacher. He would either be a lunatic–on a level with the man who says he is a poached egg–or else he would be the Devil of Hell. You must make your choice. Either this man was, and is, the Son of God: or else a madman or something worse. You can shut Him up for a fool, you can spit at Him and kill Him as a demon; or you can fall at His feet and call Him Lord and God. But let us not come with any patronizing nonsense about His being a great human teacher. He has not left that open to us. He did not intend to" (C. S. Lewis, *Mere Christianity* [New York: Macmillan Co., 1960], pp. 40-41).

25. Colton is quoting from Matthew 11:28 as is found in the "Comfortable Words," *The Book of Common Prayer* (New York: The

Difficult to accept? Of course. But what if it is true? It *is* the way out of the Genesis III cocoon. We can stay there if we wish. Or we can put our hand in someone else's, and start the painful climb up. God left it for each of us to decide.

Church Hymnal Corporation, 1979), p. 76.

IV
Grace

Introduction

It is characteristic of Albert Colton's sermons that the beginning theme is centered around the imperfection of humanity's faculties. Colton eschews the notion, popular with many other preachers, that the benefits of the faith depend on our strengths and good works. Therefore, just as Christians can contemplate forgiveness and justification only when they acknowledge their sins, so can Christians understand, as much as is possible, grace after appreciating what it means to be lost, weak, and deficient in worthy accomplishments.

The search for the lost–honestly, haven't you ever secretly resented the cost of the search crews that go out to find some silly person who wandered too far in the wilderness? And yet, isn't it a magnificent thing that we value an individual that much? We deeply know that each life is precious and at our best we act on that faith. So each man longs, in a valid longing, for recognition.

Have you ever been lost? Of course you have! It's one of our first nightmares as a child. It has happened mentally during an examination or an interview. It happens in the endless mazes of city freeways, or in country lanes that turn into mud puddles, and we realize we have missed a turning. Fairy tales tell us this as a basic theme–lost in a haunted forest. And in such stories, why were you found? Because you were so very clever that you left bread crumbs to mark your path? (Remember, the birds ate these.) And someone had to come find you. But why did anyone even bother to look for you? Have you ever thought of that?

And here we get, in these old common-sense true to life questions–to the basic concept of the Christian gospel–to the idea of *Grace* and the words of today's epistle, "But I received mercy because I had acted ignorantly in unbelief and the grace of our Lord overflowed for me with the faith and love that are in Christ Jesus" [1 Tim. 1:13-14, RSV].

This is the gospel. You and I left by ourselves are lost. We can fumble, we can try to construct a sense of values, but they tend to crumble.

In my puzzlement, in my despair, in my pain and fear, there is someone looking for me.[1]

Colton was confident that God looks for those sorely in need of salvation. He also believed that God finds those people in the street, literally and figuratively. He mirrored the guttural characteristic of the Gospel according to Mark in that his sermons addressed those who were in the midst of bad news in some aspect of their lives. He also approached people where they were and not where some felt they should be. This allowed for the development of a theology of sacramental grace.

---

1. Sermon preached the Seventeenth Sunday after Pentecost, September 14, 1986, the Cathedral Church of St. Mark, Salt Lake City, Utah.

It is important to observe two things about [the gospel account of Jesus' healing of a deaf man with an impediment in his speech (Mark 7:31-37)]. The healed man did *nothing* to deserve this. There is no statement that he was *more* worthy, and deserved this, [rather] he was healed in the condition Jesus found him. Here we are back to one of the basic tenets of Christian theology—the doctrine of *grace.* It never hurts to dwell on this, because it is what makes the bad news good news. The idea that I can be made whole by what I do is bad news.

As Paul says in Romans [7:13-20], I already *know* the rules. You don't have to preach these to me. My *problem* is that I don't keep the rules. Salvation by faith on the other hand is *good* news, i.e., my healing has already taken place, *despite* what I do or did. God loves and accepts me where I am.

The second point [is] this healing took place in the *world,* not in a temple, not during a religious rite, but on the street in everyday life. This confirms the *sacramental principle.* God acts in and through his creation in time and space.[2]

Most people are willing to have others, equal or better than themselves, enter the realm of Heaven. However, it seems to attack the doctrine of fairness to let in scoundrels. A popular cartoon,

---

2. Sermon preached the Fifteenth Sunday after Pentecost, September 8, 1985, St. Peter's Episcopal Church, Clearfield, Utah.

which portrays a scene in heaven, shows an obviously disturbed, worn out and sweating pilgrim addressed by another who says, "You know, it seems such a pity to be saved by grace after we've worked so hard."[3] *Colton tells us that such salvation is grace, a free gift of God.*

Why *should* the Lord come? Why should he *bother?* It is here that we get to the bedrock of the Judeo-Christian concept of meaning. It is based on the sure and certain hope that the King of Kings, the Lord of Lords, creator of all there is, will never ultimately let me down, even when *I* don't give the matter a second thought.

This smacks somewhat of the great agnostic poet who was asked on his deathbed whether he thought God would forgive him. He replied, "Why not? That's his business, isn't it?"[4]

Doesn't that reply, if true, make suckers out of those who prepare so long and carefully and lovingly for his coming, when those who could care less are privileged to share the same experience.

Perhaps—but that is the Gospel—the Gospel that

---

3. Calvin Grondahl, *Sunday's Foyer: A Collection of Mormon Cartoons* (Salt Lake City: Sunstone Foundation, 1983), p. 37

4. Colton possibly was recalling the words, "God will pardon me. It is his trade" *(Dieu me pardonnera. Cést son métier).* On his deathbed, Lombroso, *The Man of Genius* (1891), pt. 1, ch. 2., in *The Oxford Dictionary of Quotations,* 3rd ed., intro. Bernard Darwin (New York: Oxford University Press, 1979), p. 136.

the King of Kings will come to each of us, and accept and love us where we are–not because we are worthy, not because we are prepared, but just because we exist as one of his own children.

The Lord *will* come to us all, whether we think that fair and right or not.[5]

Quickly on the heels of exposing God for being "unfair" in God's accepting through grace those who don't "deserve" God's justification, Colton includes us all in that same camp of "undeserving people." Our pride wishes we didn't belong. But no one "deserves" justification or the quality of being judged righteous. And yet, "unfair" as it is, all of us have been given this gift of God's love through grace. And through love, God claims and judges all as redeemed.

Groucho Marx's great saying–"I wouldn't join any club that would have me as a member."

To those who finally recognize that trying to do it all themselves doesn't work and some morning wake up on their knees asking for help–*they* are the ones who realize that the time is short, there is no favoritism (God takes us all) and His truths often overturn the judgments of earth (thank God).

There are plenty of professionally religious pietists

---

5. Sermon preached the First Sunday in Advent, November 28, 1965, St. Francis' Church, San Francisco, California. Also preached the First Sunday of Advent, November 29, 1977, the Cathedral Church of St. Mark, Salt Lake City, Utah.

who need to be reminded that heaven and the grace of God is not a private club into which they are automatically and irrevocably born.

In other words, the minute I begin to feel self-righteous about my religious faith and my own personal relationship to God—watch out! Because the gate for such people is quite narrow indeed.

This does not mean that we cannot *proclaim* the Gospel—Heaven forbid! It's the greatest liberating force that ever entered my life. But that's exactly the point! It's meant as a *liberating* force—to help you be at ease and in love with your world.[6]

---

6. Sermon preached the Second Sunday in Lent, March 2, 1980, the Cathedral Church of St. Mark, Salt Lake City, Utah.

1

Man cannot heal himself. This goes against our deepest instincts, against our ever-present concern with ourselves, our personal welfare, and our self-preservation. It is the bitterest medicine in the Christian medicine bag. . . . But Christianity is not bad news. "Gospel" means good news. And this is so, because while there is nothing that man can do, there is also nothing that he need do. Almighty God, in His infinite love, has already acted.

The Ninth Sunday after Trinity — *Grace Cathedral*
August 11, 1963 — *San Francisco, California*

1 CORINTHIANS 10:1-13; LUKE 15:11-32

The Collect, Epistle, and Gospel for this, the Ninth Sunday after Trinity, make heady wine, even for the biblical scholar and theologian—there is so much here to think about and ponder. The selections from *The Book of Common Prayer* for Trinitytide are traditionally devoted to the teachings of our Lord and of the church, and this Sunday we see this principle applied with true gusto.

Not only do these readings provide much food for

thought in themselves, growing richer by greater study, but the Epistle in particular assumes in addition substantial knowledge of the Old Testament. This is all the more remarkable when we realize that this is from part of a letter from St. Paul to the church of Corinth–to a group in all likelihood not of converted Jews but of converted pagans.

As we read this portion of his letter, we cannot help but be impressed with the boldness and breadth of Paul's thought. He did not hesitate in seeing that in the wretched death of one man there were ramifications not only for himself, not just for the Greeks of the church of Corinth, but that this event had *cosmic* significance both backwards and forwards in human history, affecting not only man but all of creation which groaned for release from its travail, and through all eternity.

Thus, St. Paul seizes upon the sacred history of the old Israel and of the great story of God's deliverance of these people of God in their exodus from Egypt, their journey through the Red Sea, and their wandering in the wilderness, and he baptizes this history. The rock from which the chosen people drank was Christ.

To many, this concept must seem like the wildest kind of science fiction, with visions of time machines sending men or ideas backwards into time. But Paul was not concerned with apparently logical difficulties. Just because he was convinced of the cosmic implications of this man Jesus Christ, he knew that God's action could not be restricted in its effect to the deliverance merely of those men who happened through no virtue of their own to be born after the first century A.D. All of this must in some way be a unity.

As a Jew, he knew that Almighty God did act within His creation–that He was a deliverer from the bondage and frustrations of this life, and that He sought to heal men and make them whole again, in the only way this can truly be done, by restoring them to a proper relationship with the ground on which their being rests–God Himself. God acted in history not by abstract propositions–thus He spoke through the prophets, who were bold to say, "thus saith the Lord."

Of these things, St. Paul, as a good Jew, was surely certain. But an ache remained. Still there was a sense of separation, of aloneness. Even with this knowledge it was there. How can we heal the gap? How? One answer is obvious, Follow the rules. Live the law. Go to church *every Sunday,* as is indeed your bounden duty anyway–the ache is still there–then go to church *every day*–observe the feasts and fasts with ever greater meticulousness, give a carefully measured tenth of your income to the church, read the daily offices, practice being humble, pray loudly and efficiently–somehow God will certainly smile, and of course He'll have to recognize our devotion and our merit–slowly we notice we are indeed changing–remembering the parable of the sheep and the goats, we feel ourselves becoming more sheep-like, or is it perhaps that we notice it is really that our less zealous, more benighted friends are becoming more goat-like? We lift our spiritual skirts as they draw near so as to avoid contamination–and we note with pride–what's that?–with pride? In a flash our house of cards falls in–far from being a sheep of the Lord, we have become a crashing, pompous, prideful hypocrite. What a cruel pardon. We realize that the proudest man of all is he who thinks himself humble. And pride is the queen of all vices–it is this which exhibits our selfishness–which sets us apart–which increases our separation and makes shared communications impossible. The world to such a man is a vast nursery school in which there is no real play, because this assumes a giving and sharing. It is a world of three-year-olds engaged in parallel play, in which you are only vaguely aware of others except when you see something they have and you want it or when you defend your things from them. Who is the god of the selfish man? Himself–in his zealous search for God he has only deified himself, and this is hell–this is death. Religion has become an ultimate sanction for his dearest desires. Thus the way to God through rules is bankruptcy and death, as St. Paul saw.

But what then? What can I do? St. Paul had realized in a blinding instant that there was nothing he could do to heal this aching pain.

He was face to face with one of the most uncomfortable truths of human existence, as our Collect for today says, "We who cannot do anything good without thee . . . "[7] This goes against the grain of everything our culture stands for–it destroys all conceptions of a do-it-yourself religion. To those who find their religious solace in a life fairly well lived, with a minimum of obvious errors, and with a maximum of achievement, it says, "My son, these are as ashes." You too must stand naked and exposed. In the eyes of Almighty God, all, in our pathetic and frenzied striving, must be judged alike. We are unprofitable servants. And it is here that any true religious journey must start, depressing and degrading as it might seem.

What bad news. What a counsel of despair. And indeed it is. Man cannot heal himself. This goes against our deepest instincts, against our ever-present concern with ourselves, our personal welfare, and our self-preservation. It is the bitterest medicine in the Christian medicine bag. But it is either a true statement of the human predicament at its deepest level, or the rest of the Christian world view on which it is based collapses with it.

But Christianity is not bad news. "Gospel" means good news. And this is so, because while there is nothing that

7. *The Book of Common Prayer* (New York: The Church Pension Fund, 1928), pp. 200-201.

man can do, there is also nothing that he *need* do. Almighty God, in His infinite love, has already acted. "But when he was yet a great way off, his father saw him, and had compassion, and ran, and fell on his neck and kissed him" [Luke 15:20, KJV].

We are all such a great way off. And yet it is not our frantic clawing after God, but his running with compassion to us, that heals the breach. This knowledge of God's nature is no longer an abstract theory or something transmitted to us through some prophetic medium. This amazing truth was put into a focus that all men, or any man, could understand. God came to us in our humanity in the person of one man, a Jew, with the not uncommon name of that time of Jesus. His love and concern for you and me was so great that the creator of the universe "emptied himself taking the form of a servant, being born in the likeness of men" (Phil. 2:7 [RSV]), and suffered and died, and the gap between man and his ground of being, the Almighty, Everlasting God, is closed. God did what we fallen men could never do. He freely gave, of his own choice, that which is most precious to all mortal men, his own mortal life, to lovingly help someone else.

What an astounding claim! It is no wonder that the world has found it difficult to accept. There is an "overmuchness" to this which is a bit offensive to us. Consider the effusiveness of the father's greeting of the prodigal son with its oriental emotionalism. After all, wouldn't a good firm handshake do just as well? I am reminded of a maiden aunt of mine who used to shower me with wet, juicy kisses which I accepted in a state of trauma and vigorously wiped off as soon as possible. Or as any parent knows, there comes a time when the son makes it clear that he is now far too old to be receiving kisses from his father, or even in public from his mother. Men are not supposed to cry, even in deep grief, and any acknowledged dependence on someone else is viewed uneasily, as a sign of weakness.

But our need is that great. And indeed until each individual is brought to a sense of need–of desperate need–and on his knees is willing to accept his own tragic ineptitude at meeting this need by himself–the Gospel of Jesus Christ will have no relevance to his life. He must say, "I cannot do anything good without thee."

Paul Tillich, in one of his greatest sermons, suggests to people who have difficulty with the traditional jargon of the Christian faith, that they discard all else and start with one assumption–that they are accepted. Despite who they are and what they have done, they are accepted joyfully and fully. We are accepted, to use his term, by the ground of all being, by the source of all value, the sustaining source of all life. Accept our acceptance, and see what a difference it makes. No more need at pretense, no more frenzied scrambling up that slippery hill.[8]

And the strange, paradoxical, mysterious thing is that when this is done, there is a sense of peace and power that makes us climb even higher and more noble hills, not to earn a thing, but out of the sheer joy and exuberance released in response to this truth. In the paradox of grace the Christian man is convinced that every good thing he does is somehow not wrought by himself but by God, and yet he has lost none of his personality or responsibility. In fact, never has he felt his actions to be more truly and fully personal nor more perfectly free.

But this is far from an easy thing to do, simple as it sounds. To accept my acceptance means that I have to accept the fact that I need to be accepted. I must admit that I'm really not the life of every party, that the world doesn't count it as a privilege just to have me around, and that life is not one long feast where wherever I sit is the head of the table.

Moreover, this whole thing is a continuing problem throughout our lives. This cruel cycle has a way of repeating itself. In a flash we may see that all our striving is for naught–or indeed we may be made uncomfortably aware of this through the observations of some friend (now a former friend)–but so often we pick ourselves up again, dust ourselves off, salve our wounds with a little ointment of self-pity, and start climbing the hill again all by ourselves.

---

8. Paul Tillich, *The Shaking of Foundations* (New York: Charles Scribner's Sons, 1948), p. 162.

But whenever we think we have reached the top of the mountain, beware! "Wherefore let him that thinketh he standeth take heed lest he fall" [1 Cor. 10:12, RSV]. It is for this reason that *The Book of Common Prayer* requires a confession each time someone wishes to approach the Holy Table for Communion. We all start from the foot of the mountain. From this requirement no one is exempt.[9]

But we constantly forget this. St. Paul tries to point this out by a lesson from the past history of the Jewish people. Despite the mighty acts which God has done in the past, and is always doing to help us, to deliver us, to nourish and strengthen us, there are many who fall away, who murmur and cause dissension, and become idolaters.

An idolater is, after all, merely someone who puts his ultimate reliance upon something which is less than ultimate, and is therefore unable to recognize and accept his total dependence upon Almighty God. He is unable to say,

9. Colton preached this sermon during the time of *The Book of Common Prayer* (1928), in which the rubrics stated, "Then shall this General Confession be made, by the Priest and all those who are minded to receive the Holy Communion, humbly kneeling" (p. 75). The rubrics of *The Book of Common Prayer* (New York: The Church Hymnal Corporation, 1979), pp. 330, 379, read, "A Confession of Sin is said here [between the "Prayers of the People" and the "Peace"] if it has not been said earlier. On occasion, the Confession may be omitted" (pp. 330, 379).

"I cannot do anything that is good without thee," because this is never true of a limited God.

Israel's history is our history. It is in one sense the story of each one of us. We are all, or at some time have been, idolaters in one way or another, whether your idol be money, or job, or family, social acceptance, or what have you.

And so we are called upon each day of our lives, to examine ourselves and make our choice. Is our God to be a limited thing, or one who makes absolute and total claim upon all that we are?

Each of the billions of human beings now living on this earth must make this decision for himself. All are aware of at least two undeniable facts: First, that he was born as he is through no choice of his own; and Second, that he will die. From this, and the wealth of past and present experience of his fellows, and his own personal life, he must carve out some sense, something that will satisfy him, or he will go insane.

All men have some world view, whether it be nothing more profound than "that's the way the ball bounces" or the paradox that "no generalization is always valid including this one." Some search deeper than others. Some are satisfied with superficialities. Some take another's answer without question and use it as their own. Some keep searching without finding.

But many, many millions have at all times and in all

places chosen to give thanks to the Lord, the Holy Father, the Almighty Everlasting God for the gift of His only Son in whose life and death the tensions of the cosmos have been resolved, and who can give depth and meaning to life to all those who, acknowledging that they cannot do anything good in His absence, accept His gracious gift.

2

I am free to choose hell if I wish (although personally I do not believe that ultimately my selfishness can prevail over infinite love). Left to my own devices, I would choose hell every day, it might be a subtle and sophisticated hell, but to the extent it meant choosing a world centering around myself as my ultimate concern, it would still be hell.

The Second Sunday in Lent | *Grace Cathedral*
February 23, 1964 | *San Francisco, California*

1 THESSALONIANS 4:1-8

From the collect for this Sunday: "Almighty God, who seest that we have no power of ourselves to help ourselves . . . "[10]

The Anglican church is Augustinian in its Prayer Book, but completely Pelagian in its conduct. If conversation ever begins to lag at the next party you attend, you might try this statement out. I assure you that you will get *no* response. You will *not* be the life of the party. It obviously

10. *The Book of Common Prayer* (1928), p. 127.

sounds like a bit of theological jargon that has absolutely no relevance to anything.

It will be my attempt this morning to try to show that it has a very great deal of relevance to a very great number of things, such as the basic way we view life, and why we do some of the things we do.

But first, of course, we have to peel off some of the jargon or at least to refresh some of our memories as to what, say, "Augustinianism" and "Pelagianism" are.

The St. Augustine (or "Augusteen" if you wish; it doesn't make any difference, scholars tell me) we are talking about when we say Augustinianism is the author of the well-known *Confessions* (the reading of which in one of the several good modern translations now available in paper back might make a good Lenten discipline for some of you). He was Bishop of the See of Hippo in North Africa in the first part of the fifth century. He was not only one of the most remarkable Christians who ever lived, but one of the most remarkable men in history. He was an immensely prolific writer, and many of his writings which have come down to us have tremendously influenced not only Christian thought, but the philosophy of history and political science as well.

This Augustine (of Hippo) should not be confused with another great St. Augustine (of Canterbury), the first Archbishop of Canterbury, who landed on the British Isles some 150 years after Augustine of Hippo's death, and whom we commemorate in one of our de Rosen murals in this Cathedral church [Grace Cathedral, San Francisco].

Pelagianism is a term for the manner of theological thought of Pelagius, a British monk, who came into prominence during the lifetime of Augustine of Hippo, and eventually into marked conflict with him.

These men lived in troubled times. The Roman empire was seen by most as an institution which would endure forever; its long life was attributed by many, including a number of Christians, to divine protection. Then, horror of horrors, in the year 410 the city of Rome was sacked by the barbarian Alaric. The empire was toppling. Pelagius, who had made his way to Rome, had established himself there as a good and pious man, fled with thousands of other refugees to North Africa where he encountered the Bishop of Hippo. Pelagius, just because he was a good and pious man, was shocked at the low state of morality in Rome when he arrived. He set himself the task of preaching a more stirring morality, and like most moralists, he stressed the possibility of men being able to put themselves right if only they made the effort. All men needed was a little more will power, a little more character.

We have all heard this appeal before–whether as a pep talk at a sales convention, or before a football game, or at a high school graduation where "I am the captain of my soul" [from "Invictus," by William Ernest Henley] is recited, or even from the pulpit. But as Christians we must be careful here. Look where we may be leading.

If I, by the exercise of my free will alone, can change myself, then my sins are nothing more than mistakes–choices I make to follow a bad example rather than a good one. If I am exposed to sufficient good examples I will mend my ways, or at least, I can do so if only I choose.

This whole line of thought is of course based on an immensely optimistic conception of human nature. It is no surprise that we see Pelagius and his school rejecting the conception of original sin. Moreover, it is of course a highly individualistic conception of man. My problem is my problem, thank you, and yours is yours. Adam's failure to properly exercise his free will in separating himself from God affected only Adam, not anyone else. Each of us starts this life with a clean slate, and it is up to us to make something out of it.

It sounds appealing and sensible, doesn't it? This is probably because we are steeped in a humanistic culture that is strongly Pelagian in its orientation. And it is little wonder that Pelagius was quite upset when he read the statement in Augustine's *Confessions,* "Grant what Thou dost command, and command what Thou wilt."[11]

---

11. St. Augustine, *The Confessions of St. Augustine,* trans. F. J. Sheed

Augustine spoke from a completely different point of view—from the point of view of the convert, dramatically seized with the good news of Jesus Christ after a life of dissolution and meaningless wandering. He could never forget that event—and the marvel of his present life in the church. Why? What had he done to deserve this good fortune? As he pondered, he realized he had done nothing at all. He had not kept a stiff upper lip and sought to be good, as Pelagius would have counseled. He had the strong and awesome sense that in some way he had been chosen, through no act of his own—that God had reached out and touched him, unworthy and undeserving as he was. God reached him first, even before he could will a response, and indeed even the will to respond in love instead of rejection was the result of God's action.

But, you may well ask, wasn't Augustine merely conditioned by his own experience? Is *either* Pelagius' or Augustine's view one that can be universally applied to all of us? The Church said, after careful weighing, one was right and one was wrong and condemned Pelagianism as heresy.

Let us see if under deeper examination Pelagius' thought, tempting as it is (and all heresy is tempting) can be applied to any of us. Does not his over-optimism

---

(New York: Sheed and Ward, 1943), p. 237.

about human nature lead to ultimate despair? Does it not place upon me a burden of responsibility which I am not able to bear? If my capacity to be a better person is completely dependent upon my having sufficient gumption to be a better person, then why in the world am I not better than I am? I have difficulty in keeping even a minor Lenten discipline–what is wrong with me? Why can't I always think positively? My sense of guilt and inadequacy begins mounting and growing. I am, by Pelagian thought, *willfully* defying Almighty God, and my weakness is no excuse.

Moreover, because my capacity to use my will power is my problem, I am tempted to forget compassion for others, and the grief and suffering of others becomes unimportant. Thus, to the Pelagian the solution of the problem is fairly simple. All we need to do is exercise enough will power. If the negro juvenile delinquent in Hunter's Point [San Francisco] would only bestir himself he wouldn't be in that fix. But I think we can all see the inadequacy of such a solution–among other things, it overlooks the corporate sense of the demonic. A negro born illegitimately in a slum ghetto, raised in poverty and ignorance, rebuffed and rebuked whenever he seeks to break out of the social ghetto our society assigns to him, is bound to be affected by the sins of all of us who created this situation.

But you and I, as persons, are the products of a

thousand forces over which our will power had no bearings—our parents, who created and raised us, the schools which educated us, the culture which helped mold our values.

We certainly don't become Christians by ourselves. I only knew of Jesus Christ because someone told me about Him. I cannot baptize myself. This is done by others who wished to bring me into this group. I cannot receive the sacraments except in the context of the gathered Christian family. It may be only two or three of us, but these two or three represent the entire body of Christ at that particular time and place. As a Christian I am involved with other people whether I like it or not, merely in the fact that I am a Christian.

Pelagius, with all his piety, lost sight of the essential truth that all of us, whether we acknowledge it or not, are creatures–not creators–creatures solely and ultimately dependent upon Almighty God. Ash Wednesday represents this. There is, if you think about it, a wonderful miracle in the very fact that you and I are alive here together at this very moment. But the Christian faith goes further than this. The gospel is not the story of man's search for God, it is the story of God's search for man, a search so intense, so profound, so concerned, that Almighty God gave his only begotten son to the end that all that believe in Him should not perish. As our collect says, and St. Augustine would surely approve, we have no power of ourselves to help ourselves. This power too is a gift of God.

But we are not automatons either, or marionettes, manipulated at God's whim and caprice. The dangerous extreme to which Augustinianism can and at times has been pushed is a sort of double-barreled predestination whereby the human being is seen as little more than a puppet, created to be either saved or damned at the sole discretion of God alone. Or, in the pagan world (which appears in every daily paper), because he is born under a certain celestial sign, his conduct for even this day is predetermined. Or in the Marxist's world, with his rigid sense of economic and historical determinism–they all fall into the same trap.

We need not go this far. We acknowledge, without becoming a Pelagian, that free will is an important part of our life. But perhaps this is true only in a negative sense, i.e., we are free to reject God. We are free to choose to separate ourselves from our brothers and crawl back into our womb of selfishness.

But I can only do the positive thing. I can only reach out and touch in love because God helps me do so. I cannot will to love. I love to the extent that Christ is working in me.

This, therefore, does not eliminate the need for exhortation. I hope that many of you have already decided to come to the discussion of this sermon in our adult class after this service and point out that despite what I have said, the very epistle which follows this collect for today is filled with exhortation. We are exhorted to abstain from immorality, "For God has not called us for uncleanness, but in holiness" [1 Thess. 4:7, RSV]. Isn't this just what Pelagius was trying to do?

I suggest not. We ourselves do not and cannot *help* ourselves in any ultimate sense in God's eyes. We were already completely loved and accepted by Him even before we were old enough to do anything. Our free will is not a tool which we can use to earn God's love. That love is already and always there. But we *can* will and choose to separate ourselves from this love, and every time we separate ourselves from someone else, we separate ourselves from God.

In other words, I suggest that hell is a state where those who are there *wish* to be. They have chosen, of their free will, this separation.

I am free to choose hell if I wish (although personally I do not believe that ultimately my selfishness can prevail over infinite love). Left to my own devices, I would choose hell every day, it might be a subtle and sophisticated hell, but to the extent it meant choosing a world centering around myself as my ultimate concern, it would still be hell. I can go to hell without even knowing it. As C. S. Lewis wrote in his *Screwtape Letters,* "Indeed, the safest road to Hell is the gradual one–the gentle slope, soft underfoot, without sudden turnings, without milestones, without signposts."[12] No muss. No fuss. So simple.

I am incapable of escaping this hell by myself. The preachments of dear old Pelagius merely aggravate my basic problem by focusing even more on myself, either by giving me a false sense of my own capacity or by plunging me into despairing introspection and self-condemnation.

But God can save me from the hell of my "selfness." The mere awareness of his presence turns me from my exclusive self-concern. But moreover, through his gift, if I merely appropriate it, I can be helped actively out of this morass. And I surely trust that a little exhortation along this line to ourselves and others is never out of order.

But the sequence is crucially different. To Pelagius, we might see an order of exhortation, which leads to a better life, which leads to God. To the orthodox Christian, we see exhortation which leads to God through Jesus Christ, which as a *result* should reflect a better life.

Thus we do not pray "without myself, I cannot help

---

12. C. S. Lewis, *The Screwtape Letters and Screwtape Proposes a Toast* (New York: Macmillan Co., 1973), p. 56.

God." But rather, "without God, I cannot help myself." Thanks be to God that his help is there.

This sermon was also preached:

The First Sunday in Lent ανδ *The Second Sunday in Lent*
February 27, 1977 *March 6, 1977*
The Cathedral Church of St. Mark *St. Barnabas' Church*
Salt Lake City, Utah *Tooele, Utah.*

3

It is pretty obvious that a person can't get perspective on himself by himself. Even if he tries, he ends up merely kidding and deluding himself.

Quinquagesima Sunday
(the Sunday before Lent)
February 20, 1966

St. Francis' Church
San Francisco, California

We Christians live in very strange times. The other night a Roman Catholic priest condemned the growing Communist influence within the College of Cardinals. When pressed he explained that he felt that the slightest change, for example, in the emphasis paid to the Virgin Mary led to a vacuum in the minds of the common people, which Communists were anxious to fill. Thus, anyone who changed the Church in the slightest was helping the Communists. At the other extreme we have a substantial body of Protestant-Christian thought that has for many years maintained that the very doctrine of the Virgin Birth itself is mythology and irrelevant.

We have a fascist rebel government in Rhodesia which claims that one of its reasons for existence is to "preserve Christian civilization," and yet this very government is called by the Christian bodies of that area an insidious tyranny. The Church's courage to speak out requires great courage and may well lead to martyrdom for many.

We have certain elements of the Christian Church who are frantically trying to adapt the church and, in their words, make it more "relevant" to life. At the extreme end of the group are those described by Dean Fitch of the Pacific School of Religion in a recent article of The Christian Century as follows:

> As the Sunday morning service begins the minister enters, not from the chancel but from the back of the church. Everyone now understands this bit of symbolism: the pastor is coming out of the secular world. There is only one little question in the minds of a few of the faithful: will he ever make it, really, to the altar, to the pulpit, to the lectern that holds the Word of God?[13]
>
> For this preacher takes pride in being abreast of the times. His doctrine is an honest-to-God theology of a God who is dead. His prayers are an autoerotic exercise in complacency with the contemporary. If there is a new play on the stage, all maudlin with confusion and self-pity, he finds in it a revelation. If there is a fresh musical composition, all wrenched by disorder and

---

13. Robert E. Fitch, "The Sell-Out or The Well Acculturated Christian," *The Christian Century*, Feb. 16, 1966, p. 202.

dissonance, he will fit it somehow into his liturgy. There is no poem so garbled, no painting so chaotic but he finds it rich in significant meaning. There is no emergent immorality in his secular city but he hails it as the dawn of a new freedom. And so an acculturated clergyman presents an acculturated Christ to an acculturated congregation.[14]

And when this happens, Dean Fitch suggests, we have the "Age of the Sell-Out."[15] We are a new Esau who has sold his spiritual birthright for a secular mess of pottage.

It all somehow seems as crazily mixed up as the story in *MAD Magazine* of the absent-minded professor who tucked his TV dinner into bed and ate his son. In his grief he and his wife went to church to light a candle. The professor kissed the top of the candle tenderly and set fire to his wife's hair.[16]

Where in the world *are* we going as Christians? What is important and what isn't? Surely in the plethora of divergent views within the Christian community itself *someone* is pretty badly mixed up—someone is tucking the TV dinner into bed and eating his son.

We must begin to ask ourselves whether in our con-

---

14. Ibid.

15. Ibid.

16. Citation uncertain.

temporary frenzy for renewal modern Christian man has really become liberated, or merely unbuttoned.

Next Wednesday will mark the beginning of Lent; Ash Wednesday, along with Good Friday, are the two most solemnly penitential days in the Christian calendar. Most of the world will pay it little heed. Even most Protestants have given up any particular form of observance on this day.

And yet, God willing, on this day most of the people of this little parish will come to one of the three services on that day where we will perform a ritual 2,000 years old, and will read lessons which the Church has been using at that time for many, many centuries. Many of those attending will choose to come up to the altar rail after the service for the Imposition of Ashes on their foreheads, to the intonation of the solemn words "Remember, O man, dust thou art, and unto dust shalt thou return"[17]—words so ancient that their source is lost to us in the antiquity of a by-gone Near Eastern civilization.

How wildly irrelevant this all is! How preciously antiquarian and other-worldly! Or *IS* it?

---

17. While words similar to these are found in *The Book of Common Prayer* (1979), at the time of the writing of this sermon, Colton took this phrase from "The Blessing and Imposition of Ashes On the First Day of Lent," *A Manual for Priests of the American Church* (Cambridge, MA: Society of Saint John the Evangelist, 1961), p. 243.

I would quarrel with this "other-worldly" handle anyway—even though I'm only a fellow who works one day a week arguing with those who see the "real" world all week long. But rather than being "other-worldly" I suggest that Ash Wednesday, for example, is one of the most worldly, realistic, relevant observations of life. It deals with guilt, with finitude and limitation, and dependence. The person participating in such a service is confronting these questions. He is facing them head-on. Nor are there any sugar-coated words to make this confrontation more palatable. And the person who truly participates in such a service of confrontation with guilt, with finitude and limitation, and with an acknowledgment of our dependence upon Almighty God and other people, must be honest with himself and face himself. This is usually not a very easy or comfortable thing to do.

Of course, if, as the result of such confrontation, a man can say he has never done anything he regrets, has never out of his own selfishness caused harm and pain to others, senses no need for love and acceptance and renewal of life, then I would think that the same honesty which brought him there would compel him to get up and leave—for such a man has no need of Ash Wednesday, nor the Sacraments, nor indeed of the saving news of the gospel.

I have never met such a man. I personally believe he doesn't exist, which explains perhaps the ease of the dispensation.

Now Ash Wednesday has been criticized for many reasons. Some feel it is too morbidly concerned with our short-comings, and I can understand that in a world which tends to soften the word "sin" into the word "mistake," that such basic confrontations as this would make some uncomfortable. But "other-worldly" it is *not! Too* worldly for those raised on a softer diet it may be.

This is not to say that I don't think we need a good dose of other-worldliness once in a while—we do. It is important however to define what we mean by "other-worldly." By it I would suggest something which transcends and speaks from a frame of reference of a larger perspective than merely the here and now, but I would also add that it must be something which in order to be understood at all must touch and relate directly to the here and now.

Let me illustrate. Bishop Kilmer Myers, Suffragan Bishop of Michigan, spent many years of his priesthood in the slums of New York City. His book *Light the Dark Street* is as "worldly" a book as you would like to read. Bishop Myers knows life and he is in the forefront of our church's fight for social justice. He is in this sense a worldly man with a strong feeling that the Church must renew herself in a secular age. But he is also an other-worldly man. Thus he writes in a recent article:

Catholic means that when the Mass of Christ is offered

> its effects move through and beyond the Table and its guests into the cosmos, as Chardin suggested: that the movement of the Mass is the movement of life from its primordial beginnings to its end in God Himself. *Catholic* means that the first and fundamental altar stone is the world itself, and that the Church, the Body of Him Who fills all things, is the earnest of that event when the whole human family shall gather at the one Table. . . . The vistas opened up by the word *Catholic* are terrifyingly beautiful![18]

He sees the true validation and perspective given to the here and now only by the perspective of eternity. It is difficult for us to see this. I don't think it comes naturally. We innately think of life as the moment and that moment shall validate itself. Take a small boy sitting down alone to a table loaded with cake and candy. What a moment! And too much will be consumed too fast with the awful judgment of the stomach ache coming only later. Judgment *does* come–the gastronomical eschaton is inevitable–and yet the little boy at the moment of eating is too busy being a thorough existentialist. Babies, when they want something, want it *now*–right this minute–they aren't interested in

---

18. Three experts on the writings of Bishop Kilmer Myers all agree that "this certainly sounds like something he would say" but were uncertain as to the citation's source.

what the wisdom and meaning of a longer perspective would give them.

And is not secular man much like the baby who wants what he wants now, without concern for values which transcend and go beyond our present situation?

Dean Fitch makes the statement: "The fact is that those who have been exclusively interested in this world are precisely those who have been least able to do it good."[19] Fitch argues that it is the so-called "other-worldly" who are the great reformers, and that there is a direct correlation between other-worldly concern and social reform. He continues:

> One of the most dramatic examples in the 20th century is to be observed in the contrast between the careers of John Dewey and of Reinhold Niebuhr. Dewey was an apostle of sweet reasonableness who never understood the heights and the depths, the angel and the devil, the heaven and the hell, that are in man. His vision could never transcend the earthly, secular city. So Niebuhr went way beyond Dewey in making an impact on public affairs and in fertilizing the minds of countless scholars who could not share in the Christian faith. I have heard some of those scholars explain that Niebuhr's "otherworldliness" was something that could be left out of the reckoning. They could not see

19. Fitch, p. 203.

that it was precisely this "otherworldliness" that gave him a more powerful and searching perspective on this world.[20]

This last I would suggest is one of the great crying needs of this day–perspective on this world. It is pretty obvious that a person can't get perspective on himself by himself. Even if he tries, he ends up merely kidding and deluding himself.

And yet we hear the cry from many modern Christian writers that the Church must adapt its message to the thought forms and symbols of the day. I have no objection to using current thought forms and symbols. I'll stoop to *MAD Magazine* and maybe, under extreme duress, even Edgar Guest [poet, 1881-1959], to try to make a point. But I always thought the object was to use and mold current thought forms and symbols into tools to express the Christian faith, rather than trying to jam the Christian corpus into the limiting and restricting strait-jacket of current idiom. Some modern thinkers sound like old Procrustes, who, you will remember, made beds and hoped they would fit people. But in those unhappy cases where the bed and the person didn't fit, he cut the person to fit the bed.

This is nonsense. The Christian church has, throughout the centuries, shown the capacity to baptize and use

20. Ibid.

secular or pagan thought forms and symbols. Christmas is a perfect example of borrowing, using and baptizing–from the date itself to the mistletoe. The wedding performed in this church yesterday, from the giving away of the bride to the wedding ring itself–these are all pagan symbols which the church has taken, baptized and used, and the process transformed and transcended them.

It is, of course, true that to some extent circumstances change those things we are interested in. Paul Tillich would suggest that in the earliest days of the Church man was principally concerned with death and finitude or limitation; later concerned with guilt, and today principally bothered by anxiety and meaninglessness.[21] Perhaps so–perhaps today our principal concern is lack of meaning and despair–but this doesn't mean that all these other problems have disappeared. Each one of these is still a legitimate area of concern to each one of us.

Christianity in a very real sense is, for those of us still alive and kicking on this earth, the dealing with worldly things in perspective. The perspective we have as Christians has been given to us as a gift. I don't believe man

---

21. While Colton does not cite one of Tillich's works at this point in this sermon, a general discussion of this subject is found in Chapter Two, "Being, Nonbeing, and Anxiety," esp. "Types of Anxiety and Periods of Anxiety," in Paul Tillich, *The Courage to Be* (New Haven, CT: Yale University Press, 1952), pp. 40-63.

unaided would have found it. It is the perspective of a gift of comfort and refreshment in travail, of eternal meaning to life this second, and of eternal life after this second. It is the perspective of the power of giving, sacrificing love.

There is no price to be paid for this gift–it has already been paid for–that's what Good Friday is all about. That's the price God paid. Wednesday we start the march to Good Friday. As Good Friday is the day of God's giving for us, so Ash Wednesday is the day when *we* say whether we are willing to accept this gift–and to walk this way. All we need do is to be there and ask–we need bring nothing else–we already have the answer from the psalm read on Ash Wednesday:

> For thou desirest no sacrifice . . .
> . . . thou delightest not in burnt offerings . . .
> The sacrifice of God is a troubled spirit:
> a broken and a contrite heart,
> O God, thou wilt not despise.[22]

---

22. Psalm 51:16a, 16c, 17, as found in *The Book of Common Prayer* (1928), p. 404.

4

The proof of our justification, the fact that we are met and accepted where we are, is the symbol of the crucified one–who came to us, endured us, loved us, and let us kill Him. No love and acceptance can be more tangibly expressed that this.

The Seventeenth Sunday after Trinity *St. Francis' Church*
October 2, 1966 *San Francisco, California*

"We bless thee for our creation, preservation and all the blessings of this life; but above all, for thine inestimable love in the redemption of the world by our Lord Jesus Christ; for the means of grace and for the hope of glory."[23]

Last week we discussed the question of Christian birth enacted in the sacrament of baptism.

Birth, as we noted, is really a miraculous thing and a very puzzling thing too. One need not be a Christian to be puzzled about it. Our life today revolves around the context of the year of our Lord 1966. We know about the year, say 1066, only by what we read in history books. Yet, of

23. From "A General Thanksgiving," *The Book of Common Prayer* (1928), p. 19, or *The Book of Common Prayer* (1979), p. 71.

course, we had nothing to say about this. We could have easily been born in the days of William the Conqueror as now. In other words, there is an element of election beyond our control that we can't avoid going to the very root of our being, our birth.

Most of us were baptized in infancy and so the analogy of election or being chosen through no act of our own is as valid in supernatural birth as in natural birth.

But birth is of little moment except that it provides the opportunity for life, and life is seen by the Christian as a great opportunity, a great gift. Thus in the General Thanksgiving of our Prayer Book, we begin thanking God for our creation. God did not *have* to create us, but indeed he not only did this, but as the general thanksgiving continues, he preserved us, and gave us "the means of grace and the hope of glory."

In the terminology of daily life, we would describe our span on earth as birth, life, and death. In the jargon of theology, birth is sometimes known as "justification" and Christian life as "sanctification." Birth as justification is an event. Life or sanctification is a process.

No one *deserves* to be born. Indeed, as St. Paul analyzed the situation, if you took the mess that man makes of himself, the only thing he really deserves is death, because even the finest codes of ethical and moral behavior are either disregarded or perverted. Men know what they *should* do, but they do not do it. Or if they make their code of moral laws simple and undemanding enough (e.g., don't beat your wife or kick your dog, or cheat too much on your taxes, and try to be a good guy) they end up either making a god of this unsophisticated world view (and when the chips are down, all inadequate gods let you down, but then it's too late). Or they become insufferably self-righteous because they have kept their adolescent little code, and the state of original sin (self-centeredness and pride) into which we are all born is merely fed all the more, and we are off into the path of self-deification.

But the joyous news of the Christian faith, as St. Paul saw it, was that despite all of this, God was willing to accept us as though we were worthy, knowing full well that we aren't. God comes to meet us and embrace us decrepit and bedraggled as we are, as the parable of the Prodigal Son reminds us.

This is the gift of justification. We who are unrighteous or not just are accepted and given birth and the means of life, even though we deserve nothing of the kind. We are treated as just.

The proof of our justification, the fact that we are met and accepted where we are, is the symbol of the crucified one–who came to us, endured us, loved us, and let us kill Him. No love and acceptance can be more tangibly expressed than this.

And just as Easter tells us that the death of this man was not an end but only the beginning of real meaning and power, so our birth through baptism and our vicarious participation in this very death and resurrection is our opportunity to participate in real meaning and power.

Our birth through baptism offers us "the means of grace and the hope of glory" *if* we want them. Of course, before we want something we must know what it is. The fact that we are born does not assure us that we will learn anything about what life really is. This depends upon others who will care for us, tell us, nurture us. St. Paul again, in his relentless logic, puts it very clearly, "How then shall they call on Him in whom they have not believed? And how shall they believe in Him of whom they have not heard? And how shall they hear without a preacher? And how shall they preach except they be sent?" (Rom. 10:14-15 [KJV])

Our God-given freedom permits us to reject God if we wish–because freely given love must always have as its correlate, the God-given freedom to reject.

Some reject because they have never really heard. Others reject because after they have heard, they still reject.

The other night driving home from a meeting I heard on the radio Ira Blue talking to some woman about mother love. The woman stated that mother love was the closest thing to God's love that we know.

Ira Blue pontificated, as only he can, "I don't agree. Mother love is even more wonderful than God's love.

God's love is too ethereal, too abstract and removed. Mother love deals with the real blood, sweat and tears of life."[24]

And I thought of the cross; the symbol of God's love in the ultimate blood, sweat and tears of human pain and death. And I wondered, and I guess I will never know, whether it is possible that Ira Blue has never really heard of this, or more likely that he has heard of it and used his God-given right to reject it even as a possibility.

"The means of grace and the hope of glory." Christian life gives us the opportunity for growth to grow holy. It takes working at. When someone asks me, "Brother, are you saved?" I'm just not sure. The process of sanctification is a pretty slippery hill. Some days it seems that you climb two steps forward, only to slip back three. There come awfully dry periods when God and God's love seem awfully far away. There come periods of great cynicism when you

---

24. Ira Blue was a radio personality on KGO Radio, San Francisco, California. As one of the original "phone jockies," he prompted considerable reaction to his broadcasts from the "Hungry i" carried by KGO from 10:00 p.m. to 1 a.m. In the March 7, 1965, *Santa Cruz Sentinel*, columnist Wally Trabing said, in "Mostly about People," "Personally, I can't stand the opinionated bum . . . [but] minutes later I am throwing kisses toward the car radio as he champions a cause of mine, telling off some bigoted ignoramus in the brilliant scathing tones of a hungover tzar" (from KGO Radio 81 Press Clipping, "KGO Radio's Ira Blue: ' . . . top dog of the phone jockey craze . . . '").

wonder if this whole business of the Christian Church isn't the great hypocritical force that some outsiders paint it to be.

But here is where the means of grace comes in. God's grace of the gift of his presence comes to us in our daily life in many different ways, but in no more significant way than through the sacrament of Holy Communion. At God's Holy Table we are fed and nourished to go out into the world.

The person who neglects to eat properly and neglects his body will find eventually that his body will begin to disintegrate. This is also true of our spiritual life. Neglect and failure to properly nourish this will lead to gradual disintegration.

Now, this often has nothing to do with how a person *feels.* We have all eaten many a meal without being overwhelmed with any great sense of satisfaction. What, for example, did you have for breakfast last Wednesday morning? Yet, we eat many, if not most of our meals, not because of the emotional feelings associated with them, but in order to *survive.*

Much the same thing is true of our religious life. Our own subjective feelings can be tricky, unreliable things. I shall never forget my first communion, after I had returned to the Church from paganism–nor indeed the communions that I made in the months that followed. I had a sense of peace and serenity, difficult to describe and as the years went on sometimes difficult to recapture.

I happen to believe that my Lord is truly and objectively present in these elements of consecrated bread and wine. If I am right, then of course it doesn't matter how I personally feel about it. At some times I may be more aware of His presence than at others, but my feeling doesn't change the fact that He is there.

Paul Tillich summed up the first basic step in becoming a Christian as accepting the fact that you are accepted.[25] But in all honesty this is sometimes one of the hardest things in the world to do. We know ourselves too well. It seems impossible to believe that anyone could accept us, especially if they knew what we were really like.

And here, I think, we come to the core of much confusion. Belief is not a state of emotion and feeling. It is an act of will. Belief in its soundest sense is the conscious commitment of ourself to a particular thing and then acting upon that commitment.

Take belief in our country. I am sure that at this very moment the great majority of the over 300,000 men we have in Vietnam are not overwhelmed with sweet sentimental thoughts about how wonderful it is to be an Ameri-

---

25. See Chapter Nineteen, "You are Accepted," esp. p. 162, "Simply accept the fact that you are accepted!" in Tillich, *The Shaking of the Foundations,* pp. 153-63.

can. (I'm sure most of them would just as soon be an American some place else.) But for better or worse, they are Americans and have been told that this is their particular duty. The issue is not whether they like to do this or not. The test of their belief is whether they accept this commitment and act upon it.

Indeed, there are cases where belief based upon feeling and belief based upon will can come up with completely different answers. Take an example I used in the adult confirmation class last week. I believe that the world is round. Now my feeling would tell me that I am stupid to believe this. Anyone who has taken a good long hike knows that this is nonsense. The world is obviously flat. And yet because other people whose opinions I respect, tell me that the world is round, and because despite my own feelings this theory seems to make more sense than any other theory, I commit myself as an act of will to the belief that the world is round.

The Christian faith is basically the proclamation of a fact that God so loved the world that He gave, humbled Himself, restricted Himself to the dimension of a man, to the end that ALL men could be healed and have a whole and full life. It is a proclamation of the fact of God's action in time and space.

Our whole life is a response to this fact. We may, in the freedom God has given us, make no response at all. Although this is a response. Or we may, by an act of our will, commit ourselves to this statement of fact and act upon it, because it makes more sense about the problems of life than any other.

At the end of this month, we are going to ask each member of the parish to make a commitment, as an act of will, to sign a pledge card promising to pay so many dollars a week for the support of this parish and the church at large. This is a tangible test of our belief, of our willingness to make this act of will. This should not come as news to anyone. Since the beginning of time the church has been dependent upon the financial support of its members and has regularly organized and asked for this.

It is a necessity of which, if we are wise, we can make a virtue. This is a time of confrontation and of testing ourselves. What is the nature of our commitment? How strongly are we willing to make our act of will?

We have, I believe, an alive and vigorous parish family at St. Francis'. We are blessed with able and conscientious lay leadership at many different levels and areas.

But the signs of the times are all about us. This is no time for summer soldiers in the Christian church. An uncommitted or shallowly committed person never converted anyone, including himself.

We have been given the gift of life, "the means of grace and the hope of glory."[26] The confrontation which will be ours at the time of this parish's "Every Member Canvass" can be one more step in our journey to sanctification, or it can be just another confrontation we evade and another slip and fall back down the slippery hill.

What will we WILL this year? How will we respond to the proclamation of God's love? We should start thinking about this *NOW.*

---

26. Colton returns repeatedly in his theology and sermons to this line from "The General Thanksgiving" in "Morning and Evening Prayer" found in *The Book of Common Prayer* (1979), pp. 71, 101, and 125.

5

O.K. So where does all this get us? Once I have developed my sensitivity, I am left face to face in the shaving mirror with the true rat that I am.

The Fourth Sunday in Lent
March 20, 1988

The Cathedral Church of St. Mark
Salt Lake City, Utah

When I told my wife that the Dean [the Very Reverend William F. Maxwell] had assigned me to preach on meekness and temperance, she burst out laughing. That was something, she suggested, like me giving a lesson on how to play par golf.

These are the last of the Christian virtues discussed by Evelyn Underhill, that great English writer on spirituality, in her book *The Fruits of the Spirit,* which have been our sermon topics during Lent.

My uneasiness in approaching these subjects, and my wife's laughter, are possibly because these words, "meekness" and "temperance," have been distorted. By "meekness" I tend to think of someone who is an ineffectual Casper Milquetoast; or a hand-wringing, cringing Uriah Heap. The word "temperance" reminds me of English

Temperance houses which are not temperate at all. They are hotels which absolutely prohibit booze.

My mind was put a little more at ease when I began to actually read Underhill's book, in which she summarizes meekness and temperance as "quiet, creaturely acceptance of our own particular limitations and callings,"[27] or as she says elsewhere it is "knowing our own size and our own place."[28]

"Knowing our own place" can also bring up bad memories of racial and social bigotry. My wife taught fourth grade in England in the late 1940s. One day she asked the class what they wanted to be when they grew up. One little boy proudly said, "I want to be a scout, just like my father." "Scout" was a glorified word for "janitor" at Oxford college.

No ambition for upward mobility there. In fact, I recall the newspaper account of a sermon preached in Oxford to a group of scouts, in which the preacher in a most condescending manner reminded those assembled that society depended on good and humble servants.

---

27. Evelyn Underhill, *The Fruits of the Spirit* and *Light of Christ (With a Memoir by Lucy Menzies)* and *Abba–Meditations based on the Lord's Prayer* (New York: Longmans, Green and Co., 1956), p. 8.

28. Ibid., p. 35.

This is a far cry from the *American* fourth grader who is supposed to respond to that question, "I want to be President of the United States."

There are problems at each end of the spectrum reflected by these two different responses. If Martin Luther King, Jr., had been content to keep in his own place, American blacks would not have today the civil rights they enjoy and the possibility of a Jesse Jackson would have been ridiculous.

Yet, at the other extreme, unbounded ambition can be a heart breaker. After all, only one person can be President of the United States at one time and the road to that exalted office is littered with the bodies of the unsuccessful, some who can take defeat more gracefully than others.

Reality does indeed objectively keep us in our place. Coming from a family of doctors, I was expected to become a physician. Just a few pre-med courses disabused me of this idea. If I had *really* persevered perhaps I could have made it—but I think of the lives that have been saved by my decision not to.

We all live with certain objective limitations—a tone deaf person cannot become a great opera singer. Ultimately, as *The Book of Common Prayer* reminds us, we live in this "transitory" life.[29] Evelyn Underhill is not

29. "And we most humbly beseech thee, of thy goodness, O Lord,

talking about this obvious fact. She talks rather about *knowing* our own place, our own limitations, and *accepting* these.

This is no easy task, because the human ego is so massive. Ramses II ordered colossal statues of himself erected everywhere, as did the Caesars, and every twentieth-century despot. This idea of trying to preserve our identity, to escape our transitory place is not limited to mighty rulers. It is reflected each time some kid puts his initials in wet concrete on a sidewalk.

Returning to Underhill's first definition, meekness and humility involve quiet, creative acceptance of our own particular limitations and callings.

But of course, before we can *accept* these things, we must be *aware* of them. For me to glibly say, "I'm O.K., you're O.K." isn't enough, nor is it true.

I will never forget sitting in a boat on Hebgen Lake one summer evening with a friend. He said, "I've never done anything I'm ashamed of." Now while he was a decent enough fellow, that statement seems to me to show a tremendous insensitivity.

As Roland Bainton wrote, "Only with a developed

---

to comfort and succor all those who, in this transitory life, are in trouble, sorrow, need, sickness, or any other adversity" (in the prayer "for the whole state of Christ's Church," *The Book of Common Prayer* [1928], p. 74, and in *The Book of Common Prayer* [1979], p. 329).

sensitivity does a sense of unworthiness emerge."[30]

This may explain why as societal values become more superficial and insensitive, the less sense the culture can make of Christian concepts of sin.

Underhill is not advocating excessive grovelling and mortifying self-examinations. In fact, she quotes from a writer who nearly destroyed himself by excessive introspection, wondering whether he had ever properly confessed his sins, whether he was making *progress* in his spiritual state.[31] Underhill's response is good common sense, merely "know yourself for the childish, limited and dependent soul that you are."[32] " . . . God is a realist. He likes home-grown stuff."[33]

O.K. So where does all this get us? Once I have developed my sensitivity, I am left face to face in the shaving mirror with the true rat that I am. All this does is to create "ESTian" despair.

But here is where the Christian proclamation comes to

30. Citation uncertain.

31. "Humanity and moderation at the heart of our prayer quiet the soul and protect us against the spiritual itch. 'It sometimes comes into my head,' says De Caussade, 'to wonder whether I have ever properly confessed my sins, whether God has ever forgiven me my sins, whether I am in a good or bad spiritual state. What progress have I made in prayer or the interior life?'" (Underhill, p. 40)

32. Ibid., p. 41.

33. Ibid., p. 39.

the rescue. Paul Tillich in one of his essays sums it up this way: Forget all the credal statements and theological niceties. *"Simply accept the fact that you are accepted"*—as you are—accepted by that which is greater than you and the name of which you do not know.[34]

As Tillich says, "Nothing is demanded of this experience, no religious or moral or intellectual presupposition, nothing but *acceptance.*"[35]

A person who can accept this acceptance from another, infinitely greater than he is, can then in turn truly accept himself. Then, "he who has learned to overcome self contempt has overcome his contempt for others."[36]

When this happens we are, in other words, truly free agents, afraid of nothing—life, death, dominion, or power.

We have a plaque in our kitchen, as do millions of others, attributed to "St. Paul's Church," otherwise unidentified. It's probably a Hallmark type sentimental fraud, but it has some wisdom. "If you compare yourself with others, you may become vain and bitter, for always there will be greater and lesser persons than yourself." But then it says,

34. Tillich, *The Shaking of the Foundations,* p. 162.

35. Ibid.

36. Ibid., p. 158.

"You are a child of the universe–you have a right to be here."[37]

This is a healthy set of statements.

But I suggest they can only be made when God's grace gives us first the sensitivity to see where we really are, and then, in God's grace through the cross of Jesus Christ, we understand that we are still accepted and that nothing we can conceive can deprive us of the power and joy that this gives.

If this is meekness and temperance, turn on the faucet of these gifts, and let's all get ourselves bathed in what this means!

---

37. From the poem, *Desiderata.* The second portion of the poem that Colton quotes actually says, "You are a child of the universe, no less than the trees and the stars; you have a right to be here." "*Desiderata,* which is usually said to have been copied from an inscription "found in Old Saint Paul's Church, Baltimore; dated 1692," was actually written by an Indiana poet named Max Ehrmann and registered with the Copyright Office of the Library of Congress early in 1927. Copyright was renewed after the author's death by his widow, and the work still is protected by the United States Copyright Law. Thus this popular philosophical statement is neither anonymous nor ancient, having both an author and a fairly recent date. Nonetheless, "what it says remains timeless and reserves for its author a niche in that poetical pantheon to which belong those writers who have, at least once, seen an eternal truth clear." This information and the portions of the poem found in Colton's sermon are from (Max Ehrmann) *Desiderata* (Boston: Crescendo Publishing Company, n.d.), n.p.

V
Despair and Suffering

Introduction

Difficult things happen in our lives. As a lawyer, Albert Colton made much of his living by being involved with the adversarial situations which confronted his world. Were the world a pacific place, he would have starved as an attorney and most likely would have steered clear of the ministry and Christianity all together. Adversity, finitude, alienation, travail, agony, and affliction seemingly drove him deeper and deeper into his faith. Rather than deny that bad things happened in his world, he began much of his theological contemplation from the posture of suffering and despair.

> A friend of mine in social work, after a particularly depressing day, filled with a parade of horror stories of human misery, said, "I hate that phony Christian faith of yours. What relevance does it have to *real* life?" Obviously he never got the message, never got the point.
>
> To me, the Christian faith is the *only* way I can see that one can make any meaning or sense out of the parade of horribles that life often consists of. Somehow we fail to communicate what the gospel really is, and to understand it, we must recognize it in its *totality*.
>
> The tragic pattern of human life, from birth to death [contains] the fickleness of friends, the apparent

triumph of evil over good, the loneliness of pain of death, the grandeur of unselfish giving, but opportunity dissolved in futility. *It's all there*–nice guys finish last.

It is a pattern each one of us has followed and will follow. It certainly describes the world of my social worker friend–it is real. But if the story stopped there, it would only be a tale of despair and hopelessness. The Easter event of the resurrection turns this all around. God and his love are stronger and more abiding than anything else, and it can and does ultimately conquer everything else.[1]

Colton would not divorce himself from the reality of despair. However, he seemed incapable, at least in the formation of his theology, to consider suffering without contemplating Christ as a constant companion with the sufferer. Those who deliberated on despair, without considering despair's greatest foe, Christ, only saw half of the picture, and the weaker half at that.

A significant number of his sermons contain a yearning for his "unchurched" and "pagan" friends to give the faith a chance in making life more meaningful. That they did not avail themselves of the gospel or that they rejected it saddened him.

In light of this fact, the miraculous influence this single life [of Jesus] has had on an entire world, it is all

1. Sermon preached the Sixth Sunday after Epiphany, February 17, 1980, St. Paul's Church, Salt Lake City, Utah.

the more puzzling why more people do not come at least to make inquiry about this man, let alone pay Him homage. Three kings made a journey to Him 2,000 years ago when He was an obscure, unknown babe. Yet on this night [Christmas Eve 1967], 2,000 years later, millions stay away or are unconcerned about commemorating His coming.

On second thought, I guess this should not be too puzzling. There was not room at the inn 2,000 years ago. The world's business at that time left no time to make room for an extra baby in a busy world, no matter who he may be. This is still true, too many are wholly concerned with their own desires, their own definitions, and their own prejudices. There is no room in their inn.

I can only grieve for such people, for think of what they are missing! If it is true, as we Christians believe, that in some miraculous way the fullness of Almighty God dwelt in this little child, then that very fact tells us more than a thousand volumes of theology about the nature of God.

The miracle of Christmas is that we have been given the chance to meet the Almighty Father in the flesh. He has come to us as man and dwelt amongst us. We have been given the chance, if we will take it, to see and know exactly what this God, the Almighty Father and creator of Heaven and Earth, is in terms which we can understand.[2]

---

2. Sermon preached the Eve of the Nativity of Our Lord, December

And this is who this man was, and this makes all the difference in the world. [Jesus] was that man who showed us what God is–not because He was such a good and perfect person that He opened Himself to the ground of all being and let God's love flow freely through Himself–because this suggests that His uniqueness was the result of His human volition–you, too, could be Jesus Christ. But because God chose to show us what He is in terms that we can understand; but even more than this. This was not Prince Bountiful coming to a party in the slums of London, dressed modestly as the other boys were, and acting modestly as the other boys weren't, and leaving promptly at 10:15 in his Rolls Royce to return to the splendor of Buckingham Palace. This was a Prince Bountiful who *was* a slum boy, who lived day in and day out the life of a slum boy, who had slugged it out in the alleys of life, and who suffered personally the torments of injustice and wrong, and who through it all, could love and forgive, even as He was being murdered.

And it was not because He was so good that those who knew Him felt He was a god–this happens in history not infrequently–but it was the awesome sense of those who had encountered Him that this *was* God, the Father Almighty, Creator of the Universe. It didn't make any sense, but there was not another way to explain it. And the joyous news was that this man who was God was *good,* He was fun. He could love and

---

24, 1967, St. Francis' Church, San Francisco, California.

accept us when we knew we were really unlovable and unacceptable–and He also suffered, more deeply and more profoundly than we do–He was also the Man of Sorrows–but His suffering was for you and for me–His stripes were for our healing. And these men sensed that if they could but retain communion with this man they would retain communion with the ultimate meaning of all life, and so strengthened could, without fear, face and touch with joy the world of God's creation. And in strange words He promised that this could be so in the breaking of bread and in the sharing of the cup in His name He would be there. And when He had died and faced the phantom which ultimately finds all mortal flesh, death, He showed that through Himself all who wished to identify with Him could conquer even this, the great leveller and confirmer of our finitude.[3]

Almighty God has reached into our world and touched it in the only terms we can really understand. We now can know of a certainty what the nature of the ground of all existence is like. And we know to what extremes He will go to try to reach and touch us.[4]

Colton had difficulty with churches that did not display a crucifix. He believed that such communities disregarded, at least in part, the tremendous length God went to love us so sacrificially.

3. Sermon preached the Third Sunday after the Epiphany, January 24, 1965, St. Francis' Church, San Francisco, California.

4. Sermon preached the Eve of the Nativity of Our Lord.

He also believed that the absence of a crucifix hid the ultimate certainty that we, as well, would have our own cross to carry. The Christian, who acknowledged the cross, would appreciate the "companion," Christ, when the way of the cross came into his or her life.

> We live in a world which has not only happiness but tears and pain and sorrow also. The cross is our reminder that tears and pain and sorrow are a very real part of what we call reality. A Christian faith without the cross becomes either non-realistic spiritualism, ethical culturism, or reverts to Old Testament legalism.
>
> Historic Christianity never said that the cross would disappear either in its proclamation of Jesus Christ, or in the individual lives of his followers. Each of us has a cross to bear. The Christian faith merely helps us to carry it in this life–it does not remove it.
>
> Tears are real. We cannot nor should not ignore them. But we know that God in his loving power shall wipe them away.[5]

Colton did not shy away from tough examples. He offered an illustration of how terrible things could be in one's life. He offered such an example, not to challenge the comfort offered by religion, but to confirm the depth of Christianity's power.

---

5. Sermon preached on Septuagesima Sunday (the Third Sunday before Lent), February 2, 1969, the Cathedral Church of St. Mark, Salt Lake City, Utah.

I just finished reading *Sophie's Choice* and one hideous moment will stand out—when Sophie at Auschwitz is told by the drunken Nazi physician (who had earlier thought of entering the ministry) that she must choose which of her two little children should go first to the gas chamber. And her eight-year-old daughter was led off with her beloved flute and teddy bear.[6]

Sophie began World War II as a practicing Christian. She finished the war a confirmed atheist. She felt that whatever God there was had left and abandoned her. I have heard other people who have experienced or observed some of the more hideous aspects of human life express the same thing. This has always puzzled me.

. . . Christianity tells us of a suffering God who loved so much that He *gave* His life. The old spiritual states "Oh, nobody knows the trouble I've seen. Nobody knows but Jesus."[7] Christianity does portray a Godhead who knows, because He has been there, and He need not have been there except He willed it for Himself. Certainly one of the great strengths of Christianity is the sure and certain faith that no matter how dark it is, we will never be abandoned.[8]

---

6. Cf. William Styron, *Sophie's Choice* (New York: Random House, 1979), pp. 482-84.

7. "Oh, Nobody Knows the Trouble I've Seen . . . ," in *The New Blue Book of Favorite Songs* (Chicago: Hall and McCreary Co., 1941), p. 220.

8. Sermon preached the Fourth Sunday in Lent, March 13, 1983, the Cathedral Church of St. Mark, Salt Lake City, Utah.

Colton believed that when we found ourselves in the darkest hour, the deepest despair or the gravest suffering, we need only admit that we cannot endure by ourselves in order to tap the strength found in Christ.

> And this is when God comes to me–when I am in my despair, loneliness, guilt and anxiety. He comes in a form I can understand, as a man. As an obscure man who gave, who loved, and out of this giving and loving, suffered and died.[9]

At that very point in our most desperate vulnerability, Colton held that Christ enables us to defeat despair, suffering and death. Ultimately, the faith destroys the fraudulent power of alienation or sin.

> On Good Friday night I watched an awesome sight. An eclipse of the moon, a "blood moon" it is called, and coming as it did on Good Friday following the past few days of grief and chaos, it seemed an evil portent indeed. But as I looked out my window at the darkened moon, I could also see the cross on the top of Mt. Davidson [San Francisco], brilliantly lighted. I knew that even in celestial shadow there was hope.[10]

---

9. Sermon preached the First Sunday after Trinity, June 20, 1965, St. Francis' Church, San Francisco, California.

10. Martin Luther King was assassinated on April 4 and race riots in Chicago, Baltimore, Washington, and Cincinnati, during which thirty-one people died, broke out the day of his funeral, April 9. This sermon was preached on April 14, 1968.

A Christian, a new person, should be able to shout for joy down the somber, dark corridors of existence, and others trudging along the way can look up with weary eyes surprised to find that joy can have a place, to hear that the universe at its base is not hostile, but that it makes sense and has an ultimate purpose.

Today Easter may seem as out of place as joyous laughter at a funeral. But this is exactly what it is. This is the Easter story.

It is the gentle laughter of forgiving love in the midst of our man-made grief, which is affirmed and echoed in the ancient cry:

Alleluia, the Lord is Risen!
He is risen indeed, Alleluia![11]

11. Sermon preached on Easter Day, April 14, 1968, St. Francis' Church, San Francisco, California.

1

Keep away from controversy. Be one of the bland leading the bland. And when the confrontation comes, the answer is easy, "Oh yes, I knew Him. I was baptized and confirmed. But I'm not a follower. You know me better than that. After all, one has to be practical."

Good Friday
April 16, 1965

St. Francis' Church
San Francisco, California

Who was a follower of the Man? It all depends, doesn't it? There were of course those who had known Him way back when and had literally followed Him wherever he went, teaching and proclaiming. These were called disciples. We can even remember some of their names. A mixed bag they were, united in common loyalty to this man. This man was a great puzzle to them. His teachings were sometimes hard to understand, and He himself was hard to categorize. He didn't seem to fit any established pattern. He was a good and kind man. He was a holy and devout man. He had great and awesome power when He chose to use it. But He rejected the titles they tried to give Him. A puzzling person.

But there was no question as to loyalty of this small group. No sir. Some might fall away. That rich young fellow wasn't able to discipline himself to this new life. But as Peter had said, "We have left everything and followed you" [Luke 18:28]. And this was true; although it is difficult to say to what extent he was swayed by the promise that he "who has left house or brothers or sister or mother or father or children or lands for my sake . . . will receive a hundredfold now in this time" [vv. 29-30]. It would seem like a good investment anyway.

But things weren't turning out that way. Something had gone terribly wrong. Judas was the first to sense this. Men have been betrayed before and since this time and it's fascinating but fruitless to seek to analyze the motives of this man. But it may be safe to say that like all traitors, he had carefully rationalized his conduct at the time. He had a reason to justify his action. I shall betray this man, or this country, or this principle, for a higher good, to punish or to reward or to change. The quality of a Judas lurks to some extent in us all.

And we have Peter–good, solid, stout-hearted, strong, impetuous, and perhaps not too bright–but with a heart as big as he is. A follower? I should say so! "To the death, Lord" [Luke 22:33]. But then came the great moment of truth, the acid test when you are called upon to witness. And there is the cold sweat and hard knot of fear and of panic as the confrontation of the world comes unexpectedly, catching you unprepared. And he lies. "I know Him not. I've never seen Him before" [vv. 57ff]. The threat is over. Personal unpleasantness is avoided, and the life goes on as before. But there is one difference. We now know that we are liars, and that we are cowards and we weep bitterly, as Peter did, primarily perhaps not at this denial of a friend (after all, what difference could this have made to Him?), but at the humiliating blow this has to our ego. We can avoid this whole problem, of course. Just don't get involved with people like that. Keep away from controversy. Be one of the bland leading the bland. And when the confrontation comes, the answer is easy, "Oh yes, I knew Him. I was baptized and confirmed. But I'm not a follower. You know me better than that. After all, one has to be practical."

And these followers left Him to die alone. They had a choice and they took it. But sometimes in life we have no choice. Events reach out and seize us. We are caught in situations we cannot control. An automobile hurling at us across the center line; a sudden illness; or the directive of a superior to do a certain thing; or, more subtly, the influence of a friend which leads you to a completely different group than you had planned.

How Simon of Cyrene must have hated *his* experience. A pious Jew who had made the long trip from Africa to eat the Passover in the Holy City. Caught in the crowded streets as Roman soldiers approached, he moves dutifully aside to let them pass, marching three poor wretches to their death. He avoids their eyes but freezes in his tracks as he hears an officer bellow at him, "Here, you, help carry this cross" [Luke 23:26]. How degrading! Why did the blasted officer have to single *him* out? "If any man would come after me, let him take up his cross and follow me" [9:23]. But Simon didn't want to be a disciple of Jesus Christ. He just wanted to be left alone. Yet he had to bear a cross all the same. The cross was thrust on him. The only alternatives open to him were accepting it willingly or accepting it unwillingly. He could carry it, cursing his bad luck every step, or he could carry it, accepting the duty that had been forced on him, or even welcoming the opportunity of lowering his pride and self-conceit.

We aren't told how Simon felt. We are told in St. Mark's gospel that he was the father of Alexander and Rufus, and St. Paul greets Rufus in his letter to Rome. It would be nice to believe that he became a Christian. There are many who become followers through no direct choice, but because a cross has been given them whether they want it or not, and they find that when they carry it with this man, the yoke is easy and the burden is light.

I imagine each of us here today professes to be a follower, or we would not be here. Also each has within us a pinch of Judas, and a dab of Peter, and a cross which has been given us whether we wanted it or not. And we stand before the cross of God this day to ask that this man of sorrows and suffering forgive us and cleanse us so that we may truly follow Him. I want to be a follower. Help me to do this Lord, and forgive me.

2

If the man does not recant, he must be punished. And all of the bishops and rectors and wardens and vestrymen nodded their heads.

Good Friday	*St. Francis' Church*
April 16, 1965	*San Francisco, California*

Everyone wants authority, but few want responsibility. I like to boss, but I don't like to be blamed. And after a little while on this earth each of us gets pretty good at ducking blame. Johnny threw the ball through the window because his brother told him to. Little George cut down the cherry tree because the hatchet slipped. Eichmann gassed to death thousands of Jews because a superior told him to. Johnny and George would get short shrift from their mothers even if what they said were true. Eichmann got short shrift in his argument from the Israeli courts, even though he doubtless was working under orders from superiors. Buck-passing is an ancient and honorable art, but somewhere the buck has to stop. Somewhere responsibility must be fixed.

Where does the buck stop on Good Friday? Who *did* this thing, anyway? The centurion and his soldiers? But he was merely acting under orders. Pontius Pilate? But he is on record as saying this man was innocent. He *tried* to save Him, and then publicly washed his hands of the whole thing. It was the Jews that screamed to crucify Him. But it wasn't the Jews who screamed–it was *some* Jews–the high church dignitaries who inflamed the mob. The Man Himself was, after all, a Jew as were His followers, and Nicodemus the Pharisee defended Him in the Sanhedrin itself, and Joseph of Arimithea, another member of the Sanhedrin, was a secret disciple of the Man. Well, then, it must have been the fault of a few malicious Jewish leaders–although they could rightly point out that they had no power to execute anyone. Only the Roman government could issue such an order. And this, too, is true. And so we are back where we started.

Can anyone really blame the Centurion for what he did? He was merely carrying out orders. If he refused (and a career soldier probably couldn't conceive of refusing anyway) he, himself, would have been broken and punished. He probably didn't relish the execution detail, but in the army you get all kinds of jobs and you do what you're told. Moreover it is apparent that he was deeply moved by the event. Pious legend has it that he later became a Christian, and after all, didn't St. Paul participate in the execution of St. Stephen? Don't blame the centurion, he just works there.

Pilate had his problems, too. It was his job to maintain

law and order amongst this fanatical, hysterical people. He was sitting on the powder keg of revolt, and any slight spark would ignite it. Thus, while he detested the Jewish High Priests, he knew the power and influence they had. He, too, had been impressed with the prisoner. Pilate was too cynical and wise in the world to be deeply concerned about what he said, but his wife, too, had been strongly influenced by this man. But, after all, when you weigh the cost of one life against the possibility of a general uprising, who has to be blamed? This would not be the first time innocent blood would be spilled for the common good.

The High Priest had a point, too. It was his job to protect religious orthodoxy. The Jews had the most highly developed religious consciousness in the world. They were devout monotheists and this man was making claims to divinity. This was obviously ridiculous. How could a man be divine? The Lord is One God and Him alone shalt thou worship. Indeed, this was blasphemy. If the man does not recant, he must be punished. And all of the bishops and rectors and wardens and vestrymen nodded their heads. Can we blame them because the significance of this man's claim was beyond their comprehension? Isn't it beyond ours as well? Can we blame them for wishing to avoid disrupting influences in their religious life? Do we not wish this as well?

Very complicated, this problem of blame. We have seen that we cannot absolve even the followers of this man.

They all ran away. But at least we have dear old Nicodemus and Joseph of Arimithea, at least they stood up against this outrage. But did they? Read again. They made an attempt to persuade the Sanhedrin against taking this action, but when the vote was taken, they were not there to be counted. Of course, they could say, of what earthly good would it have been? We were clearly outvoted. As the German said under Hitler, "What possibly could I do–one person against vast legions?" It would have been a useless gesture.

This is really a complicated problem. But wait, I get the picture. *Nobody's* to blame. This is just the way the cookie crumbles. "Don't blame me, lady, I just work here, and those are the rules of the company." You see, all of this was predetermined. All of the people were helpless puppets in the hands of fate. It's "the system" that was the executioner, and God runs the system, so if anybody is to blame, blame God.

Not bad. It's a rather comforting thought, too. We pass the buck back to where it belongs, to Him who started life in the first place.

Of course, there *is* another possibility. It is possible that *all* of these people were the executioners and that all people participate in this guilt who crucify goodness for all of the right reasons. I don't think I like *this* idea very much because it means that I, too, am guilty and when I am asked, "Were you there when they crucified my Lord?" I must answer, "Yes." And it means that on this day I must kneel before this cross and ask forgiveness, not for a group of wicked other people, but for myself. I have to ask God to have mercy upon me, a miserable offender. And I have to realize that pride and selfishness contaminate us all and that these are infectious things. They are a disease which man by himself is powerless to stop. Man must kneel before the cross in contrition and say for himself and for all men: "Father, forgive, for we knew not what we have done" [c.f. Luke 23:34].

3

I am free of carrying my burden of myself and I can rejoice that this load is lifted. But perhaps your load, which I will help bear, is even heavier. It is a lot like the game of hearts where you pass along the worst cards in your hand to the person next to you. There is that moment of joy when you pass along your discards, but it is followed by the sobering view of the monsters that have been handed to you.

The Second Sunday in Lent *St. Francis' Church*
March 10, 1968 *San Francisco, California*

"Almighty God, who seest that we have no power of ourselves to help ourselves . . . "

These words from our collect for today[12] were written in Italy in the sixth century at a time when the native populace was under invasion by the barbarians and also when there were a number of pestilences, earthquakes, and famine. Those were times of deep trouble.

12. *The Book of Common Prayer* (New York: The Church Pension Fund, 1928), p. 127.

I cannot help but think that our times are analogous as we hear continued bad news from Vietnam, attempt to assess the terrifying implications of the Presidential Commission's Report on Civil Disorder, and note in a front page article of our daily paper a quotation from the Director of the National Institute of Mental Health [Dr. Stanley F. Yolles] that the "'alienation' which is a major underlying cause of drug abuse, is deeper and more diffused now than in any other previous period of American history." He describes the problem and our culture thus: "rebellion without a cause, rejection without a program, and a refusal of what is without a vision of what should be."[13]

To make matters even gloomier, I finally got around to reading a paper from a Stanford biologist [Paul Ehrlich] sent to all clergy of the Diocese. (Incidentally, in a time when the role of the parish ministry is under great criticism and re-evaluation, I think an ever more effective argument can be made for the need of the religious community to have a trained person paid to, among other things, read, mark, digest, and attempt to communicate, in religious perspective, the myriad and overwhelming body of information coming to us.)

The point of this paper was not what are we going to

---

13. "Drugs and Alienation–An Urgent Warning," *San Francisco Chronicle*, Mar. 7. 1968, p. 1, cols. 1-2.

do to avoid world famine, but rather what are we going to do when it inevitably arrives within less than ten years. He puts it this way:

> A locomotive is roaring full throttle down the track. Just around the bend an impenetrable mud slide has oozed across the track. There it lies, inert, static, deadly. Nothing can stop the locomotive in time. Collision is inevitable. Catastrophe is foredoomed. Miles back up the track the locomotive could have been warned and stopped. Years ago the mud-soaked hill could have been shored up to forestall the landslide. Now it is too late.
>
> The locomotive roaring straight at us is the population explosion. The unmovable landslide across the tracks is the stagnant production of food in the undeveloped nations, the nations where the population increases are greatest.
>
> The collision is inevitable. The famines are inevitable.[14]

Ehrlich goes on to say:

> The U.S. Department of Agriculture estimates that America can continue to feed the developing countries until 1984 . . . We are the only country which will be in

---

14. Ehrlich is quoting from William and Paul Paddock, *Famine! 1975* (Boston: Little, Brown and Co., 1975), pp. 8-9, in Paul R. Ehrlich, "Population, Food and Environment: Is the Battle Lost?" *Texas Quarterly* 11 (Summer 1968): 45.

> a position to *give* food to starving countries, and the amount of food which we will be able to donate will fall short of world-wide needs. We will be forced to choose who will live and who will die.[15]

He quotes one solution proposed [by the Paddocks]:

> that we place each country in one of three categories based on the method used to classify wounded entering a military hospital:
>
> Those that will die regardless of treatment.
>
> Those that will survive regardless of treatment and regardless of the agony they may suffer.
>
> Those that can be saved, if given prompt treatment.[16]

Only by radical surgery, he suggests, can we have any chance of survival.[17] For example, he suggests "(a) good way to start would be to urge the Vatican to bring its policies [concerning birth control] into line with the desires of the majority of American Catholics."[18] (A similar plea to the Pope was deemed "impertinent" by some prominent leaders at our last Diocesan Convention). More drastically, he states that grain exports to India have actually harmed rather

15. Ibid., p. 45.
16. Ibid., pp. 45-46.
17. Ibid., p. 54.
18. Ibid., p. 53.

than helped Indians in the long run,[19] and that we should announce that we will no longer ship food to countries where dispassionate analysis indicates that the food-population imbalance is hopeless.[20]

And if this did not give me enough food for thought for one week, I happened to see the superb TV documentary on "The Rise and Fall of the Third Reich" (which almost made the price of my set worthwhile). But it is a shattering, sickening commentary on our twentieth-century world. A father phoned in to a radio talk show and said that he had let his children watch the series, but found himself unable to answer their obvious question, "But, Dad, why did this happen?" Why, indeed?

It is enough to make one long for the good old relatively untroubled days of the sixth century. Somebody else's wars, famines, earthquakes, and moral upheavals always seem more benign than your own.

But, of course, I can't settle for some old sixth-century problems. I have to settle with the ones given to me right now. They won't go away by my ignoring them.

I happen to be what is called a "twice-born" Christian. I was baptized in infancy, fell away from the Faith in my

19. Ibid., p. 46.

20. Ibid., p. 53.

college and post-college years, and returned to the Church in my maturity.

I returned, doubtless, for many reasons, but surely one of the most important was that the Christian faith *made more sense* out of the problems of life than any other I could find.

It does not give me all of the answers to each specific problem, but it fit them into a context, into a world view, which had greater logical and emotional consistency than any other religion.

And as I have said before, I interpret religion in a very broad sense. Charles Kean said, religion is "any working principle of interpretation that men use to explain the ambiguities of their experience, to provide the answer to the tragedy and anxiety they encounter in the course of daily living (and invariably involving a strong allegiance to that interpretation)."[21]

Thus, the question is not *whether* you are going to "get religion," but only *what* religion are you going to choose.

I am a Christian because I believe I am a realist—I see a world around me in which I live, move and have my being which with all of its wonder and occasional joy, also has plenty of pain and suffering and problems.

---

21. Charles Kean in *Christianity and Property*, ed. Joseph F. Fletcher (Philadelphia: Westminster Press, 1947), p. 160.

I cannot realistically ignore these problems–because I am involved in them. It would be "like telling a fellow passenger 'your end of the boat is sinking.'"[22] Each of these problems involves me, whether I like it or not.

Now to me, one of the first virtues in the Christian faith is the fact that it recognizes that evil does exist, that there is darkness and destruction loose in the world. As Charles Williams, author of *All Hallow's Eve,* and a devout Christian, observed, "The universe is always capable of a worse trick than we suppose . . . but at least, when we have known this, we are no longer surprised."[23]

Moreover, without trying to give some pat and easy answer as to why such problems do exist, the Christian can affirm the fact that suffering through problems *can* transform itself into knowledge and growth.

This is not always so–pain and suffering can warp and break a person–but it is a possibility. As Dr. Carfagni pointed out very eloquently to our Thursday morning Lenten class last week, we are a culture that

22. Ehrlich, p. 53.

23. C.f., "The universe is always capable of a worse trick than we suppose, but at least when we have known it, we are no longer surprised by anything less," in Charles Williams, *All Hallows' Eve,* intro., T. S. Eliot (Grand Rapids: William B. Eerdmans Publishing Co., 1989), p. 237. The discrepancy may be due to Colton's using an early, unavailable edition.

seems to run away from pain, as the millions of pills and drugs sold and consumed every day attest. Yet pain is a part of reality. Without knowing pain you have not known life.[24]

The word "suffered" is inserted in the Creed for a purpose. The super-pious had felt it was in some sense undignified or impertinent to suggest that incarnate God experienced pain.

Yet, if the audacious concept of the Incarnation means anything at all, it means that God has shared life with me in the limitation of humanity that I know and these limitations include pain, suffering and problems. And so the appropriation of suffering by God is not only not viewed as undignified and impertinent, but the symbol of all symbols for the Christian is exactly that–the cross, a thing of suffering and of pain.

The Christian then acknowledges the reality of pain and problems and assumes the existence of a God who is not only aware of these, but in His willed

---

24. The March 3, 1968, Sunday bulletin for St. Francis' Episcopal Church, San Francisco, California, said the following about this speaker: "THIS THURSDAY MORNING AT 9:45 DR. ARTHUR CARFAGNI, a psychiatrist and Director of the Immediate Psychiatric Aid Center at San Francisco General Hospital, will speak on 'Narcotics in San Francisco.' Dr. Carfagni is an expert on the dangerously increasing narcotic use in our community and proved to be extremely effective and helpful when he spoke to our young people a few months ago."

humility took upon Himself pain and problems. Of course, your pain is not my pain; your burden is not mine. But I do know that I cannot carry the burden of my pain and problems by myself. I know that as a *Christian*. As a pagan I have trouble admitting that. Somewhere in a pagan ethic I am expected to carry my own burdens and solve my own problems. I am ashamed to admit that I do not measure up and shape up, because the only reward for such confession is judgment and rejection. And so I bury these things and I try to hide them from others and even more seriously, I try to hide them from myself.

As a Christian I can be honest and say I can't bear this burden but then, if I can't who will?

Answer: Someone else. The burden I can't bear can perhaps be carried by you and you and you. This doesn't mean I have nothing to carry through life because, in fulfilled reality, I must carry something. The only rule of fulfillment is that the load I carry can't be my own. My own load only grinds me into myself and I become obsessed only with my own problems and myself. I become a big ball of groaning, complaining egocentricity.

Again as Charles Williams put it, "Nobody can carry his own burden; he only can and therefore he must carry someone else's. Whose burden in particular he shall carry is up to him to decide: usually this choice is dictated by his character and his social circumstances."[25]

This truth was recognized by the Christian community of the sixth century as our collect for today reminds us, "We have no power of ourselves to help ourselves."[26]

Help comes from outside ourselves. It comes from letting others help with our burdens and our shouldering theirs. Obviously in such a concept is implicit a sense of community and interdependence. There is, in this sense, no such thing as "my" problems or "your" problems. They are "our" problems, all of them.

This, in a way, is an immensely liberating and joyous concept. I am free of carrying my burden of myself and I can rejoice that this load is lifted. But perhaps your load, which I will help bear, is even heavier. It is a lot like the

---

25. While this citation is uncertain, Williams did say, "But if you will be part of the best of us, and live and laugh and be ashamed with us, then you must be content to be helped. You must give your burden up to someone else, and you must carry someone else's burden." Charles Williams, *Descent into Hell* (Grand Rapids: William B. Eerdmans Publishing Co., 1973), p. 99. See as well the discussion leading up to this on pp. 98-99.

26. "Almighty God, who seest that we have no power of ourselves to help ourselves; Keep us both outwardly in our bodies, and inwardly in our souls; that we may be defended from all adversities which may happen to the body, and from all evil thoughts which may assault and hurt the soul; through Jesus Christ our Lord." *The Book of Common Prayer* (1928), p. 127.

game of hearts where you pass along the worst cards in your hand to the person next to you. There is that moment of joy when you pass along your discards, but it is followed by the sobering view of the monsters that have been handed to you.

Taking on someone else's problems is not solving them, to be sure. It may possibly be that some problems have gotten beyond our capacity to solve, e.g., that millions of people are going to starve no matter what we do.

We recall that our Lord did not *solve* the problem of the cross. It did not go away. But he went *through* that horror; he did not avoid it.

Whether we *solve* the problems or not there is no question but that part of our duty of burden bearing is to *try* to find resolution. One of the deep tragedies of existence is the spectacle of good men sitting back and doing nothing.

Our little efforts applied to a particular problem might seem to be pathetically feeble ones, and a solution to some problems hopeless. Yet, we can never tell when some little act, some little event, echoes down through the stately halls of eternity.

The world around us shows us plenty of problems with which we need help. Today's collect reminds us of two correlative points about such problems. First, that by ourselves we cannot help ourselves–*we* need outside help;

second, that just as I need help from you, you need help from me.[27]

All people carry burdens. The only real issue is whether you will let someone else help bear yours, and whose burden you will then assume. This we can do now. We will do it faithfully and imperfectly. We may betray confidences given in love and trust. We may fail to fulfill responsibilities assumed. But the process is right and it is true.

Our failures in such an attempt are made holy, however, in the context of our ability to acknowledge and appreciate what our Lord said. "Come to me, all who labor and are heavy-laden, and I will give you rest. Take my yoke upon you . . . and you will find rest for your souls. For my yoke is easy, and my burden is light" [Matt. 11:28-30, RSV].

The daily papers show us that the inventory stock of burdens is at an all time high. You can have a wide range of selection as to size and color. Which ones are you going to choose to carry?

27. From the Collect for "The Second Sunday in Lent," *The Book of Common Prayer* (1928), p. 127.

4

And this, the last Sunday of Easter in the Church calendar, is a good time to remind us of what Easter says: It says that pain, suffering and death (often unjust and unfair) really do exist. That is the reality of Good Friday, and these realities cannot be avoided. They are a part of the miracle of life, and they will not go away.

The Seventh Sunday of Easter
May 31, 1981

The Cathedral Church of St. Mark
Salt Lake City, Utah

"Why do the innocent suffer? Why do the young die? If God is a God of love, as you say, how can he allow this to happen? The hell with you and your God!" said the father of a young girl who died of leukemia and he never went to church again. Somehow God had taken his daughter.

I became a Christian because it presented the most realistic world view I could find to the facts of life as I observed them. It dared to face the *hard* questions. I'll try to tackle one of these questions today about innocent suffering. I can't "answer" them, but I hope to be of help in putting them in proper context.

"*Answers.*" A church that has all the answers isn't asking the right questions. A great deal of the problem comes from a misunderstanding about what Christianity is and what it is not.

If you have not suffered, you will never understand the cross. But many who have suffered still do not understand. Indeed they reject the very cross which is the answer to the problem.

Let's start with reality. The reality is that all people die. If you have any doubt, go back and read this morning's obituary section, and the reality is that people die differently. Some die peacefully after a long, full life; some violently and suddenly; some slowly and painfully. And people die at different ages. Some die after only a few days of life and some run the chronological gamut to even four score and ten or beyond. Through medical science, we have extended the average period of what we call life, but the disparity as to when and where still remains. This is a fact, and it has always been a fact.

But there is another fact, equally undisputed, which we too often ignore or take for granted, i.e., the opposite of death is *life*, and each of us here today is alive.

Life is where the Christian message starts, and what an incredible miracle it is! Each of us went to bed last night and for a period of time became unconscious, but during that time we call sleep, our heart kept beating, our lungs drawing oxygen from the air to replenish our blood, which coursed through our body, our cuts continued to heal, and then we awoke. And for most of us this meant opening our eyes to see. (Seeing–what a miracle in itself.) Within an hour of waking, we had heard (another miracle), tasted and went about the affairs of the day without much more thought.

And yet we have just witnessed a portion of the miracle of life. Now the Christian sees life not as something which just happened, not something deserved as a matter of fact, but as an incredibly wonderful gift. The theological word "grace" means in part "a freely given gift." The Christian sees God as creator, and the "Lord and giver of life."

So this miracle we all enjoy is a free gift and of course in all fairness we should not object when a free gift given to us to use for a while, must be given back. We didn't do anything to earn this right to experience life. Admittedly, each of us would, if we were the giver, have done a little more fine tuning or improvement on this bag of bones we call a body, the medium through which we exist. I would have preferred Clark Gable's nose. Some of us have been given far more serious impairments, but that does not take away from the incredible significance of this force called life.

The Christian further says that this marvelous free gift was given for a purpose–to be enjoyed to be sure; but enjoyment in a much deeper sense than sheer hedonism.

The "General Thanksgiving" of *The Book of Common Prayer*, sadly not used too much anymore, sums it all up pretty well: "We bless you for our creation, preservation, and all of the blessings of this life."[28] Our life, to be fully enjoyed, is to be lived in relationship to the loving creator who gave it to us in the first place.

Next, we must consider the relationship of quantity and quality. They do not necessarily go together. Bigger isn't always better, although we Americans usually tend to think so, and longer is not necessarily better. Some people live into their eighties and nineties, and yet have not really *lived* one day of their life. And yet our Lord Himself died in his early thirties. Other people of genius have made indelible marks in our world who have lived only a very short time. No one dies laughing and very few willingly (unless they are very disturbed). But the fact remains that length of life and quality of life are not related.

Next, the Christian does not say that pain, suffering and death are good–Jesus wept at the death of Lazarus. But the Christian *does* say that pain, suffering and death are *real*–they exist.

When we dress up a cross with jewels, and surround it with flowers, we tend to forget that this cross, the principle

28. *The Book of Common Prayer* (New York: The Church Hymnal Corporation, 1979), p. 101.

symbol of the Christian, is really a sign of pain, suffering and death. It is in a sense a "sick" symbol–like wearing a small hangman's knot or a minuscule electric chair around your neck as an ornament.

Christianity does not say that pain, suffering and death have disappeared. Indeed, to the contrary, the cross reaffirms their reality. But what the cross and Christianity *do* say is that God chooses to *share* in that reality, that He is with us when that reality comes close to home. This we know because in a unique act of love, He chose to limit Himself and to actually participate in that very experience.

However, that is not the end of the story. We are shown that even hard, bad, indeed, evil things can be turned into good, indeed, triumphant news. Joseph sensed this possibility many centuries before when he addressed his brothers, who out of jealousy had sold him into slavery, when they came to him in supplication as he had become Pharaoh's right hand man and was in a position to help them. "You meant this for evil, but God used it for good" [Gen. 50:20].

And this, the last Sunday of Easter in the Church calendar, is a good time to remind us of what Easter says: It says that pain, suffering and death (often unjust and unfair) really do exist. That is the reality of Good Friday, and these realities cannot be avoided. They are a part of the miracle of life, and they will not go away.

The triumph and meaning of it all does not come from avoiding this reality, but in going *through* it to the assurance that an even greater miracle than earthly life lies ahead of this.

In other words, Christianity does not deny the cold hard facts of life, nor does it assert that it will change this reality (rather, the symbol of the cross *affirms* this reality), but what it *does* say is that it can fit this into a perspective which we, from our threatened, finite, short-lived place in the universe, could never suspect.

Because pain, suffering, and death are part of the reality which I have already partially suffered and which I will inevitably face, as a price of the gift of life, I have no business shouting and shaking my fist at anyone. That may be the price of the ball game that I didn't have any choice but attending but I have heard very few people complain about the fact that they are alive and well.

Now the first step of anyone who wishes to find an honest "religion" or world view is to accept this reality (although a number of religions try with might and main to deny it).

You can say, facing this reality, that life is a great crap-shoot, and your object is to keep the dice as long as you can, and then give them up gallantly as a "gentleman" or a "lady." Most *honest* pagans espouse this, and live their *personal* lives consistent with this principle. They get rocked, however, when *reality* makes itself known to someone *else* to whom they are closely bound.

There is another option, however, once you are realistic and courageous enough to face ultimate reality. You can accept the Christian faith.

This is not just to say that in facing the ultimate reality of pain, suffering and death, there is pie in the sky bye and bye. (Although I won't allow that put-down for the Easter proclamation, which attests to the fact that there is *ultimate* and *everlasting* meaning to each and every human life.) It is to say that *because* of this, there is no reason I should not be a freer, more open, forgiving, loving person during the time that I have been given this gift of life.

It is to accept this concept of grace and then to live freely, joyously and unafraid within it that makes one a Christian.

This is the witness which the Christian facts of reality show us to be true. Yet, this witness is hard to follow, not because the rules are so rigorous (there are no rules except to accept reality and God's ever-present love as shown in our Lord), but they are hard to follow because we have all been taught "there's no free lunch"[29] and "there's a sucker

29. The phrase "There ain't no such thing as a free lunch" is from Robert Heinlein's novel, *The Moon Is a Harsh Mistress* (New York: George Putnam's Sons, 1966), a discussion of which is found in Edwin G. Dolan's *TANSTAAFL* (New York: Holt, Rinehart and Winston, Inc.,

born every minute,"[30] and of course there is truth in each of these statements.

We are hardened, tough cynics and even when we hear this message, we want to justify ourselves. I find myself doing this constantly.

So it is a great tension even we Christians are within. We hear the song, and indeed I believe it *does* make sense. But as my soul soars with Clay Christiansen's music,[31] a sermon from the Dean [Maxwell], or the majesty of the Eucharist, or the quiet peace on occasion in my own solitude, I always sense there are other forces which prevent everyone else in this city from breaking down the doors to enter and share with us these great moments.

One such force is our personal failure to accept reality. Another such negative force is our own open unacceptance of this proclamation.

Let me put this another way: *I* believe in everything I have said in these past few minutes, as do I hope most of

---

1971), chap. 1, esp. p. 14.

30. For an interesting discussion on P. T. Barnum's quotation, see M. R. Werner, *Barnum* (New York: Garden City Publishing Co., Inc., 1926), pp. vii-viii.

31. Clay Christiansen was the Organist-Choirmaster of the Cathedral Church of St. Mark when this sermon was given. Dr. Christiansen now serves as an organist in the Mormon Tabernacle on Temple Square, Salt Lake City, Utah.

you; but my life and your life do not always reflect this. This is important, but not critical. The *essential* thing is to *also* admit *this*. Because if I truly believe, and am truly repentant, then my own admission and confession and continued adherence only add to the honesty and reality of this proclamation.

Plaster saints do not write sermons. Sermons are preached by sinners to sinners, to help us explore together, at its most basic, the mysteries of life and death.

And to sum up what I have been trying to say—I am talking about the *cross*—it is the sign of the world's eternal pain and the sign of the world's eternal salvation. It is *BOTH* of these things!

Those who reject the pain of life have never really lived. To those who accept and are willing to take into themselves not only their own, but the suffering and pain of their brothers and sisters, we Christians can offer an omnipotent God who created all there is, yet wept, suffered and died as one of us.

And at the end could say, so that we *all* can say *Alleluia*!

VI
Death

Introduction

When Albert Colton died on November 7, 1988, much was said about his death. Colton would have wanted it that way. He would have been very upset had people talked about "his passing," "his departure," "his demise," "his parting," or "his being deceased." He felt those words reflected a round-about-way of viewing death. Christianity is not "round-about." Rather, it meets death head on and defeats it. As real as death is to the one who dies, so too is resurrection and the faith of the Church.

> [Every Ash Wednesday] we hear something we do *not* want to hear: "Remember that you are dust, and to dust you shall return."[1] But it is also something that is *true*.
>
> The Gospel means "Good News." But to really appreciate the scope of the overwhelming goodness of this proclamation, we have to face some sobering realities, just as we have to go through Good Friday to get to the triumphant Easter message.
>
> The Christian message asserts the reality of death, of our finitude, but of course the incredible

1. From the Ash Wednesday Liturgy, *The Book of Common Prayer* (New York: The Church Hymnal Corporation, 1979), p. 265.

joy and wonder of the resurrection promise really only hits home when we face the cold but truthful message of Ash Wednesday.

We are not evergreen trees that go on forever through our seedlings (a Masonic funeral symbol). "You're dead, you rascal you!" That is truth.[2]

Thus people "die." They don't "pass on" or "pass away." Death is a very real thing.[3]

The reality of death becomes painfully apparent when one begins to face it with some regularity. Colton, in his own middle age, felt the sense of seemingly being affected by death more poignantly than most.

The middle-aged person is on the firing line. He has lost in the process of having to make realistic decisions what he thinks is the often simplistic idealism of the young. He must act in a realistic world where he has learned from bitter experience that bad decisions usually have bad consequences.

He is not used to death, but by this time it is seldom a total stranger to him either. He is bound to experience it with his own parents at about this time, although often he can rationalize this as a "release."

---

2. Sermon preached on Ash Wednesday (otherwise undated), the Cathedral Church of St. Mark, Salt Lake City, Utah.

3. Sermon preached the Twenty-sixth Sunday after Pentecost, November 12, 1978, the Cathedral Church of St. Mark, Salt Lake City, Utah.

It seems to occur more frequently with those people he knows who are a little bit older than himself–his boss, the president of the club, "old" Mrs. Smith down the street etc.

But the bite begins to come with old friends. Suddenly the phone rings and you are told that Jim is dead, not "old" Jim, but your Jim, your friend, with whom you had lunch last Tuesday. Not a pain, not a problem, and he is gone. Six months later you still remember his office phone number and you want to call and talk to him, but he is gone and there is a void. You miss him.

Then, just because you are middle age and have lived that long, the actuarial table begins to catch up with you, and the specter which keeps the actuary in business comes close to home. Figures and statistics become painful, terrible realities. The family which has experienced the death of turtles and dogs and kittens and goldfish and guppies, experiences the loss of someone deep and dear, a brother or a sister, a child or a spouse, and the hard work and the treadmill and the injustice well up in a great big black ball in the midst of our body, and we don't know where to strike out or who to hit, or what to do.

But we do that which all human beings in middle age have done. We go on.[4]

4. Sermon preached on Good Friday, April 12, 1968, St. Francis' Church, San Francisco, California.

Colton recognized that it was popular to assume that "going on with life" required bravery and a sense of strength seldom tapped. He believed nothing could be further from the truth about surviving the death of a loved one or facing one's own death. The Christian was not to be brave for such bravery depended on his or her own strength and such strength is marginal at best. Rather, the Christian could be vulnerable for it is in such a state that the faithful can grasp the undeniable fact that Christ died for our salvation. In that, sufficient strength can be found in Christ to cause the power of death to take flight.

> "Christ has died; Christ is risen; Christ will come again."[5] This is in a sense a capsulated Christian mini-Creed. It states what we believe to be historic fact [the first two statements] and historic hope.
>
> But it does not take this (a fuller answer to questions about death) as the historic Creeds do . . . "for us and for our salvation"[6] these historic events occurred. Christ died for me, for us. God came to us and said, "I will show you what death can be–a long dark tunnel usually full of pain" (so far he tells us

---

5. These three phrases are said by the congregation every time "Eucharistic Prayer A" is used. The phrases are found in *The Book of Common Prayer* (1979), p. 363.

6. "For us and for our salvation" continues with "he [Jesus Christ] came down from heaven; by the power of the Holy Spirit he became incarnate from the Virgin Mary, and was made man." Found in "The Nicene Creed," in *The Book of Common Prayer* (1979), p. 358.

nothing that all men have not known). But what is new is that God says, "I know that tunnel, my beloved, I have been through it and I show you that through this and beyond this I offer to you a life that has gone through a refinery, burnt and cleansed of dross through heat and pain, but that is the way you find me–the way of the cross–death to yourself in this life and ultimate death of that bag of bones we carry around and identify by a name, a social security and telephone number, and an address."

That is pretty heady wine. I am not strong enough to die to myself every day in this life. [Even] the monk given a medal for his humility had it taken away the first time he wore it. But the Gospel, the good news, isn't that God only takes the absolutely good and righteous with Him. (He wouldn't have any passengers.) The good news is that he will take me where I am, warts and all, provided that I am willing to put my hand in his and walk through the tunnel of life and death, dark as both may be, knowing with a sure and certain faith that no matter how many barks on the shins, how often I stumble and fall, I'll be picked up, dusted off, and be pushed and shoved and led onward.[7]

I made the statement the other day that Christianity

---

7. Sermon preached the Twenty-sixth Sunday after Pentecost, November 12, 1978, the Cathedral Church of St. Mark, Salt Lake City, Utah.

is a life and death matter, and I am afraid I sounded like an old black crow croaking nothing but gloom and doom. I was particularly conscious of the question of death because in that week we had had five funerals recorded in our parish [St. Francis' Church, San Francisco] register. But I will stick by the statement, and perhaps paradoxically assert that it is just because Christianity *is* a life and death matter that it can lead to such a great zest and joy in life. This is true because the Christian faith can look unafraid at the specter of death itself. Anyone who has attended a Requiem Eucharist knows the joyous serenity that comes even at a time of the deepest grief and sorrow.

Christ did not remove death or the sorrow of that parting. But he removed the sting and the finality of death, and by so doing gave new zest and meaning to earthly life while we have it.[8]

Many preachers, during a funeral, are tempted to explain why a person died with lines of thoughts ranging from "God needed our friend in Heaven" to "It was time for him or her to go." Colton resisted such ideas. Instead, he tried to center his sermons around giving thanks for the life of an individual and praising God for the defeat of sin and taking away the sting of death. His sermons speak of a simplicity of death permeated with

8. Sermon preached on Trinity Sunday, May 24, 1964, St. Francis' Church, San Francisco, California.

a confidence that God knew what God was doing with the invention of death.

It is not our church's custom to give extended eulogies at funeral services. Our rationale for this is that the Lord already knows all, loves all, and accepts all; and those here [the Cathedral Church of St. Mark, Salt Lake City] by their presence are expressing love, concern and support which needs no supplement from a preacher.

Thus the Anglican funeral service has a certain detached objectivity. Yet for the committed churchman the Holy Eucharist (or Communion, Lord's Supper, Sacrament, or the Mass) is the one act which can be done both at the time of greatest joy and greatest sorrow. Dom Gregory Dix wrote of this as follows:

> Was ever another command so obeyed? For century after century, spreading slowly to every continent and country and among every race on earth, this action [the celebration of the Holy Eucharist] has been done, in every conceivable human circumstance, for every conceivable human need from infancy and before it to extreme old age and after it, from the pinnacles of earthly greatness to the refuge of fugitives in the caves and dens of the earth. Men have found no better thing than this to do for kings at their crowning and for criminals going to the scaffold; for armies in triumph or for a bride and bridegroom in a little country church; for the proclamation of a dogma or for a good crop of wheat; for the wisdom of the Parliament of a mighty nation or for a sick old woman afraid to die; for a

> schoolboy sitting an examination or for Columbus setting out to discover America; for the famine of whole provinces or for the soul of a dead lover; in thankfulness because my father did not die of pneumonia; for a village headman much tempted to return to fetish because the yams had failed; because the Turk was at the gates of Vienna; for the repentance of Margaret; for the settlement of a strike; for a son for a barren woman; for Captain so-and-so, wounded and prisoner of war; while the lions roared in the nearby amphitheater; on the beach at Dunkirk; while the hiss of scythes in the thick June grass came faintly through the windows of the church; tremulously, by an old monk on the fiftieth anniversary of his vows; furtively, by an exiled bishop who had hewn timber all day in a prison camp near Murmansk; gorgeously, for the canonization of S. Joan of Arc–one could fill many pages with the reasons why men have done this, and not tell a hundredth part of them.[9]

So we gather here today to break bread and share the cup in remembrance of Richard [Richard Ure, longtime friend of Albert Colton], to give thanks for the life and love he shared with us, to offer support and companionship for those who must deeply feel his loss and who cared for him and loved him in his last days of suffering.

The Christian faith accepts death for the reality it

9. Dom Gregory Dix, The Shape of the Liturgy (London: Dacre Press, Adam & Charles Black, 1945), p. 744.

is, and does not minimize the sense of loss this reality brings, nor does it give a facile answer to the "why" of this, nor of what might have been.

So in facing the reality of death head-on, the Christian faith does emerge with a proclamation of hope and triumph, because we assert that death is not the end, but rather a new beginning. We can assert that Richard is now at peace, that he is lovingly accepted in a realm which we, still on our earthly journey, cannot begin to comprehend. Easter proclaims that there is hope and meaning beyond this sad moment.

This message is called the gospel–the *Good* News. It gives us assurance that the frustrations, limitations and sufferings experienced in earthly life are merely *our* cross that does not end at our Good Friday–but in Easter hope.[10]

Colton consistently preached the theme that the Christian is not immune to hardship, sorrow, loss, pain, and separation, even separation at death. At the same time, however, the Christian is privy to a confidence which transcends the anguish and sorrow so common at the death of a companion, spouse, member of the family or friend. That conviction grounds itself in Easter. As such, the Christian can speak with a certainty common as life itself.

I have a story about a much beloved priest who was

10. Sermon preached on December 28, 1982, the Cathedral Church of St. Mark, Salt Lake City, Utah.

dying. (I loved him very much.) A priest friend of mine went to him to administer the last sacrament and he got all choked up in the administration. The old priest said, "Hell, boy, give *me* the book. You don't understand, I'm going *home*!"[11]

11. Sermon preached at a funeral on February 12, 1985, the Cathedral Church of St. Mark, Salt Lake City, Utah.

1

All people who think at all about the meaning of their life have developed some attitude toward their death. With the tremendous variety of approaches to it, one can only safely say that* somebody *is going to be very surprised!

The Octave of All Saints — *Grace Cathedral*
November 2, 1961 — *San Francisco, California*

PSALM 23; DEUTERONOMY 34; 2 TIMOTHY 4:1-8

We have just passed, for another year, the season of ghosts, skeletons, and trick or treat, and I assume that we who answered the door gave a sigh that the new generation has been beautifully conditioned to forget what the word "trick" traditionally meant.

Probably not one out of a thousand little spooks who rang your doorbell could have told you that all of this business arose originally from a great Christian feast day commemorating the faithful departed, the Feast of All Saints.

One of the reasons for this of course is that death itself is not a subject often mentioned in present American culture. While in the good old days any church attender might count on at least one rip-snorting sermon a year in which death was painted in the most graphic colors, this custom has gone out of date. Reference to death is considered to be in bad taste, even from the pulpit. Like birth, death today is an event that seldom happens in our presence. The mortician strives to make it as inconspicuous a part of the funeral as possible, and we tend even to drop the word from our vocabulary. People "pass away," "pass on," or "depart," but they never seem to "die."

And yet, of course, we are talking about the one event which will be common to all of us sitting here. Despite Ben Franklin, it's even more common than taxes. This attitude certainly says something about our world, particularly when we know that the threat of *mass* death, for the first time in man's history, is not much further away than any particular lunatic with some scientific knowledge.

I would suggest that to avoid the concept of death is to avoid an extremely important dimension of our life. Indeed it is our inevitable death that gives a great deal of meaning to our life, just as, for example, the boundaries of a football field describe the field. It gives dimension and perspective to our brief time span as a creature on this earth, and helps us to answer the great question, "Why, and for what purpose, are we living anyway?"

Death defines our attitudes toward life. For those who believe, as Bertrand Russell said he did, that "I believe that when I die I shall rot, and nothing of my ego will survive,"[12] it is understandable that he would also say that he would rather be "Red than Dead." With such an attitude, by definition, there could be very few things that would be more precious than one's own life.

And yet one does not have to be an avowed atheist to marvel at the tremendous insignificance of *any* human life, let alone our own. In one hundred years the economic titan of any community, be he bank president, corporation head, or labor leader, will be forgotten even by his own family. In not too many years after that, the President of the United States will be, to most people, only a name to memorize to pass a particular examination. John O'Hara once wrote what I thought was a very touching short story. It was the obituary of a *very* insignificant man written as though it were front page news. He extolled the efficient way that the deceased could operate a mimeograph machine, how he enjoyed his bowling league (where his team won fourth place), and how he was once assistant–assistant secretary of his fraternal lodge. Pathetic accomplishments, O'Hara suggests, and yet whose aren't?[13]

The lessons read for today all speak of death: the 23rd

12. Bertrand Russell, *Why I Am Not a Christian and Other Essays on Religion and Related Subjects*, ed. with an Appendix on the Bertrand Russell Case by Paul Edwards (London: George Allen and Unwin, Ltd., 1957), p. 43.

13. Citation uncertain.

Psalm, the death of Moses, and the 2nd letter of Paul to Timothy, which includes the great words "the time of my departure has come. I have fought the good fight, I have finished the race, I have kept the faith" [2 Tim. 4:6b-7, RSV].

These passages remind us that death is a part of our Christian life. Despite our personal insignificance, our life and our death have eternal meaning. Indeed, in our modern day, it is the Christian who is best equipped to face this specter. In a world that prides itself on being "realistic," it is the Christian who is the most realistic of all about the really basic stuff of existence. It is the Christian who at death is the least concerned about the trappings. One of the great glories of *The Book of Common Prayer* is that it is the same service for the lowliest and the highest. It is a common pall that covers the coffin of all of God's children.

Yet like lots of hard problems, we tend to put off thoughts of death. Nevertheless, we read with fascination stories in the paper about a person who knows he has only a given time to live. What is he going to do with this time? I recall reading that the passengers in the two airlines which crashed over the Grand Canyon had almost three minutes from the time of collision until the planes hit the ground. What did these people do in this period? And yet, of course, in one way or another we *all* have just three minutes to live, give or take a few years.

The Prayer Book litany asks that we be delivered from

"sudden death."[14] What is meant here is not delivery from death itself, but from a death that is unprepared, unforseen, and unprovided for. In some cases, it is true, a great crisis does bring a person to a search for truth when this search had never been undertaken before. But tragically and pathetically, it is also often too late to make such a search. Even if it is not ourselves that are involved, but someone we love deeply, we find that in the shock of imminent or actual loss, we can only revert to our established patterns of thought and ways of viewing things. It is often asking too much for us to strike out anew at times like that.

A man once dying of cancer told his priest visitor, "I haven't bought any of this Christianity business for sixty-five years, and don't think I'm going to be one of those snivelling death-bed converts." He was probably right, although for a reason he hasn't thought of. It's terribly hard to shake off the encrustation and patterns of sixty-five years and look at a problem afresh in a crisis like this.

This is meant to be a practical sermon. I am not trying to explore the theology of death. In fact in one sense there

---

14. "From lightning and tempest; from earthquake, fire, and flood; from plague, pestilence, and famine; from battle and murder, and from sudden death, *Good Lord Deliver Us.*" From "The Litany," *The Book of Common Prayer* (New York: The Church Pension Fund, 1928), p. 54, and "The Great Litany," in *The Book of Common Prayer* (1979), p. 149.

is not one little theological cubby-hole into which we fit death. The meaning of life and death is inherent in the Christian message. Anyone who leads a full Christian life already knows all that needs to be known about this.

Rather, I would like to remind you, because it is not frequently done, that death is an adventure ahead for us all. It is also something we will be faced with in the loss of others. I can only suggest that at such times the comfort of the Christian faith and of your church is immeasurable. Parenthetically, may I suggest that at such times it is perfectly proper to call your minister before anyone else. The very word "minister" suggests that part of his vocation is to do that very thing in times of crisis. He should be of help to you not only in the emotional and religious problems involved, but in handling practical details as well. It is appropriate to have a service in your church. It is appropriate to have a Eucharist and to sing your favorite hymns. It is appropriate to have people to your house afterwards, to be yourselves, to laugh and cry about old remembrances, and if it is your custom, to provide refreshment. To the Christian this is a parting, not an end.

All people who think at all about the meaning of their life have developed some attitude toward their death. With the tremendous variety of approaches to it, one can only safely say that *some*body is going to be very surprised! But if Christianity is what it says it is, it gives us the meaning of life, and of death. There is much about death that remains a great mystery. But it is an event that we should face realistically as part of God's loving plan for us. As a friend of mine suggested, we can view it either as a comma or as a period.

We are now in the Octave of All Saints. One of the glories of the church calendar is that it calls particular questions to our attention now, while there is still time, and not during the pain and sorrow of an immediate personal crisis. It is perhaps a time when we can indulge in a little self-examination. We can ask ourselves whether our thoughts on this subject square with a belief in a God who says, "I am with you always," and who died for us that we may live eternally.

Let us remember the glorious words of the Order for the Burial of the Dead:

> I am the resurrection and the life, saith the Lord: He that believeth in me, though he were dead, yet shall he live: and whosoever liveth and believeth in me, shall never die.
>
> I know that my Redeemer liveth, and that he shall stand at the latter day upon the earth; and though this body be destroyed, yet shall I see God; whom I shall see for myself, and mine eyes shall behold, and not as a stranger.[15]

---

15. *The Book of Common Prayer* (1928), p. 324, and in *The Book of Common Prayer* (1979), p. 469.

This sermon was also preached:
The Octave of All Saints
The Twenty-third Sunday after Pentecost
November 2, 1980
All Saints Church
Salt Lake City, Utah.

2

. . . death is not a nasty word. It is a fact. Don't duck it or cover it up with euphemisms. To avoid this is to avoid reality. After all, pets in your house "die" (they don't "pass away" or "depart").

The Third Sunday in Advent
December 11, 1966

St. Francis' Church
San Francisco, California

In the midst of life we are in death. The Lord gave–The Lord and Giver of Life. I am the Resurrection and the life. To show us how far we have come from traditional Christianity, the classical sermon subject for the four Sundays of Advent were death, judgment, heaven, and hell. That's a far cry from the cheery tunes we now hear from the commercial media. (And to be good and non-sectarian, the pitch is now not "Merry Christmas," but rather the more innocuous "Happy Holidays.")

But in an attempt to keep to the older tradition, I should like today to share a few thoughts about death. Death will occur to each one of us sitting here today. It will happen to all of the people now on this earth. It is the necessary correlation of birth, and yet, while we accept birth without question, while we accept the magnificent gift of life as our "right," we somehow reject and feel cheated about the other end of this journey.

In the burial office of this church at the grave side we say, "In the midst of life we are in death,"[16] and there is no one there to say to us nay, because this is an obvious fact. Earlier in the burial office we quote from the book of Job (as we do in much of the Burial office and in much of what is truly deep about the meaning of life and death) where we say "The Lord gave, and the Lord hath taken away; blessed be the name of the Lord" [Job 1:21, KJV].[17] And if we back up a little further we come to the beginning of the burial office, to the great ringing words of affirmation, with the triumphant stamp of certitude given to us by the witness of the Resurrection in the New Testament, "I am the Resurrection and the Life, saith the Lord: he that believeth in me, though he were dead, yet shall he live; and whosoever liveth and believeth in me shall never die" [John 11:25-26, KJV].[18]

The Christian faith is a hard boiled article. It doesn't promise the absence of fear, of sickness, and of death. Take *The Book of Common Prayer* [1928]. Take its "womb to tomb"

16. *The Book of Common Prayer* (1928), p. 332.

17. Ibid., p. 324.

18. Ibid., pp. 324-37.

section starting on page 271.[19] It will take you through every significant event in your life.

And constantly we are reminded of the relationship here between life and death. To talk of death we must first talk of life. What a fantastic miracle life is—the very fact that we exist. No one of us had a thing to say about the fact that we are here today. Creation is a gift. That's Genesis I. But creation is an on-going gift. Think of the miracle of healing.

I gave my finger a first-rate gash last Thanksgiving trying to carve the turkey. I used an electric carving knife, which is a wonderful example of a Christian precept that technology will not necessarily bring salvation to anyone. It depends on how you use the technology. It can bring great comfort and ease, or it can bring great harm, depending upon the capability of the person using it. But in any event, I watched my index finger with fascination through the process of healing—through the first night of throbbing pain, the body's use as protection the piece of unnecessary fingernail and layers of skin, and thus its discarding of these, and the miracle that underneath a good number of layers of skin on the end of my finger another layer of skin, tender and sensitive, with, in the most amazing sort of way,

19. By "Womb to Tomb," Colton is speaking of the ministration of Holy Baptism together with The Office of Instruction, The Order of Confirmation, The Solemnization of Matrimony, The Thanksgiving After Child-birth, The Visitation of the Sick, and The Burial of the Dead.

the same fingerprints (unique only to me, the F.B.I. tells me, of all the people in the world) pushing up to take their place as part of those two stubs which type out this sermon.

This is a small illustration, but a true one. I had nothing to do with this. Some fantastic process took a pretty well split finger and knit it back together, and all I had to do was sit by and watch. This is a miracle, and yet we take this as an everyday occurrence, which it is, just as our life itself is.

And yet there come those times when that which is rent asunder cannot be put back together. A young man who has not regained consciousness from heart surgery five days ago; an old woman being kept alive through tubes and injections; a little girl wasting away from an incurable cancer.

And we cry out in anger. Why are these things, "O Lord and Giver of Life"? What a farce. You give, just to take away. You gave life, let us say, but only to give pain; you give freedom only to breed guilt; you give love only to make hate possible–and in the end of your crazy game, you take it all away anyway in death, removing from us the object of our love, the means by which we expressed this, and ultimately ourselves, the only frame of reference that we know, and without which we cannot conceive of anything. These are the natural cries of bitterness at our limitations. We resist these and in a sense cannot even conceive of them.

2. THE THIRD SUNDAY IN ADVENT, 1966.

A short story I read some years ago told of a man who was to be executed before a firing squad in some military situation in the Balkans. And in his pre-execution fantasy, he imagined the honest dignity and contempt with which he would face this moment. But then he began to develop his thoughts further, and he realized that despite his great and moving last speech, and the undoubted dignity with which he would face this moment, the men in the firing squad would go back to work, and at the end of the day go down to the village for a few drinks and a few girls, and they would be hungry and complain about their dinner, and go to sleep, and their life, and that of the village, and surely that of the rest of the world, would go on exactly as before.[20]

Or, in a wonderful book, *Shantung Compound*, the author, one of the editors of the *Christian Century*, describes a group of Caucasian people in China who were being rounded up by the Japanese after Pearl Harbor to be taken to a concentration camp. They had been warned that they must only assemble with them what they could carry. Langdon Gilkey writes:

> That warning had been issued in earnest. At noon sharp a Japanese officer shouted through a megaphone that everyone must pick up his own belongings and

20. Citation uncertain.

> carry them by hand to the railway station. A horrified gasp swept though the crowd. Every elderly person, every father of a family, every single women thought of the station a mile away and then looked in near panic at the mountain of stuff at their feet.[21]

At our hour of death we will be like these people, unable and unwilling to comprehend parting with the accumulation of earthly life.

And yet by contrast, we have a man named Paul of Tarsus who wrote to some people in Phillippi, "For his sake I have suffered the loss of all things, and I count them as 'refuse' (Revised Standard Version) 'dung' (King James Version) 'garbage' (New English Version) in order that I may gain Christ" [Phil. 3:8b, RSV].

"In the midst of life we are in death"[22]; this is true and has nothing to do with one's religious beliefs. And here advice can truly be universal. Because it is a fact, a truth, it is one that should be faced and acknowledged. All men, to my knowledge, acknowledge the obligation (if not practice) to live responsibly and die responsibly. This means, of course, without morbidity and over-dwelling on it, to think about this eventuality, and to make responsible plans

---

21. Langdon Gilkey, *Shantung Compound* (New York: Harper and Row, 1966), p. 3.

22. *The Book of Common Prayer* (1928), p. 332, and *The Book of Common Prayer* (1979), p. 492.

for it. In the old days words of wisdom were passed along through the last will and testament. Modern lawyers, unfortunately, seldom ask the client about these, because it already takes twenty pages to type up a so-called "simple" will with some modest trust provisions.

But if I may be bold enough to suggest, you can accomplish the same thing outside of the harsh abstract coldness of a will. Write down and tell those you love what you feel, and what you would like (and I would suggest that you do this every year, and tear up and burn what you did the year before); but for heaven's sake don't tie this up with conditions relating to property or money in the will itself. I shall never forget a weeping thirty-five-year-old woman in my law office who couldn't pay her rent or buy food for her four children, yet she would inherit one million dollars when she was sixty. Her parents, both dead, had put the money into a trust because they didn't trust her use of money, and wanted to be sure that she was taken care of in her old age. We should never play God with what we have to give. If we have not given basic values by then, how fruitless a job it is to nag from the grave. But a letter, or if we know we are dying, a good talk–what a great and wonderful memory it can be.

And death is not a nasty word. It is a fact. Don't duck it or cover it up with euphemisms. To avoid this is to avoid reality. After all, pets in your house "die" (they don't "pass away" or "depart"). Not to discuss this with your children is to deny them one of the basic facts of existence.

And now we come to the sentence, "The Lord gave." Here we begin to separate the sheep and the goats. Life, as the theist sees it, is a gift of God. We do not "deserve" life, or have a "right" to life. It is something which has been given to us to use. Even a long life of eighty years or more is but a short time in the total scheme of things. If all time since creation were seen as a twenty-four-hour day, the entire period of mankind's existence would be measured in a few seconds. This means that by the measurement of time alone a single life exists on one of the lesser planets of a vast universe for the merest fraction of a second.

Now we can conclude from this either that man is so obviously insignificant that a single life has no meaning at all, or if we affirm with the Jew and the Christian that each individual life is a sacred gift of infinite value we must also say that time is therefore not the total measure of value. There is a dimension of depth and quality which is even more important than mere quantity. There are moments when we can pierce the veil of time into eternity; fleeting seconds on the time line that give meaning to all else. We know this in our own lives–moments of great happiness, flashing insights, which we treasure, look back upon and use as a frame of reference in the regularity of the rest of our time.

The Christian therefore does not see time as the limit

of all things. Time is important, because man lives for this moment in it, but it is not the total measure. There is meaning beyond time, which, after all, is itself merely a creation of God's. The Christian affirms life. It is good because it is a gift of God. But there are also things worse than death. Men can have hell here in time as well as beyond.

But it is in the triumphant opening of the burial office that the Christian stands alone. "I am the resurrection and the life saith the Lord: he that believeth in me, though he were dead, yet shall he live."[23] This is not a vague, general principle of immortality, or the search for symbols such as the evergreen, but the triumphant assertion that an individual's personhood and capacity for loving growth is not limited to a few years of earthly time and a particular bag of bones he has been given to wear for that period.

So, as the initial fact of life is a gift of God, so is the gift of eternal life. This is a very different thing from saying that death does not exist. The Christian sees death as a very real thing, and without God's second great gift, that would indeed be the end of meaning. In other words, eternal life is not a general principal built into the system and thereby a claim or right which goes along with the contract of earthly life itself. It is rather a special gift purchased for us

---

23. *The Book of Common Prayer* (1928), p. 324.

by the blood and sweat of Calvary. I am not *entitled* to eternal life, but I am offered it from the hands of the man on the cross.

And the burial office holds in tension the bitter-sweet Christian attitude toward death. There is unquestioned sorrow, loss, and loneliness. There is separation for the moment which may stretch on for many years. And the greater the love, the greater the ache over such separation. But there is also the note of triumphant joy. It is most appropriate to sing hymns at a funeral, and there is no more fitting hymn than the great Easter hymn, "The strife is over, the battle done, the victory of life is won; the song of triumph has begun. Alleluia!"[24]

The Christian affirms that even in the loneliness, the pain, and the fear of death itself, he is never alone. The man who descended into hell is there to walk through this moment with us too. As St. Paul wrote in his letter to the Romans:

> In face of all this, what is there left to say? If God is for us, who can be against us? . . . I have become absolutely convinced that neither Death nor Life, neither messenger of Heaven nor monarch of earth, neither what happens today nor what may happen tomorrow, nei-

24. "Hymn 91, V. 1," G.P. Sante da Palestrina, adapted with Alleluias by William H. Monk, trans. Francis Pott, *The Hymnal 1940* (New York: The Church Pension Fund, 1961).

> ther a power from on high nor a power from below, nor anything else in God's whole world has any power to separate us from the love of God in Christ Jesus our Lord! [Rom. 8:31, 38-39, Phillips]

And the result is portrayed in the graphic picture language of that strange last book of the Bible, Revelation, in the passage used as the epistle on All Saints' Day: "They shall hunger no more, neither thirst any more; neither shall the sun light on them, nor any heat. For the Lamb which is in the midst of the throne shall feed them, and shall lead them unto living fountains of waters: and God shall wipe away all tears from their eyes" [Rev. 7:16-17, KJV].

3

Quite naturally in an Easter sermon you expect me to mention God, and I fully intend to. And I would suggest to you that if you ever start down the road of inquiry about the real meaning and purpose of your life (which I hope you all do) then I think you must postulate the existence of God–or there is no meaning at all.

Easter Day
March 26, 1967

St. Francis' Church
San Francisco, California

"Now the eleven disciples went away into Galilee to the mountain to which Jesus had directed them. And when they saw him they worshipped him; but some doubted" [Matt. 28:16, RSV].

I was driving home late one rainy night on a freeway north of Sacramento [California]. My windshield wipers were going full speed, and it was still difficult to see. The traffic was heavy and going at a good clip. I noticed the car in front of me start to weave, first into the far right lane, then across to the far left, and then suddenly whip around and skid sideways.

I turned to the right to avoid the car and fortunately there was no car in that lane, and as I whipped by afraid to apply my brakes for fear of skidding myself, I glimpsed another car smash into the first, and I heard another car hit those two. The traffic was so heavy it was not even possible to stop, and I drove on, my heart pounding, realizing that I had been a few seconds or a few feet from death or serious injury.

At another time, while hiking with some friends of mine in the high Uintah mountains of Utah my feet slipped on some ice and I went shooting down a cliff, finally coming to rest only a few short feet from a sheer precipice.

Each one of you, if you have lived any time at all, have doubtless had similar experiences. You have stared death in the face. Now I am not going to tell you that during these two events I found Jesus–the only thought I recall having in either case was, as I sailed down the cliff, "What a totally absurd way for me to die."

But I am interested in how each of us analyzes such an event afterward, and how he fits it into his own frame of values.

The Prayer Book says, in the Burial office, "In the midst of life we are in death,"[25] and this is surely true. Do we merely shrug this off, or try to ignore it? What do we see as the meaning of our life, and what does the existence of

25. *The Book of Common Prayer* (1928), p. 322, and *The Book of Common Prayer* (1979), p. 484.

death have to say, if anything, to that meaning? Is life just a racket, and social responsibility just a joke, as some of our youth suggest? WHAT *IS* IT ALL ABOUT?

Quite naturally in an Easter sermon you expect me to mention God, and I fully intend to. And I would suggest to you that if you ever start down the road of inquiry about the real meaning and purpose of your life (which I hope you all do) then I think you must postulate the existence of God—or there is no meaning at all.

The Rev. Robert Capon, an Episcopal priest from Long Island, has written a strange and uproarious book called *An Offering of Uncles*. In it, he put it this way:

> There is only one person you can blame (or thank) for putting meaning into the world: God is the only possible author of history; man didn't make himself any kind of an animal, let alone a priestly one. But there are two people you might blame for taking meaning out of the world: God—*and man.* Of these two, however, only man can sensibly be faulted. For if the confusions of history are God's doing—if God raised up meaning on a Friday and kicked the stuffing out of it a week later, smiling an un-ruffled inscrutable smile all the time, then meaning simply has no meaning. Shape is nice, and so is shapelessness; gardens are nice and so are tangles, and life is nice and so is death; and history is non-history and good is evil; and nobody is to blame for anything, and away we go into the great Oriental Nothing, or

All or Whatever that doesn't give a damn. I don't know about you, but I can't buy that. It doesn't sound like much of a God to me; and it certainly doesn't sound like the God of Abraham, Isaac and Jacob.[26]

But even if you concede Father Capon his point; this does not get you to Easter as he suggests. There are many ideas of God that do not include or even require Easter in them.

Indeed, it might be interesting to compile a list of forms of non-Easter in our own culture, but first we must be sure we agree on what Easter is.

Easter is the proclamation that one person, whom we call Jesus Christ, and whom we describe as both fully God and fully man, did indeed suffer and die upon the cross on a specific day about 2,000 years ago and that he rose from this death preserving his individual identity, and will continue to live and reign, world without end. Easter is also the proclamation (and this is what makes it good news for the rest of us) that God offers to share this gift of eternal meaning with us–that indeed is the reason he suffered and died.

If you could just stand here with me through the

---

26. Robert Farrar Capon, *An Offering of Uncles: The Priesthood of Adam and the Shape of the World* (New York: Sheed and Ward, 1967), pp. 74-75.

past three years [1965-67] watching the bodily remains of beloved parishioners being brought into God's house for the last time, and to have the assurance that this is not the end of meaning for these people but rather the entrance into a newer and fuller life in light and joy in the holy fellowship, then you could see the tremendous exultant power of the Easter proclamation: "The strife is o'er, The battle done . . . Let shout of holy joy outburst, Alleluia."[27]

And contrast this to the hopeless, grey grief of the pagan funeral with its frantic and pathetic attempts to find meaning and to stay the inevitable in opulent displays which we know moth and rust will corrupt sooner than we like to think.

What a joyously incredible thing it is to know that I shall be with my Lord, that I am taken as I am and because of this my life here and now takes on a newer and deeper meaning. Our joy is not just to earn another dollar tomorrow. What we do tomorrow is to be seen in the perspective of eternity, and while seen from that perspective, it might still be the appropriate thing to earn another dollar tomorrow. We must do our duty to provide. It might just also be the appropriate thing to go fly a kite with your son, or pay a call on a sick friend who is just as lonely as you are, or

27. Hymn 91, Vv. 1, 2, *The Hymnal 1940.*

read that book you've been too busy to look at, or say a prayer, or thank your wife for just being your wife.

When all the world is playing it safe, plagued by fears and dreads, Easter tells us just the opposite. Easter lets us play life to the fullest.

And yet it is strange and wondrous what lengths people will go to to avoid this good news. One way is to deny that there's any problem. One such form of denial is born out of modern technology, the other as old as the hills.

The technological way to bob and weave around the importance of Easter is to say that while we haven't got this problem of death licked yet, we will, if we just apply a little more scientific elbow grease. One grotesque example is the idea that we can take bodies and put them into a deep-freeze; then when science has solved these problems, we can have a resurrection—but into what? Surely not into a world of light and joy and the fellowship of the saints, but a strange and unknown world, with no one we loved or ever knew, no familiar sites, sounds or smells—the wonderful, intangible strands that tie us to *our* family, or town, our friends, our school—a world of loneliness and separation. I suggest man-made Easters can become instead man-made hells.

The other age-old way of ducking Easter is through some idea of the immortality of the soul. I will go on, some way, because that's just the way things are, either as myself or as part of some vague general principle of continuity.

The latter variation sounds for some reason much less comforting when it comes close to home. Do you want to become a vague general principle? The other, "and that's the way things are," is a variation on the theme of "Good old God." A friendly, benign grandpa, handing out sugar candies in his senility. But such concepts deny at least two important things, Good Friday and Judgment. And what about those who have not gone through a personal Good Friday and who have never known the weight of judgment (or who have not judged themselves) . . . well, who are these people? I have never met one of them. Easter meets and faces both judgment and Good Friday and if I am looking for a realistic analysis of life, I would opt for Easter.

But, then, what if this whole Easter business is a monstrous fraud? We preachers were saved last Easter by the *Time* magazine cover story "Is God Dead?"[28] This year we have the book by Hugh Schonfield, *The Passover Plot*,[29] which suggests that the whole story of the resurrection was a big farce, a big fraud, carefully rigged to euchre the ignorant country-folk. It's kind of a turn-of-the-century snake-oil salesman gimmick. The book has now sold over *100,000* copies.

---

28. "Is God Dead?" and "Religion: Theology: Toward a Hidden God," *Time*, Apr. 8, 1966, cover and pp. 82-87.

29. Hugh J. Schonfield, *The Passover Plot–New Light on the History of Jesus* (New York: Bernard Geis Associates, 1965), pp. 158-82.

But let me let you in on a secret. There's not a thing new in Mr. Schonfield's book. From the very day the resurrection occurred, people doubted. People figured out ways that it could have happened as a trick.

St. Matthew's gospel even contains one of these stories–that the body was stolen while the soldiers were asleep.

St. Matthew's gospel comes to its conclusion with the story of the eleven remaining disciples coming to meet their risen Lord where He had told them to find Him–and then we have the short phrase, "but some doubted."

Of course some will doubt, God bless them. I can't blame them. I doubted too. How can you *not* doubt something you have never heard of before, and by definition will never happen again?

But what if it is true? If it is, how else would it have been reported? How could you have reported this event any other way? There is an exciting variation in details in the four accounts we have preserved in our Bible–surely true to life, if you've ever heard four different accounts of an important event seen by four different people.

But all reports were united in their conviction of the overwhelming impact of this event. If I asked you what you were willing to die for, I believe you would weigh this fairly carefully. And yet these witnesses were willing and did die for their conviction of the truth of this event, as millions have since then.

Many will doubt. Most, hearing the news for the first time as an adult *should* doubt. To accept this is the most significant decision they will ever make, and such a decision should be made with great concern.

Nor can this thing be proved or shown conclusively to those outside the circle. We can never prove scientifically something that by definition happened only once.

The proof comes from faith in its truth, and the good Lord has left each of us in our divinely given freedom to decide that for ourselves.

But let's take a good long look at our lives through a long time tunnel and then examine the options. One would be that God does not exist at all and individual meaning therefore is restricted to the narrow limits of a life span. Another is that God exists, but that an impassable gulf exists between God and man. In this option, we would have a God so transcendent and inscrutable that He has little to say about the daily round of joy and sorrow and only the vaguest concern about individual birth and death.

Or we have the Christian option of a God who comes to us as we are where we are, who hears our sorrows, offers us healing of our wounds when we cannot heal ourselves, and promises us eternal meaning.

Too good to be true? Perhaps. But act upon the presumption that it is true, and see what happens. *Good Friday is a reality of life.* It comes to each of us, often many times.

It can't be avoided no matter what religious or non-religious world view we hold.

But to the Christian, through the dirge of Good Friday, comes inevitably and irresistibly, faintly at first perhaps, but swelling into a triumphant chorus, the mighty fanfare of joy:

> The powers of death have done their worst
> But Christ their legions hath dispersed . . .[30]

And this we can say, because "The Lord is risen; He is risen indeed, Alleluia!"

This sermon was also preached:

The Sixth Sunday in Easter and	*April 1975* (otherwise undated)
May 19, 1974	*Bountiful Community Church-*
St. Stephen's Church	*Church of the Resurrection*
West Valley City, Utah,	*Bountiful, Utah*

30. Hymn 91, V. 2, *The Hymnal 1940.*

4

Since Easter, no great tombs are necessary. Pace: Agamemnon, and Pharaoh, and Hadrian and Lenin. A pine box contains within it the power and promise of eternity.

Easter Day — *The Cathedral Church of St. Mark*
April 7, 1985 — *Salt Lake City, Utah*

"Alleluia. Christ is risen. The Lord is risen indeed. Alleluia."[31]

Easter, the great ultimate pronouncement of the Christian faith; without it Christmas is just the beginning of another life and Good Friday is just the end of another life (unjustly ended, but no one ever said that life and death were fair).

And while department stores don't pipe Easter hymns endlessly as they do carols at Christmas, religious music of the Easter event far over-powers in scope and majesty the admittedly wonderful music of the nativity event.

An example is Handel's "Hallelujah Chorus" which we will be hearing shortly.

---

31. *The Book of Common Prayer* (1979), p. 355.

4. EASTER DAY, 1985.

Easter is far more than another miraculous event–after all, pulling a rabbit out of a hat is fun to see, a man walking on water would be an awesome sight. And a man rising from the dead? Well, I've seen that in science fiction.

None of these touches me, affects me, moves me, except as a spectator. I like to see a pretty woman sawed in half and put together again to prance off the stage with her magician husband. But, although temporarily entertained, *I* go back to *my* life, to *my* anxieties, fears, occasional joys, and grey routine.

What say you of *this*, oh great Easter day magician? "A great deal," says the person whose triumph we commemorate this day–because this is not the rabbit out of the hat to entertain us spectators in the audience. *This* rabbit out of the hat is truth for *all* of us.

Each one of us knows that we will die by accident, illness, or just running out of gas. Because our whole world has centered around ourselves and it is through ourselves that we know of existence, we really can't conceive of this, of our own non-existence. But we know it will happen.

We can laugh and joke about it, we can try to forget it, or to use a football term, we can punt, and try to kick the whole thing as far away from ourselves as possible. But the truth is that particular ball will always come back to us, ultimately behind our own goal line. In football jargon, being caught behind your own goal line is called a "safety."

That's not a bad metaphor for what life *before* Easter

means. I'm caught behind my own goal line (we each have a Good Friday). That's *bad* news. But the good news is that Almighty God knows this, and views our plight with loving concern.

As the great opening collect of the Eucharist (written by Charlemagne's prime minister Alcuin over a thousand years ago) states: "Almighty God, unto whom all hearts are open, all desires known, and from whom no secrets are hid . . ."[32]

To pursue the football metaphor, after you fall on the ball and take your lumps, after you have admitted your failure, you get a free kick from the twenty-yard line, and you're back in the ball game only two points down.

The Christian analogy to that story is fairly simple. It doesn't mean that you'll "win," but, crazy thought, "winning" the game isn't what it's all about. Oh, I know, show me a good loser and I'll show you a loser.

That's in football. But life isn't a football game with points and winners and losers. To that extent my little analogy's really a bad one. Indeed, I suggest that if you play your life as a game, with pluses and minuses and winners and losers, whether it be your marriage, your career, or any relationship, you are doomed, at least if Easter and Christianity are correct.

32. *The Book of Common Prayer* (1979), p. 323.

After all, Good Friday proclaims a loser. As Deuteronomy (21:22-23) pronounces: "if a man . . . is put to death and you hang him on a tree . . . (this) hanged man is accursed by God" [RSV].

In other words, forever cursed is one who is crucified. This scriptural anathema made it doubly difficult for a devout Jew to accept Jesus Christ as the Messiah.

However, the early and medieval Christian couldn't care less about this Old Testament curse. In those times a person considered himself lucky if he made it to age thirty. Death was all around–from childbirth, through an age of violence, to middle age without penicillin.

The promise of Jesus Christ's resurrection was for *them*. He said from the beginning, "this is for *you* also." Earthly misery, yes; but hope beyond this, *also* yes!

But in our modern western culture this point no longer seems to have much appeal. For most of us our life is no longer one of constant misery and early death. When we look to the future *pensions* are the big thing. Death and judgment are of no concern–rather a bigger and better golden parachute to see us through the sere and yellow leaf.

Yet if Christianity is truth for all cultures at all times (which I believe) then it must also speak to a twentieth-century world that says it is not interested in death.

For those of you who believe that a continuing life in community after your bodily death is unimportant, let me try *this* Easter theme. "I came that they might have life, and have it abundantly" [John 10:10, RSV].

The Greeks had two words for time–*chronos,* or clock-time, and *kairos,* the significant, meaningful time.

Our Lord was here giving us the assurance of a *kairos* life, by means of which each moment can become hallowed, not in some future state, but *now.*

It is a life lived in freedom because it has been forgiven and is therefore hallowed, however shaky it may be in its externals.

The frustrations, the guilts, the sense of inadequacy that each of us carries around, no longer need concern us. I am forgiven, and eternally valuable.

The proof? Not only a proclamation, not only a nice thought, but the proof is that death, the ultimate assignment of all of us to anonymity, has been overcome.

I have taken to walking in the city cemetery which is below our house. There are acres and acres of monuments. There are some wonderful tombstones. One commemorates Mr. and Mrs. Snowball. Another has carved on it a cement-mixing truck, remembering someone who was in the Redi-mix business.

However, and it is typical of most cemeteries, there is little proclaiming of joy and Easter. There is no great "free at last, free at last" exclamation such as is on Martin Luther King's tombstone.

Tombstones themselves don't last very long. Within a

hundred years many are indecipherable. But they reflect the innate desire within all of us for permanent remembrance. (I am sure that many of us when we were young could not resist the temptation to put our initials in wet concrete.)

Yet have initials in wet concrete or an elaborate tombstone after the fact given us *abundant* life? Of course not. But these acts do express our yearning for something *more*.

Our Lord's life and death proclaim that something more. The Resurrection of the first Easter morning puts the ultimate stamp of authority on the truth of this.

Since Easter, no great tombs are necessary. Pace: Agamemnon, and Pharaoh, and Hadrian and Lenin. A pine box contains within it the power and promise of eternity.

So what is Easter? Evelyn Underhill, a great Anglican religious writer, refers to "the whole psychological zoo living within us, as well as the embryonic beginnings of artist, statesman or saint."[33] This embryonic beginning is proclaimed in Easter.

Easter proclaims not only something more than the yearnings portrayed by our initials made in wet concrete or an elaborate tombstone. It proclaims triumph of life *today* and forever.

---

33. Citation uncertain.

Handel in his great *Messiah* selected verses from the Book of Revelation for the Hallelujah chorus to make this proclamation:

> Hallelujah, for the Lord God omnipotent reigneth [Rev. 19:6], . . .
>
> The kingdom of this world is become the kingdom of our Lord and of his Christ; and He shall reign forever and ever [v. 15],
>
> King of Kings and Lord of Lords, Hallelujah! [v. 16]

VII
The Ministry

Introduction

The Episcopal Church's Book of Common Prayer (1979) says, in the service of the ordination of a priest, "My brother [sister], the Church is the family of God, the body of Christ, and the temple of the Holy Spirit. All baptized people are called to make Christ known as Savior and Lord, and to share in the renewing of his world. . . . As a priest, it will be your task to proclaim by word and deed the Gospel of Jesus Christ, and to fashion your life in accordance with its precepts."[1] Albert Colton saw the vows of ministry, for both clergy and lay people, as exposing the world to Christ and witnessing to the power of God's grace.

> Show me there is really a Christ crucified who died for me, and by rising from the dead offered us all eternal life and meaning. Further, show me this makes a *difference*.[2]

For Colton an immediate problem with ministry was its being

---

1. *The Book of Common Prayer* (New York: The Church Hymnal Corporation, 1979), p. 531.

2. Sermon preached on the Feast of St. Thomas, December 21, 1976, the Church of the Good Shepherd Church, Ogden, Utah, on the occasion of the ordination of the Reverend Richard Henthorne to the Sacred Order of Priests.

seen as "people helping people," or doing good works from a humanitarian point of view. Drawing upon a continuing theme, he believed good pagans could do nice things for one another as well as be extraordinarily caring. The Christian, however, engages in a rather unique ministry. True, the Christian cares and serves. But at the same time, the Christian sees the world radically different from the view of the good humanitarian. Quite simply, the humanitarian works hard for the sake of humanity. The Christian serves Christ, and thus all others for the sake of and in the name of Christ.

> If we can draw a lesson from the secular world, this is the time we fly our colors highest and most proudly. There can be no question that we must relate to the world around us–be concerned and involved in its problems, its pains and its suffering, and do what we can to alleviate them.
>
> The Christian must see these concerns through the knowledge of the fallibility of *all* men, the perspective of eternity, and the knowledge that in the end result, it is *God* who saves and not we ourselves.
>
> Like the Jew of the diaspora, we must live and participate and work in a secular world (we have no choice, and God is surely working there too). But in doing so, we should never forget that we do so as Christians–our concern must start from the altar. This is the place we receive our commission. This is the place we receive our strength. This is the place to which we return to lick our wounds and recuperate. This is the place from which we go out to do battle.

And the day we forget this, we are merely another Elks Club without as nice facilities (although admittedly lower dues), or another social action group, rising or disbanding with the interest shown in the particular cause.

This is our common task . . . to claim this city for God and enter into its life in order to play our part in making that claim good.[3]

It seems obvious that "ministry" is not complete without a clear recognition that Christ is the fulcrum of all that ministry represents. Service in the name of Christ is inherently different than service in the name of humanity. Along the same lines, ministry in the name of Christ is not complete unless it incorporates the Body of Christ in total. Colton was adamant that "the ministry" was not viewed exclusively as "the diaconate, the priesthood and the office of bishop." All baptized Christians were part of the ministry.

When Colton said that all baptized Christians were part of the ministry, he really meant it. By that, he claimed that when one examines who has been called to ministry, one finds the rolls of the ministry filled with a wide range of people including even those imperfect people known as sinners. As all laity lacked perfection, so the same held for clergy.

3. Sermon preached in October 1966 (otherwise undated), Good Samaritan Mission, San Francisco, California, for the introduction of the Reverend Arden Clute as Vicar.

Therefore, the Church could not be praised or blamed because of the actions of one individual. After all, everyone baptized in the Name of the Father and of the Son and of the Holy Spirit had a stake in what happened with and in the Church. And because God had claimed everyone in baptism, all were commissioned to a station of responsibility in the life and action of the gathered community.

How often have you heard someone say, "I came to church with all of my concerns, but Father X did not do a thing for me." The other evening at one social gathering I heard three people say words to this effect (and interestingly, not one of them was talking about the same Fr. X). The evening was capped off by a fellow who told me that he had joined the church because he was a successful business man and he had noted that the church needed to be run more like a business. So he had volunteered his ample talents (he did not mention his money) but he admitted to discouragement. Some of the brethren had not welcomed his talents.

Now, good Christian people, there is a heresy in this little cameo, and a massive misunderstanding as to what the Christian faith is all about.

The heresy is the case of bad, or ineffectual, or insensitive, or stupid, or irrelevant, or nasty old Fr. X–who does not do anything for us–Fr. X, whom we also compare to some idealized concept, a pastiche of remembered good things, whom we call good old Fr. Stoutheart–a fine, genial, spiritual man, who always had the right word, always remembered names, and always had a peppermint candy and a kind pat for the children, and *never* asked for or preached about money.

I will let you in on a secret. Every clergyman already knows full well that he is not Fr. Stoutheart, and hard as he may try, he realizes he will not become one. He spends considerable time on his knees well aware that he is merely brand X.

Fr. X's only solace is the love of God and some knowledge of Christian history–because you see, very early in the Church people became aware that all clergy were to some extent Fr. X's–as indeed were all the people in the pews. Mr. X's. ordination did not automatically make a man holy or charismatic. It gave him a commission on behalf of the rest of the body of Christ to go out and do a job. One of the truly holy acts he performs, the celebration of the Holy Eucharist, is, thank the Lord, made neither less nor more holy by the particular priest's worthiness or unworthiness. If our faith is right, God is uniquely with us in this act of the breaking of bread regardless of our merit–and it is this reassuring truth with which many a priest in his hours of discouragement and self awareness has literally clung to the horns of his altar.

You see, Fr. X is not the Church. We together are the Church–comforting, strengthening and sustaining each other, for better or for worse–sharing both joys and tears, as St. Paul says is the task of each Christian. In these very troubled and discordant times in the Church I think it is well to ask the critics of our poor old Fr. X's, "What have *you* done to minister to him in his time of need?" For I am convinced that without a rebirth of awareness on the part of our *laity* that this is *their* church, that they are not merely passive recipients, that our canon law gives them great responsibility, and that they must stand up and be counted on issues and then be willing to abide the consequences of an honestly arrived at decision—until that day comes we will flounder with clergy trying to fill the vacuum of leadership, who are then crucified for their attempt to do so. Clergy *must* lead in certain areas of the Church's life—this is one part of their marching orders. But without the active check and balance of an involved and informed laity, we will have lost our sense of what the Church in its fullness can become.[4]

In the final analysis, Colton saw the ministry as a wonderful menagerie of people exercising the prerogatives given them by virtue of their baptism. The strength of Colton's concept of the Church was seen in the many who gave their imperfect best to try and serve their Lord.

" . . . you are Peter, and on this rock I will build my Church . . . " [Matt. 16:18a, RSV].

The text clearly is a bestowal of the role of leader-

4. Sermon preached the Twenty-third Sunday after Trinity, November 9, 1969, the Cathedral Church of St. Mark, Salt Lake City, Utah.

ship upon Peter. "Rock" was used in the Old Testament as well to characterize a basic foundation.

"Behold, I am laying in Zion for a foundation a stone, a tested stone, a precious cornerstone, of a sure foundation" (Isa. 28:16 [RSV]), and "Hearken to me, you who pursue deliverance, you who seek the Lord; look to the rock from which you are hewn . . . " (Isa. 51:1 [RSV]).

In the secular world, the Episcopal Church has always exercised leadership far disproportionate to our members as shown by the numbers of them in Congress. We even have a priest in the U. S. Senate [Senator John Danforth, Missouri]. The Vice-President [then Vice-President George H. Bush] and the Secretary of Defense [Secretary Caspar Weinberger] are Episcopalians. But the Episcopal Church has never had *one* rock on which it stands or falls–Peter, Luther, Calvin, or Wesley–rather a wonderful succession of rocks strengthening through the generations.[5]

5. Sermon preached the Eleventh Sunday after Pentecost, August 23, 1987, the Cathedral Church of St. Mark, Salt Lake City, Utah.

1

This mighty act of God's coming into the world as the man, Jesus of Nazareth, not only gave meaning and healing to all men, but in some sense it was the focal point of* all *creation. . . . What an incredible assertion!–By this reasoning, the cross had an effect upon the entire cosmos. The effect of the cross did not depend upon whether, to use the wonderfully pictorial language of the Psalter, the floods did clap their hands or the hills did sing for joy together (Ps. 98:9), any more than the effect of the cross is dependent upon its* acceptance *by the world of men.

The Fourth Sunday after Trinity — *St. Francis' Church*
June 21, 1964 — *San Francisco, California*

"For we know that the whole creation groaneth and travaileth in pain until now" (Rom. 8:22 [KJV]).

Today in our Cathedral Church [Grace Cathedral, San Francisco], a number of men will be ordained to the sacred ministry, making their vows and receiving the laying on of hands from our chief pastor and pastor of pastors, the Bishop of this Diocese.[6]

6. When Colton wrote this sermon, women were not yet ordained

This is an exciting and climactic day for these men and it represents the culmination of years of wrestling with a critical decision and further years of training.

If you looked at this group of men yesterday in their civilian clothes, they would look the same as any other group–there is no fanatical gleam in the eye or charismatic glow that they exude. Nor is there necessarily any immediate and awesome sense of in-flowing power at the moment that the bishop lays his hand on your head. (In an ordination to the priesthood this is a different matter, because at that time all priests who are present join with the bishop in laying on hands and if you have ten or so men participating, the ordinand is made physically aware by reason of pressure alone that this is a weighty office indeed.)

But despite the absence of any inner subjective sign, this ordinand will never be the same again. He is ordained to the Sacred Ministry and will remain so the rest of his life–no matter what he does or what is done to him, he has been commissioned and set apart. He may later become a Zen Buddhist (as one Anglican priest has done), he may renounce the church completely; he may have serious

---

to either the diaconate or the priesthood. The first ordination of a woman to the diaconate took place later on in the year this sermon was given, 1964. The first ordination of a woman to the priesthood was in 1974.

moral or theological lapses which force the Church to seek his deposition, i.e., prohibiting him from exercising his office–but he is still a member of the Sacred Ministry. This concept is called that of the indelibility of Holy Orders. Once a man is ordained he remains ordained.

Much the same is true of Holy Baptism. The Church teaches that this act is done only once and for all. There is no way you can become *un*baptized. You may do serious harm to your baptismal vows. You may fall away completely from the Christian fold, but your baptized status in the eyes of the Church remains the same.

Now these are not just mystical assertions handed down from on high. They are conclusions which the historic church reached after wrestling with specific problems and attempting to square them with the basic conceptions of the Christian faith.

At the beginning of the fourth century the Church underwent a serious persecution by the Roman government. Government officials raided churches and demanded that the clergy hand over to them for destruction sacred vessels and books. Many clergy refused and were put to death or imprisoned as a result. Some clergy, through weakness, fear, or a hundred other reasons complied, and handed over what was demanded. Still others sought to trick the officials and handed over worthless things, telling the unknowing pagan officials that this was what they sought.

Fortunately for the Church this persecution did not last long, and in 311 A.D. an Edict of Toleration was promulgated. But the Church's problem had only begun. In adjusting itself to the period of peace, a number of Christians, especially a group in North Africa where the Church at that time was quite strong, refused to have anything to do with clergy who during the persecution had sold out to the government. Those were traitors or *traditors*, and it was argued that because of their weakness they had forfeited their orders.

The position of this group, called the Donatists, raised some very basic questions: Does the unworthiness of a minister affect the validity of his orders? If a sacrament is celebrated by a person of doubtful character, is its value therefore impaired or destroyed? How worthy do you have to be to be a Christian.

The Donatists considered themselves a gathering of the pure and undefiled. They did not wish to associate with those churchmen who in their eyes were backsliders and undesirable. (It is an ironic sidelight that it was later proved that many of the Donatists' bishops themselves had been *traditors* during the persecutions.)

The conclusion of the Church, after a series of investigations and councils, was clear and unequivocal. Ordination was valid even if the bishop who performed it was a traitor. A person retained holy orders and his celebrations were valid even if he had been a traitor or otherwise proven disloyal to his church.

And could the conclusion have been anything else? If we are honest, who ever is worthy? Who is there who has not sinned? An honest priest is the first to admit that he is completely unworthy to assume his office. It is not because of his superior worthiness that he alone is authorized by the Church to celebrate the Eucharist (there are many saints in any congregation far more worthy), but because the historic church has always held that one from its number shall be duly authorized to do this. Indeed, in reality, it is, of course, not the priest who consecrates the bread and wine at Holy Communion but Almighty God Himself, acting through this particular man. Holy Communion is a free gift from God, just as our Lord Himself was. We earned neither.

A man in holy orders has hands no less undefiled to receive the sacramental body of Our Lord than anyone else in the congregation who humbly and contritely approaches the Altar Rail. And it is for this reason, among others, that our Prayer Book specifically provides by its Rubric, which is part of our Canon Law, that the Host shall be received by each communicant into his hands.

This is not to say that any man in Holy Orders should not do everything in his power to lead a life which is a godly example for his flock. Woe to one who forgets this. But it is to stress again the objective nature of the Christian Faith as delivered to us from the truly Catholic tradition.

A man is set apart for the office of deacon, priest or bishop by certain outward and visible signs. He is not what the theological textbooks call a self-authenticated charismatic. A man does not enter the sacred ministry merely because he has a sudden urge to do so. He enters it only with the formal action and approval of the rest of the Christian community by forms and procedures handed down from earliest times.

This is but a long way of getting to a very basic point. Being a Christian is not only just the way you feel, and just the way you believe, but it is also the way you *do*—outwardly and visibly. One of the great heresies of our time is the belief that religion is a purely personal affair. This may be true of some religions (especially the religion of secular humanism), but it certainly is not true of Christians.

Christianity is incarnational and sacramental in its very base—because God indeed became a man and lived in a completely earthy sense, we know that things of this world have real significance. Thus the Christian is not only required to feel and to believe certain things, but to do certain things. He is required to worship God in His house every Sunday (a timely reminder as our pews begin to empty for the summer)—not to think pious thoughts in his hammock, but to be physically present with his body to join with his brethren in corporate praise. He is required to receive Holy Communion at least three times a year. He is required to give not only of his time and his prayers for the spread of the kingdom, but also of his hard-earned money. A faith which does not reach the most prized thing each of us has (our money) is obviously irrelevant to the most important things in our lives–in other words, it's a fringe benefit and not a very important one.

It is certainly true that the mere fact a man does certain outward acts is not necessarily proof that his inner motives are pure. One of the deepest sins of all is hypocrisy, and our Lord was the first to attack this with unusual bitterness. But let's be sure just who he is attacking. He was attacking those who were already doing the prescribed external things, but doing them for the wrong reasons. Thus He condemned those who tithed meticulously of even their household herbs, but who neglected justice and the love of God (Luke 11:42). This does not mean He condoned those who didn't tithe at all–He merely demanded that those who were already keeping the external law plumb even deeper into their basic motivation. The fact that religious hypocrisy existed did not justify one from withdrawing completely from corporate religious activities. It is no solace to the "God on the golf course" religion. It is a mandate perhaps to cleanse the temple, but not an excuse to withdraw from it.

Not only does the Christian Faith speak to our life of external attitude and conduct as human beings, but as St.

Paul sensed, there was something about this cross that affected not only our lives, but all of creation. This mighty act of God's coming into the world as the man, Jesus of Nazareth, not only gave meaning and healing to all men, but in some sense it was the focal point of *all* creation. St. Paul was a city boy, and was less impressed with the wonders of nature than one who was raised in the country. He used rural analogies sparingly and sometimes made mistakes that would make the farmer of his time hoot. But he sensed and saw that the plight of man, his sense of emptiness, frustration, and guilt and lack of wholeness, was not confined to mankind alone. There was an "out of jointedness" shared by all of creation, which groaned and travailed in pain.

"Until now"—"Until now," when through the life, death, and resurrection of this one man *all* things were given new meaning. Nature itself could be healed.

What an incredible assertion!—By this reasoning, the cross had an effect upon the entire cosmos. The effect of the cross did not depend upon whether, to use the wonderfully pictorial language of the Psalter, the floods did clap their hands or the hills did sing for joy together (Ps. 98:9), any more than the effect of the cross is dependent upon its *acceptance* by the world of men.

The cross stands as an objective fact—the fact of God's ultimate love for us despite our unworthiness. The cross remains as truth as to the ultimate meaning and purposes of life whether any particular minister abuses the sacred commission which has been given him or not. The cross remains whether each baptized person remains loyal to his church or not.

We cannot get rid of the cross any more than we can scrub off or eliminate the gift given us by our baptism, or the commission given to some in ordination.

It will not go away. It is there. The only variable is how *we respond* to this fact. And our mandate here is clear—knowing our unworthiness, we are asked to respond in thanksgiving, not only with our lips but with our *lives*. We are asked to accept the tangible and outwardly visible reality of our life as we lead it each day.

We appropriate this cosmic yet earthly truth into everyday actions of our own very earthy lives—so that, to use St. Paul's words, "creation itself will be set free from its bondage to decay and obtain the glorious liberty of the children of God" [Rom. 8:21, RSV].

2

In spite of its many defects, the parish church is still one of the few remaining places in an age of specialized interests where a group composed of CPA's, plumbers, and bird watchers can gather together. It is one of the few places left where disparate peoples can communicate.

Septuagesima Sunday
February 11, 1968

Church of the Redeemer
San Rafael, California

The Occasion being the Institution
of their Rector, The Reverend Angus Dun, Jr.

I love San Francisco, but one of the things I still miss there are the great summer thunderstorms of my mid-western youth. One can see the clouds build up, see the great cracks of lightning in them, and then hear the long roll of the thunder as the storm approaches. The wind builds up just before the storm hits, and for a short period you have wind, seemingly coming from every direction at once, lashing the trees and bushes into a frenzy, dust sailing in little eddies of air. Then comes the rain, settling the dust, clearing the air. And often within an hour or so the storm has passed over with a few drum rolls of thunder and dull red flashes in the distance. The sun comes out again, and if you are lucky you see a rainbow.

I sometimes think the Church today is in a period similar to that just before the storm hits–with short blasts of violent wind coming from every direction at once lashing those things it encounters into a frenzy.

It is a difficult enough task to describe the role of the church in such a period. It is even harder to describe the role of the priesthood and the parish ministry that will not be violently blown about by some wind–whether of erroneous and strange doctrine we cannot tell at the moment.

We can start with some obvious facts. The number of participating members in the fellowship of Christ's Church in this country is not only declining in a relative ratio to our population growth, but indeed in many cases is declining absolutely (and in the recent Gallop poll showing the first increase in years of a downward trend still does not apply in the same way to churches in our cities). The day when the minister was the parson–literally "the person" of a community, listened to with awe and respect, who wielded authoritarian power, is obviously long gone. The day when it was still at least the socially appropriate thing to do to go to church is ended. The faithful church attender is the exception in a community, and even he finds himself challenged in some of his deepest ideas and beliefs not only by his pagan neighbors but from the pulpit of his own church and his fellow parishioners.

A recent book quite critical of the institutional church was called *The Comfortable Pew.*[7] I have yet to find a comfortable pew, and it is quite certain that the present winds a-blowing are going to cause more squirming than ever in pews that never *were* designed to be comfortable. The word "pew" derives, after all, from the old French word for balcony or parapet, and many pew sitters today feel that they are hanging precariously on a parapet of a fortress which is under serious attack.

One of the most interesting attacks presently going is that against the church as an institutional structure. For some reason the very words "institution" or "structure" make some people froth at the mouth. "I don't need any organization to tell me about God." "I don't have to get together with any formal group of phonies to find meaning to my life." "I'm as good a Christian as anyone else, and I find God in my garden." "Rectors and vestries have sold their souls to preserve meaningless institutional structure."

Such assertions often start with "I" and usually revolve around "I" in their essential thought. Totally absent from such expressions is any idea of the value of *collective* wisdom. Several teenagers in our recently concluded Camp St. Francis expressed great anger that their parents gave

---

7. Pierre Berton, *The Comfortable Pew–A Critical Look at the Church in the New Age* (Toronto: McClelland and Stewart Limited, 1965).

no weight to their opinions, but on further questioning they conceded that they felt no obligation to listen to their parents either (or any other adult, for that matter) because they were all stupid. One fifteen-year-old boy told me that he felt he knew as much about the war in Vietnam as Secretary [Robert] McNamara [U.S. Secretary of Defense, 1961-68].

Collective wisdom is of course a very threatening thing. It carries with it the possibility of judgment against the individual. He could be judged wrong, and this is embarrassing. Such judgment sets limits, it defines our boundaries, it reveals our own inadequacies and limitations–and limitation and finitude are the hardest things in life to live with.

I am not suggesting that the majority in an organization is always right, but rather, that a group of responsible people who wrestle painfully and within the limits of their honesty to a conclusion are more likely to be right than a single individual, however brilliant. This I understand to be one of the basic arguments for a democratic form of government. Plato's idea of a philosopher king was a swell idea, but he ignored the problem of individual sin and our amazing capacities at self-seduction.

There have indeed been a few individual prophets who have properly rocked the collective wisdom. But for every such prophet who makes it, there are a thousand flashes in the pan who at the moment made a very bright light, who are later totally ignored and forgotten.

We hear many say within the church that the time has come to choose up sides. Each side has its own slogans: "Reform and relevance vs. WASPish reaction"; "prophecy vs. institutionalism"; "content vs. authority"; "All-American orthodoxy vs. pinko do-goodism"; "true Catholicism vs. heresy"—all of the slogans loaded, all suggesting that there is an easy choice available, and all resulting in division and polarization.

My problem is that outside of cowboy movies I have never yet met a "good guy" or a "bad guy," or for that matter I have seldom run into a complete black and white issue or decision. Yet I am also enough of a sinner to know that if I am *forced* into making a decision, I will then do everything I can to justify that decision, because I would hate to be wrong. I would think that at times like this we should tread warily through slogans and shibboleths—and of those winds which tend to divide and polarize us into positions we cannot get out of—we must learn to distinguish very carefully between criticism of one another which is legitimate and might be helpful and that kind of undermining of one another which reveals too often envy and malice.

The Christian faith sometimes confuses people by its apparent contradiction. For example, it affirms the total and ultimate value of each individual life, and this value as an individual does not remain merely through this veil of tears we call life, but through eternity. In this sense Christianity is an extremely individualistic world view. Yet the Christian also says that Christians are bound together, part one of the other–one body, linked mystically to Jesus Christ. I am your brother–more than brother. I am part of you and you of me. We are a holy friendship, you and me. What I say and do affects you, and you affect me. We are born together of a common baptism, and we are fed together of the same bread, we confess together the same Lord.

There are no outward signs which show this bond. You can take a picture of any group and there's nothing external that will tell you who the practicing Christians are–no halos, no pious looks–on the outside they look, all of them, Christians and non-Christians, as they are in one sense–all God's creatures, each different, each the same in God's love.

This is true of all Christians, layman or priest or bishop. This diocese has an annual clergy conference. All of the bishops and priests make it a point to attend in the *least* clerical looking outfits possible. I've often looked at this group in their wild sport shirts and without benefit of clerical collar, and wondered if I took a photograph, what other people might guess this group was. Was it a gathering of CPA's, plumbers, or bird watchers? Looking at the incredible variety of sorts and conditions of men present, I just don't think you could guess.

Until this crazy assortment of men walks into a chapel together, then you get in a deafening way the thrilling sense of a corporate response of praise to God who has called them to this particular form of ministry in their Lord's church. It is the corporate response which brings the Christian out of the photograph. It is surely the corporate response of which the priest is both leader and symbol—to make the people of God under his care and cure aware of their common bond and responsibility for each other.

In an age of increasing specialization the parish priest is probably one of the last of the general practitioners. His duties run the gamut of human existence. In spite of its many defects, the parish church is still one of the few remaining places in an age of specialized interests where a group composed of CPA's, plumbers, and bird watchers can gather together. It is one of the few places left where disparate peoples can communicate. It is the task of the parish priest to assist in this process of communication—to assist this mixed bag of people in realizing the unity which flows from the common cup and common bread; to give them a sense of "holy fellowship."

Your vicar now to be installed is an exceptional man in many ways, not least of all in that he is a fish (if he will excuse the analogy) swimming against the current. At a time when men are leaving the parish ministry in ever increasing numbers for either secular or non-parochial work, he is a priest who leaves a church institution for parish work. He is a man with great gifts of warmth and compassion, possibly because he knows what anguish and personal suffering are.

I trust that you will take him and his family to your heart and not for granted. As he will support and lead you, I am sure that you will be supportive of him. At a time when the parish ministry is under increasing pressure, the supporting pat on the back is more needed than ever.

In a divided, frightened world, our common obligation to reconcile and unify assumes a terrifying importance. Recall the words of the psalmist, "Behold, how good and joyful a thing it is, for brethren to dwell together in unity!" [Ps. 133:1, based on Coverdale Translation in *The Book of Common Prayer* (New York: The Church Pension Fund, 1928), p. 509]

3

The Church is one of those few places left where the big, ultimate questions are still asked, and where the answers and experiences of millions of people over thousands of years are available for those who seek them.

The Tenth Sunday after Trinity — *St. Francis' Church*
August 18, 1968 — *San Francisco, California*

The Articles of Religion define the visible church as a congregation in which the word of God is preached and the sacraments are duly administered.[8] Three elements—the gathered community, the preached word and the sacraments.

Of these three, surely the concept of preaching is the one which is held in the least regard by even the faithful today and with the exception of a few sensationalists, such as Bishop Pike [the late Bishop of the Diocese of California], preaching is truly a voice in the wilderness to the unchurched. (Indeed while Bishop Pike can indeed "pack

8. Article XIX, *The Book of Common Prayer* (1928), p. 606, and *The Book of Common Prayer* (1979), p. 871.

'em in" on a one-shot basis, I doubt if very few in his audiences would undertake the discipline of listening to him *every* Sunday.)

Part of the problem is of course the quality of the preaching itself–superficial, inadequately prepared and poorly delivered sermons are unfortunately far too prevalent in all churches.

But without discounting this, I would suggest that the deeper problem today is with those who listen. For a number of reasons we are no longer a culture that wishes to listen. In fact there is a certain resentment of anyone who tries to tell us anything from a position of authority.

Learned and superficial journals alike actively attack the idea that content should be transferred as content from one person to another. It is ridiculous, they suggest, to see learning as the transference of one bag of faults and information from the brain of one person to that of another. And we see a tremendous interest today in small group therapy and non-verbal communication.

Now I am the last one to knock the power of non-verbal communication. Indeed that is one of the reasons I am a high-churchman; because I am sure that the use of music, color and even the sense of smell can evoke a sense of God's presence and majesty far more effectively and permanently than an eternity of sermons.

But what I am deeply concerned about is that non-verbal communication is seen as an adequate substitute for the other. If I take six people and put them in a small group and tell them to discuss a certain problem–and if not one of them knows the slightest thing about that problem–then that problem just isn't going to get solved. The group may have had a wonderful time together, feeling each other, rolling around–they may have all sorts of profound changes in their personal relationships–but as to the specific problem before them it is I think still true that 0 + 0 + 0 can go on forever and still equal only 0.

Every person who has ever lived has certain basic and common problems. We come into this world through no choice of our own and we start out on a journey which we know will terminate with our death. No one of us takes exactly the same journey or follows the same route but we can learn from others that much of the scenery is remarkably the same and we can learn, if we wish, from others who have made the trip before us, how to avoid certain problems or at least to be prepared for them. And each of us at one time or another, in some way or other, must surely ask himself the deep and ultimate question, "What is this journey all about and is there any purpose, significance and meaning to it beyond merely the taking of the journey itself?"

The Church is one of those few places left where the big, ultimate questions are still asked, and where the answers and experiences of millions of people over thousands of years are available for those who seek them.

3. THE TENTH SUNDAY AFTER TRINITY, 1968.

The corpus or body of knowledge and experience, which gives meaning and direction to all others on the "journey" is known to Christians as the gospel of Jesus Christ. It is the assertion that there is meaning, not blackness and void beyond the end of the journey and that meaning beyond the journey speaks to and gives value to the actual journey itself.

But this meaning and value is not self-taught or self-discovered. It is transmitted from one person to the other, recounting the experience of God's action upon the world of others on their journey and the response of other men to God's mighty acts. The gospel, in other words, is at its base rooted in history (this is what distinguishes the Christian faith from simple philosophy) and can only be understood if one is willing to learn from something outside himself.

Surely part of the Church's problem today is that even so many practicing Christians are religious illiterates. They don't know what their faith is about, and of course one can't proclaim something he himself doesn't understand. We can do something about this if we wish, although first we have to recognize that it is a problem. Some obviously don't. Thus a man told a neighboring priest the other day that he would have to withdraw from parish activities because he had become a Mason, and as he said, "You know *that* requires a lot of study." It is little wonder that the world pays us so little heed. A housewife buys a new appliance, or a man a new car and reads the service manual from cover to cover so that he can get the most out of his new acquisition and yet some of the same spend less time on reading, thinking and learning about what they at least profess with their lips to be the meaning of life.

But there is the bigger problem for the Church today. There is not only the Church's own religious illiteracy, but this exists in a world which seems not interested in listening–where particularly so many young people now believe that value is self-authenticated without the need to listen or learn from anyone else.

Their plight can be described in parable form. There were once three blind men who set out on a dangerous journey that they had never made before. They came from a country where all people were blind and thus did not know of people who could see. On their way they met a physician who observed their condition and said to them, "See here, it is ridiculous for you three to be on such a dangerous journey in your condition, when by a simple operation I can make you see." "Will this operation be painful?" asked one of the blind men. "Of course," said the physician, "but all things worthwhile involve some pain." "I will not suffer pain," was the reply. The second blind man asked, "Will it take a long time, this operation?" "That depends upon what you think a 'long time' to be. There will be a period of recuperation and you would have to wait and interrupt your journey for that. But anything worthwhile takes a 'long time'!" "No, no, out of the question," the second man said, "We must hurry–we're late now." The third blind man said, "That's right. After all, what's wrong with being blind?" "I agree, there is nothing 'wrong' with it," the physician replied, "but it is so tragic when unnecessary. However, I see I cannot explain the miracle of sight to you when you have never experienced it or care to listen to what it is." His voice trailed off because the three blind men were already rushing and stumbling on down the road. Later they met a wise old man who said, "Let me help you." They felt his beard and said, "But you are an old man and we are young. How can you help us?" "Because I have made the trip you are making many times myself and I have maps made by others who have also made it, and I could interpret the maps for you." "No, no, we don't need you." "But then," the old man said, "if you are blind and have never made this journey before and won't let anyone else help you, how in the world are you going to find your destination"? "That's easy," the first blind man said triumphantly. "The three of us will take a vote."

And I guess all the wise man and the physician can do is keep themselves in readiness and good condition for the moment when the cry for help comes–to cure and guide a blind world which can never cure and guide itself–to be prepared when the world is once again prepared to listen.

But we who are here now–are we prepared to be quiet and to listen?

This sermon was also preached:

September 1974 (otherwise undated) *St. Stephen's Church West Valley City, Utah,* and *The Tenth Sunday after Pentecost July 27, 1975 The Cathedral Church of St. Mark Salt Lake City, Utah.*

4

He glanced at the crucifer, Zack Bronson, who, resplendent in his unwrinkled white alb, was at one and the same time yawning, looking at his watch, and scratching his buttocks. Zack, who had not the foggiest idea of what was to happen, was the boy who had come to Iscariot yesterday to tell him that he wished to be a priest, after he finished Yale. Dear old Zack, whose I.Q. would only crack 100 on some beneficent day when the computers were nodding.

1968	*The Cathedral Church of St. Mark*
(otherwise undated)	*Salt Lake City, Utah*

In a whole world of discussion about the intolerance of priests, I am always amazed that no one ever asks the priest details about his actual priesthood. I am not talking now about his private devotions or his political or sexual life and desires, his personality, his ability to relate to his people (or any people), his failings and his ambitions, his knowledge, his stereotypes—I am talking about the guts of his priesthood. Something he does that is truly different.

No one, even in this age, seems to have the interest to inquire why it is that thousands of men, each day of the year, walk into a small room, put on some strange clothing, walk to an altar, intone some words over some bread and wine, eat some of this themselves and then distribute the rest to a few people who are gathered around them, and then see each person present leave to go about their business. And yet few priests see this as anything but the most significant and unique thing they can do.

Why in the world does a priest do this? What does he really think while he is doing this? For what possible purpose is it done? It is here that Christians start, and unless we can communicate why it is that Christians start here, we are in deep trouble.

Of course, this is asking a man why he loves his wife. If he in fact does, the words that come out in response to such a question are hopelessly shallow and inadequate. They never, in the poor loving husband's pathetic way, do justice to a devotion and a concern, a life shared, a sorrow and a joy mingled together and a knowledge of a common devotion.

But perhaps one of the things a priest must do today is to try to explain this whole thing.

The world seems to understand when we hear a great musician or actor or painter or dancer or sculptor explain, in understandably inadequate ways, the motives, means and emotions whereby he seeks to express himself. But for some reason, the Christian priest, who indeed uses all of these art forms, is never consulted or listened to, in his search to express himself, for purposes which, if he is right, are far grander.

* * *

John Iscariot stood before his altar. He had not looked at the congregation and thus did not know how many of his flock were there. It did not matter. For this moment, dressed in vestments made with the hands of many faithful ladies of his altar guild, he prepared to start the service.

Around him and upon him were things given by other people. Given for mixed motives, with relative degrees of abstract taste and beauty, to be sure, because the sanctuary and choir of the typical parish church was a thing of many persons.

He prepared to read words, written by others long dead. Tested and tried in time through thousands of years, polished into many languages, in this case English, they had a cadence and a ring and a meaning, the hearing which he never tired of or found boring.

Yet he cast his eyes to his right and saw Sam Boanerges, one of his acolytes. He wondered why Sam was really there beside him. Did Sam ever begin to realize what they were going to do together? Oh not in a mystical, other-worldly sense in which most explanations are made (although they are also true), but does he, Sam Boanerges, see this as a thing of great beauty for now–for this moment, with value in itself? And in the wonder of it, which he doubts Sam senses anyway, does he also see the need for excellence? Does Sam realize what any artist who has done the same thing hundreds of times still realizes—that each time is different, that each offering is unique, and that while those who merely observe may never distinguish, you who do participate do know—has Sammy ever felt the sawdust taste that comes with the knowledge of rote and routine performance?

Oh Sammy, with your socially aggressive mother and poor hen-pecked father, pushed beyond your capacities in the world outside, yet here this morning of your own will—do you, Sam, know what we are about to do?

Iscariot was aware of Peter Granite on his left. A handsome boy, black as the ace of spades, quiet, incredibly attuned to liturgical choreography, always gracefully present at the right time, mercifully never under foot at the wrong ones. The only child of a widowed mother—the understandable apple of her eye—one of the few negro families in this white congregation—oh, how Iscariot hoped that Peter understood!

He glanced at the crucifer, Zack Bronson, who, resplendent in his unwrinkled white alb, was at one and the same time yawning, looking at his watch, and scratching his buttocks. Zack, who had not the foggiest idea of what was to happen, was the boy who had come to Iscariot yesterday to tell him that he wished to be a priest, after he finished Yale. Dear old Zack, whose I.Q. would only crack

100 on some beneficent day when the computers were nodding.

Iscariot did not have to look at, in order to be aware of, his two supporting priests, now at their places in the sedilia. This was their third service together of the day. Each of them had a chance to celebrate. Now it was his privilege to fill that role. He knew that they would be bored with the sermon the third time—who wouldn't? But he did not have even the slightest doubt as to why they were here—he and they at least shared this understanding. He knew that they were with him in the search for beauty and meaning even in doing precisely the same thing three times in four hours.

Iscariot loved them, and he felt they loved him, although there certainly couldn't have been three more different men on the face of the earth.

And as thoughts can come and go in far shorter time than it later takes to express them, he marvelled at the fact that in all of the turmoil of the modern church, he had never heard of a priest using this service which he was now beginning as a method of personal protest. Many a priest had lost the faith, many had left in anger, but in a time when almost every symbolic gesture had been made in protest of something, no one had used this moment to throw the chalice or hurl the bread—nor had he heard of this ever happening, ever.

And so as the opening hymn concluded, he cleared his

throat, made the sign of the cross, and began saying aloud the words of a prayer undiminished in their grandeur by at least twelve centuries of use.

And as he raised his hands to the *orant* position of priests in supplication used long before the earthly birth of his Lord, he unconsciously sought to gather toward the altar with him Sam, and Peter, and Zack, his priestly brethren, the people in the pews, and indeed all of the company of heaven in this, another imperfect attempt of a creature giving thanks to his Creator—made glorious and whole by the sure and certain faith that the Creator asks only this, and in our doing of this is already here with us.

VIII
Witness

Introduction

Albert Colton had a strong sense of witness. While he intensely "felt" Christ in his life, he rarely attested to that. He had a great fear of confusing the attributes of the self with the attributes of Christ. He was not an "I've found it!" type of person. In fact, he was suspicious of such preachers. There seemed to be too much emphasis on the "I've" for his comfort. Colton was more of a "Look at what and who I've found!" individual. That "something and someone wonderful" delighted him and moved him to witness.

This focus on someone other than himself was not due to an overly developed sense of modesty. Colton was very aware of himself and very happy with whom he saw in this creation of God's. But he ultimately and significantly knew that the redemption of himself was due to the one whom he had found and therefore he elected to gaze intently on that one, the Christ.

It is as though you and a companion were standing on a bluff overlooking a pounding surf and observing a magnificent sunset, and your senses savor the sound and smell and the gorgeous coloring, and then you are reminded with a jolt that your companion is blind. While he may be moved by the sound and smell, he cannot fully partake of the experience in the same sense that you can. The great gift to the Christian is that he can live life fully. He has been given an added dimension to his world of experience.[1]

Again, Colton tried to focus on God rather than on our ability to become accomplished at spirituality.

What a wonderful thing! What an astounding thing! Is it any wonder that people find it hard to believe? Or is it any wonder that those who have chosen to believe can both fall down on their knees in wonder and rise to their feet in joy, at the knowledge that God has sought us out, and shown us Himself in terms which we can at least partially understand.[2]

Colton showed a frustrated side in his faculty of observation when he noticed most painfully that many of his friends were part of the masses which did not consider nor appreciate the revolutionary side of Christianity. For them, it was not the radical and pivotal fulcrum of their lives. In fact, the impact of the faith on their lives was minimal.

So I am left with the First Epistle of Peter [1 Pet. 4:12, 19], wherein he speaks of persecution and a fiery ordeal for a Christian to witness to his faith. Persecution is a common religious theme. Remember Daniel

1. Sermon preached on Christmas Day, December 25, 1963, Grace Cathedral, San Francisco, California. It was preached again in 1974, St. Stephen's Church, West Valley City, Utah, and in 1975 and 1978, the Cathedral Church of St. Mark, Salt Lake City, Utah.

2. Ibid.

in the lion's den; Shadrach, Meshach and Abednego in the fiery furnace. In Rome, the Christian martyrs were torn to shreds by wild animals to the delight of the crowds and the Emperor. Today, Idi Amin, massacring in cold blood an Anglican bishop. There were Bonhoeffer and the Christian martyrs of Adolph Hitler. But in much of Western civilization since the 4th century, it may be said that something terrible has happened. Christians became respectable.

I remember the hiring partner of a law firm I applied to asking me what religion I belonged to (no longer a proper legal question). Thinking he thought I was Jewish, I replied, "I'm an Episcopalian." "*Good,*" he said, "that's a gentleman's religion."

We face something far more demonic than a coliseum full of lions. We mainline Christians face a *cultural condescension, indifference, smooth orthodoxy, superficial piety, and lip service.*

We see smooth orthodoxy all around us. Our president's [President Reagan] frequent references to the deity are unblemished by an attendance at a service of worship (except where required by state occasions).[3]

Perhaps a most significant reason why so many in the world take Christian disciplines either superficially or not at all is due

3. Sermon preached the Seventh Sunday of Easter, May 18, 1980, the Cathedral Church of St. Mark, Salt Lake City, Utah.

largely to the lack of quality and intensity in our witness, observed Colton.

The other day I was visiting a woman in the hospital who was painfully ill. I asked if I could bring her Holy Communion on Palm Sunday. She looked over, embarrassed, at the woman in the other bed, and said, "No thanks. I think that would make me a bit too conspicuous." It was too late and inappropriate then for me to deliver a little sermon on the problem. I could only regret that we the church in this case had not taught well enough. And this is even more tragic because this woman has participated hundreds of times in a service in which she has formally acknowledged that it is this sacrament which feeds and sustains us to get through life–by which our deepest selves are fed, and by which we are assured that by this means that we are very members incorporate in the mystical body of Christ.[4]

I guess what I am suggesting is this: You are commanded, if you bother to come here [to church] at all, to manifest the light of Jesus Christ in your life (however uncomfortable that may make you). To make manifest this Epiphany you ought to know what you are talking about (and if you really don't, find out). We will never *force* anyone to believe anything. God willed us to be free, and to respond to Him only in freedom.

4. Sermon preached on Maundy Thursday, March 26, 1964, St. Alban's Church, Albany, California.

We must remember that Christianity is by its very nature a *proselyting* religion. It is meant to show forth its light to the rest of the world, and it proclaims that it has something *unique* to say about the nature of God and His relationship to man.[5]

Colton believed a second consideration as to why witnessing was so difficult or unfruitful could be seen in the "cult of open-mindedness" which was really not open-minded at all.

It is an ironic thing when the day comes that a proclamation which terms itself the Good News, heralding the arrival of the Prince of Peace, to bind up and heal the wounds of life and to wipe away its tears–it is an ironic time indeed when such a message is viewed with disinterest, distrust or hostility.

All of this [in this case, not exposing children to Christianity] is usually done under the guise of so-called "open-mindedness." "I believe in letting my child make up his own mind, and I don't want to prejudice him." There is, of course, an obvious fallacy in the cult of open-mindedness, because to decide not to choose is nevertheless to choose. A traveller comes to a fork in the road, and unable to decide which way to go sits down at the crossroads and spends the rest of his life there, only deluding

5. Sermon preached the First Sunday after the Epiphany, January 13, 1980, St. Paul's Church, Salt Lake City, Utah.

himself that in so doing he hasn't committed himself to a decision.

Man, by the nature of his existence cannot avoid making choices. This does not mean that choices are easy. People will use a great deal of mental and nervous energy in avoiding a decision. . . . Yet the irony is that the so-called open-minded are often those minds through which every conceivable breeze can blow without hindrance. In a world of empty values, new and improved demons can move in and out at will. If a man refuses to take responsibility for his own decisions, then he is a patsy to be manipulated into making decisions with which he still must live and which mold his life.

We should start addressing ourselves to the world where it is right now—to help these people realize that belonging to the "non-church of the open mind" is really only a delusion. Such vacuums will be filled and therefore the question is really what is the nature of what it is filled with.

We owe it to our world to make clear to them the choice that is set before it.[6]

Colton lamented the fact that witnessing to Christ often suffered because individuals within the Body of Christ were fighting with one another about comparatively insignificant

---

6. Sermon preached the Third Sunday in Lent, February 26, 1967, St. Francis' Church, San Francisco, California.

issues. While those issues were weighty to the life of the Church (the revision of The Book of Common Prayer, *women's ordination, the ordination of homosexuals, etc.), they were not, in his eyes, as significant as what he saw as the "basic Christian proclamation." Had equal energy been spent on the proclamation centering around the liberating nature of Christ, resolution of the other issues naturally would have followed. The Christian manifesto made it possible to deliberate on the salient issues found in the Church. However, Colton believed such discussion, argument and final deliberation of issues within the church should never cause one to leave the fold or at least leave it alone.*

> If we want to get bothered and upset, let's not do it over the little things–let's get bothered and upset about the *big* things. Here's something that can really get someone upset and bothered–the basic Christian proclamation. The Christian faith as universally proclaimed, whether by Billy Graham, Pope Paul, the Archbishop of Canterbury, or the Vicar of Fleabite, Utah, states:
>
> God exists.
>
> That God is love.
>
> That love is the most powerful force in the world.
>
> That our life has eternal meaning.
>
> That this God of love loves and accepts each one of us where we are.
>
> All of this is not just pious conjecture, but has been proven and shown by the entry of God into space and

time, where he suffered, died, and then conquered death for all of us.

All of this is free. . . . Let's not waste our time and that of others on whether we can or cannot accept trivial little aspects of the church, or of any other church. Think for a minute during the rest of this service whether you can really accept the *big* assumption. If the Christian faith is correct, we are free to accept or reject this. Most simply put, can you make this statement:

> I accept a Lord of Lords and King of Kings
> Who accepts me where I am
> and I accept this acceptance.[7]

Finally, Colton believed we ought to jettison any tendencies to be aloof when we witness. Our mannerisms should well serve the message.

Stiff-upper-lip-Anglicanism has its drawbacks. There's nothing wrong with "enthusiasm." Christianity ought to be the most exciting thing since the prettiest girl in your class said, "I love you."[8]

---

7. See Paul Tillich, *The Shaking of the Foundations* (New York: Charles Scribner's Sons, 1948), pp. 153-63. Sermon preached the Sixteenth Sunday after Pentecost, September 18, 1977, the Cathedral Church of St. Mark, Salt Lake City, Utah.

8. Sermon preached the Fourth Sunday after Epiphany, February 3, 1980, the Cathedral Church of St. Mark, Salt Lake City, Utah.

1

Our job, each of us, is to bear our witness in those parts of the world our lives take us and if our witness is at all honest, it will mean that we will bear a cross. And this can be lonely business, because we should always remember that it was the same crowd who shouted "Hosannah" on Palm Sunday who cried "crucify Him" a short time later.

Palm Sunday
April 11, 1965

St. Francis' Church
San Francisco, California

This is a day of dramatic liturgical contrast. We start with all of the pomp and circumstance of a solemn, triumphant procession and we sing "All glory, laud and honor to thee, Redeemer King!"[9] This is indeed a festal occasion in which we commemorate our Lord's triumphal entry into Jerusalem. But then the Eucharist itself commences, and the purple vestments remind us that this triumphal ride was not to earthly glory, but to a lonely and hideous death. The gospel recounts the passion of our Lord as told by St.

9. Hymn 62, St. Theodulph, tr. John Mason Neale, *The Hymnal 1940* (New York: The Church Pension Fund, 1961).

Matthew. And we sing, “Ride on, ride on in majesty,”[10] to a mournful tune which points to the bitter irony of the palm procession—the words of the hymn express this well—“Ride on, ride on in majesty! In lowly pomp ride on to die.”[11] And we realize that this day marks the beginning of Holy Week, The Way to the Cross.

I was asked last week whether we were not laying too much stress on the cross. After all, I was asked, was not the real basis of the Christian faith the resurrection? And of course it is true that the focal point of the Christian calendar is Easter Day, not Good Friday.

But let us also remember something very basic to the Christian faith, and to life generally, “Without the cross, there can be no resurrection.” There is no resurrection without the crucifixion. There is no Easter without Good Friday.

This is a hard saying. We instinctively wish it were not so. Even Christians find it hard to take, especially in this country. Thus, we find many more empty crosses than we do crucifixes, and the theological rationalization for this is that the crucifix (that is, the cross on which the body of our Lord hangs) is only half the story—the *Good* news is that the

---

10. Hymn 64, Graham George (copyright 1941, the H. W. Gray Co.), *The Hymnal 1940*.

11. Hymn 64, v. 2, *The Hymnal 1940*.

cross is now empty, and the empty cross portrays the Risen Christ. Perhaps so. But why then are so many uncomfortable at the sight of the crucifix?

Why is it that we cling so to the doctrines of immortality of the soul, and avoid the use of the word "death" and use euphemistic substitutes like "passed on" and "passed away"?

We resist the idea that this life is all there is, and we seek solace in the idea of some vague sort of immortality which happens willy-nilly, just in the nature of things. If the human soul is immortal, then this means that no matter what happens, death is merely waking up the next morning in a different room. It is a comforting ideal. It removes any sense of personal accountability on my part and it avoids the cross. If we're all immortal anyway, why worry about that corpse on the cross? As the barroom or drug store philosopher says cheerily, "It really doesn't matter what religion you've got. After all, we're all going to the same place anyway."

It is a comforting idea. No muss, no fuss, no messy cross to scare and bother us. But what if it isn't so? What if when you die you are dead? What if this is the end–the end of existence for this person? This is surely just as plausible, and many claim that they can make their peace with this just as easily as any other view. Bertrand Russell says in the book *Why I Am Not a Christian*, "I believe that when I die I shall rot, and nothing of my ego will survive.

I am not young, and I love life. But I should scorn to shiver with terror at the thought of annihilation. Happiness is none the less true happiness because it must come to an end, nor do thought and love lose their value because they are not everlasting."[12] Many others profess to find comfort in the fact that what they have done in their life will in its small way affect lives still to come, although this view is usually restricted to the *good* we have done. It is a little less comfortable to contemplate the evil we have done which will also continue on.

Thus, the doctrine of immortality of the soul avoids the cross. The doctrine of death, as the end of individual meaning, could retain the cross, but stops there–the end of life is at Good Friday, not Easter.

But what if there were a third alternative? What if death really were death, the end. But what also if a *new* life were given us as a *gift*, not because we deserved it, or because it was the nature of things, but because He who created us wished us to have this if we wanted it. And this new life had very little to do with the present physical shell we inhabit and through which we express our individuality. This new life I can have now as an individual, and this new life I will retain as an individual even after the time that this won-

---

12. Bertrand Russell, *Why I Am Not a Christian and Other Essays on Religion and Related Subjects,* ed. Paul Edwards (London: George Allen and Unwin, Ltd., 1957), p. 43.

drous machine I inhabit and call a body is worn out and moldering in the grave.

This is the Christian option. It offers a life of meaning and relationship in *this* life (indeed it affirms the sanctity and meaning of *this* life) as well as the gift of individual meaning and relationship beyond this life.

But this is not just built into the system. It is a *gift* God offers, a gift of meaning purchased by the cross. This is the one cross of Calvary which was the price paid sufficiently once and for all. This is where the critical battle was fought, and Easter shows us that victory is assured. But, as in any war, the crucial victory seldom means the end of hostilities. There is mopping up to be done, and we are each handed our own small crosses to complete this job.

It would be nice if Easter did not require Good Friday. It would be nice if His Good Friday eliminated the need for mine and yours. But God has not chosen to work this way. You and I are co-ministers with Him in the process of the healing of man.

I remember, as a child, receiving a large shipment from my grandmother, of my father's boyhood books written at the turn of the century. There were great stories, and the theme of most of them, Horatio Alger to Tom Swift, was about the same. The hero was brave, industrious, kind and courteous, and after a number of mishaps, he rose to a position of great prominence and success. The formula of life seemed simple enough–work hard, be brave, kind and courteous, and success will be yours. I could never understand why the "bad guys" in these novels didn't understand this. Why didn't everyone act like this?

And then, as I grew older, I began to see men who had worked hard, and were brave, kind and courteous, who were *not* in positions of great prominence and success. And I also met men who were in positions of great prominence and success who were *not* industrious, brave, kind and courteous. Most men I met were mixed bags of all these qualities. And I learned that it was *hard* to be brave, because this often meant that you must suffer, and it was not any fun to suffer.

Shelly Berman has a routine about a trip to the dentist. He wonders why it is that dentists ask you if you want novocaine. As he said, "Of course I want novocaine. In fact, I want novocaine so I won't feel him giving me the novocaine."

No one likes pain. If they do, the psychiatrists have a word for them. And very often to be brave, to do what you feel is right, involves pain. Nor is it true that despite the suffering, eventually the world will recognize and applaud your bravery and you will emerge a hero in a position of great prominence and success. Any politician or professional athlete knows this—hero today, heel tomorrow. They are hissed and booed by the same crowd that only days before was pushing and shoving for their autograph, or strewing palm branches in their way. "In lowly pomp ride on to die." Anyone who plays the game only for the roar of the crowd cannot be a brave man but rather a phoney and often a heart-broken man.

It takes courage to witness to what is right, or to use the words from our baptismal service, "... not be ashamed to confess the faith of Christ crucified."[13] Profiles in courage need not be restricted to those men who bravely decided great matters of state. It often requires a great deal more courage to witness to Christ crucified in the niggling little petty details of everyday life because here we do not even have the comfort to know that history is looking over our shoulder and that it might at some future day vindicate us. For most of us, in most of our decisions, history books could not care less.

But the principle is the same in either case. Our job, each of us, is to bear our witness in those parts of the world our lives take us and if our witness is at all honest, it will mean that we will bear a cross. And this can be lonely business, because we should always remember that it was the same crowd who shouted "Hosannah" on Palm Sunday who cried "crucify Him" a short time later.

And if on occasion we have not regretted the fact that we are Christians because of the demands this makes on

---

13. *The Book of Common Prayer* (New York: The Church Pension Fund, 1928), p. 280.

us–whether it be to witness to Proposition 14 or racial justice generally, whether it means ordering fish when others have steak or climbing out of bed a bit bleary eyed to get to church when you know that others at the same party are still in bed, or whether it means giving sacrificially of your money to your church when you know others who obviously don't–if on occasion we have not regretted these things, then we ought to wonder whether we really are carrying our crosses as we should.

St. Paul, as usual, sums up the problem well, and he says it in terms of the cross:

> For the word of the cross is folly to those who are perishing, but to us who are being saved it is the power of God. . . . For Jews demand signs and Greeks seek wisdom, but we preach Christ crucified, a stumbling block to Jews and folly to the Gentiles, but to those who are called, both Jews and Greeks, Christ is the power of God and the wisdom of God (1 Cor. 1:18-24 [RSV]).

2

I do know this: if I have the worst looking lawn on the block, my neighbors aren't going to spend much time listening to me preach on how to be a better gardener.

The Seventh Sunday after Pentecost *St. Mary's Church*
July 22, 1979 *Provo, Utah*

From my recent reading, I have run across two quite different religious points of view:

The first was a quotation in a recent *Wall Street Journal* involving Dr. George Crane, the father of Republican presidential candidate Phillip Crane. It said:

> "Jesus," observes George Crane approvingly, "gave only one church picnic."
>
> Jesus wasn't a liberal-leaning, welfare state "mollycoddler," Dr. Crane explains. Jesus could have performed his loaves-and-fishes miracle many times, yet he performed it only once. He could have set up soup kitchens, a welfare program. "Yet he let thousands starve within the sound of his voice." Jesus helped those who helped themselves.
>
> "And Jesus didn't make house calls," the doctor continues, warming to his theme. "He didn't heal people unless they had the ambition, the faith, to come

to him. In the final analysis, he separated the sheep from the goats."[14]

The other is from William Manchester's book on the life of Douglas MacArthur. He quotes MacArthur as saying vaguely that "although I was brought up as a Christian and adhere entirely to its teachings, I have always had a sincere admiration for many of the basic principles underlying the Oriental faiths. Christianity does not differ from them as much as one would think. There is little conflict between the two, and each might well be strengthened by a better understanding of the other."[15]

Both of these quotations, I submit, show a remarkable lack of knowledge of the basic fundamentals of the Christian faith.

To summarize Dr. Crane, "In Christ, there is no free lunch."[16] This statement is totally contrary to the basic concept which marks Christianity "the gospel," or the

---

14. Dennis Farney, "To Know Phil Crane, You've Got to Know His Father, George," *The Wall Street Journal*, 13 July, 1979, p. 1, col. 4.

15. William Manchester, *American Caesar* (Boston: Little, Brown and Co., 1978), p. 512.

16. As has been noted previously, Colton has in mind, "There ain't no such thing as a free lunch," popularized by Robert Heinlein's novel, *The Moon Is a Harsh Mistress* (New York: George Putnam's Sons, 1966), a discussion of which is found in Edwin G. Dolan's *TANSTAAFL* (New York: Holt, Rinehart and Winston, Inc., 1971), chap. 1, esp. p. 14.

"good news." The basic message is that there *is* a free lunch. God so loved that he *gave*. He meets us where we are, *not* because we are deserving, to the contrary, he comes to us knowing that we are *not* deserving.

This is illustrated so well by the great parable of the Prodigal Son. Yet, when he was still a far way off, the forgiving father ran to embrace and accept his no-good son. The parable is not popular with some, who tend to agree with the hard-working brother who had stayed home and caused no trouble, "It's not fair."

The same issue is illustrated in the parable of the workers in the vineyard–the last hired got the same pay as those who had worked hard all day. "It's not fair."

Of course, it all depends on how you look at it. If we are the good son, or the worker that has labored all day, it *isn't* fair, but if we are the prodigal son, or the last hired, while it still might not be fair, it certainly is good news.

Each of us has to examine our hole card on this. We should remember that Christianity is not an absolute sanctuary for saints, it is a hospital for sinners.

I personally have no doubt where I fall. I'm a Christian because I am a selfish sinner who needs help. Dr. Crane, on the other hand, implicitly sees himself as a sheep, not a goat. He abhors "mollycoddling" because he feels no need for mollycoddling himself. He assumes he has made it, and made it on his own. He doesn't need anything free. But the feeding of the five thousand is an illustration of the fact that there *is* a free lunch, and that lunch, contrary to Dr. Crane, was not offered just once and for all, but it is offered every day of the year; that's exactly what we are doing at this very service. We are participating in God's free lunch.

As to house-calls, again this is basic to the gospel message. God is not an austere physician who we can see only by supplication and after paying a fee. He is always present, always available and all for free, if only we will let Him in.

Indeed, sometimes we don't *want* Him in. "Unto whom all hearts are open, all desires known, and from whom no secrets are hid . . . ,"[17] of course, turns traditional thinking upside down, and it is this which makes General MacArthur's statement, as bland and tolerant sounding as it is, inaccurate. As Manchester comments, "No serious theologian could endorse that. It was Rotarianism, Norman Vincent Peale-ism; a man with MacArthur's intellect should have been reasoning on the level of Reinhold Niebuhr. And his affirmations of piety might have carried greater weight had he joined a congregation."[18]

Christianity, at its basic core, is unique among all of the

---

17. *The Book of Common Prayer* (New York: The Church Hymnal Corporation, 1979), 323.

18. Manchester, *American Caesar*, p. 512.

religions and philosophies of the world. There are many common strands among the world's religions, especially in the area of ethics, thus, almost all religions put restraints on the taking of human life.

But the concept of a loving, suffering God who made the ultimate and willing sacrifice for us when we did not deserve it, this is a *uniquely* discovered truth of the Christian. Christians are constantly tempted to change this, e.g., the Roman Catholic Church with its abuse of the concept of indulgences for a time came dangerously close to perverting the faith, and some other present-day versions of Christianity, e.g., Mormonism says, "Be good, do good things, and then you will earn God's love," i.e., salvation by works.

But these are distortions of the basic Gospel message which is: God loves and accepts us even when we are most unacceptable, and therefore, *because* of this acceptance, we should try to act in a way which makes us worthy of this love, i.e., salvation by grace and faith.

This is not to say that God is not at work in other faiths, but we Christians are forced to say that we have been exposed to the workings of God in their fullness. So often we take this all for granted. "[G]ood old God . . . forgiveness is his business . . . ," forgetting the truly incredible nature of what it is we proclaim, or probably, it is that we have never really *heard* this Good News.

There is no arrogance in the Christian claim of uniqueness, because by its very nature it is to be *shared* with others. Of course, we don't really have to consciously *sell* anything. If we live our life in the full comprehension of what it is that Christianity proclaims, *this* will show forth, and others will say, "That seems to make a lot of sense to Joe, and he's a sensible fellow. Perhaps there's something there I better investigate."

I do know this: if I have the worst looking lawn on the block, my neighbors aren't going to spend much time listening to me preach on how to be a better gardener.

But we Episcopalians in Utah have rather a unique commission–whether we like it or not, and whether we want to or not–our very existence is a witness to historic and traditional Christianity as it has come down through the centuries. We can only start by truly understanding what it is that we proclaim, which is, "Yes, Dr. Crane, there really *is* a free lunch. Come on and join us in partaking of it. The only thing it costs you is your pride."

3

Remember, Jesus said, "Come unto me, all ye that travail and are heavy laden, and I will refresh you" [Matt. 11:28].[19] He did* not *say "Come unto me all ye that are holy and pious, and I will love you because you are so good."

The Feast of the Epiphany
January 6, 1981

All Saints Church
Salt Lake City, Utah

The word *Epiphany* means, at its root, a showing forth or a manifestation. Its significance for the Christian is illustrated by the preface to the fourth gospel, which proclaims the appearance of God as a tangible reality in the world–"the world knew Him not" [John 1:10, KJV].

St. Paul was one of the first to truly sense that in the life and death of this baby was a meaning and a message not just for a few people, but for the whole world. This is why he called himself apostle to the gentiles and why the feast of St. Paul is appropriately celebrated during Epiphanytide.

19. From the "Comfortable Words," as found and translated in *The Book of Common Prayer* (1979), p. 332.

The concept of Epiphany is illustrated by the story of the "Three Kings," symbolizing this manifestation to the entire world.

There is an inevitable collision course of the Incarnate Godhead and the world around Him. The baby Jesus didn't stay in the cave, secure and sheltered from the world. Nor could He, for the world sought Him out even before He was capable of going out to it. And this is told in symbolic form in the story of the three kings or wise men representing in ancient legend the different races of mankind, all of whom came to see and pay homage to the new-born Christ.

The result is that despite all of its problems and weakness, Christianity is today the largest single religious group on the face of the earth. There is almost no place one can go that has not been touched to some extent by this proclamation.

The event of Epiphany is one that, beginning with the wise men's visit, was bound to continue until the end of time. The world will always be pressing in upon the Church and the Church in turn interacting with the world. The Church is not able to hide from the world, nor should it. Once God entered the world as man, the Church and the world were forever intertwined.

This doesn't mean they are the same thing. To quote from St. Paul's good advice in his letter to the Romans (Phillip's Translation), "Don't let the world around you squeeze you into its own mold, but let God remold your minds from within" [Rom. 12:2]. In other words the Christian's task is to work with the world he is in, not let it work on him.

We can't run away from Epiphany. Like all events we commemorate in the Church year, they are just not things that happened once upon a time (although they did that too), but they occur again and again. Thus, for example, the miracle of creation did not happen just once, with God brushing off his hands and walking away. God's creation re-occurs again every second. It is part of God's process. It occurs with the miracle of the conception and birth of each child.

And every child must be taught anew, to read, to write, to speak, and to acquire a sense of value. No person born and living alone on a desert island could, for example, be a Christian, because he would have no touch with the community of continuity, the Church, which preserves the Christian message.

Thus the truth of the Incarnation can occur again and again as its significance is grasped within the heart of each individual, but it comes only when it is taught to that person by others. And in the same manner, the *event* of the Epiphany must be enacted over and over again, or the Church and the faith it propounds would perish from the earth. We then, as members of the Church, are God's instruments to see that Epiphany is constantly kept–that this truth is shown forth, made manifest.

As we start a new secular year, we have a good chance to see how each of us is doing with his personal Epiphany. How much witnessing to the gentile world around us have we done?

How has our witness been to ourselves? How seriously *do* I take my faith? Do I see it as a framework within which I fit *all* of my heart, soul, and mind? How many competing gods do I have that push the faith into a comfortable "religious" corner? Ambition, popularity, comfort. Am I really honest about this faith which I am supposed to manifest? If I have doubts and concerns, do I honestly wrestle with them and seek a resolution, or do I forget it as not too important anyway? You know, we *do* wrestle with things that *really* bother us such as an income tax return that doesn't balance, or a question the boss asked us which we couldn't answer.

How has our witness been to our families? As to our children at least two things are clear: (1) they are molded to a terrifying extent by their parents' values; (2) they are not fools. They know those things which are meaningful to their parents and those which are not, and they know that the things parents sometimes say are important aren't necessarily what they believe are important. If the life of a Christian isn't important to you, you will have a tough time trying to tell them it should be important to them. Epiphany starts at home.

It is not only in the so-called "churchy" things that we make our Epiphany, but in the whole question of the maintenance of *value*.

Paul Tillich once said of "religion" that everyone has one, whether he knows it or not. He defined "religion" as that which a particular person held as *ultimate concern,* and as he observed, we all "epiphanalize" or show forth in our life what our ultimate concern is.[20]

To many the ultimate concern is not terribly well thought through. It is a hodge-podge of half-baked generalizations, often one conflicting with the other. In the ordinary day-to-day flow of events we can operate fairly well with this type of intellectual and emotional machinery, just as a badly out-of-tune car can go along on a straight-away.

But it is in the time of crisis that the test comes—those moments when some cold hard reality hits us, and hits us

20. The discussion of "ultimate concern" is spread liberally throughout Tillich's three volumes of *Systematic Theology*. A definition of "ultimate concern" is found in Tillich, *Systematic Theology – Volume One* (Chicago: University of Chicago Press, 1951), pp. 11-12. The sense that every person has a "religion" is developed in Tillich, *Systematic Theology – Volume Two* (Chicago: University of Chicago Press, 1957), pp. 25-26. Further development on the subject can be found in Tillich, *Systematic Theology – Volume Three* (Chicago: University of Chicago Press, 1963), pp. 130-31.

hard. It is a terrifying feeling when at such moments we look down for help to our hole card and find there is nothing there.

An article by a Roman Catholic priest brought me up short the other day. He was writing about Sunday school and Christian education for children. He argued that it all ought to be abolished as a waste of time. Because, he said, Christianity is not a children's religion, and they cannot really understand it. It is only, he said, when we have grown up and suffered and know something about the real height and depth that the human condition can reach that the Christian message can say anything to you.

His thesis is overstated, of course, but there's something to it. We see so often children raised in the Church who drop away upon attaining maturity. So often this happens not because they have rejected the message, but because they never really understand and heard it in the first place.

Thus, some people express shock, surprise and disgust that there are hypocrites within the church. But the Catholic tradition never said otherwise. St. Augustine fought this out in the fourth century when he maintained that the Christian Church was not an exclusive club of the holy and super-pious, but rather that it was a hospital for the lame, the halt and the blind who admit they need help and ask for it.

Remember, Jesus said, "Come unto me, all ye that

travail and are heavy laden, and I will refresh you" [Matt. 2:11].[21] He did *not* say "Come unto me all ye that are holy and pious, and I will love you because you are so good."

The Christian body is not a group that because of its superior excellence builds a pathway to the stars. It is a group that realizes the awesome miracle that the stars have already come to him where he is.

This does not mean that the true Christian is a sluggish, passive non-entity. As history has shown and personal experience will attest, there is a tremendous dynamic freeing of spirit and energy when we finally realize and accept the fact that we are free to be ourselves. We need no longer prattle and pretend.

This is the message for which we are called to make Epiphany–to show forth not only with our lips but in our lives.

Albert Mollegen in his book *Christianity and Modern Man*, wrote that he felt the crisis of our time was "the terrible shrinking of the area of Western civilization, the West's deep unbelief in itself, and its lack of missionary passion."[22]

This is perhaps true to some extent because we have

---

21. *The Book of Common Prayer* (1979), p. 332.

22. Albert Mollegen, *Christianity and Modern Man–The Crisis of Secularism* (New York: Bobbs-Merrill Co., Inc., 1961), p. 158.

let the world's values impose too much on those of the outrageous, audacious proclamation of God's entry into time and space, and we have watered down the incredible assertion, "Behold, I make all things new" [Rev. 21:5, KJV].

Once a person has let this message really sink into his bones there is no longer any need for exhortations to go out and make Epiphany. Once this good news is grasped and ACCEPTED, it will come bubbling out of its own accord.

How this bubbling forth is manifested differs with how each of us is made up, but mark my words, other folks will know about it.

And that is what Epiphany is all about.

4

Then suddenly a large man in snorkeling gear burst out of the lagoon and in a loud voice and a Brooklyn accent he said to his wife and all that could hear: "My God, this is the most fantastic experience of my life. You all should try it."

The Second Sunday of Easter
April 26, 1987

The Cathedral Church of St. Mark
Salt Lake City, Utah

"We believe in one God, the Father, the Almighty, maker of heaven and earth, of all that is, seen and unseen."[23]

This is a sermon to the Doubting Thomas in each of us who has ever had trouble saying these first words of the Nicene Creed. This pulpit is dedicated to literate people preaching to literate people to the glory of God. We restrict our power to communicate because of this and we speak to a limited group of our community. They must be able to read and to appreciate liturgical beauty. Now we well know that those who do not have these attributes are equally loved by our Lord.

---

23. "The Nicene Creed," *The Book of Common Prayer* (1979), pp. 326, 358.

But let's be honest; while the Episcopal Church doesn't speak very well to the followers of Brother and Sister Bakker, we admit we are only *one* branch of the Holy Catholic Church of Jesus Christ. Yet we stress certain things more, that other portions of Christ's body do not.

Thus, we emphasize an understanding of history and liturgy. (For example, as we stood during Lent through the seemingly eternal Great Litany, it is perhaps helpful to know that this was the *first* part of the Roman Catholic's services which Henry VIII ordered to be done in English, well before the first *[The] Book of Common Prayer* in 1549. Henry added a plea for deliverance from the "detestable enormities of the Bishop of Rome," a request which a more tolerant age has omitted.)

This sense of the need for Christian history is lost on those who think that Karl Marx was one of the four Marx brothers–who think that Columbus sailed to America after 1750–who can't date the Civil War within fifty years–who can't identify Stalin or Churchill and who think that FDR was president during the Vietnam war.

As *Newsweek* states in its April 20th [1987] issue and last Sunday's *60 Minutes* [CBS television program] reaffirms, unless someone gets really concerned about these lapses, and the students who gave the answers didn't seem to care, "civilization may perish simply because nobody bothered to pass it on."[24]

This is desperately important for Christianity, because Christianity is a pass-it-on world view. You can't become a Christian by yourself. Someone else has to tell you about it. Someone else has to baptize you. An Anglican priest celebrating the Eucharist may not receive communion by himself. Unless there is at least one other person present, he folds his tent sadly, completes ante-communion and goes home. Fortunately, I've never had this happen. So what happened before you and I arrived on the scene is essential to being a Christian. Christianity is not just a nice warm feeling. It is a proclamation of historical fact.

Some of my dearest life-long friends would rather be caught dead than state, "I believe that Jesus Christ is my Lord and Savior." Some say this because they believe it is in bad social taste and obviously such a confession is not a clincher to a cocktail party argument.

But most of these folks I know are not embarrassed, they just don't care. Why we are here, what our purpose is, what our ultimate destiny is–these do not seem to be issues of concern.

In World War II, the propagandists said, "There are no

---

24. David Gates, "A Dunce Cap for America," *Newsweek*, Apr. 20, 1987, p. 72.

atheists in foxholes." Those who were there would respond with one of the Federal Communications Commission's seven forbidden words (I'm dying to see these in print so I know what they are).

How does anyone believe in anything? I had heard of snorkeling. We took our children to a small hotel in Cozumel, Mexico, and I looked at the lagoon before me and the blue water beyond it. The beach sand was warm and I read a Dorothy Sayers detective story. I was in a world I understood and the margarita in my hand was a known fact. Then suddenly a large man in snorkeling gear burst out of the lagoon and in a loud voice and a Brooklyn accent he said to his wife and all that could hear: "My God, this is the most fantastic experience of my life. You *all* should try it." I promptly rented some snorkeling gear, waded into the lagoon, and put my head under water. There was indeed a totally new world, existent the whole time I was baking my carcass on the beach, but of which I was unaware. Magnificent sea creatures of incredible beauty, of all shapes, sizes and colors, darting, lazing, lurking–in silence only marred by my own snorting. These creatures viewed me with mystic disdain, keeping just out of my reach. This was *their* world, one which I only a few feet away had not, until this moment, even dreamed existed.

I think there is a good religious analogy here. For about twenty years I have celebrated the Wednesday 7:00 a.m. Eucharist at our Cathedral Church [of St. Mark, Salt Lake

City, Utah]. Most of the year it is dark when we start our service. Our group numbers from ten to a high of twenty. By the time we finish and adjourn for coffee and always a treat, the city has begun to bustle—most obvious near us are the Mountain Fuel [Supply Company] people getting to work by 8:00 a.m. We are snorkelers. We have found a new and alive world, different from, yet always a part of the world that we travel every day. We meet our Lord and each other in a brief, quiet service that is totally different from the asphalt world outside. I am still waiting for someone to jump out of that lagoon at the Cathedral and cry out, "Hey, Myrtle, this is one of the great experiences of my life—you should *all* try it." But if he or she won't *I* should.

This is, of course, the pragmatic approach to a doubting Thomas. It is where *I* came from. The Christian faith makes more sense of the human condition than any option I know.

I am thereby disregarding several ancient approaches to the Church and to the conversion of our doubting Thomas. Another Thomas, Aquinas, and the Scholastics, thought that they could rationally *prove* the existence of God, and by an even bigger and more tremendous jump, the uniqueness of the Christian gospel. But as one theologian at least has observed, this school of thought ignored the classical Christian understanding of human nature as fallen and flawed. This, of course, would include our ability to reason our way to an answer unaided. One of the great bits of genius in our Constitution is the founding fathers' great distrust of human nature. I can rationalize myself to any result I want, and thus believe in it. So too can an Adolph Hitler, a Joseph Stalin, or any bigot and zealot. So much for the concept that I understand, and *then* I believe.

An early Christian Tertullian tried another tack. "I believe because it is so absurd."[25] A total divorce of reason and belief is not a good working hypothesis for our daily lives but it is true that in worldly values the Gospel is sometimes absurd. The hypothesis that fits me best is the

---

25. As has been mentioned earlier, Colton quoted Tertullian as saying, *"Credo quia absurdum."* However, some doubt that Tertullian actually said this. For example, Arthur McGiffert wrote: "We are to believe the rule of faith not because it is true and not because it appeals to us, as expressing the mind of Christ, but because it is commanded. The more unreasonable it appears to us, so Tertullians seem to think, the greater the merit of our faith (f.n. 3, cf. Adv. Marcionem, II.2; V.5). In his tract, *On the Flesh of Christ*, he declares, 'The Son of God died: it is absolutely worthy of belief because it is absurd (f.n. 4 *Prorsus credible est, quia ineptum est.*). And having been buried, he rose again; it is certain because it is impossible' (f.n. 5 *Certum est, quia impossible est [De carne Christi, 5].* The particular words, *Credo quia absurdum*, often attributed to Tertullian are not his.)." In Arthur McGiffert, *A History of Christian Thought* (New York: Charles Scribner's Sons, 1947), Vol. 2:16. As has been noted earlier, Tertullian did not say these words but rather said, "The Son of God died; it is absolutely worthy of belief because it is absurd."

Latin, *Credo, ut intelligam*–I believe so that I can understand.[26]

I like this because it fits my observation of how you and I work. We start with a hole-card, from wherever, and then build up our rationalizations and justifications around it.

President Eisenhower once said, "I don't care what people believe, as long as they believe in something."[27] He couldn't be more in error, because if my thesis is correct, *belief* is of importance. "Ideas have consequences," as Richard Weaver said.[28] Hitler's belief in anti-semitism led to the murder of six million Jews.

---

26. *"Neque enim quaero intelligere ut credam, sed credo ut intelligam. Nam et hoc credo: quia 'nisi credidero, non intelligam.'"* ("For I do not seek to understand so that I may believe; but I believe so that I may understand. For I believe this also, that 'unless I believe, I shall not understand.'" In St. Anselm, *St. Anselm's Proslogion*, trans., intro., and phil. com. M. J. Charlesworth (Notre Dame: University of Notre Dame Press, 1979), pp. 114-15.

27. It is difficult to know exactly what situation Colton remembered for this quotation. It probably is from the following portion of the text of President-elect Eisenhower's speech to the Directors of the Freedoms Foundation at the Waldorf-Astoria in New York City in December 1952: "In other words, our form of government has no sense unless it is founded in a deeply felt religious faith and I don't care what it is." "Eisenhower Promises Study To 'Get Facts' on Segregation–President Elect Says Soviet Demoted Zhukov Because of Their Friendship," *New York Times*, Dec. 23, 1952, p. 16 L, col. 5.

28. Richard M. Weaver, *Ideas Have Consequences* (Chicago: University of Chicago Press, 1948), cover.

Now in saying that faith starts the whole business, I guess I'd better define what I mean. Albert Mollegen, one of our few twentieth-century American Anglican theologians, gives this illustration that the faith of revelation need not be factually true:

> Let me illustrate this. Suppose someone asked me, "How do you know that your wife loves you?" I would begin to talk personally and dramatically, describing what she says and does in order to make manifest her revelation to me. I would say; "Look at all the things she does for me. Last Wednesday she cooked my breakfast, she got my children off to school, she cleaned the house, she brought me my mail, she got my lunch"–and so on, right through the day. And then I might relate some of the words that she said: "At an odd time of day she caught me long enough to make this direct statement–'I love you.'" So I would say to my questioner, "In and through these actions and words a loving personality was made manifest, and I responded to her. That's the reason I know she loves me."
>
> Then my wife would speak up and say: "That's all very well, but remember–last Wednesday you were out of town!" And I would say: "Oh my goodness, that's right!" Then I would have to correct my dramatic, personal narrative. "Well, it must have been Tuesday," I would say.
>
> "No, it wasn't Tuesday. You were out of town all day Tuesday, too," she would recall.

> "Well, what day was it?"
>
> "I don't know. It was a usual day. But I don't know which day last week it was."
>
> My narrative has a certain amount of factuality. It is datable fact, but the date is lost to historical investigation for ever and anon—and yet it happened. It might be that I put a Monday breakfast and a Wednesday lunch and a Friday supper all on the same day. But there *was* a breakfast, and there *was* a lunch, and there *was* a supper.
>
> Insomuch as the Biblical record can be corrected by historical research, let's correct it. Insomuch as its pictures cannot be corrected because there are no data, or because no data have as yet appeared, let's be reverently agnostic about the exact historiographical accuracy of the narrative—and still understand that there *is* photographable fact there, although it may not be identical with what is alleged by the narrative. The major purpose of the narrative is the communication of the personal revelation, not the preservation of the visible, audible, tangible events through which the revelation came.[29]

In other words, the *facts* of my belief may be a bit scrambled and uncertain, but the *truth* my belief conveys is certainly untainted.

---

29. Albert Mollegen, *Christianity and Modern Man—The Crisis of Secularism* (New York: Bobbs-Merrill Co., Inc., 1961), pp. 120-21.

Anglicanism, in defining necessary faith, generally avoids arguments from mystical experience. The Virgin Mary may well have appeared weeping on a water tower in Gary, Indiana, but, doubting Thomas, I will not require your belief on that basis.

I will ask your belief, doubting Thomas, first on an honest assessment of where you presently stand, and I mean an *honest* assessment. Obviously, you have not met by one hundred percent every standard you have set, or if you have, your standards are phoney and inadequate. How have you worked your way out of this dilemma? It does no good to pound the rules into you once again. Aren't you just like St. Paul who wrote "For I do not do what I want, but I do the very thing I hate" (Rom. 7:15 [RSV]). He *knew* the rules, yet he finally was honest enough to realize that the rule book by itself only led to guilt and despair.

Would you, doubting Thomas, acknowledge that on occasion you need help from some place else? A spouse or a good and trusted friend? (Remember the fellow that wrote: "My head is bloody, but unbowed. . . . I am the master of my fate; I am the captain of my soul"?[30] He was William Ernest Henley, 1849-1903. He committed suicide.)

30. William Ernest Henley, "Invictus," lines 8, 15, 16, in *The Literature of England–An Anthology and a History, Volume Two,* Rev. ed., eds. George Woods, Homer Watt, George Anderson (New York: Scott, Foresman and Co., 1941) p. 936.

Would you, doubting Thomas, consider then asking for additional help from a community that has existed for two thousand years for that very purpose, offering help. The hundreds of millions who have done this over the centuries were not all dopes, Thomas. A lot of them were much smarter than you are.

You are now old enough, Thomas, that I cannot ask you to accept something just because it is in your family tradition or your cultural heritage. Yea, indeed, the Anglican tradition of the Christian faith assumes you will ask questions–every day if you wish.

But doubting Thomas, I ask you to take a leap of faith with me, if I have described you correctly. Come snorkeling with me into a new world. Bring your guilt, your inadequacies, your frustrations with you, and get into that water.

In that new perspective, you will see there is no need for that baggage and you will see that you can give it up. And I think that if you respond as I did, you will jump out of that water and yell to everyone in sight, "Hey, I've found something wonderful."

IX
Stewardship

Introduction

Albert Colton was celebrated in the Diocese of Utah, as well as the Diocese of California, as an apologist for Christian stewardship. While he did not shy away from an occasional gimmick in training people to engage in a canvass drive or in surprising a congregation with a humorous, albeit thoughtful skit, Colton was grounded in the Holy Eucharist for his theology on stewardship.

> The Eucharist is the taking of what we have, acknowledging with thanks that it is given to us by God, offering it, and then having God return it to us for our use.
>
> The Eucharist assumes certain things. First, it assumes what we call the sacramental principle, that is, God acts through his creation. He *uses* the stuff of life. Thus, for example, the Christian sees great significance in history. It is not an endless cycle, it is not meaningless, but rather is the story of God working His purpose out in time and space. We say that the principle of God acting through people was shown uniquely in one person, Jesus Christ, who became intimately involved in the pain and suffering of the world, and was one who *gave*–gave completely of Himself–"For God so loved the world, that He gave his only begotten son . . ."

[John 3:16, KJV]. It was He who gave the command that in the commonest things of life, in bread and wine, when offered in remembrance of Him, would bring His presence in a very real sense to us.

A second basic assumption of the Eucharist is that one must give in order to receive. This rule is of course contrary to our basic instinct, which is first to make sure of our own situation and then (we say) we can then do some giving, i.e., we tend to say, receive, and *then* give. "You like me first, and then I'll like you." And the liturgy of the Christian says that this instinctive selfishness must be nipped in the bud at the very beginning. The rule should be "first you give, and *then* you receive." Now many feel this is highly unfair. How do I *know* I'll receive? Am I not just being played for a sucker? The people who get what I give may use it improperly. Or even more basically, I can get hurt this way. And of course this latter point is quite true. Involvement means vulnerability. The opening of yourself and the giving of yourself means that you can be hurt. But the Christian says that you must run this risk in order to be a full person.

The liturgy thus acts out the pattern of life, a cycle of offering and return. This is really what makes a thing holy. I take what I have (or rather, of course, what I have been given) and I give this to God. Now I actually can't give it directly to God. No celestial hand reaches down for it. In a sacramental world I give it to the outward and visible sign of that inward and spiritual grace. So I give this to people, or to institutions (which are really people).

To which person or group of persons we give we must each decide for ourselves–the beggar at the gate, the March of Dimes, or the Holy Catholic Church (which also consists of flesh and blood people). And we give without any strings–not in hope of a reward, not because if I scratch your back, you'll scratch mine. I just give.

How much do we give? Realistically we can't give all. We have obligations, including to ourselves. We need a *standard,* as we do in other aspects of our religious life, e.g., *when* to worship: "All persons within this Church shall celebrate and keep the Lord's Day, commonly called Sunday, by regular participation in the public worship of the Church . . ." (from Canon Law).[1] *How* to worship: we use *The Book of Common Prayer* as adopted by our church.

How much to give? "Give till it hurts"–but pain thresholds are low; "Your fair share"–but that's cart before the horse. We *need* to give, whether we have an oil well in the church courtyard or not; in one sense it doesn't matter what the Church needs. A table, bread and wine are enough. The *tithe* is a biblical, fair, and possible [standard for giving] (al-

---

1. Title II, Canon 1, of the Canons of the Episcopal Church, *Constitutions and Canons of the Episcopal Church* (New York: The General Convention of the Episcopal Church, 1982).

though it makes us stretch), and it is easily determined–just look at your Form 1040.

Forget details, i.e., net or gross; church or world–once you have accepted the concept, you will find these to be unimportant.

The point is that we give something that is significantly representative of what we are and what we have.

And then comes the miracle of the liturgical action. What we have freely offered, without strings, is *returned*. Not only what we have is returned, but it is blessed and sanctified, and it is returned for our use.[2]

Colton knew that some believed it inappropriate to talk about money in church and were offended when particulars about giving, such as the tithe, were addressed. He thought such an opinion was nonsense and he forged ahead. Stewardship was an act of prayer. He strongly felt that the Christian should not limit his or her comments to the efficacy of prayer alone, but also talk about the method of praying.

Let's disabuse ourselves of any idea that it is inappropriate to talk about money in God's house. This is a sacramental universe. Our Lord redeemed and gave meaning to all His creation. His body, the Church,

2. Sermon preached in October 1984 (otherwise undated), St. Paul's Church, Salt Lake City, Utah. This sermon was also preached the Twenty-first Sunday after Pentecost, October 20, 1985, the Cathedral Church of St. Mark, Salt Lake City, Utah.

> because it lives and works within the context of this world, uses and must have the things of this world to do its work–whether it be for the bread and the wine which nourish our souls at the Eucharist, the alms which are given to the needy and desperate, or for the glorious ornamentation we use to show by tangible symbol our praise and thanksgiving to our Creator.[3]

In a world filled with preachers, many of whom are on Sunday television programs and who link salvation with the amount of money you give to their religious efforts, Colton reflected a solid difference of opinion. One could not buy salvation or redemption precisely because salvation had been given freely already to him or her by God. No one can take that away nor can one claim to own a heavenly franchise regulating the distribution of such grace.

> And let's be sure of our theology of giving. No one is promising the substantial giver a reserved seat in the celestial kingdom. Even when we have done all we can do, we know that it is very little and very inadequate indeed. Our wedding garment is still a rather sad looking thing to wear before the king.[4]

---

3. Sermon preached the Twentieth Sunday after Trinity, n.d., St. Francis' Church, San Francisco, California. The sermon was again preached in 1970 (otherwise undated), the Cathedral Church of St. Mark, Salt Lake City, Utah, and in 1974 (otherwise undated), St. Stephen's Church, West Valley City, Utah.

4. Ibid.

> Giving isn't going to earn you God's love, because that love is there totally whether you give one nickel or not. I do so wish, at canvass time, that we could threaten you with hell fire and brimstone if you don't tithe, but we can't, because that's bum Christian theology. Because I tithe does not guarantee me a reserved seat on the celestial fifty yard line. However it is, if done for the right reasons, some indication that I have heard the proclamation.[5]

Colton firmly believed that Christians, once contributing financially to the world of the Church, did not have as an option to express an opinion, the cancellation of their pledge. Specifically, he felt that being angry or disappointed with the Church does not warrant the reduction of a pledge. Giving to the Body of Christ is not dependant on the relative omnipotence, omnipresence or omnificent abilities of the choir, clergy, vestry, sexton or others in the membership. Rather, giving to the Church is a recognition that God "whose power, working in us, can do infinitely more than we can ask or imagine" [Eph. 3:20, JB]. Colton believed, therefore, that one must give to enable Christ to work through the imperfect ministers and ministries of the Church.

---

5. Sermon preached the Ninth Sunday after Pentecost, September 28, 1986, the Cathedral Church of St. Mark, Salt Lake City, Utah. The sermon was also given on November 17, 1985, to the Elim Lutheran Church congregation at their Stewardship Luncheon, the Ogden Hilton Hotel, Ogden, Utah.

In a playground you can always, when you lose, take your marbles and go home. A lot of people try to play the rest of their life this way. But for emotionally adult churchmen I would suggest that there are at least two reasons why this option is not available: First, because it is always possible that we are wrong, and the outside possibility that we are *dead* wrong, and that God the Holy Spirit is saying things through the church that are true about us and that make us squirm; second, because you can never really take your marbles and leave your family. A child can rebel against his parents; parents can do things which embarrass the child. The child may consider himself much smarter than his parent (and sometimes he is). But there is flesh of "fleshness" in a family that rebellion, embarrassment or intelligence cannot remove.[6]

Colton was not willing to compromise on his belief that belonging to the Church included serious obligations prescribed, in part, by the Catechism of the Episcopal Church. "The duty of all Christians is to follow Christ; to come together week by week for corporate worship; and to work, pray, and give for the spread of the kingdom of God."[7]

---

6. Sermon preached the Twenty-first Sunday after Trinity, n.d., St. Francis' Church, San Francisco, California. The sermon was again preached on November 1974 (otherwise undated), St. Stephen's Church, West Valley City, Utah.

7. *The Book of Common Prayer* (New York: The Church Hymnal Corporation, 1979), p. 856.

We have no right to claim the privileges of God's kingdom if we are unwilling to assume the responsibilities admission to it involves. The twentieth century martyr, Dietrich Bonhoeffer (who was hanged by the Nazis on the last day of the war) has written about the scandal of what he calls, "cheap grace,"[8] the sickness that permeates so much of modern Christianity, the taking for granted of one's religious faith and heritage.

You are asked by your church to give financially for the support of your church. You are asked to give substantially, not in a token amount, for the work of Jesus Christ. You are asked to commit yourself in advance, as an act of faith, to a written pledge of your giving, measured by the standard of the tithe, or ten percent of your income.

You can of course say "no" to this request. We are dunned for our money on every side, and we can dismiss this as just another appeal for funds. There are many, many, many jokes about passing the plate in church services. But in saying "no," good Christian people, let us at least be honest with ourselves. What we are then really saying is that the Church, and the work of Jesus Christ, is just not that important to us.

8. See "Justification as the Last Word," in Dietrich Bonhoeffer, *Ethics*, ed. Eberhard Bethage, trans. Neville Horton Smith (New York: Macmillan Publishing Co., Inc., 1965), pp. 120-25, esp. p. 125. See also Dietrich Bonhoeffer, *The Cost of Discipleship* (New York: Macmillan Co., 1963), Chap. 1, pp. 45-114, esp. pp. 45-60.

We want cheap grace. We do not want to go to the trouble of putting on our wedding garment.[9]

Christians, by virtue of their baptism, have abundant life. And here, for Colton, is where the subject of stewardship met and embraced the mandate of evangelism and witnessing. By having the Gospel, Christians are called to share that over which they have been made stewards. It is not just treasure, talent, and time which make up stewardship. It is the sacramental uses of those resources to build up the Body of Christ which foster stewardship. All of this serves as a response to the grace of God.

A man once lived who taught me that I could walk through the veil of tears, joyous and unafraid, because even in the valley of the shadow of death he was with me. He also said, "I came that (you) might have life and have it abundantly." If we accept this, we must learn to share this abundant life (John 10:10, RSV].[10]

9. Sermon preached the Twentieth Sunday after Trinity.

10. Sermon preached the Ninth Sunday after Pentecost, September 28, 1986, the Cathedral Church of St. Mark, Salt Lake City, Utah.

1

We do not love God abstractly. We express this love materially, through acts of concern through the giving of ourselves and of what we have. By the fruits of our giving the real nature of our concern is shown.

The Twelfth Sunday after Trinity — *Grace Cathedral*
September 9, 1962 — *San Francisco, California*

"And He took him aside from the multitude, and put His fingers into his ears, and He spit, and touched his tongue; and looking up to heaven He sighed, and saith unto him *Ephphatha*, that is, be opened. And straightway his ears were opened, and the string of his tongue was loosed, and he spake plain" [Mark 7:33-35, KJV].

To many it is a story of this sort which is the most embarrassing thing about Christianity. Not so much because of the healing itself, but because of the unquestionably materialistic means used in this story to affect his healing. "He put his fingers into his ears . . . he spit . . . touched . . . said." Surely if you as Christians say, this man was Incarnate God, why did he have to go through this superstitious, magical sounding mumbo-jumbo? Couldn't he merely have willed it so, and it would be so?

Why *does* this story of the healing of the deaf mute make some uncomfortable? We must first ask whether there really is a "superior," more "highfalutin" way in which Almighty God should act within His creation. Are the use of bodily matter, gestures and words "inferior" means of conveying God's power and strength?

Of course we know the answer as far as we ourselves are concerned. We can do nothing without the use of our bodies. There is no doctor who ever treated any patient without the use of some mechanism of his body, whether it be merely the use of his vocal cords over the telephone. The material things of this world (of which our bodies are a part) are the sole means whereby we can even communicate with one another. Our body is what sets us apart from everyone else in the world, but it is also the means whereby any relationship with these others is possible.

Precisely in this way, the Christian church says, God chooses to relate Himself to His creation through the means of that very creation itself. Indeed if God wishes to relate to His creatures, He must do this in a media which His creatures understand–their own creatureliness.

And yet, throughout the centuries the human creature has resisted this concept of Deity. Even assuming one believed God existed, He was and must be, we often feel, "out there," aloof and removed. Instinctively we tend to draw up our own Emily Post book of how God should act. He should be a nice old man who only comes around on stated occasions when he is invited–such as baptisms, marriages and funerals.

We can see therefore, how astonishing and blasphemous is the message of Jesus Christ. It was, as St. Paul tells us, a scandal to the cultivated world of the Roman Empire and it still is. Here is the assertion that the Lord God Omnipotent, Creator of all there is, not only deigned to use the rude things of ordinary life, but our very manhood itself, to show Himself to His creation.

Not only this, but what a man He chose to be. Far from a genteel, philosopher king living a serene life of detached meditation, He was born into poverty, associated principally with crude, unsophisticated men, used gestures, touching, spittle and obscure phrases to effect His purposes, and died a hideous criminal's death.

Note here that our gospel story today is not about magic. Magic is the manipulation of the supernatural by the material–it is the assertion that by the doing of certain things God *must* respond. Christ's message is completely the opposite of this. It is that God uses matter to effect his purpose.

But even this we push away from. We want to "spiritualize" God and remove Him from the specific. I was fascinated in finding myself half way through Edwin O'Connor's Pulitzer Prize winning novel, *The Edge of Sadness* (Boston: Little, Brown, 1961), which portrays the life of an American Roman Catholic priest, when it occurred to me that I had not seen the words "Jesus Christ" once. I finished the book looking for this, and while I may be wrong, I do not think the words appear anywhere in the book. And yet it claims to be a searching analysis of the inner life of a Christian priest. To be sure, the words "God," "prayer," and "grace" abound. But without making too much of this perhaps this is an example of the reluctance of authors, and all of us, to accept the specific concreteness of the Christian faith as centered in Jesus Christ.

To the Christian, like it or not, the words "God," "prayer," and "grace" are all centered in what he believes is the ultimate revelation and manifestation in the man, Jesus of Nazareth.

I am reminded of a friend of mine whose religious life was a nice culling of lowest common denominators from his religious heritage, who, on one of his rare visits to church on Christmas Eve, remarked when asked about the service, "Well, frankly, there wasn't enough Christmas, and too much talk about Jesus Christ."

But the Christian says that God has sanctified materiality supremely in Jesus Christ. This is what gives value to human life. It is far from empirically provable by reason alone that "all men are created equal." Rather, it is because each man is of equal value in God's eyes that we can justify this statement. Otherwise it is merely a bit of illogical sentimentality.

1. THE TWELFTH SUNDAY AFTER TRINITY, 1962.

We of course accept without thinking the use of material things in expressing our regard and concern between ourselves, most obviously in the giving of presents. There is probably not a married woman here who does not wear on her finger a costly and from a practical point of view completely useless bit of metal and precious stone. Why? Because deep down in our culture is the concept that love can be symbolized and expressed by means of a concrete object. The marriage service of our Prayer Book expressly refers to a ring. It does not describe the ring to be used. And yet of course we feel that this ring should be costly, expensive. The husband we feel, should give this in a way that costs him something. We do not want this relationship to be cheap or easy. Love is nothing if it is not costly. The ring symbolizes not only the marriage bond, but the costliness of this bond, reflected in the ten thousand and one daily acts of giving and consideration in the healthy marriage.

We reflect our love of *God* in the same way. We do not love God abstractly. We express this love materially, through acts of concern through the giving of ourselves and of what we have. By the fruits of our giving the real nature of our concern is shown.

To whom or to what do we give? There are many worthy causes, many great needs. How do we choose? One way is to treat all good works alike: symphony, church, hospital, education, and then merely to sprinkle our largesse, whether it be our interest, time, talent or treasure equally amongst them all. This is the sprinkle theory.

Another way, of course, is to ignore the demand altogether. Spend our time and talents completely on our own satisfaction and take the blanket deduction the Bureau of Internal Revenue gives us for good works. This is the "look out for good old number one" theory. (The real tragedy of it is that it isn't a prudential approach at all, but a sure road to death.)

The Christian choice is more complex. By his baptism the Christian becomes a member of the body of Christ. The fellowship in his church is the continuation of Christ's work in time and space. It is this which makes prior claim on him. To be sure the work of Christ is not restricted to the formal church as there are many secular agencies doing the work of the Lord. But, to use a legal term, the *presumption* to the Christian must ever rest with the formality of Christ's Body, the Church, as the object of his attention.

Christians in various ages have been called to give different things. Not infrequently, especially in the early centuries, the Christian was called upon to give his very life. The call to martyrdom rings a bit hollow today, interesting reading, but alien to the comfortable acceptability of the Christian church in this culture. Today it is the state, not the Church, which trains youth to be willing to give their lives for it.

The Body of Christ has frequently grown stronger in

those times of overt persecution, when only those who truly *dared* made the leap of faith. It has frequently softened in times of complacency.

Therefore it is in a way heartening to note that the call to heroism has not disappeared, nor has the danger to Christ's body. It has merely changed its nature.

We have been called a materialistic culture. To the extent this means men can live more comfortably and fully, we can only praise God for this. But the problem comes in the baptizing of the materialistic bounty.

This morning we will offer to God symbols of ourselves, our alms, and bread and wine. This is done in the liturgy through the collection, and through the movement by the acolyte (representing all of us) carrying the bread and wine from the credence table to the altar.

We are not asked to sacrifice our lives for our faith–in a complex world we cannot even give too much of our time, as we are mostly obligated to work at secular pursuits to support ourselves. (Our Cathedral [Grace Cathedral, San Francisco, California] rises to the glory of God largely with the *physical* efforts of our congregation.) But there is an intriguing way in which each era has its own particular demand of heroism. We Americans do have a chance to be heroic. And heroism is *always* costly. In our case our chance for heroism comes in the giving of that which is of primary concern to each one of us, our money.

I'm well aware that the Church has been bitterly criticized because it always seems to have its hand out for money. In some way this is considered bad taste.

But is not a great deal of this uneasiness really because we have failed to completely grasp the basic unity of the material and spiritual as shown in Jesus Christ? There is no real separation of "material" and "spiritual" things.

It is because of this truth that the Christian is asked to give—because the every-day stuff of life is part and parcel of the meaning of eternity. Because God has given Himself for me I *respond* by giving myself to Him in every way that I can. Not that I *owe* Him anything, or that He needs anything that I have. It is simply that in sheer gratitude for the meaning that has been given my life through Jesus Christ and for His many other gifts, I want to respond and return these gifts in some small way. The only means I *have* to respond to God is through what I am and what I have.

When this response permeates *every* aspect of our being—our reason, our friends, food, raiment and all of the other comforts and conveniences of life, then we can understand the incredible meaning of the Christian message.

Almighty God loves us and gives to us all the means of sanctification. Not just of our soul, not just of our heart—but all of us and all of creation. Thanks be to God.

2

If you double or triple your pledge this year I will not promise you that your scrapbook won't go into the garbage can. I won't even promise that your name will be spelled correctly in your obituary. And God will love you just as much whatever you do.

The Twentieth Sunday after Trinity *St. Francis' Church*
October 8, 1967 *San Francisco, California*

The house didn't smell of death, and well it shouldn't, because the children had been reorganizing things ever since father was buried three days ago. Most of the furniture had been labeled and tagged. Mary and Joan were in the kitchen each trying to be courteous and yet foxy in a sisterly way dividing up the last pieces of mother's china and kitchen ware.

John was in the living room at father's desk negotiating a listing of the house with the real estate agent. He had flown out from Chicago for the funeral and had only yesterday been able to talk to father's lawyer, who told him that the will left everything in three equal shares. Household effects were best handled, the lawyer suggested, by the three children sitting down and dividing them up. It saved a lot of technical trouble that way.

But John was exhausted. He had not realized that Mary and Joan had already been at work, at least mentally, in the dividing up, and he wished that his wife were here so that he would know whether he was being short-changed when he ended up with the silver nut bowl, and Mary and Joan each flourished and labelled as their own something that looked bigger and better. His wife had told him at the time of his mother's funeral, that mother had really acquired some very lovely and valuable things. He wasn't sure whether the silver nut bowl was one of them, and he had a faint feeling that he had been conned by his sisters.

Joan and Mary emerged from the kitchen, Mary carrying a large scrapbook which she dropped on the desk. "This requires a decision," said Joan. John broke off his conversation with the real estate man and started leafing through the book. It had been carefully and lovingly kept–page after page of pictures and clippings of the lives of mother and father, and at the end many newspaper articles about father, who had become quite a significant figure in the community. John looked at his sisters. "Well, who wants it?" "I already have copies of the family pictures–I think all of us do," Mary said. Joan, the practical one, said that she felt that scrapbooks were a lot of sloppy sentimentality anyway, and that she would prefer to remember mother and father as they were, not as a book of press clippings described them. John, who would really have rather liked to keep the scrapbook was afraid that his sisters would use this as a credit against something else of real value, so looking at the faces of his sisters, he took the book and put it into a large wastebasket, and turned again to the real estate man; the sisters returned to the kitchen to continue their sorting.

The pathetic thing about this story is that father was really quite a man in his day–a president of his bank, mayor of his city, governor of his state, captain of his lodge's bowling team. Describe this in any worldly terms you wish. He had legions of friends, but in his last years they had gradually died off. His closest friend, his wife, had died six years ago. And it was not that his children did not love him, they did, indeed, and had been most tender and loving in his last illness. But now they had lives to lead, and all were concerned about getting home to their own families. Life had to go on.

This is also the worldly story of you and me, give or take a few variations in the details. It does not matter much whether your obituary notice is a paid ad inserted by the undertaker or front page news. Within a few years we will have been forgotten save for the few who loved us very much, and even those memories fade, as indeed they themselves fade away.

It is almost impossible for us to conceive of our own non-existence, and whether we say or even believe that we are afraid of death or not, each person lives under the greatest of philosophic tension: the tremendous importance of ourselves to ourselves vs. our tremendous *in*significance in the totality of things.

There are various ways to try to handle this tension. One is the hard-boiled so-called realistic view of a professed atheist such as Bertrand Russell, who wrote:

> I believe that when I die I shall rot, and nothing of my ego will survive. I am not young, and I love life. But I should scorn to shiver with terror at the thought of annihilation. Happiness is none the less true happiness because it must come to an end, nor do thought and love lose their value because they are not everlasting.[11]

Now of course I cannot logically and conclusively prove to an atheist that God exists, any more than he can prove that He does not exist. What Lord Russell's view *does* do when carried out logically is to come down heavily on the tremendous insignificance of an individual life. In Russell's book, *Why I Am Not a Christian*, there is a debate between him and a Jesuit priest. The priest asked Russell if he were morally shocked at the conduct of the commandant of the Belsen concentration camp in Germany. Russell replied

---

11. Bertrand Russell, *Why I Am Not a Christian and Other Essays on Religion and Related Subjects,* ed. Paul Edwards (London: George Allen and Unwin, Ltd., 1957), p. 43.

that he was indeed shocked, but at least to me the reasons he gave for his moral outrage were pretty inadequate. Basically, he said he was shocked because he *personally* felt that this was a morally wrong thing to do.[12] His standard was his own feeling. But quite obviously the commandant of Belsen and Adolf Hitler and a number of others did not feel morally shocked at all—any more than Sheriff Bull Conner[13] felt morally shocked by what he did. By Russell's argument what could be morally wrong with making soap out of a few million people if it were felt that this would be to the ultimate benefit of the majority?

Moreover, can you really accept a view of the world in which you are merely another ant in the anthill? Here today, gone tomorrow, with even the "hereness" merely sound and fury signifying nothing?

At least a Christian must give people like Bertrand Russell credit for facing and wrestling with the basic issues of life. Most people choose another option. They try to run away from confrontation or avoid it. Death is never men-

---

12. See debate between Bertrand Russell and Father F. C. Copleston, S.J., in "The Moral Argument," in Russell, *Why I Am Not a Christian*, pp. 120-25, esp. p. 125.

13. Eugene "Bull" Conner perhaps is best remembered for the events during his tenure as the Commissioner of Public Safety in Birmingham, Alabama, in 1963 when fire hoses and police dogs were turned on black protesters.

tioned. People don't "die," they "pass away" or "depart." Perhaps some people today honestly don't think about death. Harvey Cox's brilliant book, *The Secular City*, suggests that modern urban-secular man just doesn't ask himself ultimate questions about life or death.[14] Perhaps so, although I doubt it. But this doesn't necessarily affect the great tension I had referred to earlier. So pathetically often we see people who boldly articulate a hard-boiled philosophy in which they admit the obvious insignificance of individuals in the totality of things, and yet their whole heart, soul and mind are obsessed with the overwhelming significance of themselves. This can be summed up in the tone of the self-pitying martyr who says with a snivel, "You go out and enjoy yourselves. I'll stay here. After all, I don't matter." Obviously what such a person really means is that he thinks he matters a very great deal.

There is another choice available to deal with this problem; but it assumes a miracle. One dictionary defines a miracle as "an event or effect deviating from the known laws of nature, or transcending our knowledge of these laws."[15] Our empirical common sense would lead us to agree with Orwell's cynical maxim in *Animal Farm*: "All

---

14. Harvey Cox, *The Secular City* (New York: Macmillan Co., 1965), pp. 79-84.

15. Citation uncertain.

animals are equal, but some animals are more equal than others."[16]

Our miracle would be that all human creatures are truly equal and of infinite value, not because they are all of the same virtue (they are clearly not), not because they have the same talents or intelligence (they clearly do not have these similarities), not because they necessarily have any characteristics which the standards of this world can define as making them equal, but for the miraculous reason that the God who made them loves them equally, and it is this love and the potential to respond to this love which gives them value–nothing else. On this basic postulate hangs every humanitarian movement of modern history, whether it be abolition of child labor and slavery, public hospitals, universal free public education, civil rights, or the movement for the abolition of capital punishment. This is the great issue in the debate over the abortion laws–the sanctity of each human life.

By this miracle each life in this church today is a Great Story. Each life is the great American novel. The only way we really experience ourselves is as stories. When we try to

16. The Seven Commandments of Animalism which concluded with "All animals are equal" were replaced with the single commandment, "All animals are equal but some animals are more equal than others." In George Orwell, *Animal Farm* (New York: Harcourt, Brace and Co., 1946), p. 12 and p. 113.

understand and evaluate ourself, the "self" we have to work on is our past history, strung together in a series of events in past time. We are also unfinished stories, at least insofar as we ourselves can tell the story.

The miracle is that *your* story is the great story. It is as important as any other story that will ever be told. History books recall only the slightest fraction of the millions of people who have walked this earth. The Christian claims equal significance, not only for the heroes, but for each of those now totally forgotten by the living. This in itself turns our customary value structure upside down. Columbus's discovery of America has possibly less permanent significance than the fact that one of his crew, now forgotten by the history books, nursed a sick shipmate back to health. Your relationship to your spouse has every bit the same significance as some of the great romances of the history books. Your decision to quit your job and open a new business may have the same fateful consequences as Caesar at the Rubicon. No one will ever again have to make the decision Harry Truman made to drop the bomb on Hiroshima but my decision to deliberately hurt or offend a neighbor may ring through the halls of eternity with an even more jarring sound.

The big question, if this miracle is true, is, "How are you going to write your story?" You have been given the freedom to write it as, unfortunately, most men have written it. You can draw a circle with yourself in the center, and your story will be a tale of how big a dot the center of the circle can become and how many satellites, whether people or things, you have been able to attract to revolve around your orbit.

Or you can do something dramatic and exciting with your story. You can give instead of take. You can try to measure by what goes out rather than what comes in. You can do something wonderful, exciting and good. Get out of the rut of your prudential concerns and write a *different* story!

The end of each life story, however you choose to write it, is the same—an obituary. No obituary will ever set forth the really important events as you saw them (you'll be lucky if they spell your name correctly), and my opening story about the three children and the scrapbook will apply just as well to a Christian saint as to a militant atheist, a generous giver and a selfish miser. Within a short time few living even remember that you existed. If we write our story merely for what the world at the moment thinks of it, we are as pathetic as the fading movie star I saw at an airport the other day, old enough to be my mother, trying to look sexy.

Very few will remember, one way or the other. But as St. Paul knew, this really doesn't matter. "If God is for us, who can be against us?" [Rom. 8:31, Phillips] He did not mean by this, I am sure, that at some post-obituary period God would give extra special celestial lollipops to the children whose earthly life had been made so drab and painful because they had been "good" (and you will note that in this sermon I have not mentioned life hereafter). St. Paul was convinced of the resurrection and life everlasting, as I am, but he was also concerned about life here and *now* and he knew that a life story could be an obituary even before physical death. This makes such a story no less important in God's eyes, but surely it makes it more tragic, because as we are now, unless we do something about it, we shall become.

Lest any vestryman think I am selling them short, this is indeed an Every Member Canvass Sermon on the most basic level that I know how to give one. Here is a description of you and me given by our kids: "pleasure-leisure-love locksteppers, well meaning money-making machines, naked in our imperial new clothes."

There come a few moments each year and each day when we have the choice as to whether we want to rewrite our story and get out of the lockstep. I honestly believe that the Every Member Canvass is one of these. When we are requested to do something big, not just for the Church of Jesus Christ, not just for the work it does in the world, not just for dear old St. Francis' parish [San Francisco, California], but for ourselves and the story we are writing.

The bulk of us are token pledgers. We pay less than it would require to get our families to the local movie house once a week. This is a fact. It is my hope that each year at

Canvass time we can reach a few more–to take this confrontation not as a threat, not as another request for a hand-out, but as a chance to get out of the lockstep, to change your story into one which breaks from the mold.

The Canvass is by no means the only way such confrontations are made. There are plenty of others. But I have found that people who have cracked the barrier of tokenism in one, have also done it in other.

If you double or triple your pledge this year I will not promise you that *your* scrapbook won't go into the garbage can. I won't even promise that your name will be spelled correctly in your obituary. And God will love you just as much whatever you do.

But I do promise that to the extent we can crack the barrier of our own selfishness and give, our apprehension of God's love is enhanced and our understanding of its meaning grows.

A good ending for my life story is the word of the psalmist: "Yea, a joyful and pleasant thing it is to be thankful" [Ps. 147:16, Coverdale, in *The Book of Common Prayer* (1928)].

3

Have you ever thought of the incredible fortune bestowed upon us? With few exceptions this congregation is white, middle class WASP. We* could *have been born an Ethiopian. Our chance in this world* starts *with a head start. Few of us speak a second language fluently, but fortunately for us the rest of the world, including every air line flight control terminal in the world, must speak* our *language. We haven't had to stretch.

The Nineteenth Sunday after Pentecost
September 28, 1986

The Cathedral Church of St. Mark
Salt Lake City, Utah

AMOS 6:1-7; PSALM 146; 1 TIMOTHY 6:11-19; LUKE 16:19-31

I find myself assigned to preach on a Sunday where the appointed Gospel contains another of those exclusionary parables similar to the narrow and closed door I was given to wrestle with a few weeks ago.

In today's Gospel, we are told little of the personal ties of the two principal characters, the rich man (frequently called Dives, which is Latin for "rich man") and Lazarus, except that Dives was a rich man who lived very well "clothed in purple and fine linen who feasted sumptuously every day" [Luke 16:19, RSV], and Lazarus was a beggar who lay at Dives's gate, desiring to be fed from what fell from Dives's table. He was covered with sores.

Our other lessons for today also dwell upon the well-to-do. Amos warns of the smug complacency of luxury. "Woe to those who are at ease in Zion . . . Woe to those who lie upon beds of ivory and stretch themselves upon their couches . . . who drink wine in bowls and anoint themselves with the finest oils" [Amos 6:1, 4, 6, RSV].

Our passage from 1st Timothy concludes:

> As for the rich in this world, charge them not to be haughty, nor to set their hopes on uncertain riches but on God who richly furnishes us with everything to enjoy. They are to do good, be rich in good deeds, liberal and generous, thus laying up for themselves a good foundation for the future, so that they may take hold of the life which is life indeed [1 Tim. 6:17-19, RSV].

Our psalm for today reminds us that the Lord lifts up those who are bowed down. He sustains the widow and orphans. He keeps his promise forever.

Our Lord loved twitting the rich. The rich man's chances of heaven are compared to those of a camel getting through the eye of a needle. We are told of the young man who was told to give up everything to follow Him–and he went away sorrowing, for he had much riches.

The main body of the Christian Church has never

taught that a Christian must part with all his worldly possessions to be a follower. Communal sects have arisen but they have not survived. Certain Christian orders have taken vows of poverty, but this has always been seen as a special vocation for a chosen few.

Indeed, one of the great blots upon the history of the Christian Church is its accumulation of great worldly wealth, which is often flaunted even in the face of surrounding stark poverty. This occurs until a collective religious and secular consequence rises up to squash such acquisitional arrogance.

But is to be rich, in itself, an unforgivable sin and to be poor and covered with sores a great redeeming virtue? A first reading of the parable of Dives and Lazarus would suggest this: between them there is a great chasm fixed. It sounds like a classic Marxist text–the class struggle–death to the bourgeois and the aristocracy! If not now, then in the unforgiving hereafter!

As with the last exclusionary text I had to preach on, by coincidence I was out in the wilderness the weekend before with a group of friends, again all of them unchurched.

I read over the parable several times and asked them what it said to them. We discussed the fact that there was apparently no description of the rich man as evil (unless being rich was per se evil) and Lazarus was poor. But did

Dives even know Lazarus existed? (Although he must have seen him each time he went from his house.)

Then one of my friends said, "Read to me again what Dives said to Abraham when he was in Hades." "Father Abraham, have mercy upon me, and send Lazarus to dip the end of his finger in water and cool my tongue; for I am in anguish in this flame" [Luke 16:24, RSV].

So Dives *did* know of Lazarus. He even knew his name. And what did Dives do? Even though circumstances had completely changed, his mind-set had not. "Boy, fetch!" Lazarus was the obvious instrumentality to do something *for* him and it becomes equally obvious that in his lifetime Dives had never even considered doing anything *for* Lazarus. In this regard, Lazarus did not even exist.

In this context, the parable takes on a different meaning. It is not an indictment of wealth *per se,* but of arrogant, unmindful possession of power without responsibility.

Now, I know all of the perfectly valid arguments against giving to the Lazaruses of the world: You encourage begging. You make a nation of loafers. He should go out and get a job.

Yet the other day a man out in front of one of our Utah Socialist Liquor Stores showed me his money and he needed another twenty cents to buy a bottle of muscatel. I gave him a quarter to aid him in another night of oblivion. Was I an aider and abetter in promoting social misery?

A friend of mine told me about a flight, non-stop, from

Salt Lake City to New York City. He was flying first class and drinks were free. But in those days they had a ration of only two drinks to a person, no matter how long the flight. After the fourth hour he noticed that the fellow next to him had not ordered his quota. My friend asked him if *he* might have his drinks. The man's response was, "Of course not, I am president of Brigham Young University." Did he really think that this refusal was going to change any moral climate in the supplicant?

Surely our small gifts are not going to change the world. My twenty-five cents only added to its misery. But at least I parted with *something*.

Our food bank at this Cathedral Church [of St. Mark, Salt Lake City] asks for no credentials of worthiness. We give to those who ask. The State of Utah tried to put conditions on giving away Federal surplus food–I.D., Social Security numbers, etc.–a lengthy form purportedly to stop "free cheese loaders."

Thirty percent of this country is fundamentally illiterate. They can't even *read* this form. Rather than this incredible bureaucratic demand, we should have an *enraged* populace which demands literacy from our public schools and a basic literacy test as a condition of parole from our penal institutions.

If I am lost in a world in which I cannot cope and I have no Dives who at least shows an interest in my existence, where am I? In hell on earth.

3. THE NINETEENTH SUNDAY AFTER PENTECOST, 1986.

O.K., you and I are not Dives. We are not clothed in purple and fine linen and feast sumptuously every day. But guess what? We really are. If you compressed the world proportionately into the town of Manti, Utah, Americans, a small portion of the world's now four billion people, would be incredibly rich. Living high on the hill, with 98 percent of the rest in miserable slums below. From a prudential view (forget a moral point of view) guess what will ultimately happen? These folks down the hill are going to decide that the accident of fortunate birth is no justification for this prestigious position, and some folks are going to try to change this.

Have you ever thought of the incredible fortune bestowed upon us? With few exceptions this congregation is white, middle-class WASP. We *could* have been born an Ethiopian. Our chance in this world *starts* with a head start. Few of us speak a second language fluently, but fortunately for us the rest of the world, including every air line flight control terminal in the world, must speak *our* language. We haven't had to stretch.

The parable for today tells me that we had *better* stretch. You and I are Dives. The twenty-five cents to a bum isn't enough. Lazarus needs more than that. What at least I should have done is ask the man who he was, where he came from, what was his immediate problem, what were his plans. I did not do this, and to this extent I was only a tad better than Dives. I just wanted to get away and go about my business.

I would not have changed the world by such inquiries: Old con artists know well how to bring a tear, and to give you the answers you want to hear.

But this was a human being I bought off for a quarter so that he would not bother me any further.

I have guilts about that. The parable in today's Gospel bothers me as of course it should. Does it bother *you*?

In the grace and love of our Lord Jesus Christ, I hope it does.

4

"The Tough Nut"

The Twenty-sixth Sunday after Pentecost
November 16, 1986

The Cathedral Church of St. Mark
Salt Lake City, Utah

[Note: This skit, written by Albert Colton, preceded his sermon that Sunday.]

VOICE OFF: The elegant home of the widow Mrs. G. Woodingham Gotbucks – a Sunday afternoon.

Mrs. G: (Humming at her knitting)

(Bell rings)

Mrs. G: Who is it, Geoffrey?

VOICE OFF: Someone who says he is a canvasser from St. Mark's Cathedral, Madame.

Mrs. G. Someone selling canvass to see me on a Sunday afternoon–how bizarre!

VOICE OFF: No, Madame, he says something even more distasteful–he has come to ask for money.

Mrs. G. Oh, dear, now I remember–all those

[Mrs. G:] letters I've received. Well, show him in, Geoffrey.

How do you do young man? Sit down. Geoffrey, bring the young man some champagne and some of the caviar pizza.

Times are getting harder for poor old widows, young man. Our cuvée is running dry.

But you don't have to say a thing, young man, I know why you're here. I have been a member of the dear old Cathedral since before you were born. Dear old Dean humph, humph, and dear old Bishop humph, humph, He confirmed me. I don't get around much anymore, as the song says. (You didn't think I was that "hip," did you, young man?)

Haven't been to the old place in years, but I certainly hear things, not good, either. We have a new bishop and I hear he's too tall. I always preferred short men, myself. They are more sincere and you can push them around more easily (like my dear Harvie. He was only five feet, two inches, you know). You have a new Prayer Book, a new Hymnal, you let

[Mrs. G:] women do things publicly (someone told me you are even ordaining them, but I can't believe that), and I hear you read the Bible out of translations other than the blessed "St. James" version.

Well, "Toujours the change," as the French say. (Or does that mean "keep the change"?) Anyway, young man, I won't take a minute more of your time. Just renew my pledge at the same old amount.

(Pause)

No, it isn't $100 a week, it's one dollar a week. Nobody gives *that* much money!

(Pause)

You say two people in the parish do, and others are close behind? Well, they must be knee jerk liberal saps or silly clergy who take these things seriously, that's all I can say.

(Voice gets tough) Look, young man, here's some advice for your old age: "waste not–want not." That plus a $5 million inheritance got me where I am today.

You can renew my pledge for $1.00 per week.

[Mrs. G:] Why, you're tearing up my card–
come back here!!!

(Door slams)

Geoffrey, what did he say as he left?

VOICE OFF: He said he felt sorry for you, Madame, and he had tears in his eyes.

5

As with the whole process of our Lord's ministry of proclamation, teaching, feeding and healing, these functions after Pentecost were left in the hands of the fallible people who together constitute the Christian church.

The Eighth Sunday after Pentecost August 2, 1987 — *The Cathedral Church of St. Mark Salt Lake City, Utah*

As we raced to the car to begin our long trek to the Wind River Mountains [in west central Wyoming] last weekend, I picked from the shelf a paperback entitled The Great Depression. So much of this bleak story I had forgotten–"long lines of patient, hopeless, humiliated men shuffling forward slowly to receive a bowl of watery soup and a crust of bread from charity kitchens."[17] By December 1931, unemployment had reached one-third of the American labor force.[18] "In some respects, it was the

17. Robert Goldston, *The Great Depression–The United States in the Thirties* (Greenwich, Conn.: Fawcett Publications, Inc., 1968), p. 49.

18. Ibid., p. 52.

children who suffered most. Millions of them dropped out of school, hundreds of thousands lost their families."[19]

Those of us in our cabin discussed those days. We had all been fortunate enough to have avoided the real nightmares of those days. We were all relatively comfortable.

Today we still have the hungry and the homeless about us, even in Salt Lake City, and it struck me that those of us in this Cathedral congregation are generally like our little group in the mountain cabin. We are relatively comfortable as this condition exists around us.

It is easy to try to shut our eyes and rationalize this problem. President Hoover is quoted in the book I mentioned as saying that he had heard of one hobo who received ten free meals in one day.[20] You recall President Reagan's story of the woman who drove up to the store to use her food stamps in a new Cadillac. It is easy to point out that the few dollars that Canon Wirth deals out to indigents dozens of times a week does nothing to cure that person's underlying problem.

Our gospel for today is St. Matthew's version of the feeding of the five thousand. When one-quarter of the

---

19. Ibid., p. 53. See as well Chapter two, "Brother, Can You Spare a Dime," pp. 45ff.

20. Ibid., p. 59.

human race routinely goes to bed hungry each night, and when between 13-18 million people (75 percent of whom are children under five) die of starvation each year, it can be asked, "If this caring, loving God could feed five thousand people plus women and children *then*, why doesn't he do it now?"

Of course, we must remember that during his earthly ministry our Lord did not feed *everyone*, nor while he did do some healing, he did not heal everyone–only a select few received these benefits. Remember that St. Paul, even after his conversion, continued to have what he called his "affliction."

As with the whole process of our Lord's ministry of proclamation, teaching, feeding and healing, these functions after Pentecost were left in the hands of the fallible people who together constitute the Christian church.

They were to carry out these ministries in his name, but seldom with miraculous powers, rather working within the restrictions of physical laws and further and more significantly, working with human beings who each, whether Christian or not, had the innate tendency to be far more concerned about their own welfare than those of others.

One of the most mind-boggling matters I have ever encountered is that of agricultural economics–subsidies, cross-subsidies, surplus seen as an evil, millions upon millions spent to store food stuffs to keep them from the market. In this vast land of plenty, farmers are being forced from their land by foreclosure. As I say, I cannot begin to fathom the whys and the wherefores of all of this.

But I do know a few basic facts. As a report issued by our last General Convention stated: God has really given this world of ours bountiful resources. "Approximately 1,500 million metric tons of grain are produced globally each year. If *equally* distributed among the world's 4.7 billion people, it would give everyone some 3,000 calories per day including ample protein." It is estimated that it would cost $17 billion per year to purchase and accomplish this distribution process (this figure would also include education and housing for everyone in the world). This admittedly is a huge sum, but ironically the world spends this amount in arms every two weeks.[21]

This in itself ought to tell us something about our priorities.

The famine in Ethiopia illustrated further problems. We found that shipments of relief goods were being fun-

---

21. *The Blue Book–Reports of the Committees, Commissions, Boards, and Agencies of the General Convention of the Episcopal Church: The Report of the "Standing Commission on Human Affairs and Health"* (New York: The General Convention of the Episcopal Church, 1985), pp. 126-27. A fine creation centered spiritual and theological discussion of this can be found in Matthew Fox, *Original Blessing* (Santa Fe, New Mexico: Bear and Co., 1983), pp. 9-29, esp. p. 14.

neled off by corrupt middle men and that the communist oriented government was often distributing this relief in ways to further its own political purposes. But one Roman priest said, "Look, these starving kids aren't political."

The feeding of the five thousand was an act of pure grace. There were no qualifications for getting fed. Those who came to hear Him received sustenance. As the central proclamation of the good news, the gospel, is that God takes us where we are. God so loved that he gave–without strings.

But there is also the strain of judgment in Jesus' teachings–remember the sheep and the goats; the wheat and the tares, etc. The tension between grace and judgment is reflected in the old preaching axiom: Your function, preacher, is to comfort the afflicted, and to afflict the comfortable.

Dietrich Bonhoeffer, the World War II German Christian martyr, coined the term "cheap-grace" in which he pointed out that while grace was indeed free, there is a *cost* of discipleship involved as well.[22]

Cheap grace is reflected in the death-bed exchange reported of Gertrude Stein–someone asked her, "Do you

---

22. Dietrich Bonhoeffer, *The Cost of Discipleship* (New York: Macmillan Co., 1963), Chap. 1, pp. 45-114, esp. pp. 45-60.

think God will forgive you?" To which she replied, "Of course, that's his business."[23]

As we gather here this morning for *our* free meal, I hope you will give some thought as to how you can exercise your discipleship. One obvious and simple way is to make a contribution to the Cathedral [Church of St. Mark, Salt Lake City, Utah] food bank administered by Mr. Rush Duer. Anyone can come and receive food–no questions asked. It is estimated that about 5000 people were fed last year.

So you see, you too can participate in an act of grace. You too can literally participate in the feeding of the five thousand some two thousand years later–checks, yes, made out to the Cathedral Food Bank, but no fishes, please.

---

23. Colton may well have read that Gertrude Stein had said that. However, he might have been remembering the words of Empress Catherine the Great when she said, "I shall be an autocrat: that's my trade. And the good Lord will forgive me: that's his" ("*Moi, je serai autocrate: cést mon métier. Et le bon Dieu me pardonnera: Cést son métier*"), in *The Oxford Dictionary of Quotations*, 3d ed., intro. Bernard Darwin (New York: Oxford University Press, 1979), p. 244.

X
Church, State, and Law

Introduction

Albert Colton believed the complex issue of church and state was something which demanded considerable energy and time. He made it a point to preach upon the subject when the occasion demanded it. The Very Reverend William F. Maxwell, Dean of the Cathedral Church of St. Mark in Salt Lake City, said of Colton, upon his death, "As a priest he was a superior preacher, a loving pastor, and a great Christian. He was also an attorney who was widely respected in the legal community. I think these two parts of his life were wonderfully integrated. . . . [He was] a unique example of the union of the sacred and the secular."[1]

As an Anglican who lived and studied the law and observed the Church in both the United States and England, Colton had a perspective on the church-state issue which was well informed, experienced, and, indeed, integrated.

While he was integrated in his academic, vocational, and professional life regarding church and state, Colton remained unequivocally opposed to confusing the roles and boundaries of church and state.

Attempts at theocracy, that is rule by men of God,

1. William F. Maxwell, quoted in "Albert J. Colton Dies at 63, Priest, Attorney, Scholar," *Salt Lake Tribune*, Nov. 8, 1988, p. D1, cols. 1-2.

have been attempted throughout known history. Portions of early New England underwent this experiment. This [Salt Lake] valley was settled with this assumption in mind, and sometimes with more and sometimes with less subtlety, attempts are constantly made to bring this to fruition.

What could possibly be wrong with any politician who urges a "return to spiritual values"? How could anyone from a Christian pulpit take issue with this being a good idea?

Well, I for one will give it a try, because I think this concept of the way men should be governed, *given the nature of men*, can be one of the most demonic of all forms in which we can live together.

Our Lord Himself never suggested the establishment of a theocracy. Indeed he constantly rejected suggestions that he assert a worldly kingship. " . . . render to Caesar the things that are Caesar's . . . " [Mark 12:17, RSV]. St. Paul carefully refrained from rattling the cage of Caesar and was in fact quite proud of his Roman citizenship.[2]

Being an Anglican in the predominately Mormon setting of Salt Lake City, Colton was very aware of being a part of a minority faith and was sensitive to that situation as a lawyer, as a citizen, and as a church person. He was wary of others as well

2. Sermon preached the Fifth Sunday of Easter, May 13, 1979, the Cathedral Church of St. Mark, Salt Lake City, Utah.

as himself establishing and therefore defining the accepted standards of conduct which one would normally find in a theocracy.

> *Who* is to define what is "Spiritual"? Is it unspiritual for women to wear western dress? The Ayatollah Khomeini thinks so.
>
> Is it unspiritual to drink a glass of wine? Our LDS [Church of Jesus Christ of Latter-day Saints] friends think so.
>
> Roman Catholicism in the heyday of its political supremacy asserted, "error has no rights" and "error" was of course defined as anything which contradicted Roman Catholicism.
>
> The Church of England pushed through Parliament the *Act of Uniformity* imposing upon all the people of that country not only one religion (the Christian Faith) but also only one way to express that religion.[3]

Colton became quite alarmed when issues of morality were placed before the citizens for consideration in an election.

> Another type of question being raised in this election . . . is this year's Proposition 16, the so-called "Anti-Smut" or "Clean" proposition. . . . Proposition 16 clearly radiates wholesomeness and goodness. A twelve-page newspaper supplement, in color sponsored by the Schick razor company and appearing in

3. Ibid.

papers throughout California and mailed to most clergy, puts it squarely on the line. A "Yes" vote is a vote for decency, or as the last page of the supplement says, "Happiness is voting yes on Proposition 16."

The issue seems so clear cut. Who in the world would vote in favor of smut? Well, Bishop Tippett of the Methodist Church for one, the Board of Directors of the Northern California Council of Churches for another, a conservative newspaper as the *Los Angeles Times* for a third, also the Archdiocese of San Francisco and the San Francisco Chamber of Commerce. All have urged a "no" vote, and these are hardly figures of lascivious evil. Rather they are concerned about the means suggested for such control which they feel denies basic constitutional safeguards and liberties, and the lesson that history has frequently taught us that the use of "good" in the hands of the overzealous can lead to witch hunts where the good suffer with the evil.[4]

While distrusting zealots, Colton also exposed watered down belief and sentimentality as a dangerous fraud and would have no part of it either.

It is not that I feel that what we believe is not important–it is desperately important, because ideas

4. Sermon preached the Twenty-second Sunday after Trinity, November 6, 1966, St. Francis' Church, San Francisco, California.

have consequences in the way we live, whether we know it or not.

One of the most foolish statements ever made was attributed to President Eisenhower: "I don't care what a person believes in, so long as he believes in something."[5] Doesn't that sound tolerant and broad-minded? But of course if Ike had thought it through, he would see how silly it was. Of *course* he cared what a person believed. Does he, for example, take no position about the Adolf Hitlers of his world who believe in making soap out of millions of "inferior" people? The Eisenhower dictum does indeed reflect a moral bankruptcy. . . . It is reflected in Main Street Christianity, "I'm as good a Christian as anyone else. I don't bother about the Creeds or churches, but I don't kick my dog and I try to be a good guy, and good old God, he'll take care of me."

But the crux of the matter is that the Main Street Christian is *not* a good guy, nor is anyone else.[6]

And yet Colton was convinced that the church had a place in the state. That place for the church was in the "state of prayer and prophecy."

---

5. As has been already noted, while the citation is uncertain, President Eisenhower did say, "In other words, our form of government has no sense unless it is founded in a deeply felt religious faith and I don't care what it is." In *New York Times*, Dec. 23, 1952, p. 16 L, col. 5.

6. Sermon preached the Fifth Sunday of Easter.

The (American) *Book of Common Prayer* recognizes the Fourth of July as a special day, showing the felt need for God's help to us as a nation.[7]

The Church has always been concerned with the State, because in a sacramental world it is impossible to divorce the two. Thus for those who object strongly to the Church's new-found voice on political and social issues, they should be reminded that we say prayers for the President, the government and those who govern at each public service. If we feel sufficiently that our prayers for the President and the State have value, then surely we can be honest enough to say aloud not only *that* we pray for our government, but *why* and *what* we are praying about.[8]

Colton saw that prayer as "activity." And therefore, any and all activities in which the state had a part or role were fair game for prayerful contemplation, intercession, and action. Piety could not be silent.

Election time is upon us, as our bulletin for today reminds us. I suppose there are a few who might even find the bulletin offensive. "The church should have nothing to do or say about the dirty world of politics,

---

7. See *The Book of Common Prayer* (New York: The Church Hymnal Corporation, 1979), p. 242, for the Collect for Independence Day. See also pp. 16-17 referencing Independence Day as a Major Feast Day.

8. Sermon preached on Independence Day, July 4, 1970, the Cathedral Church of St. Mark, Salt Lake City, Utah.

and should confine itself to spiritual affairs" [they might say]. But the problem is that the Christian Gospel makes no such distinction between things temporal and spiritual, and we would not only have to scrap such Sunday bulletins as this which come from such a conservative diocese as the Diocese of Chicago, but we would have to pretty well revise *The Book of Common Prayer* and the Bible itself.[9]

To the contrary, the Church and her members are a part of the world and should be concerned about life in all of its aspects and we can no more legitimately eliminate the political world from our concern than we can any other.[10]

The role of Christianity, in considering the state, had to include reflection on values, issues, and personalities.

[Some suggest] the Church's right and responsibility starts and finishes in a democratic society when it does what it can to urge people to exercise their right of franchise. This is summed up in the slogan, "We don't care who you vote for, just as long as you vote."

9. In 1966 the bulletins of which Colton was speaking were published by the Public Relations Office of the Diocese of Chicago. They were edited by the "Partly Printed Parish Papers Editorial Committee," of which the Dean of St. James' Cathedral, Chicago, the Very Reverend William F. Maxwell, was a member. In 1978, Dean Maxwell began his rich partnership of ministry with Colton at St. Mark's Cathedral, Salt Lake City.

10. Sermon preached the Twenty-second Sunday after Trinity.

But this is a little silly, if you think about it, and comes close to the old saying, "I don't care what you believe in as long as you believe in something." Both statements assume that the Christian Church is not concerned about *VALUE*, which is of course, nonsense. If a person has not taken the slightest interest at all in either issues or candidates, and casts his ballot on an "eeny-meeny, miny, mo" basis, I could rather imagine the Church saying, "For heaven's sake, please *don't* vote!" If you are going to exercise this right, then exercise it responsibly. If the Christian Church has any role in a time of disintegrating value, it is surely one of emphasizing the need for responsibility in action and conduct.

Another suggested answer is that the Church has a right to speak out on political issues but never on personalities. But this creates problems too. There are, to begin with, certain issues on which I think the Church has no real business speaking because they raise only the barest possible type of moral question (although in looking through Tuesday's ballot, I found fewer clear examples than I thought). One example of this might be Proposition 11, dealing with *technical* changes in the Boxing and Wrestling Initiative Act. (Although I do think the Church might have something quite legitimate to say about the *substantial* aspects of professional boxing and wrestling.) And while it is a pretty good rule of thumb to say that the Church should stay away from personalities, there does come a time when a person and an issue are so clearly identified that it would be impossible for the Church to speak on the one without the other.

To complicate the problem even further, it is true that in most cases the *issue* in question is sufficiently complex that reasonable Christian minds can differ about it. Take the question of the war in Vietnam or abortion. It is impossible to say that there is a definitive Christian answer to this, because Christians of unquestioned commitment disagree radically in their approach to it.[11]

Colton recognized that Christians could disagree about what values were true and important, what issues were most needing attention, and which personalities needed scrutinizing. He did, however, offer two components of the faith he believed were universally Christian considerations of society.

First, the Christian is obligated to see that he has made use of all the materials before him. He is expected, in other words, to do a good job. As Dorothy Sayers has pointed out, our Lord undoubtedly in his youth assisted St. Joseph in his carpentry.[12] We have no record of what he did, but of one thing we can be sure–if he made tables, he made *good* tables. There is nothing slip-shod or half-baked about the power of

11. Ibid.

12. Citation uncertain.

God, and one of the greatest scandals to the Body of Christ is not corruption or venality or even heresy, but the absence of a standard of excellence.

Second, and this is perhaps the hardest thing of all, we must analyze ourselves in the light of the Christian concept of man. You and I are sinners, that is, we are innately selfish, and left to ourselves, will think instinctively first and foremost of ourselves. The Christian Church would further say that man in this state of selfishness is never truly fulfilled, and the reason that the Gospel is truly GOOD NEWS is that it makes available to us the means of escaping from the prison and hell of self-pity and self-concern. A fulfilled person is a giving person who can give of his love, concern and (as we have spent a few weeks stressing) of his money to others.

But sin is a wily devil and it comes at us in its most demonic form clothed as an angel of light. We each have a most marvelous capacity to seduce ourselves, and we clothe such seduction in the most marvelously glowing robes of grandiose principle![13]

Given the above demands upon society, Colton suggested three phases for the Christian in political involvement.

We often seek to spout pious generalizations or retreat to "basic principles" to justify action we take out of selfishness, fear and ignorance.

13. Sermon preached the Twenty-second Sunday after Trinity.

So the first step in a Christian lesson in politics is to *recognize* this trait in ourselves. (It might also be helpful to recognize that this is true of all men, including candidates. As the aphorism goes, the difference between a man and a statue is that the statue gets bigger the closer you get to it.)

This first step gets us at least to the second step which is the General Confession in the liturgy,[14] and using the liturgy as a pattern of life, we have to start on our *knees*, recognizing our inadequacies and resolving to try to do something about them.

The third step is to try to do something about them. Our recognition of some concerns helps us here. Perhaps, for example, in reviewing a proposition dealing with the police force, we find that we have strong personal prejudices about the police. Rather than react automatically and emotionally along the line of our prejudice, let us make that prejudice stand on its own feet and defend itself on the merits of a particular case. Let's assume a little caution when we find ourselves automatically voting a position which merely confirms our prejudices and our own selfish interests.

Then after as honest an examination as we can make of the man and issues, we must make a decision.[15]

---

14. *The Book of Common Prayer* (New York: The Church Pension Fund, 1928), p. 75.

15. Sermon preached the Twenty-second Sunday after the Trinity.

Colton believed that making a decision, as a Christian, was not an easy task. How Christians dealt with the laws, actions, and opinions of the state could drive them to moments of frustration, loneliness, and despair. But one thing was for certain. A Christian could not hide from the world and the intricacies of living in a community.

The father of a late friend of mine, an austere, extremely dignified man with a brilliant mind and a sometimes acid tongue, and a lifelong Episcopalian, once wrote a letter to his son which he shared with me. The gist of it was that this gentleman felt very strongly that he did not come to church to hear sermons on texts from Time magazine, which he felt perfectly competent to read on his own.

I can understand his feelings. There comes a time when we are sick and tired of being reminded of the mess we live in, and we want just a few moments respite; we need a place where we can be quiet and regain our composure before venturing forth into the world again.

This is a most understandable and perfectly valid desire, but I am not sure that Epiphanytide is the appropriate time to exercise it. To the contrary, Epiphany is that time when we commemorate the collision of the Incarnate Godhead with the world around Him. The baby Jesus did not stay in the cave, secure and sheltered from the world. Nor could He, for the world sought Him out even before He was capable of going out to it. And this is told to us, perhaps in symbolic form, in the story of the three kings, representing in the ancient legend the different races of mankind, all of whom came to see and pay homage to the new-born Christ.

The event of Epiphany is one that, beginning at that moment, was bound to continue until the end of time. The world will always be pressing in upon the Church, and the Church is not able to hide from the world, nor should it. Indeed its very commission is exactly the opposite–the Church's role is to go to the world of the Gentiles and to make its message manifest.

The collision was inevitable once God entered the world as man. Church and world were inextricably intertwined.[16]

---

16. Sermon preached the First Sunday after the Epiphany, January 7, 1968, St. Francis' Church, San Francisco, California.

1

The flag is a symbol just as the cross I wear is a symbol. The flag, I believe, is a more fallible symbol, but this does not mean it is not significant.

The Sixth Sunday after Trinity — *St. Francis' Church*
July 2, 1967 — *San Francisco, California*

"O Eternal God, through whose mighty powers our fathers won their liberties of old; grant, we beseech thee, that we and all the people of this land may have grace to maintain these liberties in righteousness and peace; through Jesus Christ our Lord."[17]

One of the tests whereby the Romans ferreted out the early Christians was to make them burn incense before the altar of the emperor. The Christians were by conscience forbidden to do this–not because, as they tried to explain, they were not necessarily not loyal to the emperor, and not because they would not pray every day for him and for the empire, but because they could not, in this symbolic fashion, recognize the emperor as God. The emperor too was under God's judgment.

---

17. *The Book of Common Prayer* (1928), p. 263.

Thus, Polycarp, Bishop of Smyrna, was tried by the Roman proconsul in the year 155, and asked to "swear by the genius of Caesar and curse Christ." Polycarp responded, "We have been taught to render to authorities and powers ordained by God, honor as is appropriate. . . . but this, I cannot."[18] Polycarp was burned to death.

One of the basic problems of any Christian is the tension he must bear between his loyalty to his nation-state and to his Lord. It is a proper tension, and one we should be particularly aware of in the commemoration of our Independence Day.

After the American Revolution, when the Anglican

---

18. Another rendering of this conversation is found in *Butler's Lives of the Saints–Concise Edition,* ed. Michael Walsh (San Francisco: Harper and Row, 1985), pp. 56-57. "He (Polycarp) was led to the tribunal of the proconsul, who exhorted him to have regard for his age, to swear by the genius of Caesar, and to say, 'Away with the atheists,' meaning the Christians. The saint, turning towards the crowd of ungodly people in the stadium, said, with a stern countenance, 'Away with the atheists!' The proconsul repeated, 'Swear by the genius of Caesar, and I will discharge you; revile Christ.' Polycarp replied, 'Forescore and six years have I served Him and He hath done me no wrong. How then can I blaspheme my King and my Savior? If you require of me to swear by the genius of Caesar, as you call it, hear my free confession: I am a Christian; and if you desire to learn the doctrines of Christianity, appoint a time and hear me.' The proconsul said, 'persuade the people.' The martyr replied, 'I address myself to you; for we are taught to give due honor to princes, so far as is consistent with religion. But before these people I cannot justify myself.'"

church in the United States realized that it must either become an independent part of the Anglican communion or perish, it set to work to adopt its own independent *Book of Common Prayer*. It had received the gift of the episcopate in a concealed and obscure fashion from the small independent and persecuted Episcopal Church in Scotland. This took place after the Church of England had refused to consecrate a bishop for this new nation because any such bishop quite obviously could not fulfill the then legal requirement that all consecrated bishops would swear allegiance to the British crown. Fortunately, within a few years Parliament repealed this requirement, and the Archbishops of York and Canterbury participated in the consecration of two Americans three years later, in 1787. Thus the American Anglican Church had at that time three bishops from two different lines of succession.

The argument over the new Prayer Book was at times an extremely heated one. Americans would not and could not accept, lock stock and barrel a simple duplication of the English book.

It was customary in the liturgy of England to specifically remember the Sovereign, and to commemorate certain state occasions. (This was also the liturgical custom of all other Christian churches with fixed liturgical forms of worship.)

Obviously American Episcopalians could not offer formal prayers for George III to the neglect of Episcopalian George Washington, and they had no intention of doing so. Indeed to the contrary, it was proposed that the new American Prayer Book contain on July 4th special lessons and a collect, epistle, and gospel for the celebration of the Holy Communion, this to be entitled "A Form of Prayer and Thanksgiving to Almighty God for the Inestimable Blessings of Religious and Civil Liberty." It was hoped that this day would be "observed by this church for ever."[19]

It was no secret that a number of Anglican clergy had remained loyal to the crown during the revolutionary war, and the Presiding Bishop at that time, who had himself been a loyal supporter of the Revolution, bitterly resisted this insertion in the Prayer Book as something which would divide rather than unite his church.

The 4th of July commemoration was thus eliminated by the new American branch of the Anglican communion and was not made a part of our Prayer Book until 1928, when Bishop Edward Lambe Parsons was commissioned to write the collect for Independence Day which appears in the present Episcopal Prayer Book, together with a special epistle and gospel lesson for the offices.

Of course even very few Episcopalians hear these

---

19. Massey Hamilton Shepherd, Jr., *The Oxford American Prayer Book Commentary* (New York: Oxford University Press, 1950), p. 263.

things read in church on the 4th of July (probably most of *them* are not even aware of their existence), and I recount this story of our own church only because I am sure that in a small way it illustrates the deep tension sincere Christians feel between the pull of church and state.

We sometimes forget, in the stained-glass way in which scripture is read to us, that our Lord really at times had a very dry sense of humor. Thus when he said, "Render therefore to Caesar the things that are Caesar's and to God the things that are God's" (Matt. 22:21 [RSV]), he had really tossed the ball right back to those who asked the question and told them to answer it.

Most Christian Churches in this country will at one time or another display the American flag on some formal occasion. For those who have taken this for granted, let me remind them that is an extremely delicate act. The Church is being bitterly attacked as just another salesman of jingoistic western imperialism–Christianity as just another product that followed a flag, like Coca Cola, canned beer, and conducted tours.

There is no question but that the Church has used the flag and that the flag has used the Church, although it takes two to tango. We wince at the times in which a nation has proclaimed that God is on its side, or the times in which the Church has become embroiled in its own structure in the "beholdeness" of national power of appointment. (Roman Catholics should remember that the United States is one of the few countries where to this day the state does not insist on exercising some right of concern over the appointment of their bishops.)

But I am concerned about the superficiality and naivete of those who condemn any relationship of flag and church so unequivocally. It is not as simple as that. Our Lord Himself tossed this problem back to us to solve. There are plenty of pagans who wrap themselves in the American Flag, and use this shield as a launching pad for every form of hate and intolerance. The very term "un-American" is not only poor English usage, but has come to mean in the popular mind, thanks to our super-patriots, something which is intrinsically evil and demonic. The word itself means simply that which is not American.

Surely we cannot say that all things which are not American are therefore intrinsically bad. Indeed, there are many things in the United States which are bad and not good.

But on the 4th of July I will have the American Flag in our church beside the altar—not because we think that God is an American Episcopalian, not because we believe that God loves Americans above all others and holds a heavenly picnic on the 4th of celestial July, but because our ministry and our congregation happen to be predominately American, and because we must meet God where we are now, and because our country and our people need God's help where we are now.

1. THE SIXTH SUNDAY AFTER TRINITY, 1967.

In our parish church we administer wine to several hundred people a week, in the sacrament of the Eucharist, the Holy Communion, the Lord's Supper. We are aware of what wine can do to men. It can send them to a living hell, as any visit to skid row will show you. But paradoxically it can also not only be that vehicle which the Psalmist said "maketh glad the heart of man" (Ps. 104:15 [KJV]) but the very instrument of God's presence itself.

Almighty God gave us the freedom to create both nation-states and wine. We can use either one for our damnation or we can use them as instruments of our salvation and our healing. God has given us the freedom to use those things of His creation, and with this God-given freedom we are required to make decisions.

These decisions will never be easy, and we have no assurance that they will be right. We Americans, at present the strongest, the most mighty nation on earth, are caught in the morass and quick-sand of an enervating, frustrating, seemingly thankless war in an appendix of the continent of Asia. I recently read a book written in 1955 about the same war, and if we could exchange the words "French" for "American," the book could have been published yesterday. Sincere Christians and non-Christians disagree over where this country should go from here.

In the debates in the Security Council and the General Assembly of the United Nations I have heard "God" used on both sides to defend and justify the positions that have been taken by both the Arabs and the Israelis.

I have strong feelings on these issues, as of course you do. But I have no easy answers. Adlai Stevenson once wrote: "I don't recommend a working trip around the world to anyone who likes to keep cool, sleep in the mornings or take Sunday's off. But I strongly recommend it to anyone who thinks the world's problems are simple and that we can solve them all."[20]

Beware if you think you have easy answers to any problem. But also be aware that you have certain symbols and allegiances into which you were born. They are the context of your life, the skin around your bones and like your skin and bones themselves, while they may be and indeed are defective and ultimately perishable, they are the only instrument God has given you at the present time which makes you you.

The American flag is a symbol of our "corporateness," as a nation, as a group of people who either by accident of birth or by choice have chosen this national symbol in a world where each man must choose a national symbol.

I believe that when history is written one thousand

---

20. Adlai Stevenson, "The World I Saw," *Look,* Sept. 22, 1953, p. 46.

years from now that with all of its blemishes, it will generally be regarded as a rather remarkable symbol of a rather remarkable people.

Each of us has our anecdotes, but I remember two quite well: we were having tea in England in an obscure little village with an obscure little vicar in 1949. He said with a wonderful, warm smile, "You know, you are the first Americans we have met since the Marshall plan went into effect. I want to *thank* you for what you are doing." His wife responded icily, "George, that I think they understand. After all, we fought the war before they came, didn't we?" I found out they had lost a son in 1941, before Pearl Harbor. The wife's response was true and understandable, but the vicar's thanks (not often repeated) was also a valid recognition of the uniqueness in history of a victorious power not seeking spoils from its conquest, but indeed sending billions of dollars not only to its destitute allies but to those nations it had conquered.

The other anecdote is a 4th of July party in the American embassy in Prague. We sang the "Star Spangled Banner" (only a great country should tolerate such an unsingable tune), raised the flag, and knowing that we would go back to our hotel and the then constant security checks of the state police, thanked God that we were lucky enough to be Americans.

I can get as teary as the next man about the American flag. It is the symbol of a heritage into which I am born, and of which I am proud. I cannot of course absolutize this symbol, for to do this is to make it a god. Unlike some Congressmen who would send people to prison for burning the flag, I would think that we should recognize that such legislation will only be another example of man's tragic belief that he can by dictation turn a man's heart. Men have spit upon the cross when by torture they were forced to; men have also kissed the cross when by bribery it was to their advantage to do so–and what did either prove?

The flag is a symbol just as the cross I wear is a symbol. The flag, I believe, is a more fallible symbol, but this does not mean it is not significant. We live in a world of symbols. Those pieces of paper you carry in your pocket at this moment (or in your purse) are symbols which are given value only because the United States government says that they have the value imprinted upon them. You have a symbol at the present moment in your bank account, a number, which will dictate what you can and cannot do tomorrow.

If I understand the Christian faith, it says that God came to me, not only two thousand years ago, but that He comes to me in every moment of my life–right where I am–and asks me where I am going, and offers to show me a way. He doesn't meet me in clouds or in visions, but confronts me where I am, and judges me by the heritage that I have been given.

1. THE SIXTH SUNDAY AFTER TRINITY, 1967.

As in my baptism I was born into, both a wonderful privilege and responsibility. So indeed, by the grace of God and through no choice of my own, I was born an American. Both of these are heavy burdens to carry. Last July 4th, we had our flag close to our altar, where it needs to be.

Corny as it may sound, I hope each of you will go out and buy a flag if you don't have one and fly it. Don't fly the flag just in pride, but in the sense, and with a prayer, that we may use the power which it symbolizes to the glory of God and that it will be a symbol of a nation of righteousness and peace because if we fly it to our own glory, there will be a long, long judgment we will face in the years to come.

2

What I am concerned about is . . . the assumption that a Christian's decision to violate the law can be made solely upon the dictation of his personal conscience and that such obedience is obedience to the voice of God.

The Second Sunday in Advent — *St. Francis's Church*
December 10, 1967 — *San Francisco, California*

Advent is a traditional time for preaching about serious themes, and I wish to take advantage of this tradition to preach on a subject which has given me a great deal of concern recently. Preparing sermons gives me an excellent chance to think through questions and hopefully this preparation will be of assistance to you as well.

I will start with a few assumptions. One is that the moral crisis this country faces today is far deeper than the question of our involvement in Vietnam. For after Vietnam is resolved, one way or the other, the *manner* in which it and other pressing problems before us are resolved will be with us—they will indicate what our national character has become.

Long after Vietnam we will have to see how concepts

of justice, order, true freedom, and moral concepts of right and wrong can survive in periods of crisis.

In this statement I am quite obviously taking issue with certain anti-war positions such as the statement made the other day that "ending the war in Vietnam transcends everything else, and is therefore far more important than abiding by all the traditional rules including preservation of an orderly America."[21] I would agree with an editorial from the *New York Times* that some recent outbursts, including those not directly related to Vietnam protests, are "appallingly reminiscent of the behavior of Communist and Nazi hooligans in pre-Hitler Germany" and make a mockery of the ideals such demonstrators profess.[22]

Before proceeding further, let me reiterate what I have

---

21. "From Dissent to Disorder," *New York Times*, Nov. 26, 1967, p. 12E, col. 2. The context of the quotation is as follows: "Defending such actions which turned a recent local demonstration against Secretary of State Rusk into a nightmare, the leader of a group at Columbia University called The Resistance, declared the other day: 'Ending the war in Vietnam' transcends everything else and is therefore far more important 'than abiding by all the traditional rules,' including preservation of 'an orderly America.'"

22. Again, "From Dissent to Disorder," the context of the qoutation is as follows: "Their contemptible attacks on government officials, physical assaults on police and violent interference with the peaceful pursuits of other citizens appallingly reminiscent of the behavior of Communist and Nazi hooligans in pre-Hitler Germany–make a mockery of their professed ideals."

said many times before from this pulpit: Christianity is a proclamation of fact, not a code of ethical behavior. It is the proclamation that God entered this world to save us from ourselves, and to heal the separation we have created between man and man, and between man and God. It is the Good News of God's action, not a celestial Emily Post of rules for man's action. This means that Christians can honestly and sincerely disagree over certain courses of action, and be no less Christians because of it.

But this does not mean that certain courses of conduct have not been given serious and profound analysis by Christian thinkers for many, many centuries, and the conclusions they have reached are well worthy of our consideration.

Many of the Christians who have participated in recent demonstrations have defended their stand on the grounds that a Christian has a sacred duty to follow his conscience wherever it may lead him. Our own bishop has used such language. Thus in a press release issued at the time he refused to allow Grace Cathedral to be used for a draft-card burning, he stated with regard to the selective conscientious objector: "His only moral response–once his conscience informs him that he may not cooperate in a given war which he judges unjust–is to defy the law. . . . it is . . . the clearest of Christian teaching that in such cases the Christian's conscience, i.e.

his obedience to the voice of God is higher than the human law."[23]

I choose to take respectful but serious issue with such a position, and my objection has nothing to do with the merits or demerits of our position in Vietnam. What I am concerned about is what I think is the far more serious and lasting question–the assumption that a Christian's decision to violate the law can be made solely upon the dictation of his personal conscience, and that such obedience is obedience to the voice of God.

The concept of conscience is one upon which Christian moral theologians have devoted many, many a weighty tome. It is thus all the more remarkable to note that this concept is absent from both classical Greek philosophy and also from the Old Testament. For both, actions were judged not on the basis of some personal subjective factor, but by reference to external authority, either that of the City, State, or of the Mosaic Law.[24]

However, in the last three centuries B.C., a growing individualism led to increasing references to "conscience"

---

23. Press Release of the Bishop of California, Nov. 27, 1967, p. 2.

24. J. P. Thornton-Duesbery, "Conscience," *A Theological Word Book of the Bible*, ed. Alan Richardson (New York: MacMillan Publishing Co., Inc., 1950), p. 52.

both in Stoic thought and in some Jewish writing of the Apocrypha.

Even so, the word "conscience" does not appear in any of the four gospels (John 8:9 is considered a gloss), although it does appear frequently in the writings of St. Paul and other epistles.

"Conscience" in these writings was said to belong to all men alike (Rom. 2:15). For the most part, it bears witness to, or pronounces judgment upon actions already performed (e.g., Acts 24:16; Rom. 9:1; Heb. 9:14; 1 Pet. 3:16, 21).

But even in the Epistles there are suggestions that conscience was not always the perfect guide. Thus, we have a reference by St. Paul to a "weak conscience" (1 Cor. 8:7-12 [RSV]), and in later Epistles to "liars whose consciences are seared" (1 Tim. 4:2 [Phillips]), and the statement in Titus, "To the pure all things are pure, but to the corrupt and unbelieving nothing is pure; their very minds and consciences are corrupted" (Titus 1:15 [RSV]).

In the development of the great and elaborate codes and systems of Christian moral theology of the Middle Ages, it was generally agreed that when a man, after informing himself to the best of his ability on the requirements of the moral law, acted as his conscience dictated, he was to be held guiltless, even though his actions were judged by outside considerations or by their results to be reprehensible. In such a case his action was excused by reason of "invincible ignorance." Of course, if the conscience were doubtful, then this was a very different matter.

This principle of medieval casualty is summed up in an Anglo-Catholic text, quoting Thomas Aquinas, as follows: "It is a first principal of morals that wherever conscience gives a clear ruling for or against an act, it must be unhesitatingly obeyed, even though impartial criticism holds that the conscience is erroneous."[25]

It was Immanuel Kant who developed a system of philosophy based upon the absolute supremacy of conscience in the late eighteenth century. It was the existence of conscience that Kant used as his means of "proving" the existence of God.

But of course all of this developed before the days of Sigmund Freud and the revolutionary focusing of science upon the working of the human mind which he began.

In the past few years, we have seen the developing of a new Christian ethical code known as the "New Morality" which, to over-simplify, rejects externalized norms as rules of conduct and suggests that *all* conduct is appropriate as long as it is done in love and does not hurt anyone else.

And thus, in what is surely one of the great ironies, we

---

25. Kenneth E. Kirk, *Some Principles of Moral Theology and their Application* (London: Longmans, 1961), p. 179.

have a group of old and young Turks walking hand in hand with the medievalists, both giving prime significance to the individual as his own judge of the rightness or wrongness of his conduct.

I would submit that both approaches contain serious defects: the medieval sanctification of conscience because it does not take into consideration the knowledge which psychiatry has given us of the mind, and the "New Morality" because it does not pay sufficient heed to the doctrine of sin.

Anthropologists and sociologists have shown us that the values we have are learned values, and they have also shown us that values differ from culture to culture and age to age. A psychiatrist would agree that we each have a conscience (the Freudian would call this our "super ego"—our judicial, our police self, that part of us which scolds, threatens, judges and preaches). But the point is that our conscience or super-ego scolds, threatens, judges, and preaches only on the basis of what has been fed into it. A cannibal gentleman who has never known any other way of life is not going to go to bed with a troubled conscience because he just finished a meal of missionary stew. He may have a deeply troubled conscience which will not let him sleep—but not for that reason, but perhaps he went the wrong way around the village totem pole, an action which wouldn't give you and me a second thought. A conscience is merely our ability to apply given norms to particular facts. It does not *invent* norms but takes norms supplied elsewhere. Put another way, a conscience preaches back to us only what has been fed into it to begin with. When we consider some of the values that are being fed into formative personalities today, I think you can share my apprehension at giving conscience a blank check.

Even more serious, however, is the failure of such a subjective, individualistic test of the rightness of conduct to deal with the problem of our own sinfulness. If you give me enough time by myself, I can rationalize and justify almost anything I do. I may even convince myself that in so doing I am obeying the voice of God Himself.

But we also remember chilling newspaper stories of sick and fiendish acts done by people who claim they are obeying the voice of God.

This does not mean that Christian conscience does not have a role to play in the way we make decisions. But I would suggest that the role is a negative one, not a positive one. It can tell me what not to do, and then I had better heed it. But before I decide to take some drastic positive action on the basis of my conscience, I would be wise to first seek reinforcement elsewhere.

Archbishop William Temple, in his usual sensible manner, put it this way:

> When the suggestion to act in some definite way arises, conscience approves or disapproves. That is always important, and no man who is in earnest about

> the business of right living will ignore that verdict of his moral nature. But he must not attribute to it infallibility. His moral sense requires training, and that training is never complete. . . . When conscience condemns an act, there is likely to be something wrong with that act, but that conscience acquiesces or even approves is not convincing evidence that all is right with the act. Conscience . . . is not by any means a completely reliable guide to life. It may be the best that we have got at any moment, and we must act by it, but always with a readiness to revise its judgments.[26]

I have hauled you through this discourse because I think it has a direct bearing on an extremely serious moral issue. The reliance upon individual conscience alone to justify the breaking of a law which no one I know of claims is in itself innately evil (the Selective Service Act has obvious defects both in content and application, but if the Vietnam war were ended tomorrow demonstrations would doubtless cease) is but another illustration of a growing disregard for collective wisdom and external authority and an atomizing splintering where each man becomes a law unto himself.

One of the great word pictures St. Paul coined was that of the Church as the Body of Christ. A body is a unity, even

26. William Temple, *Nature, Man and God* (New York: Macmillan and Co., Ltd., 1960), p. 179.

though certain portions of that body have different talents and functions. My right toe does not go marching off down the hill without a little advice and consent from the rest of me. The one great unique act we Christians can do is break bread in Eucharist–and quite rightly we can only do this in company, in community. A person cannot receive communion by himself.

In seminary I learned a jim-dandy, thousand dollar phrase: "a self-authenticating charismatic." It described a person with great personal charm and power who, in the early Church, led people astray from the teachings of the corporate Church by the strength of his own will. He alone, by the power of his personality and the conviction of his conscience, was to lead the Church without regard to the Church's corporate mission or mandate. Such men were rejected by the Church.

The whole basis of the Christian faith, as I understand it, is rooted in community. We Christians may be a peculiar people to the world, but we are a peculiar people together.

One of the basic reasons for the malaise that affects this diocese is surely the feeling that statements are being made and actions are taken without consultation, notice or even heed of the existence of the rest of the body of Christ.

Some of these may indeed be true prophetic voices, giving us the always jarring word of God to our complacency. We may indeed have an Amos in our midst, a prophet of social righteousness; we may indeed have another Joan of Arc who hears heavenly voices; but we may also have false prophets who divide and fractionalize the body of Christ unnecessarily.

Make no mistake. This is no apologetic for complacency. If you can look at the world around you and not be disturbed, then the Church today is no place for you. Pagan man is disturbed at the fear and hate he sees. The Christian, who sees in all of this a sacramental potential, should be far more than disturbed—he must weep, and then use those few moments God has allotted to him on this earth to do something about it.

But the world I weep over is one where many of our children seem to see no value, no check, no mandate, beyond themselves. A generation of children who see the law only as hindrance and hypocrisy. A generation who feel that all action is possible as long as one retains a sense of *personal* "honesty" and "integrity." A generation with a massive distrust of anything that smacks of Institutionalism and Establishment.

We, the older citizens, have doubtless created and are responsible for this world. The conscience only acts or reacts to what has been fed into it. Every dinner table conversation in which we have used terms of racial derogation, every act by which we put over some slight violation of the law or of established norms, every Sunday we insist the children go to church while we stay home—all a double standard between formal allegiance and actual practice—each of these is a seed-bed for distrust of all authority. However, this does not mean we must condone or encourage the results of our sin.

I am a Christian because I do not trust myself. I need you and God to help me to act responsibly. But, I have never seen God directly, and I experience Him only through you who are fellow members of His Body and through His sacraments. In any dramatic or drastic actions I would take, however my conscience might direct me, I think it would be my sensible obligation to ask and listen to your thoughts.

Christian history keeps in constant tension the relationship between the sacred uniqueness of the individual and the equally sacred collectivity of the Church. At different periods one or the other of these must be stressed—a teeter-totter can never be perfectly balanced, and never should be or you would ruin the fun, but all the weight can never be at one end either.

We in the Church have had a great orgy of individual expression. We have attempted to sanctify this with the balm of holy conscience. We have had the schizophrenic enjoyment of dashing off in all directions at once.

It is time we put a little weight on the other side of the see-saw. I believe in the Holy Catholic Church. It, in times past, hammered out its creeds together, and some heads were cracked together in the process. The Church, once it had made its decision *together*, enforced its decisions *together*.

We are small enough now. We badly need unifying leadership. But it cannot be that of a license for self-authentication which results from the free reign of individual conscience. We are a church of sinners, and we need law and we need control and direction. What the Church determines together I am willing to follow, and I am not willing to say that my only moral response, once my conscience informs me, is the voice of God and that this alone can lead me to defy the law. Our great heritage, the great heritage of Anglicanism, is that we can develop our law, direction and control together. For God's sake, let us do this!

3

The creation story of Genesis thus reminds us of two basic principles. First, that it is God's basic wish and plan for man to live in order, not chaos, and that it is our duty as God's agents in creation to help mold a world of order; knowing also that any system of order must also be flexible to meet changing times and needs. Genesis also reminds us that ideas have consequences, and in our troubled times it is critical that we do all we can to be sure that the ideologies we hold and espouse are sound and wholesome. No one can fence sit or be silent.

Trinity Sunday — *St. Francis' Church*
June 9, 1968 — *San Francisco, California*

[Note: Senator Robert Francis Kennedy died on June 6, twenty hours after being shot by Sirhan Sirhan.]

Today has been designated a national day of mourning by our President. A gallant young man so senselessly killed; a family which, despite its great wealth, has had more personal tragedy than it would seem any one family could bear. We mourn for them, but in another sense we gather together to mourn for our country. Within a few years we have gathered solemnly together in our churches three times to mourn the assassination of political leaders, all of whom were practicing Christians.

There is a deeper feeling that somehow we are a nation coming apart at the seams. Newspaper headlines have referred to a "mood of despair," of a "destructive national bent." The *Wall Street Journal* headline was "We're On a Runaway Train."[27] James Reston wrote of a "world morality crisis" and of "lawlessness which threaten modern public order."[28] The event is seen as another tragic symptom of a growing breakdown of the forces of reason and of law.

The natural reaction is to ask "why, why, why?" To some it may be just another senseless act in a senseless world. They would echo the line from Shakespeare's *King Lear*: "As flies to wanton boys are we to the gods,–They kill us for their sport."[29] To such a person, recent events only confirm his cynicism.

---

27. *"Echos of Violence* - Shooting of Kennedy Stirs Mood of Despair Among Many Americans - They View Act as Confirming Destructive National Bent: Negroes See Blow to Cause - 'We're on a Runaway Train,'" *Wall Street Journal,* June 6, 1968, p. 1, col. 6.

28. James Reston, "World Morality Crisis" and "Kennedy New Victim of Lawlessness Threatening Modern Public Order," *New York Times,* June 6, 1968, p. 20 L, cols. 7, 8.

29. Gloucester in conversation with an "Old Man" *King Lear,* Act

To others, who have put their trust solely in man's ability to progress and pull himself from the slime to the heavens, the crisis is a threat to his very base of value. Where before he had sung with confidence, "We shall overcome," now he had the haunting uneasiness that we shall perhaps *never* overcome, and that human life is perhaps only a bubbling, demonic stew.

Where do we as Christians fall? Surely in neither of these two categories. If we, as a church, have any reason for existence at all, it is to be able to face such questions without either cynicism or despair.

If we analyze our present world, it is still the church which is one of the few institutions that can face the truly deep, truly powerful forces in our life.

It is a time when we should get back to first principles, and it might be appropriate for us to turn to our Bibles, and start once more at the very beginning–with the book of Genesis and the account of creation that the first chapter contains. Here we in no way see a story that is in opposition to scientific truth. No one is required to accept this as literal truth. But its significance lies in that it goes far beyond scientific truth–however creation occurred as

---

IV, Scene I, found in *The Complete Works of William Shakespear* (New York: World Syndicate Publishing Co., 1935), p. 881.

a matter of scientific fact, this is an interpretation of value and meaning placed upon that process.

In this great myth there was in the beginning of what we call time, only God–what was not God was "without form, and void" [Gen. 1:2 [KJV]. It was chaos–confused and unorganized. Out of this chaos God created order. Thus, "God said, Let the waters under the heavens be gathered together into one place, and let the dry land appear: and it was so. . . . and God saw that it was good" (Gen. 1:9-12 [KJV]).

Two things are apparent here. First, that an orderly structuring of things was seen by God as good and desirable. For creation to exist, chaos must give way to order. Second, the act of creation resulted from the word of God. In the case of God the word was in fact the deed.

Genesis continues: "Then God said, Let us make man in our image, after our likeness; and let them have dominion over the fish of the sea, and the birds of the air, and over the cattle, and over all the earth, and over every creeping thing that creepeth upon the earth. So God created man in his own image, in the image of God He created him; male and female He created them. And God blessed them, and God said to them, Be fruitful and multiply, and fill the earth and subdue it: and have dominion over. . . every living thing that moveth upon earth . . .

and God saw everything that He had made, and behold, it was very good" [Gen. 1:26-31, KJV].

Man was thus the ultimate marvel of God's creation—made in the image of God, just a little less than the angels, specially blessed. And God gave to man a specific role befitting his uniqueness. Man was to have dominion over all creation. He was to participate with God in the continuing act of creation and re-creation. Man was to be the agency whereby God's creation continued and was governed, and as the New Testament tells us, man was also to be the instrument through which God's infinite love is made known to His creation.

Man very rapidly forgot his great commission. He accepted his rights without assuming his duties. The story of Cain's murder of Abel tells us that very soon man began to kill rather than create.

And many, many centuries later, some men still ignore the lesson from Genesis. They forgot or ignored the need for reason and order in creation, and in fact have often treated such concepts with ridicule and contempt. They speak rather of "freedom" and "the right to rebel," even when their rebellion is without purpose and goal, the only result of which might plunge us back again into chaos. They espouse slogans such as the one that a person has a "right" to violate a system of law if he is willing to pay the consequences. As I suggested in a sermon during Epiphany, this logic would justify any conduct, even assassination, and surely there is no such right in a democratic society. Such blind, irrational rebellion ignores a basic fact about true freedom. We, as finite creatures, are only truly free when we know and accept our limitations. This is summed up in the Prayer Book collect which reminds us that it is in God's service that there is perfect freedom.[30]

A simple example of this would apply to children. It means that in order for you to become real, fulfilled people, you must live under certain sets of rules. The Bible summarizes one such rule as "honor your father and mother." Now this doesn't mean that your father or mother will always be right. In fact there are bound to be times when they are unfair or just plain wrong. As you get older you will undoubtedly find certain values your parents have which you don't accept and certain things they do of which you don't approve. But what your parents know and you don't yet realize is that they *too* went through the same problems with *their* parents, as have every set of parents since the beginning of time. This whole problem is made

30. "The Collect for Peace," *The Book of Common Prayer* (1928), p. 17: "O God, who art the author of peace and lover of concord, in knowledge of whom standeth our eternal life, whose service is perfect freedom; Defend us thy humble servants in all assaults of our enemies; that we, surely trusting in thy defence, may not fear the power of any adversaries, through the might of Jesus Christ our Lord." Also in *The Book of Common Prayer* (1979), p. 57.

more difficult today because, for some reason, many parents are afraid, unwilling, or unable to assume the role of leadership which parenthood requires, and we certainly cannot blame a child for not following direction not given to him.

This is an illustration of a much bigger problem. The creation story talks of God's substitution of law and order for chaos. The enactment of human laws is merely a projection of this principle of creation, and both the Bible and the Prayer Book are full of injunctions to obey the law. But no system of law is ever perfect, and we can never treat any system as such or we would be making the law into a god. Senator Kennedy himself felt very strongly that many of our present laws were unfair or wrong or unjust. Individual Christians and the Church must, as part of the job as partner with God in the act of continuing creation, be constantly at work to change and reform and make better our system of laws. What I fear as one result of the second Kennedy assassination is an over-reaction, where emphasis upon "law and order" really means leaving things right where they are now, and this would be intolerable.

Christians, as partners with God, have too often forgotten another thing about Genesis. When God spoke, things happened. Or to put it in our more finite terms, ideas have consequences. Whether we are aware of it or not, we act out what we *really* believe in. An illustration: If I really believe that people of another skin color are not truly my equal in the eyes of God with every bit as much value as I have, then this will be reflected in what I say and do. And if I remain silent or indifferent, this will have its consequences, as indeed it already has.

If we tolerate forces in our culture that glorify violence as the way the "he-men" solve their problems, then we should not be surprised if violence erupts in the world of reality. One of the great ironies on the day following the assassination was the rescheduling by the American Broadcasting Company of two of its network TV shows (one entitled "You Have Just Been Murdered"), because it was felt that these shows were in questionable taste.[31] But surely if these shows were in questionable taste on Tuesday night, are they not inappropriate on any night?

The creation story of Genesis thus reminds us of two basic principles. First, that it is God's basic wish and plan for man to live in order, not chaos, and that it is our duty as God's agents in creation to help mold a world of order; knowing also that any system of order must also be flexible to meet changing times and needs.

Genesis also reminds us that ideas have consequences,

31. The show, "You Have Just Been Murdered" was listed as "Today's [for Wednesday, June 5] Highlights" – 7:30 PM "You Have Just Been Murdered" is the reprise for The Avengers. Two mock attempts are made against the life of a millionaire (7, 11)," *The San Francisco Chronicle*, 2 June 1968, p. 4-TV, cols. 1-2.

and in our troubled times it is critical that we do all we can to be sure that the ideologies we hold and espouse are sound and wholesome. No one can fence sit or be silent.

But there is something further that Genesis shows us. Underlying its every page is the assertion that this is *God's* world. It is God who reigns and who is active with His healing love in our world of troubles. The Bible is filled with events of senseless tragedy, because it is among other things a chronicle of a portion of man's history and history reflects many events of senseless tragedy. Yet what makes it different from all other history is that it is also a chronicle of hope. The people who are described in that book suffered no less than any other people. Baptism exempts no one from pain and grief. But the Christian is given a companion with whom to walk through the dark night. God is with us. As St. Paul wrote, "If God is for us, who can be against us?" [Rom. 8:31, Phillips]

The very cross above our altar proclaims an act of senseless tragedy, the killing of a good man. Yet the very group that uses this symbol proclaims that its message is one of overwhelming good news. Because God is with us, he can use even tragic and senseless death for his ultimate purpose.

Robert Kennedy's death is but one of many tragic and senseless deaths which occur every day. And yet the focusing upon this one event might help us to meet all other such events.

We have seen an incredible sense of moral duty and of courage. Not only in his own willingness to stand up and be counted, but in the clear sense of duty and courage he had imparted to his family–where two sons would serve as altar boys at their father's Requiem, and another would lead in carrying his father's coffin to the grave.

I remember a story of Robert Kennedy when he was Attorney General [of the United States]. He was attending an early morning mass and the priest appeared without any acolytes. Robert Kennedy walked up from the congregation and served the priest himself. He saw a need, he was able to do something about it, and he did it.

This is a pretty good job description for each one of us. If we each did this, we could send out to a world in despair "ripples of hope," to use a phrase from the eloquent and dignified statement read by Robert Kennedy's sole surviving brother.[32]

---

32. Actually, the reference, "ripples of hope," is from the sentence, "Each time a man stands for an ideal, or acts to improve the lot of others, or strikes out against injustice, he sends forth a tiny ripple of hope." Senator Edward Kennedy was quoting his assassinated brother, Robert, from RFK's speech, "To the Students of Capetown University, South Africa," given on June 6, 1966. The entire speech can be found in: Edward M. Kennedy, "Eulogy of Robert F. Kennedy," *Contemporary American Speeches*, eds. Wil A. Linkugel, R. R. Allen, and Richard L. Johannesen (Belmont, California: Wadsworth Publishing Co., Inc., 1972), p. 308.

We do not live in a time of sunshine. Dark clouds are all about and they might well become darker. Our duty is clear. God gave us our commission at the time of our creation. But duty without hope is hollow.

However, we *know* hope, a "sure and certain hope."[33]

"If God is for us, who can be against us? He that did not hesitate to spare His own son but gave Him up for us all–can we not trust such a God to give us, with Him, everything else that we need? . . . Who can separate us from the love of Christ? Can trouble, pain or persecution? Can lack of clothes and food, danger to life and limb, the threat of force of arms? . . . No, in all these things we win an overwhelming victory through Him who proved His love for us. I have become absolutely convinced that neither death nor life, neither messenger of Heaven nor monarch of earth, neither what happens today nor what may happen tomorrow, neither a power from on high nor a power from below, nor anything else in God's whole world has any power to separate us from the love of God in Jesus Christ our Lord" (Rom. 8:31-39 [Phillips]).

---

33. From the "Burial of the Dead," in *The Book of Common Prayer* (1928), p. 333: "Unto Almighty God we commend the soul of our brother departed, and we commit his body to the ground; earth to earth, ashes to ashes, dust to dust; in sure and certain hope of the Resurrection unto eternal life, through our Lord Jesus Christ."

4

I submit that this is where the* law *comes in, not as a means of salvation, but as the minimum safety net that allows sinful society to operate at all. To be a law abiding citizen is not a virtue, it is a* minimum *standard of behavior.

The Sixth Sunday of Easter
May 8, 1983

All Saints Church
Salt Lake City, Utah

I imagine that there are indeed certain occupations which are incompatible with holding the priesthood. I'm amazed that a number of people include within this group the practice of the law. "How can you reconcile the two?" I am frequently asked.

I have a somewhat facile answer to that. I have no trouble embracing the two at the same time, because I am a great believer in Genesis III.

However, the question asked forces us to address a basic issue–how does Christianity see the role and function of the law?

Law has been defined as "the principle and operation of order in the world."[34] We think of the law usually as something dealing with restraints or with prohibitions, although the ten commandments mix prohibitions with

34. Citation uncertain.

demands for positive action, e.g., honor thy father and thy mother.

Many people equate compliance with the law with Christianity–thus, "I consider myself a good Christian because I don't cheat on my taxes or my wife, I don't beat my dog, and I try to lead an honest life." Nothing could be further from the truth. There is not one word in the historic creeds, which sum up the Christian faith, not one word about ethical behavior.

We forget, or try to forget, how totally radical and revolutionary the ethical teachings of Jesus were. In preparation for this sermon, I reviewed a book on Christian ethics which carefully and ruthlessly examines our Lord's teachings and concludes that "they constitute an ethic of perfection which transcends any possible legal formulation." As the author says, the directive from Matthew "You therefore must be perfect, as your heavenly Father is perfect" (Matt. 5:48) cannot be "captured in a code."[35] This rule standing by itself can do nothing but create despair. How can *I* be perfect? I can't.

Of course, life under the law leads to a similar frustration, as St. Paul learned and preached. Some religious groups today still teach salvation by keeping the law. Keep

35. Paul Ramsey, *Basic Christian Ethics* (New York: Charles Scribner's Sons, 1954), p. 73.

this rule and that rule and because of some sort of contract with God, He will have to reward you. The fallacy of this logic is shown by the illustration of the mother who says to her child, "Be good, and *then* I will love you." That is not a good mother, but a very bad one.

But not only is salvation by the law bad theology, it just doesn't work. We *all* know what the laws are. The problem isn't in not knowing what the laws are, but that we don't follow them. As St. Paul wrote in Romans, "I do not understand my own actions. For I do not do what I want but I do the very thing I hate" (Rom. 7:15 [RSV]).

If this describes us all, as I believe it does, then salvation by the law only leads to frustration, guilt and despair. It was for this reason that St. Paul so joyfully accepted the good news of salvation by faith alone.

But wasn't Paul simply jumping from the frying pan into the fire? At least there was a theoretical possibility of keeping the laws, but to accept the counsel of perfection is sheer insanity.

I am amazed at how some of the teachings of our Lord really *bug* people. A dear friend of mine said the other night, "That parable of the Prodigal Son is the sappiest, stupidest thing I have ever heard of. The forgiving Father is a sentimental fool."

You will all, I am sure, recall this famous parable. In it the no-good wastrel son, having squandered his inheritance in riotous living, is welcomed home unconditionally and indeed receives favors which the good, honest hard-working son had never received.

I am indebted to Paul Ramsey for this retelling of the story which comports more with the common sense of the world and would be more to my critical friend's liking.

"There is some point in retelling the story of the prodigal son so as to hold the father's forgiveness within more reasonable bounds. The son, having wasted his substance in a far country with riotous living, came home penniless but full of good intentions; but the father, who knew by experience what such intentions are usually worth, met his son's entreaties with implacable firmness: 'My house is closed to you till such time as you have made good your position by honest work, and also replaced the sum that you have wasted'; the son then went out into the world, and turned over a new leaf, and when at last he returned to his father he thanked him for the strictness that had led to his amendment, unlike other fathers whose foolish laxity and weak acquiescence would have left him to continue in his bad habits . . . "[36]

True to life and common sense, this retelling of the parable may be, but Jesus taught differently. Time and time

---

36. Paul Ramsey, quoting Anders Nygren, *Basic Christian Ethics,* p. 70.

again, his parables outrageously turn upside down the common wisdom of us all.

In a sense, Jesus threw away the law books. As Paul Ramsey sums it up, everything is lawful, everything is permitted . . . with one critical and crucial qualification . . . everything is permitted *which Christian love permits*.[37] Or to put it another way, "Love and do as you *then* please." This is hardly a blank check for licentiousness, because while everything is permitted which Christian love permits, everything is also *demanded* which Christian love *requires*.

We are asked to *self* regulate. Degrees of value are not known in advance or derived from some preconceived code. They are derived *backward* by Christian love from what it apprehends to be the needs of others.

On a few good days for a few fleeting moments, I may operate in this context, but my hunch is that I am not atypical, and that most of us are in the same boat. It is not that I cannot at times grasp the outrageous, revolutionary mandate of the Gospel, but it is only there in fits and starts and the great bulk of my life is lived outside this context.

I submit that this is where the *law* comes in, not as a means of salvation, but as the minimum safety net that allows sinful society to operate at all. To be a law-abiding

37. From Ramsey saying, "Paul counters with the theme, All things are lawful for me, all things are now permitted, *which Christian love permits*." In Paul Ramsey, *Basic Christian Ethics*, p. 77.

citizen is not a virtue, it is a *minimum* standard of behavior. Contempt of the law and of legal process is the most insidious threat we face to our continuing as a civilized society.

But what of unfair and unjust laws? Our state legislature has recently been busy snooping into our homes and our private lives. Badly maligned and abused as we lawyers are (sometimes justifiably), it will be *lawyers* who will put that legislature to the test as to how far they can go.

We talk of the law mollycoddling criminals. I am reminded of another of Jesus' outrageous parables, that of the workers in the vineyard. You remember that was the story of the fellow who started work at the crack of dawn and worked hard all day, and who was paid the same wage as the fellow who was hired at noon [Matt. 20:1-16]. Bad news, we say. Yet of course it all depends on with whom we identify. It was very *good* news to the fellow who was hired last. The law's protections are for the prisoner in the dock, but remember that some day you or I could be that prisoner in the dock, and then we would be very grateful for those protections.

Our system of law is far from perfect. Although from my limited knowledge of comparative law, I don't believe I would want to exchange the heritage of the common law for any other.

The law cannot bring us salvation. Even in a land where all laws were just, and everyone abided by them, we would without more, have a cold, heartless community. We would need a dynamic, a challenge, a tension of something more. The Gospel offers us this.

Nevertheless, in a sinful world where the law of God is *not* written in our hearts, a system of law is a necessity.

In a world where there is no death, we would not need undertakers; where there is no disease, we would need no physicians; where there is no war, we would need no military.

But this is not the world we live in—and certainly one selling point of main-line Christianity is that it gives me as realistic a world view as I have been able to find.

So long as I listen to the serpent of Genesis III who tells me that I by myself can become as God (which I do) and so long as I find myself unable to put into personal practice the ethic of Jesus, the Christ, I have need of the law.

I can hope and pray that I will become less dependent upon this *bottom,* minimal judgment line. I think as we proceed through the process of sanctification that this can be so.

We accomplish that goal by painful inches. We must work every day to comprehend this. Because there is a single truth proclaimed to us: "the law was given by Moses; *grace and truth* came through Jesus Christ" (John 1:17 [RSV]).

XI
The Faith Speaks to Society

Introduction

Albert Colton, like many clergy and church people in the decade of the 1960s, was thrust into a turbulent task of trying to address the illnesses of society from the posture of a prophet. Whether one liked it or not, the faith had to speak to society and Colton had to engage in applied and pastoral theology. It was a matter of a calling rather than an option he, and many others, elected to choose.

Day of wrath! O Day of mourning!
See fulfilled the prophets' warning,
Heaven and earth in ashes burning![1]

I had intended this sermon to be a comfortable, mid-summer meditation on the parable of the prodigal son. But these have hardly been, the past few days, comfortable lazy mid-summer days. The specter of racial violence has come closer and closer to our midst–even Selma, Alabama, or Bogalusa, Louisiana, seemed a long way off, and a different culture, and here we have the same thing close, close, close to home.

---

1. Hymn 468, possibly Thomas of Celano, trans. William J. Irons *The Hymnal 1940* (New York: The Church Hymnal Corporation, 1961).

[The Watts race riot had just begun. This sermon was given at St. Francis' Church in San Francisco.][2]

Colton would have preferred lazy mid-summer days to turbulent times as would anyone. However, he believed that God will not allow the Holy Spirit to be limited to the office of comforter alone. Colton was aware that at times we are cast into controversy and turmoil, not necessarily to bring answers, but to offer meaning. We are driven to that because all of creation is God's venue and God expects us to be found even where it is uncomfortable to be.

God lives in constant relationship with his creation. (He is not just the little child who goes off to dinner and forgets about his "toys".) God is also Redeemer. So concerned is He with his creation that He became involved in it in the most intimate way possible. He became part of his own creation by becoming a man, by experiencing suffering and death, and this was the final reassurance to us of his total concern. If this is true, then it can never be said again that God is unconcerned, nor conversely, that anything we do is beyond God's concern. All of the world is caught up in one great complex of relationships to Almighty God, whether it be boiling potatoes, washing the dishes, working on the assembly line, or writing a legal brief.

All of our time and efforts are completely related

2. Sermon preached the Ninth Sunday after Trinity, August 15, 1965, St. Francis's Church, San Francisco, California.

> to God, whether we like it or not. There are no cubby-holes into which we can crawl. This is the God "unto whom all hearts are open, all desires known, and from whom no secrets are hid."[3] And this is a humiliating state of affairs. I want at least some privacy. But the God of Christianity offers none.[4]

Colton abhorred the idea that we could turn our back to problems in our society because the problems were too big or grave. "We can't save the whole world" was a sentence not found in his vocabulary for it suggested a defeatism contrary to his understanding of the power of Christ. It fell to the ministers of God not only to call the world to repentance, but to respect God's ability to address what ailed us. Rationalization of the world's problems or an unwillingness to resist evil was sinful to Colton.

> If we expect nothing more, we can not see anything more even if it came along and confronted us face to face. We have made our peace with "now," and we seem content to live with it, rationalize it, poke the lumps of a lumpy pillow around and try to get some sleep.[5]

---

3. From the "Collect for Purity," The Book of Common Prayer (New York: The Church Pension Fund, 1928), p. 67.

4. Sermon preached on Rogation Sunday, May 3, 1964, St. Francis' Church, San Francisco.

5. Sermon preached the First Sunday of Advent, November 29, 1970, the Cathedral Church of St. Mark, Salt Lake City, Utah. The sermon was also preached in December 1974 (otherwise undated), St.

But getting sleep on a lumpy pillow is foreign to the religious tradition of prophecy, thought Colton. The prophets were called to take society to task and the Christian tradition has chosen to maintain the same relationship with the state. Just as God compelled the prophets of old, and then the early church, to confront the society of their day, so is the Body of Christ today called to a ministry of Christian social action and awareness.

> The prophets of the Old Testament were men who in their time seemed uniquely gifted in their capacity to see, to ask about what they had seen, and to comment when such could be a very unpopular task indeed. There was no question raised in those days about the propriety of religious men "meddling" in secular affairs. These prophets were totally immersed in their world, politics and all. These men in an unusual way sensed the nature, the presence and the will of God, as He made Himself known to their time. But the writings of these men, intensely topical as they were, also speak to men in all times and places, and despite some early objections, the Christian Church in her wisdom incorporated their writings in its canon of Holy Scripture.[6]
>
> The world needs to be shaken and challenged. The gospel can and does do a pretty good job of that. But we must be careful that in the shaking and challenging

---

Stephen's Church, West Valley City, Utah.

6. Ibid.

we do not forget in whose name we are doing this. It is awfully tempting to revert to bad little boys who delight in shaking and challenging just to watch the expressions of horror and shock on other people's faces.

If the Christian does have a duty to shake and challenge, he must never forget who it was who gave him that mandate. It is a duty which must be exercised with responsibility and compassion, never to hurt unnecessarily, and certainly not as a means for self-righteous magnification of the one who is doing the shaking and challenging.

The Church is beginning to regain her realization that she must live and speak in the world. But in such a time it is all the more significant that we recall the words of the ancient collect, and in exercising this duty pray that those admitted to the fellowship avoid those things *which are contrary to our profession*, and also those things *harmful to its proclamation*.

But let us also remember that some statements which we feel hurt us most are exactly those things which we as Christians *must* say for the integrity of the Church and for the salvation of our own souls.[7]

---

7. Sermon preached the Third Sunday after Easter, April 16, 1967, St. Francis' Church, San Francisco, California. In this sermon, Colton was drawing on the Collect for the Day which read in part, "Grant unto all those who are admitted into the fellowship of Christ's Religion, that they may avoid those things that are contrary to their profession, and follow all such things as are agreeable to the same; through our Lord

Colton haunted his congregation with equating the actions of those who do little or nothing about the problems in society with the rich man in the story of Lazarus. He also confounded those around him who saw sin as just an issue of society needing solving rather than the state of alienation and division among people.

> [The story of the rich man, known in tradition as "Dives," and poor Lazarus (Luke 16:19-31) illustrates a common problem with social ministry which is contrary to the Christian profession.] What did Dives do that was wrong? I suggest the answer is fairly clear–in this specific confrontation, HE DIDN'T DO ANYTHING. Dives was a busy man, concerned with many problems, and it is conceivable that in his concern he may not even have *seen* the poor wretch [Lazarus] at his gate, even though he might have stumbled over him. See with his eyes? Of course. He couldn't avoid this. But to see with the heart and with concern, he did not. In seeing Lazarus, Dives thought he saw "the poor" or the "downtrodden" as an abstraction, not an individual child of God named Lazarus.
>
> And of course we all see what we want to see, and hear what we want to hear. As sinners, in our self-centeredness, we project away from ourselves all outside problems into generalities. Dives could perhaps discuss quite knowledgeably the plight of the "Ameri-

Jesus Christ." From "The Collect for The Third Sunday of Easter," *The Book of Common Prayer* (1928), p. 173.

can Negro" or the "race issue," but never even see the Negro at his own gate.

The Church too has been guilty of such failings. Endless lists of pious, well-intentioned General Convention resolutions very often succeed only in salving our conscience by a generality and blinding us to the actual Lazarus immediately before us.

The generalization might not only be a false salve to our conscience, but it can also be an excellent thing to hide behind. A good example was the lengthy statement read by Governor Wallace of Alabama at the doors of the university auditorium. In the cloud of generalities about "liberty," "sovereignty," and "oppression," he never once mentioned the specific issue, which was whether two qualified young residents of his state would be allowed to walk through that door and go to school.

But I do not live in a generalization. And neither do you. I live in a particular body, at a particular time and at a particular place. My encounters with the world around me are through specific things, not generalities. I have never seen a "race issue." I don't know whether it is blue, or green, round or square. But I do see Lazarus. I encounter him at my doorstep, which is the world I touch and feel, every day of my life.

But I return to my text. Dives was not a brutal man. Our lesson is far more subtle than this. It is easy to spot the demonic in the storm trooper, in the Ku Klux Klan. But the forces of unrighteousness are at their most dangerous when they are less easy to detect. Indeed when they use the very words and the very symbols of righteousness. The deepest wounds in the Body of Christ are inflicted in the name of our Lord Himself by those who profess to be Christians with their lips and belie it with their deeds. The deepest danger to a free democracy is the use of general phrases to justify not only a ghastly perversion of these very phrases (e.g., "freedom," "liberty," "property," "sovereignty"), but even more so when they are used to salve the troubled conscience.

Our problem is not to defend an abstraction. It is to reach out and touch with concern Lazarus at our gate, Lazarus at our job, Lazarus right beside us here and now, the same particular man as we are, who can be lonely, frightened, anxious; who did not ask to be born any more than we did, and does not want to die any more than we do; who has the same capacity to love and be loved as we do; and who reaches out to the same God, and is strengthened and succored by the same God, the same God who suffered and died to show us the cosmic value of one individual life.

Lazarus at the gate is not a vague symbol. Lazarus will be at the gate when I rise to leave this church. I will confront him in the first person I see, and in each separate person I encounter in my life. This is why Catholic orthodoxy rejects the idea of a "vertical" church, of good old God and me, a church of one person. The church is a visible, corporate body of people, in encounter and contact with each other. Finding God on the golf course is not a problem, but letting God work in my relationships with people in my office, on my job, on the street, or in my family, there is the test.

Look for Lazarus at *your* gate and when you see him, help him. And the strange thing is that from time to time through our own walls of self-interest might show forth A GLIMPSE OF ANOTHER TRUTH, that Lazarus, who cries for love, for compassion, for help, is not only not an abstraction but rather an individual child of God of infinite value. Lazarus is also you and also me.[8]

At the heart of the faith speaking to society was Colton's acknowledgment that one cannot escape judgment. While some shy away from social involvement because it means working with those with whom they feel uncomfortable, Colton identified an even greater challenge. When it came to addressing the problems in society, the Christian had to start with his or her own sinfulness. Social ministry and social action began with one's own confession and only after that could legitimate and authentic ministry begin.

Each one of us has had some share in the creation

8. Sermon preached the First Sunday after Trinity, June 16, 1963, Grace Cathedral, San Francisco, California. The sermon was preached again on the First Sunday after Trinity, May 31, 1964, St. Francis' Church, San Francisco, California. The sermon was preached again on the Eighteenth Sunday after Pentecost, September 28, 1980, All Saints Church, Salt Lake City, Utah.

of this hideous mess [the racial tension culminating in the Watts riots]. It should not cause us wonder to observe that if you take a group of people and give them only sub-standard housing, employment and education, and then tie on the lid to the kettle, that it will sometimes explode. No one can condone the demonic, barbaric conduct [of both black and white people] of the past few days, and by giving reasons for it, I am not attempting to excuse it.

Nevertheless, here is a situation where surely we cannot condemn and then withdraw from all involvement in this problem. Not only do others need our help, but those of us like the elder son who have by the luck of birth received a greater share of this world's goods, need for our own salvation to respond to this problem by addressing ourselves to it, and becoming involved in it.

Which shall it be? "This son of yours, oh God, you take care of him" or, "This brother of mine, oh God, I will try to understand and help."[9]

9. Sermon preached the Ninth Sunday after Trinity.

1

This problem is not what we as whites ought to do to help our black brothers–it is whether we are willing to let them help us. Not to condescendingly agree to extend our hand in fellowship to them, but to hope that the incredible strength and moral courage of these people will result in them still being willing to extend their hand to us, for us to cling to and pull us out of our trap of fear, hate and moral indifference.

The Twelfth Sunday after Trinity September 1, 1963

Church of the Good Samaritan San Francisco, California

I hope I may share with you some of my experiences and thoughts about the march on Washington last Wednesday in which I participated, even if I cannot find a text for today to support it.

I am supported in using this subject today by James Reston, columnist for the *New York Times*, who wrote Friday:

> The first significant test of the Negro march on Washington will come in the churches and synagogues of the country this weekend. . . . This whole movement for equality in American life will have to return to first

> principles before it will "overcome" anything. And as moral principles preceded and inspired political principles in this country, as the church preceded the Congress, so there will have to be a moral revulsion to the humiliation of the Negro before there can be significant political relief.[10]

I felt there were some profound religious insights in the whole occasion, and to see these it is irrelevant whether you believe that the march itself was or wasn't a good idea, or whether or not it will have any political impact on pending civil rights legislation.

I was fortunate enough to be included in a California group consisting of artists from Hollywood, union officials, and students. These were all people vitally concerned with the question of Negro rights. The great majority of them were not members of any organized religious group and quite honestly weren't the least interested in churches as such. Their reasons for this disinterest were as many as there were people there, but there was one question that kept coming up again and again: "Why is it that you people who call yourselves Christians don't practice what you preach?" One well-known actor recounted a conversation he had had recently with an Episcopal priest in a small southern town where the police had been using electrically

10. James Reston, "The First Significant Test of the Freedom March," *New York Times*, Aug. 30, 1963, p. 20 L, col. 3.

charged cattle prods on Negroes whom they had arrested. The priest deplored the practice, agreed that "in principle" he was in favor of equal rights for all of God's children, but then refused to serve on a committee to see what could be done to stop police brutality. I know, and you know, and the priest certainly knows, that the Church's problem in this field is a very complex one–we can't change men's hearts overnight, we are all sinners, the white congregations need ministering to as well as the black, too extreme action will only succeed in cutting you off from the group you are trying to reach, etc., etc. But still, this question must haunt us, and all the words and reasons in the world will not cleanse our conscience–"Why do we not practice what our Lord preached?"

> Dr. Eugene Carson Blake, the Stated Clerk and highest administrative officer of the United Presbyterian Church, speaking on behalf of the National Council of Churches at the Washington rally, was moving in his admission of guilt of us all. We from predominantly white Christian churches have not been in the vanguard of this movement. Dr. Blake had to admit that he could not even say he speaks for the united opinion of all Christian churches.
>
> "I wish indeed that I were able to speak for all Protestant, Anglican and Orthodox Christians . . . But that is precisely the point. If all the members and all the ministers of the constituency I represent here today were ready to stand and march with you for jobs and

freedom for the Negro community, together with all the Roman Catholic Church and all the synagogues in American, the battle for full civil rights and dignity would be won."[11]

But while "for many years now," Dr. Blake continued, most of the churches "have said all the right things about civil rights," still "as of August 28, 1963, we have achieved neither a nonsegregated church nor a nonsegregated society . . . We do not, therefore, come to this Lincoln Memorial in any arrogant spirit of moral or spiritual superiority to 'set the nation straight' or to judge or denounce the American people in whole or in part. Rather we come–late, late we come–in the reconciling and repentant spirit in which Abraham Lincoln once replied to a delegation of morally arrogant churchmen. He said, 'Never say God is on our side, rather pray that we may be found on God's side.'"[12]

I suggest that Dr. Blake is speaking great truth about us. This has not been a movement led by the conscience of the white Christian community, but by courageous Negro leaders. And the great miracle of the Negro leadership has been its Christian orientation–all the more mi-

11. Dr. Eugene Carson Blake in "Excerpts From Addresses at Lincoln Memorial During Capital Civil Rights March," *New York Times*, Aug. 29, 1963, p. 21 L, col. 1.

12. Ibid.

raculous when we see that the white support has come principally from secular, non-religious groups.

One could not help but sense the strong prophetic tone of the gathering. Frequent references were made to the bondage of God's people in Egypt and of God's deliverance of his people. And I am sure it occurred to many white Christians watching this huge crowd of people that perhaps our whole analysis has been wrong. This problem is not what we as whites ought to do to help our black brothers–it is whether we are willing to let them help us. Not to condescendingly agree to extend our hand in fellowship to them, but to hope that the incredible strength and moral courage of these people will result in them still being willing to extend their hand to us, for us to cling to and pull us out of our trap of fear, hate and moral indifference.

Our white fear was shown graphically in the attitude of the residents of the District of Columbia on the day of the march. Streets and stores were deserted. People kept indoors, and as the thousands of buses rolled through the quiet streets there was a sense of a city fearfully waiting an army of occupation. But what a different army this was than what was expected! It was a friendly, courteous, and, I felt, a happy group, proud of what they had accomplished, and extremely anxious not to give cause for offense.

We have assumed that we whites are the new Israel,

and that our problem is one of expanding the walls of this Israel to include the black man. We, especially of the Catholic tradition, have stressed the significance of the visible church, and by this we have frequently meant that church which is predominantly of one ethnic character.

But we cannot ignore the lesson of Holy Scripture. As we know from the Old Testament, God can use any group as the instrument of His judgment, and the fact that we come late, late into this fray now is a fearful judgment on white Christendom. The hard battles in this immediate crisis have already been fought and won by the white secular world and Negro Christendom.

And we can also recall from the Old Testament that people can be terribly wrong as to the composition of Israel in the first place. It is not something we can necessarily claim by inheritance alone; it is not something we can claim as a matter of right, a bargain to which we can hold Almighty God. The remnant may be smaller than we think. This point Old Testament prophets preach with united tongue from Amos and Hosea to Isaiah and Zechariah. Not only may God use the pagan as an instrument of judgment on His own people, but even amongst this group not all that saith, "Lord, Lord," shall enter the Kingdom. Almighty God more frequently than not has spoken through the poor and oppressed rather than through the High Priest in his mighty temple, and the choice to be made by the High Priest then is not one of leadership and control, but the salvation of his own soul. It may well be that the prophetic tone of Christianity is coming from this Negro leadership, and our choice is a very simple one–whether we will accept and heed this message.

Admittedly there are complications to such analysis. Negroes, like whites, have mixed motives. We are all a mixed bag of noble and ignoble aspirations. There are vested Negro interests which the success of this very movement will destroy, including the all-Negro church itself. The present Negro hierarchy will find it more difficult to compete for leadership in the more literate, highly trained community of the white *and* black than in the ghetto society where captive audiences are assured them. And we cannot ignore the moral obligation of the Negro leadership to work with their people to clean up their own house.

But when this is all said and done, we white people must accept *our* need. It is so easy to retreat to the world of fear and hate, and each time we do we become that much less of a person. While I cannot help but admire what the secular leaders of white America have done in this field, I have little patience with their contention that they can lead full and complete lives without the framework of the organized church. What they are frequently really saying is that they are too self-concerned to submit to the necessary discipline of working within the larger family except on their own terms, and only on the issues which particularly interest them. To belong to the family of God in His church makes constant demands, which must be answered often at great inconveniences to yourself—but in the answering we to that extent move out of ourselves. The same is true in the field of financial stewardship. The saying that we need to give more than the Church needs our gift is not just a Madison Avenue cliché. It is true. We must use all means available to move outside of a deification of our own self-concern. To the extent I can relinquish a substantial portion of that money which Almighty God has deigned to let me control, I have faced my need.

Today in 1963 we need to accept the hand that is being extended to us by our Negro brothers. We must accept this proffer of love, and we must thank God that the Negro will still accept us. And this is degrading and difficult. It is so much easier to couch this in terms of what we can do for them—that way we preserve our own self-esteem. But it is too late for that. The battles, the big, hard ones, have already been fought and won, and the martyrs are already enrolled on the books.

Our choice now is much less decisive in that picture, but it is critical for the salvation of our own souls nevertheless. For our own salvation, not just that of our Negro brother, we must witness in *action*, not in platitude and generality. Rabbi Joachim Prinz, President of the American Jewish Congress, eloquently stated in Washington:

> When I was the rabbi of the Jewish community in

> Berlin under the Hitler regime, I learned many things. The most important I think that I learned in my life and under those tragic circumstances is that bigotry and hatred are not the most urgent problems. The most urgent, the most disgraceful, the most shameful and the most tragic problem is silence. A great people which had created a great civilization had become a nation of silent onlookers. They remained silent in the face of hate, brutality, and mass murder.
>
> America must not become a nation of onlookers. America must not remain silent. . . . It must speak up and act, from the President down to the humblest of us.[13]

Or as James Reston observed, "If the preachers said what they really thought about this racial crisis and even half of those who heard and believed them wrote their honest convictions for or against racial equality to Capitol Hill, the political balance on racial equality might easily be transformed."[14]

I am aware that there are many white Christians who do not even accept my basic premise, i.e., that the Negro is entitled to equal dignity and the full protection of our

---

13. Rabbi Joachim Prinz in "Excerpts From Addresses at Lincoln Memorial During Capital Civil Rights March," *The New York Times*, Aug. 29, 1963, p. 21 L, col. 2.

14. James Reston, "The First Significant Test of the Freedom March," *New York Times*, Aug. 30, 1963, p. 20 L, col. 3.

laws to assure this. I am aware that their feelings are deep-seated and that no one of us is simon-pure. But such people must also realize that our church has spoken formally, collectively, and finally on this issue. The only problem open now is whether we are going to move from platitude to performance, from generalization to implementation, from ringing phrase to participation.

Our voice is late—our action will be even later. But we can still pray that in our contrition Almighty God will forgive this, and use us now.

2

Christians do not worship a set of rules and precepts. They worship the Risen and Only Son of the Living God. And if we are correct in our assertion as to the nature of this man, then it isn't very helpful as a guide to us to ask, "What would Jesus do if he were here?" because we do not happen to be Incarnate God, but rather sad sacks of flesh and bones with a rather large catalogue of very massive limitations.

The First Sunday after Easter	*St. Francis' Church*
April 2, 1967	*San Francisco, California*

With the approach of the anti-Vietnam war demonstration in this city next weekend, I believe that it is important and hopefully might be helpful to say something from the pulpit about the war in Vietnam and some of the ethical questions it raises for a Christian.

It has been a long time since this country has been involved in a war which is so unpopular with such large groups of Americans. There is no one of us who is not aware of it, and increasingly our individual lives are being affected by it–young men from our parish now serving there are increasing all the time. Increasing numbers of young men are returning dead, as I was reminded dramatically the other day when trying to make arrangements to have a body flown back to the middle west—"Sir, there's a war on, and such space is tight." Already nearly as much bomb tonnage has been dropped by us on Vietnam as we dropped on Europe in World War II. Thousands of women and children have been killed or badly burned. We are condemned and criticized for our involvement by other world powers, and despite a constant escalation of our efforts, the Viet-Cong still remain in effective control of sixty percent of the area of South Vietnam. Many people are confused and unsure.

Is there *a* Christian position in this war? Some people on both sides suggest so, but I would suggest that they are confused in their analysis of the Christian faith. Christianity in its essence is *NOT* an ethic. It is not a set of moral principles and practices. It is, rather, the proclamation of an event in history. It is the statement of God's mighty action in our world of space and time, and consequently a statement of the nature of God who is beyond space and time.

This is not to say that Christianity is not interested and concerned with what we do and what is moral, and what is right. To the contrary, Christianity proclaims a God "unto whom all hearts are open, all desires known and from whom no secrets are hid."[15] To the contrary, to the Christian, everything we do and think has religious consequence, and there is no place a man can flee from either God's love or His judgment.

But Christians do not worship a set of rules and precepts. They worship the Risen and Only Son of the Living God. And if we are correct in our assertion as to the nature of this man, then it isn't very helpful as a guide to *us* to ask, "What would Jesus do if he were here?" because we do not happen to be Incarnate God, but rather sad sacks of flesh and bones with a rather large catalogue of very massive limitations. As Reinhold Niebuhr wrote, "the moral qualities of the Christ are not only our hope, but our despair."[16]

Christians *were* given two basic ethical demands upon which hang all else, that they were to love God with all their heart, soul and mind; secondly, to love their neighbor as themselves. These two commands were like unto each other. They were tied together. A man could not really do one without the other.

But the sticky business of applying these demands to the details and endless variety of daily decisions was left for the Christian man and the Christian community to

---

15. *The Book of Common Prayer* (1928), p. 67.

16. Reinhold Niebuhr, *An Interpretation of Christian Ethics* (London: SCM Press, Ltd., 1948), p. 131.

hammer out in each particular case, using his God-given freedom.

Realistically this is the only way it could be done. No set of rules, however elaborate and detailed, could apply to the incredible variety of fact situations mankind must face. Detailed rules are pretty good for black and white situations, "but real life is very rarely black and white. Any father, trying to follow directions as to how to put together his son's Christmas bicycle, learns pretty quickly the difference between a printed and illustrated manual and the real, stubborn, defiant, and usually incomplete, collection of parts which confronts him," said Stephen Bayne in his book, *Christian Living*.[17]

What this means is that Christians can and sometimes do disagree over what is the correct way to exercise their freedom of choice according to the demand of love. Honest Christians have sincerely disagreed over many ethical questions, e.g., gambling, divorce, abortion, war (and particularly, of course, the war in Vietnam). And one of the great appeals to me of the Anglican communion is its capacity to comprehend and permit within it disagreement and differences of opinion.

There are of course those ethical situations where the

17. Stephen Bayne, *Christian Living* (Greenwich, Conn.: Seabury Press, Inc., 1957), p. 4.

permissible limits of Christian disagreement are really very narrow. There surely can be no Christian defense for the persecution and harassment of a fellow creature of God because of the color of his skin or his religious heritage. I know of no Christian theology which would allow a Christian to make any but one choice if it came to a clear decision between property rights and human rights.

Moreover in all our decisions, even the seemingly simple ones, we must be aware of the wily workings of the forces of sin. Sin is at its root selfishness, and in our primary concern for ourselves, we have an uncanny way of glossing over, of rationalizing our conduct, of seducing ourselves. We all know of someone who has committed an act of unmitigated selfishness, who can stare at us in wide-eyed innocence and say it really was for some *other* person's basic good. In our individual, and even more so, in our corporate decisions, we must ever be on guard against hypocritical self-seduction, self-righteousness, and it is my own opinion that in a sinful world there never will be total purity of motive.

One more general comment on the Christian use of force: I do not see this as necessarily inconsistent with the law of love. Jesus himself cast out the money-changers. Any parent knows that on occasion the law of love is best exercised by the force of the palm on a youthful posterior. In a sinful, selfish world, force is sometimes necessary to protect some selfish, sinful men from other selfish, sinful men. Walls and fences may indeed be a result of man's fall, but I've never known even a church or monastery without them.

Whether we like it or not, we men live together. No man is an island. My behavior affects you, and yours mine. If I were the only man in the world, I could sit under the sun and think the great thoughts all day long with no one to say to me, "nay." But, if I am a man in a capitalistic society with a wife and five children, my freedom is curtailed by their need for food, shelter and clothing. If I continue to sit under the sun and think great thoughts instead of working to provide for my family, then, of course, I am merely requiring someone else to do this. If I am alone in the world and am attacked by a wild beast, my decision to defend myself is purely my own, but in the corporate world of a wife and five children, the exercise of my conscience in making this decision must take into account the fact that if I do not repulse the attackers, either others will suffer, or someone else will have to do this for me. In our world today, what I decide to do or not to do, sets in motion a geometric progression of effects on other people, and this creates in me the Christian obligation to use my freedom responsibly.

And now, after this general background, we turn to Vietnam. I am indebted to the rector of St. Paul's Church, Charlottesville, Virginia, for an analysis which I found helpful.[18] He sees three different positions which people take in the name of Christianity.

The first is that this is a holy war. On Christmas Eve one military leader called upon all Americans to ask God's blessing of American fighting men engaged "in this most Christian of causes." I personally could never accept this. The Christian Church is still trying to live down the scandal and blasphemy of its holy wars of the past. We do not "kill a Commie for Christ." Even a so-called "just" war can never be called a Christian cause. It is never the causes which are Christian, but the people in them may be so. A Christian may have to kill another human being, and most Christian theologians recognize the necessity for this in certain situations, but these exceptions have never been termed "good" or "holy." They are the tragic result of a sinful world where no other choice is available.

The second position is at the other extreme–that of the dogmatic pacifist. There are two groups in this category, the absolute pacifist, and the pacifist who refuses to serve in the Vietnam conflict. The absolute pacifist reasons

18. The Rector of St. Paul's Church, Charlottesville, Virginia, from 1962 to 1969 was the Reverend Harcourt Edmund Waller, Jr. According to the *Episcopal Clerical Directory 1991* (New York: The Church Hymnal Corporation, 1991), p. 820, Waller died May 26, 1989. It is uncertain what analysis Colton "found helpful."

that killing of other humans is evil, that war involves killing, and that he will not participate in an evil deed.

Personally, I would agree with both of his premises, and still disagree with his conclusion. Of course war is evil, but so are many other things. As the history of Christian martyrdom attests; to the Christian, there are things worse than death. Sometimes, indeed usually, our choices are not between good and evil, black and white, but only in the selection of the lesser evil. I cannot absolutize any one particular ethical principle such as "Thou shalt not kill" (Ex. 20:13; Deut. 5:17 [KJV]) at the expense of all the others, because to do this is to make a religion of a rule. Moreover, it seems to me that in a corporate society, one man's refusal to bear an unpleasant burden merely means that another must bear it for him; and this is, I suggest, an abdication of his responsibility to share in the result of our corporate sinfulness.

Yet, much as I may disagree with the absolute pacifist, I must recognize, as our church has, that there are those who in honest and profound Christian conviction "are unwilling, for conscience sake, to take human life in war." As our General Convention has said, we must make provision for them in the Christian fellowship and perhaps learn something from their courage in making such a witness.[19]

19. It is unclear which General Convention Colton was remember-

Few would argue that the Society of Friends, the Quakers, have not been a valuable element of a pluralistic society.

Surely it is also hoped that the same respect might be conveyed the other way. It is a little difficult to understand why one-third of a crowd of 1,500 California students would refuse to stand for a moment of silence for our fighting men in Vietnam, as reported in Thursday's paper.[20] Surely no one thinks that anyone in their right mind is *ENJOYING* himself over there.

The other category of pacifist is a newer development. He is one who says his conscience can allow him to SELECT the wars in which he will serve. Thus he would fight against the demonic forces of Hitlerism, but not against the aspirations of a small Asiatic country to determine its own future. Such an argument parades before us the shabbiness of actual facts. We all should begin to squirm a

---

ing. Ironically, at the General Convention held five months after this sermon was given, there were two such resolutions. At the General Convention held in 1964, the most current convention for Colton at that time, there was made available to the House of Bishops and the House of Deputies a statement from the minutes of the Special Meeting of the House of Bishops held in 1962. That statement supports Colton's understanding of those "unwilling, for conscience sake, to take human life in war." See the *Journal of the General Convention of the Protestant Episcopal Church* (New York: The General Convention of the Episcopal Church, 1964), p. 982.

20. Citation uncertain.

little here, because there are many facts that make us look extremely shabby. We have the parade of puppets and despots we have supported. In our talk of the freedom of each nation to decide its own future, we leave unanswered the question of what we would do if their war-weary people decided to go Communist, and there is an uneasy feeling that we just wouldn't let that happen, no matter what the people wanted. We say we are concerned about the blood-bath that would occur if the Communists took over, and yet no one can measure this against the blood-bath that will continue to occur as the war continues. Are we really serious when we say that we must honor our commitments to SEATO [Southeast Asia Treaty Organization], which is basically a paper dragon, which most people don't even know exists, against the rising climate of world opinion that sees this conflict as nothing more than the classic reenactment of a large power suppressing, for its own purpose, the wishes of a smaller one? Do we remember the inevitable dehumanization that any war creates—the licensed brothels for our men, the correlative life of prostitution for thousands of Vietnamese young women and the incredible amount of supplies lost to the black market.

The Episcopal rector in Saigon (there *is* one) reports of a conversation with a young soldier who said he didn't mind coming to fight communism, but didn't care if the Vietnamese all died in the process. In such a war, it is tempting to talk of principles because it helps us forget the people. We are concerned about the discrepancy between what we are told is happening and what we later find out is happening; and we should become properly concerned when such a reputable reporter as Harrison Salisbury is called disloyal for reporting what he said he saw.[21] We are fighting a little people in a little nation with more troops than we had in Korea. We are spending over $300,000 for each enemy we kill in Vietnam, while in our domestic war on poverty we spend only $53 for each person classified as poor.

All of these are legitimate concerns. But let's analyze them. Many are the sordid truth of any war. Others suggest that our motives are not completely pure, and here is where I guess we part company with so many of our youth. We over forty are tarred with the brush of hypocrisy.

Yet I would suggest that one of the signs of maturity is not the elimination of hypocrisy but the admission of it. I think the General Confession which we all have just said pretty well lays that to rest. Let the man who has never acted from mixed motive cast the first stone.

The requirement of perfection in man's action is a hopeless thing if the Christian doctrine of the nature of

---

21. Harrison Salisbury, a *New York Times* correspondent, reported bombing damage of civilians in two North Vietnamese towns. The Defense Department acknowledged that civilian areas may have been hit but that care was being taken to avoid civilian casualties.

man is true at all. It is in itself hypocritical, because anyone who is honest with himself knows *he* has not attained it, and surely cannot expect more of others.

I delivered the valedictory address at my college shortly before the Marshall Plan was announced, and on the platform, unwilling listeners I'm sure, were General Omar Bradley, and the first Secretary of Defense James Forrestal, and the editor of the *Christian Science Monitor.* My thesis was that we had no business getting involved in Europe until we had cleaned things up at home, because this would be hypocrisy. I was wrong. If we waited to act until things were cleaned up at home, whether "home" be our nation, our family, or our own soul, we would never act at all. Perfectionism is not only an ethic of despair and unreality (because it's never attained), but it is also an ethic of inaction. If we wait until everything is just right before we act, odds are we will never want to act at all. Just because an action is tainted or defective still does not mean that it may not be the best thing to do under the circumstances.

My personal difficulty with the idea of selective pacifism is that it negates the idea of corporate responsibility. We have all witnessed in our lives family messes, and yet perhaps you share my dislike for the family member who refuses to get involved in trying to do anything about it because it *is* an unpleasant mess. There are certain things we do in life not because we enjoy them but because we see them as our duty and responsibility to others.

I may not like doing certain things I do out of duty, and there is nothing in the world to prevent me from trying to change those things which require that duty. In this country such changes can be effected by use of our rights to petition, demonstrate and ballot. But until such duties are changed, the fact remains that if I do not do my duty, someone else will be required to do it for me.

Having once said this, it must be stressed that to the Christian, there is only one absolute duty, and that is to his God. The duty to any nation can never be an absolute one. Surely it is not the role of the church to wrap herself in the American flag and become another arm of the administrative establishment. There may come a time when a man must choose between his duty to his God and his country, and our national law, with the wisdom and tolerance one would expect, recognizes this possibility. Such decisions are not made lightly, and it goes without saying that a status recognized for religious reasons by the law should surely be recognized by the Church.

Then we come to the third category, where I imagine most of us fit. We see this as neither Christ's holy war nor one so totally demonic that we become pacifists. As citizens of this country we each share in responsibility for the events that have brought us to where we are.

We know as Christians that the people of the world are made for unity and interdependence, and that war is the very antithesis of this. We know that the cries of a napalm mutilated Vietnamese child reach and shatter the halls of heaven, and we are uneasy and deeply troubled.

But one sign of maturity is said to be to realize that difficult problems do not have simple answers. Most of us therefore persevere in our support out of a sense of duty, realizing that while this is a gray business, this is generally true of difficult decisions, and feeling that the arguments for our involvement outweigh those against it.

But the burden of this choice should never rest easy upon us—we should be troubled and uneasy, nor can we forget that our responsibility continues each day the war continues. Circumstances can change and we must keep alert to these. This too is our duty. For example, this week we just lost the 500th plane over North Vietnam, representing a cost of one billion dollars.

Another sign of maturity is the ability to admit that we have been wrong, and this rule should be remembered by all three classes of Christians I have described.

Nothing illustrates the depth of man's sinfulness more than war. Surely all Christians, whatever their opinions, can join in prayers to God for his guidance of the leaders of the world to hasten a just peace; for those whose sense of duty places them in positions of danger; for those who suffer; and for the enemies of our positions as well.

On our knees we can all offer our imperfect prayers for help in a plight which should convince us, if nothing else will, that we have no power of ourselves to help ourselves, and that God's grace alone can redeem and reconcile us.

3

What if they* had *listened? What if their reaction was rather than one of fear and violence, one of painful, honest re-evaluation of all that their life stood for?

Palm Sunday *St. Francis' Church*
April 7, 1968 *San Francisco, California*

[Note: Dr. Martin Luther King
had been murdered the previous Thursday.]

Today we begin Holy Week, the most significant week in the Christian year. And during this week we will see several different emotional themes played out.

The quiet tenderness of Maundy Thursday
The black grief of Good Friday
The pleasant anticipation of Holy Saturday
The exploding joy of Easter Day

And the *irony* of today, Palm Sunday. An irony which the very pattern of liturgical worship points out. Thus we open with a great triumphal procession and sing "All glory, laud and honor To thee Redeemer King!"[22] commemorating our Lord's joyous entry into Jerusalem. But then the festal white changes to penitential purple, and we are plunged into Holy Week and the trip to the cross, and we as a congregation respond with that crowd of long ago as we read St. Matthew's passion and say, "Crucify Him, crucify Him" [cf. Matt. 27:22-23, NEB]. The man we laud today we loathe tomorrow, and within one liturgical hour we see enacted another proof of the fickleness of popularity. We see a man of nonviolence dying a most violent death. At the very moment He was being acclaimed by some, others whose hearts were hardened and who refused to listen to Him, were meeting to attempt to destroy him.

One cannot help but wonder what would have happened if these people had stopped to really listen. It would have been hard for them to do so, because this man Jesus was a country bumpkin (he was not one of the Establishment) and He said many critical and unkind things about them and their way of life. What He said seemed to threaten the very existence of institutions and values which they treasured and went deep down into primordial emotional depths.

---

22. Hymn 62, Refrain, St. Theodulph, c. 820; trans. John Mason Neale, 1854, *The Hymnal 1940.*

We know of course that they did not listen, but rather, seeing themselves threatened, lashed back with hate and violently set to work to destroy Him.

What if they *had* listened? What if their reaction was rather than one of fear and violence, one of painful, honest re-evaluation of all that their life stood for?

In the case of Jesus of Nazareth we will never know, because they did not listen. They thought that death through crucifixion would solve their problem. But as Easter shows us, Truth cannot be suppressed this way. Truth cannot be ignored, Truth cannot be suppressed, Truth cannot be permanently crucified.

The wise old man Gamaliel said to his fellow leaders of the Council in Jerusalem that was trying Peter and some of his apostles, "Men of Israel, take care what you do with these men. . . . let them alone; for if this plan or this undertaking is of man, it will fail; but if it is of God, you will not be able to overthrow them. You might even be found opposing God" (Acts 5:34-39 [RSV]).

Sound academic advice; but there come those times when the challenge and confrontation is so obvious that one cannot just "let it alone," or ignore it, because our very response is part of the very confrontation itself.

By the time Jesus of Nazareth had arrived in Jerusalem he could no longer be "left alone" or ignored. His confrontation had gone beyond this, and his impact was great enough that some reaction was bound to take place. The only question was, "What was the nature of this reaction to be?"

The parallel with the events of the past few days is, of course, very obvious. We have been confronted with a massive problem in human relationship, which would be absurd if it were not so cruel and detestable. Children of God have chosen to divide and separate themselves in the most wicked fashion on the basis of a very secondary biological distinction–that of skin pigmentation.

We have thought and acted in terms of this ridiculous system of categories until the consequences have sunk deep, deep into our emotional make-up, and the white majority has only moved with the greatest reluctance and at a snail's pace to do anything positive to stop this process–and only then when we have been pushed, and goaded.

The cries and prayers of anger and anguish arise like incense from the smoke of our burning cities; God knows we can never say that we have not heard them–but clearly we have not listened to what we hear.

Our response has been more like that of Gamaliel. Let it alone and hope it will solve itself; or in the more insane extremes on both sides, to try to resolve this matter by force and violence.

And I was appalled at the fear on people's faces Friday afternoon throughout this city–rumors and gross exaggeration apparent at every level; talk of further violence.

And we note that alongside our racial crisis we have a view of violence that marks us as a people and a country.

I have been most concerned by what has been called the "generation gap," or the growing lack of communication between our younger and older groups, and have reacted with a certain touchy sensitivity to blanket indictments of my and older generations for their alleged shallowness and hypocrisy, summed up by some teen-aged graffiti which read, "When I grow up I want to be like my dad—a bigot."

And so I have hauled my admittedly very "square" self off to see two films which are apparently our young people's bible, and which will doubtless win many academy awards, namely *Bonnie and Clyde* and *The Graduate.*

I found *Bonnie and Clyde* to be a masterpiece of technical cinema, but I was appalled at its totally amoral treatment of robbery and violence, and even more so at the giggles and guffaws that came from the audience. I would concede that one could produce a truly tragic theme about a murderer (*Macbeth* is a pretty good example) but any attempt at the classic development of character of either Bonnie or Clyde eluded me. The only moral character (or for that matter moral or *im*moral character, i.e. someone motivated and wrestling with some sort of value structure) I could observe in the film was the Texas Ranger. And yet some of the young people I have talked to seemed to feel that *he* was the bad guy. It was pointed out to me that after all the killings were only an unintentional result of robbing banks, and that Bonnie and Clyde were just doing "their thing."

So far, this is a typically "square" analysis. However, the other day I met an irate mother who went into a long attack on the terrible state we are in when our young children are allowed to see such awful things as *Bonnie and Clyde*. I replied, "You mean all of that killing and violence?" "No, no," she replied. "I don't care about the killing. I'm upset about the sex."

And I could see some youngster smiling ironically, "You see, it's just like we say. You 'oldies' are indifferent to killing, but you get all hung up about love."

Without getting into the obvious point that all sex is not love, I have to concede that perhaps there is more than a little truth in such an observation. Is it true that we have become immune to violence and physical suffering? What does it say when we become more incensed at dirty pictures than we do the casual glorification of the senseless killing of children of God?

How calloused and indifferent can we become? Apparently the answer is, "pretty calloused and indifferent indeed." The *Report of the National Advisory Commission on Civil Disorders* states, "[T]he most fundamental (problem) is the racial attitude and behavior of white Americans toward black Americans . . . white racism is essentially responsible for the explosive mixture which has been accumulating in our cities since the end of World War II."[23]

The slogan of white America has too often been, "Pull the ladder up, I'm aboard," not realizing that if we persist in this attitude the ship itself is going to sink.

It becomes apparent and clear that the lessons learned by the people of God reflected in Holy Scripture can never be taken for granted. They must be learned and re-learned by each generation and each people as they begin their own journey through life. We can never take anything for granted. We must start at the beginning–going back to the ancient myth of Cain and Abel to realize that we are indeed our brother's keeper–learning anew the lesson of Holy Week and the insanity of reliance upon violence and suppression.

The way of violence is death; the way of indifference can no longer be tolerated; we are past the time of words, pat phrases and glib generalizations; we must become new men, and this requires painful and honest re-examination of our basic values.

It is not easy to be optimistic. We have seen a systematic attack upon the forces of the center, or reason and mod-

---

23. Kerner Commission, *Report of the National Advisory Commission on Civil Disorders*, intro. Tom Wicker (New York: Bantam Books, 1968), p. 203.

eration in so many institutions, and we know that in any revolution the first group to go is that of the moderate middle. Martin Luther King, Jr., represented that group—he is gone.

But perhaps there is hope. It took cowardice, denial of responsibility and a crucifixion to make a committed saint of St. Peter. Perhaps the tragic event of last Thursday may help create such a reevaluation and transformation in us.

But it is going to be a long, hard, heart-breaking, painful journey. The acclaim for Dr. King will unfortunately fade away and in the end result we will have to solve our problems with the resources within us and with God's help.

Palm Sunday symbolizes the path before us. We wave palms to remember the temporary acclaim of the triumphant entry, but we take these palms home in the form of crosses, to remind us that there is no easy victory.

4

Wow! What a knee jerk liberal, activist sermon comes out of this parable! We are supposed to love activist do-gooders as ourselves? Ralph Nader?* Oh come on, Lord! *But read the parable again. There is no other answer.

The Eighth Sunday after Pentecost July 13, 1986	*The Cathedral Church of St. Mark Salt Lake City*

LUKE 10:25-37

When a preaching assignment comes around, the first thing the preacher does is to read the scriptural texts appointed for that day. And so, as I dutifully began that task I noted, "Oh good, I've got the 'Good Samaritan.' That one's a snap."

But something led me to re-read this familiar story a little more carefully, and to read some commentary as well, in the hope that I could get a new approach to this old chestnut.

And suddenly my eyes were opened and suddenly I realized that this parable taught something completely different than I had always supposed.

Let's get back into the context of the story. It starts with a lawyer, always the bad guys of history, asking Jesus a question "to put Him to the test" [Luke 10:25, RSV].

(An earlier thankfully discarded alternative translation of the Lord's Prayer used "put us not to the test"[24] for "lead us not into temptation"–I'm glad it was eliminated, although I don't think "save us from the time of trial" is much better.)

Well, anyway, back to the lawyer. I can see him before me–a bright man in his early forties, brown sparkling eyes, already a partner in one of Jerusalem's larger law firms, a degree from Harvard or Yale–out for a holiday walk to listen to wandering preachers as they spoke to poor, stupid folk. He was politically ambitious, probably running for alderman, and he wanted to show off a little.

So he asks what he should do to inherit eternal life. Jesus returned the question with a question, "What does the law say?" [Luke 10:26, Phillips] And our bright young man quotes the Shema and from Leviticus as combined in the Testaments of the Twelve Patriarchs, "Love God and your neighbor as yourself" [Luke 10:27].

And our Lord said, "You have answered right; do this and you will live" [Luke 10:28, RSV].

The lawyer's wife looked up at him adoringly. "Well

24. Authorized Services (New York: The Church Hymnal Corporation, 1973), p. 66.

done, Isaac, oh you of quick wit and much learning." But then Isaac committed the lawyer's most unpardonable sin, he asked a question without knowing what the answer of the witness would be. He did this "desiring to justify himself" [Luke 10:29, RSV]. (As senior counsel, I would have whispered, "Leave it alone as it is, Isaac. You'll go down in the Bible as a hero.") But Isaac would not quit while ahead. He went on, "All right, but who *is* my neighbor?" [Luke 10:29]

And the Lord told him the story of the Good Samaritan. Remember that Samaritans were despised bad guys, unlikely heroes in a Jewish story. Our Lord loved to turn things upside down.

Remember that the story was told in response to the question as to who is our neighbor whom we should love as ourself.

Who *is* the neighbor in the parable? The man in the ditch beaten by robbers? *No*! It was the man who showed mercy on him. The neighbor we should love as ourself was not the poor, the helpless and the suffering, but the person who *did* something about it.

Wow! What a knee jerk liberal, activist sermon comes out of this parable! We are supposed to love activist dogooders as ourselves? Ralph Nader? *Oh come on, Lord!* But read the parable again. There is no other answer.

Does this neglect the man in the ditch? Of course not. As the Dean [The Very Reverend William F. Maxwell] laid on us well last Sunday, we bear each other's burdens: the man in the ditch; our friend fallen on hard times; someone whose marriage has been broken; an older couple looking forward to retirement from a highly regarded public life having to watch over the death of their oldest and highly gifted child; a beautiful divorced woman with children, her eyesight failing and no support from her former husband, pleasantly and courteously plugging away at a switchboard.

Our Christian mandate is to help these people bear their burdens *not* because they are "neighbor," or "parishioner," or "Anglican," or even "Christian," but because they are God the Almighty's creatures and they are therefore sacred, each and every one, and we are mandated to feed, clothe and love them without regard to worthiness.

But back to the definition of neighbor whom we should love as ourselves as "doer." From the passive 1980s, it is interesting to look back at the extreme activism of the 1960s when even within the church if you weren't spending twenty-four hours a day doing and marching, you were considered to be beyond the pale.

Of course, there was a *stridency* and *hostility* in so much of that 1960's activism that is not present in the parable of the Good Samaritan. The Samaritan was someone like Virginia Parmalee who dedicates her widowed life to Crossroads Urban Center, or Rush Duer, recently confirmed, who runs our Cathedral Food Bank, or Meredith Simmons who bakes us something delicious to eat after every

Wednesday morning 7:00 a.m. Eucharist, or the members of the Altar Guild who spend endless hours to give us beauty (I always feel a little guilty crumbling that beautifully ironed linen lavabo towel).

Now of course whether a particular "doer" is viewed as hostile or strident depends on one's point of view. Doubtless, Bishop Desmond Tutu is viewed as such by the white establishment of South Africa (although the great irony is that *his* voice is one of moderation, and the great danger is that he will be usurped by truly radical black extremists).

Martin Luther King was viewed as hostile and strident by Sheriff Bull Connors (who set dogs and cattle prods on his followers) although King's tactics were those of nonviolence.

Certainly, we each have our stable of favorite and non-favorite doers. We should remember also that the Good Samaritan's acts of "doing" reflected mercy and compassion, the same mercy and compassion we would like to have shown to ourselves and that, I guess, is precisely the point.

I have before me a congregation I love in a church whose heritage and practices I love and the privilege of this pulpit which I honor and love.

Yet, have I been a "neighbor"? Have I *done* something as the Samaritan did, to justify your mandated love. I *do* know that I am of course at times and places a *burden* you must bear, and not a neighbor.

4. THE EIGHTH SUNDAY AFTER PENTECOST, 1986.

It is true that Almighty God, through our Lord Jesus Christ, has shown us that God loves us whenever and whatever we do. That is the Good News of the Gospel.

But once having accepted this, and indeed because of it, it is no great assignment to suggest that *we* be both doers and bearers.

Services are conducted at this Cathedral Church every day (except Saturday) for those who need help in *bearing*.

For *doers*, it is of course much easier to start acts of mercy and compassion with friends and family. But to be a neighbor, you can't stop there. The Good Samaritan had never laid eyes on the fellow in the road before.

The stripped, the robbed, and the half-dead are all around us, lying in the road and waiting for our help.

Afterword

When diagnosed with inoperable lung cancer, Al Colton wrote the following letter to the parishioners of the Cathedral Church of St. Mark, Salt Lake City, Utah, in the summer of 1988.

"THE HOPE OF GLORY"

Not many people reading this will have received notice that they have a terminal illness. That's always something that happens to other people. This is illustrated by a joke I've used a couple of times from the pulpit. The preacher stating, "Someday everyone from this parish will die." A fellow in the front pew cracked up with laughter. The priest asked him why he was laughing. He replied, "I'm not from this parish."

The Great Litany of *The Book of Common Prayer* asks that we be delivered from dying suddenly and unprepared.[1] This does not fit into our contemporary culture. I

1. "From all oppression, conspiracy, and rebellion; from violence, battle, and murder; and from dying suddenly and unprepared, *Good Lord, deliver us.*" From "The Great Litany," in *The Book of Common Prayer*

heard an avid golfer once say that the perfect way to go would be to drop dead immediately after making the most beautiful drive in your lifetime.

The wiser Christian tradition suggests that it is better to have a time of preparedness. Preparedness, first of all, in the temporal sense. Time to see that your affairs are in order, proper disposition of your worldly goods is arranged in a sensible and sensitive manner, and that steps have been taken to heal ruptured relationships with others, and that things hitherto left undone are done.

Preparation in a second sense is even more significant. It is preparation for an event that will happen to each of us. We must go through the experience alone, and it is one that is almost impossible to imagine, in that we really cannot conceive of our own non-existence.

A first and obvious question that is asked is "Why me, why now"? The obvious answer is "Why not you and why not now"? This should lead to a comparison of quantity and quality of life.

Earlier this year my wife Liz and I were confronted with a diagnosis that she had cancer. We sat down and pondered how this fit into our religious beliefs. We concluded that the Great Thanksgiving from the Prayer Book best

---

(New York: The Church Hymnal Corporation, 1979), p. 149.

summed up our response.[2] I think it is most appropriate for my condition as well.

Inasmuch as we seldom use this in public worship any more, let me set it forth for you to read:

Almighty God, Father of all mercies,
we your unworthy servants give you humble thanks
for all your goodness and loving-kindness
to us and to all whom you have made.
We bless you for our creation, preservation,
and all the blessings of this life;
but above all for your immeasurable love
in the redemption of the world by our Lord Jesus Christ;
for the means of grace, and for the hope of glory.
And, we pray, give us such an awareness of your mercies,
that with truly thankful hearts we may show forth your praise,
not only with our lips, but in our lives,
by giving up ourselves to your service,
and by walking before you
in holiness and righteousness all our days;
through Jesus Christ our Lord,
to whom, with you and the Holy Spirit,
be honor and glory throughout all ages. Amen.

–Morning Prayer II

---

2. "The General Thanksgiving," in *The Book of Common Prayer* (1979), p. 101.

So in comparing quantity and quality of life, I realize that even another 20 years could not add to the blessings I have already received.

A good and loving family, a satisfying job, so many friends, and, of course, the glue that holds all this together and gives meaning to it—the Church.

I cannot tell you how much your telephone calls, notes and expressions of concern have meant. Your prayers, of course, are the most important thing. I, in turn, think of and pray for all of you, and thus the cycle is complete—an expression of the communion of saints of the church militant on earth—a mystical concept, but one of which my experience has made me acutely aware. I have even asked a few of my pagan friends to pray for me, and I think they will.

I also pray for others who wrestle with similar problems. Foremost in this list is our Bishop George,[3] whom I have gotten to know and love very much. If cure can be effected by courage and love of the Lord, he's going to make it.

In your meditations, you inevitably are faced with a haunting thought. What if this Resurrection theory is a big fraud? What if when the curtain is finally rung down I am

---

3. The Right Reverend George E. Bates, Bishop of Utah, had been diagnosed with throat cancer. His cancer is in remission.

greeted not by a loving hand with the stigmata which I helped inflict, but a celestial cynical voice saying, "Ha, ha, ha–the joke's on you, sucker," and then eternal non-existence?

This in no way would make me regret following the Christian path and message during my earthly life because the basic message makes more sense of the human condition and gives a more profound way of dealing with it than any other world view I know. I can recognize myself for the sinner that I am and realize that the need of healing has been met. The sense of my worth, despite myself, has given me courage when I needed it, and I can accept myself when I know I was unacceptable.

But I do have "a sure and certain hope" that I will be accepted by a loving hand. I do not believe in the Greek separation of body and soul with which much of Christendom is tainted. I believe with the Jew that we as creatures are a totality. My big nose is as much a part of me as my prayer life. And when this totality dies, it dies in its totality. It is only by the grace of Almighty God that this is given meaning again.

How do I know? St. Paul conjectured. It will not be as we imagine. However, we will have an individual identity. We will again live in relationships. The sharing of the Beatific Vision would include relationships with others cleansed by this Presence from those elements which so often separate us now.

In some way I would hope that I have answers I do not now have; that I would have knowledge which I do not now have and that I would be able to love, accept and give and forgive in a way I do not now have.

I have avoided talk of judgment, hell, etc. This is because I believe from my life as a Christian in the way it is expressed in the Anglican communion that judgment is certain, but that hell is self-imposed. I have been given the means of grace and the hope of glory.

The means of grace through the sacraments of my Church has been an abiding strength. Through a succession of Deans I have had, for many years, the privilege of celebrating the Eucharist at 7:00 a.m. on Wednesdays in our Cathedral Church. It has become a small Christian community (open, I hasten to add, to anyone who wishes to share the spartan pleasure of meaningful activity at 7:00 a.m.).

I think of saints of that group, now gone, and the love those now there showed in giving me a chalice and paten on the 25th anniversary of my ordination to the priesthood.

But whether at the altar at a low early morning Eucharist, or assisting at one of our gloriously done high services, or merely sitting in the pew, the sense of communion is a truly Holy thing. Whether it has been reflected on my lips or in my life, only you can tell.

Not only have I been given the means of grace, but also

the hope of glory. The Colton family coat of arms (probably apocryphal) bears the slogan "Never despair." This hope of glory can only come after a vale of tears inevitable to the human condition. Despite this, I hope I will never despair of this hope.

About the Editor

The Reverend Canon Bradley S. Wirth was born in Great Falls, Montana, and was educated at the University of Washington in Seattle. He holds a B.A. and an M.A. in speech communications with a concentration in rhetorical criticism and theory as well as classical rhetoric. He received his Masters of Divinity degree from the Episcopal Divinity School, Cambridge, Massachusetts, with an emphasis in New Testament theology and rhetorical criticism of early church documents. He is an ordained priest in the Episcopal Church and is currently serving All Saints Church, Salt Lake City, as their rector. Canon Wirth is married to Jeannine Urback; they share their home with their two children, Christine and Jennifer, and two dogs, Oliver and Molly.